FIFTY YEARS OF *DUNGEONS & DRAGONS*

FIFTY YEARS OF *DUNGEONS & DRAGONS*

EDITED BY PREMEET SIDHU, MARCUS CARTER, AND JOSÉ P. ZAGAL

THE MIT PRESS CAMBRIDGE, MASSACHUSETTS LONDON, ENGLAND

The MIT Press would like to thank the anonymous peer reviewers who provided comments on drafts of this book. The generous work of academic experts is essential for establishing the authority and quality of our publications. We acknowledge with gratitude the contributions of these otherwise uncredited readers.

This book was set in Stone Serif and Avenir by Westchester Publishing Services. Printed and bound in the United States of America.

Library of Congress Cataloging-in-Publication Data

Names: Sidhu, Premeet, editor. | Carter, Marcus, editor. | Zagal, José
    Pablo, editor.
Title: Fifty years of *Dungeons & Dragons* / edited by Premeet Sidhu,
    Marcus Carter, and José P. Zagal.
Other titles: Fifty years of *Dungeons and Dragons*
Description: Cambridge, Massachusetts : The MIT Press, [2024] |
    Includes bibliographical references and index.
Identifiers: LCCN 2023018019 (print) | LCCN 2023018020 (ebook) |
    ISBN 9780262547604 (paperback) | ISBN 9780262377997 (epub) |
    ISBN 9780262377980 (pdf)
Subjects: LCSH: *Dungeons and Dragons* (Game)—History. | *Dungeons and
    Dragons* (Game)—Social aspects.
Classification: LCC GV1469.62.D84 F54 2024 (print) | LCC GV1469.62.D84
    (ebook) | DDC 793.93—dc23/eng/20230420
LC record available at https://lccn.loc.gov/2023018019
LC ebook record available at https://lccn.loc.gov/2023018020

10 9 8 7 6 5 4 3

To all who have found adventure or inspiration through *Dungeons & Dragons*

CONTENTS

PREFACE

The idea for this edited collection originated in late 2020 as a way to show-case some of the brilliant research and scholarship on *Dungeons & Dragons* in celebration of the game's fiftieth anniversary in 2024. The chapters are written by emerging and established *D&D* scholars, game designers, and players, all of whom are passionate about the game. We are excited to bring this wonderful group of voices into conversation, and we hope that they offer you some new or deeper insight into the histories, influences, critiques, and possible futures of *D&D*.

ACKNOWLEDGMENTS

We would like to extend our gratitude to all the contributors for their thought-provoking chapters. A sincere thank-you to Hannah McFarlane, who assisted with copyediting and proofreading the final manuscript. Thanks also to our acquisitions editor, Noah Springer, and the editorial team at MIT Press.

1

IS THIS THE GOLDEN AGE OF *DUNGEONS & DRAGONS?*

Premeet Sidhu, Marcus Carter, and José P. Zagal

Its possibilities go far beyond any previous offerings anywhere!
—Ernest Gary Gygax, 1973[1]

The hard truth is that *Dungeons & Dragons* (*D&D*) has changed. In the 1970s, *D&D* found its home in wargame and hobby shops worldwide. Armed with painted miniatures and brightly colored polyhedral dice, playing groups would meet up regularly in person to adventure in vast imagined lands guided by the rules in the three original "little brown books." Fast-forward fifty years, and the well-known tabletop role-playing game (TTRPG) can be experienced in an entirely different way. Players dial into online group video or audio chat platforms, their *D&D* games can be accented with digital soundtracks, interactive battle maps, and online character trackers. No physical interaction is required. Yes, *D&D* has changed a lot over the past fifty years—but what many of its players love about the game hasn't. Dungeon masters (DMs) and players still relish the exhilaration that comes after rolling a "natural 20," they build social relationships that often transcend the game space, their creativity is constantly tested and encouraged, and there is nothing that compares to the feeling of finally uncovering your campaign's "Big Bad" or antagonist. Although the game's rule set, narrative canon, and player base are continually evolving, it is comforting to know that many of the core elements of *D&D* remain the same. Regardless of the way you choose to play, having fun with your friends is still at the forefront. Now in its milestone fiftieth year, the game is arguably more popular and accessible than ever before—but is this the golden age of *D&D*?

MOTIVATION AND AUDIENCE

D&D today is experiencing an enormous resurgence in play. In addition to the growing popularity of nondigital games more broadly, *D&D*'s capacity to support social connectedness both online and in person—as well as the game's positive representation in popular media and content— has drawn increased interest from a new generation of players. As scholarly and public attention toward *D&D* continues to grow, we wanted to explore why the fifty-year-old tabletop game remains so popular.

To help us answer this question, we chose to showcase chapters in this book that would critically explore key parts of the game's history and development over time. We also wanted to include chapters that would highlight *D&D*'s impact on the games industry and beyond. As a result, this book celebrates the game's many achievements over the years, but it also acknowledges and discusses some of the deeply problematic issues and representations that are ingrained within the game's design and play history as well. Both are necessary to address when speculating about what the future of *D&D* could look like. By bringing together perspectives from *D&D* players and scholars, role-playing game (RPG) designers, and key figures throughout its history, we hope to provide a deeper understanding of the game's rich history, culture, and play.

This book is intended for *D&D*'s dedicated and passionate fan base— whether you're an academic, a game designer, a player, or anything in between. We believe there's something in here for everyone. Found in this book are essays that give insight into a broad range of *D&D*-related topics that add to the emerging and continued scholarship of the game in academia. Most importantly, though, each chapter offers readers the opportunity to learn more about the game and critically reflect on their own experiences, perceptions, and play of *D&D*.

CONTEXTUAL OVERVIEW OF CHAPTERS

This book contains a collection of essays that investigate some notable factors of *D&D*'s design, play, and fifty-year history. Each chapter stands alone, offering an innovative contribution to existing research and discourse on the game. However, reading the chapters together shows how *D&D* has managed to remain popular in the many decades after its initial release. All the chapters acknowledge, reflect, and speculate on various areas of *D&D*'s past, present, and future. Alongside chapters by research experts or emerging scholars, we have also included insights from key figures in the wider *D&D* community. Directly after this chapter, game designer Sam Mannell introduces us to other designers involved with *D&D* whose personal vignettes will be woven throughout the book. The rest of the chapters will be divided thematically into four parts: histories, influence(s), critical analyses and play, and future(s). You'll also find commissioned artwork by C Liersch between the first three part interludes. What follows here is a brief introduction to each of the book parts, as well as an overview of the chapters.

HISTORIES OF *D&D*

Co-created by David Lance Arneson and Ernest Gary Gygax in 1974 to address their perceived limitations of the popular wargaming genre, *D&D* was designed to be a collaborative TTRPG where groups of players met in person to role-play characters and tell stories with their friends. In most playing groups, one player would take on the role of the DM: a player who narrated the story, refereed the game, and embodied the monsters, challenges, and nonplayer characters (NPCs) that other members of the playing group would encounter throughout their gameplay. Together, DMs and players would explore their shared imagined worlds, overcome complicated challenges, and develop strong relationships—using dice rolls and player discretion to guide the outcomes of in-game actions and events. The chapters in this part explore the legacy of *D&D*'s early years on the game today.

As the social nature of D&D is often stated to be one of the major reasons why people play the game, the first and last chapters of this part both reflect on the game's social importance (see chaps. 2 and 8). Before game studies was officially established as a distinct academic discipline,[2] a lot of early discussion about games was presented in a variety of formats.[3] In the game's early years, growing interest about *D&D* inspired dedicated television segments and even "explainer-style" books that were created to give the general public a better understanding of what exactly *D&D* was—as well as unpacking some of the core concepts and mechanics of the game.[4] However, it was not until Gary Alan Fine's book on *D&D* players—titled *Shared Fantasy: Role-Playing Games as Social Worlds* (1983)—that the game's social capabilities were established in academia.[5] In chapter 2, Fine reflects on the subsequent impact of his foundational research, as well as the unexpected yet enduring social appeal of the game. Fine's research would go on to influence larger social investigations of *D&D*, such as those conducted by David M. Ewalt in *Of Dice and Men: The Story of Dungeons & Dragons and the People Who Play It* (2013), and Nicholas Mizer in *Tabletop Role-Playing Games and the Experience of Imagined Worlds* (2019).[6] We also felt that it was important to showcase perspectives of players who had experienced *D&D* in its early form and rule sets. Consequently, the final chapter of the book's first part is a reflective personal essay by Stephen Webley, whose first edition *Advanced Dungeons & Dragons* (*AD&D* 1e) playing group reconnected and rediscovered *D&D* and their friendships as a result of the COVID-19 pandemic.

In addition to covering the social legacy of the game, chapters in this part also investigate the innovation and influence of *D&D*'s rule set and design. In chapter 3, Jon Peterson expands on his previously published historical work on the game and provides a new look into what he considers the game changers of *D&D* to be: the "exploration" and "experience" mechanics.[7] As *D&D* is often referred to as the foundation of modern RPGs, Peterson argues that these pivotal elements of *D&D*'s design have been adopted and modified in many digital and nondigital successors.[8] One element of *D&D*'s design that is discussed passionately within the community is the game's combat system. In chapter 4, Evan Torner gives readers an introduction into the contentiously debated topic of combat in *D&D* and its design trajectory throughout the multiple editions of the game. Both Peterson's and Torner's chapters add to the existing work of Aaron Trammell and Steven Dashiell, who have investigated similar areas, such as *D&D*'s dungeons and the influence of *D&D*'s rule set on certain kinds of play and players—namely, "rules lawyers."[9]

Delving further into the design histories of *D&D*, the remaining chapters in this part focus on the impact of certain individuals and rule sets that have contributed to the wider accessibility of the game today. In chapter 5, Tony A. Rowe and Zach Howard recount the prolific contribution of Dr. J. Eric Holmes—the creator of the first basic *D&D* rule set (1977). The chapter adds depth to the existing biographies of key figures involved with *D&D* and extends our knowledge of relevant *D&D* paratexts and publications such as *Alarums & Excursions*.[10] Like Holmes's *Basic Rules* (1977), the introduction of the Open Game License (OGL) Version 1.0a in 2000 would improve *D&D*'s accessibility once again. In chapter 6, Michael Iantorno interviews Ryan Dancey, who spearheaded the implementation of the OGL during his tenure at Wizards of the Coast (WotC). In addition to fleshing out the history of the OGL, Dancey provides firsthand insight into the license's legal ramifications, its adoption by game designers, and the transformation of the role-playing industry at the turn of the century. Iantorno's interview supports existing work by Nicolas LaLone, who reminds us of *D&D*'s ability to be easily ported and transferred between different media.[11] *D&D*'s flexibility and adaptation in new media forms are also examined in chapter 7 by Mateusz Felczak. In his chapter, Felczak explores the impact of *D&D* on digital game modifications, which is related to the existing critical work by William J. White (2020) on *D&D* and the Forge, an online RPG discussion forum and community.[12]

D&D'S INFLUENCE(S)

Like the game's historical and design legacies, the social and cultural influences of *D&D* are widespread. The book's second part begins with a chapter by Esther MacCallum-Stewart, who argues that the role-play-heavy play styles in "actual-play" *D&D* shows—also called live-play shows, in which a group of people play a TTRPG for an audience—are influencing how players today approach their own *D&D* play (see chap. 9). MacCallum-Stewart's chapter builds on the substantial prior work that has examined *D&D*'s popular-media representations and modern resurgence.[13] Notably, it adds to the scholarship in Shelly Jones's edited collection *Watch Us Roll: Essays on Actual Play and Performance in Tabletop Role-Playing Games*

(2021), which explores how actual-play content is bridging the gap between digital and nondigital TTRPG play, as well as Stephanie Hedge and Jennifer Grouling's edited collection *Roleplaying Games in the Digital Age: Essays on Transmedia Storytelling, Tabletop RPGs and Fandom* (2021), which highlights how TTRPG players are engaging with technology to further enhance their role-playing experiences.[14]

Although *D&D* today is experiencing unprecedented popularity, there was a time when the game was implicated in the "Satanic Panic" of the 1980s.[15] Although *D&D*'s relationship to religion has been investigated previously,[16] Adrian Hermann offers a renewed investigation of religion in *D&D*. In chapter 10, Hermann discusses representations of religion(s) in *D&D* across multiple editions and gives readers unique insight into the complex relationship between the two. Like religion, *D&D*'s association with fantasy and speculative fiction has been inherent and ongoing. Drawing from her own research and professional writing experience, Dimitra Nikolaidou's chapter 11 proposes *D&D* as an influential factor in the evolution of speculative literature. Expanding on Peter Bebergal's *Appendix N: The Eldritch Roots of Dungeons & Dragons* (2021) and Curtis Carbonell's (2016) examinations of the game's literary and fantastical influences, Nikolaidou suggests that the influence of *D&D* has shaped not only contemporary speculative fiction but also the culture of the fantastic in general.[17]

The remaining chapters in this part explore the game's impact in diverse nongame environments. In chapter 12, Premeet Sidhu recounts the substantial influence of *D&D* on education and learning contexts. The chapter reviews existing work from interdisciplinary games and education scholars and argues that education is a core pillar of *D&D*'s legacy and future.[18] In chapter 13, David Harris and Josiah Lulham explore the reciprocal relationship between theatrical performance and role-play in *D&D*. Building on initial work from Daniel Mackay (2001),[19] the two discuss how *D&D* has a unique ability to generate stories through the live interactions of its players. Concluding the book's second part, in chapter 14, Jay Malouf-Grice provides an evocative exploration of how *D&D* has been employed by queer players to experiment with identity, resist hegemonic narratives, and build fantastical queer utopias or dystopias.

CRITICAL PLAY AND ANALYSES OF *D&D*

In addition to understanding the game's enduring appeal and influence, recent years have seen more directed and extensive consideration of *D&D*'s racism, misogyny, and other problematic elements.[20] The chapters in the book's third part encourage the wider *D&D* community (for example, designers, scholars, and players) to acknowledge and reflect critically on how the game has been designed, viewed, and played over the years.

In chapter 15, Amanda Cote and Emily Saidel explore the representation of "race" and race in *D&D*. Any player of *D&D* or fan of high fantasy in general is likely familiar with the common tropes surrounding different "races" or "species" of characters—from gruff dwarven miners to haughty magical elves. However, critics and scholars have long since advocated for changes to *D&D*'s "race"-based system on the grounds that many in-game "races" risk reinforcing real-world stereotypes about people of color. This issue has recently been addressed in WotC's decision to remove the term "race" in future iterations of the game.[21] In analyzing these timely tensions, Cote and Saidel prompt designers, scholars, and players to consider how progress toward inclusion in *D&D* is occurring, albeit unevenly.

With its roots in European wargaming, *D&D* would seem an unlikely context for contemporary Indigenous players to find community or positive experiences. Yet, despite the game's problematic and often deeply damaging roots in savagist and anti-Indigenous tropes, Daniel Heath Justice—Indigenous scholar, fantasy author, and citizen of the Cherokee Nation—demonstrates in chapter 16 that Indigenous people can be avid fans of *D&D*. Contributing to the critical body of Indigenous game-related work by scholars like Jodi Byrd (2018), Naithan Lagace (2018), and Beth Aileen Lameman (2010),[22] Justice's chapter considers the complex relationship that some Indigenous players may have with *D&D* and examines the ways that Indigenous participants in these gaming and fan communities challenge, contest, and reimagine the settler colonial underpinnings of mainstream fantasy role-playing.

Continuing to explore personal experiences and critical histories of *D&D* play, Aaron Trammell and Antero Garcia reflect on *D&D* through critical race studies perspectives—but with different positions. In chapter 17, Trammell and Garcia argue that although *D&D* has long printed content that imagines a particular "white male player," there has been a deliberate push recently by WotC to include content that appeals to a broader demographic of players that is not explicitly racist—such as *Tasha's Cauldron of Everything* (2020) and the revamped *Van Richten's Guide to Ravenloft* (2021).[23] Although attempts have been made to overhaul *D&D*'s content to be more inclusive and sensitive to nonwhite cultures, Kellynn Wee notes that criticisms have still tended to be made from the perspectives of players and scholars situated in Anglo- and Eurocentric spaces. In chapter 18, Wee describes *D&D*'s localization, adaptation, and play in the Southeast Asian context of Singapore. The chapter pays attention to how space and materials shape Singaporean players' *D&D* play styles as they seek to replicate a narrative experience similar to actual-play shows.

Rounding out the book's third part, in chapter 19, Victor Raymond and Gary Alan Fine explore expressions of deviance in *D&D*'s early years. In doing so, they build on the work of Sarah Albom (2021), who explored how *D&D*'s text can incentivize players to take violent actions more often than offering peaceful solutions,[24] as well as Shelly Jones's research (2018), which argues that *D&D*'s mechanics, visual components, and narrative structures all establish a unique allegory for processing trauma.[25]

FUTURES

The book concludes with a chapter that aptly explores the potential futures of *D&D* in classic *D&D* style—through tables and dice rolling. In chapter 20, Jonathan Walton presents a series of randomized tables that readers can use to generate their own possible *D&D* futures, speculating on what *D&D* could look like at 150 years old. The table format is an homage to the common tool used for procedurally generating content in *D&D* and suggests that the future of *D&D* contains countless possibilities, many of which may exist simultaneously.

CONCLUSION

In anticipation of the game's milestone anniversary, *Fifty Years of Dungeons & Dragons* showcases a collection of essays and written works that explore why the fifty-year-old tabletop game remains so popular. We hope that each chapter offers readers the opportunity to potentially learn something new about the game and critically reflect on their own experiences, perceptions, and play of *D&D.* Our introduction began with a provocative question: is this the golden age of *D&D?* Unfortunately there is no simple answer; only time will tell. As we leave you to ponder the question while you peruse the rest of the book, we do think one answer is pretty clear: it is at least the golden age of *D&D* scholarship.

NOTES

1. Gary Gygax, "Introduction," in *Dungeons & Dragons Volume 1: Men & Magic* (TSR, 1974).

2. Espen Aarseth, "Computer Game Studies, Year One," *Game Studies* 1, no. 1 (2001), http://gamestudies.org/0101/editorial.html.

3. Thomas Apperley and Darshana Jayemane, "Game Studies' Material Turn," *Westminster Papers in Communication and Culture* 9, no. 1 (2012): 7, http://www .westminsterpapers.org/articles/abstract/10.16997/wpcc.145.

4. British Broadcasting Corporation (BBC), *Heart of the Matter: Sword and Sorcery,* video file, 1980, accessed January 18, 2023, https://www.facebook.com/watch/?v=57 2990156407352; John Butterfield, David Honigmann, and Philip Parker, *What Is Dungeons and Dragons?* (Harmondsworth, UK: Penguin Books, 1982).

5. Gary Alan Fine, *Shared Fantasy: Role-Playing Games as Social Worlds* (Chicago: University of Chicago Press, 1983).

6. David M. Ewalt, *Of Dice and Men: The Story of Dungeons & Dragons and the People Who Play It* (Simon & Schuster, 2013); Nicholas J. Mizer, *Tabletop Role-Playing Games and the Experience of Imagined Worlds* (Springer, 2019).

7. Jon Peterson, *Playing at the World: A History of Simulating Wars, People, and Fantastic Adventures, from Chess to Role-Playing Games* (San Diego, CA: Unreason Press, 2012); "Precursors," in *Role-Playing Game Studies: Transmedia Foundations,* ed. José P. Zagal and Sebastian Deterding (Routledge, 2018), 55–62; *The Elusive Shift: How Role-Playing Games Forged Their Identity* (Cambridge, MA: MIT Press, 2020); *Game Wizards: The Epic Battle for Dungeons & Dragons* (Cambridge, MA: MIT Press, 2021).

8. For example, Nicolas LaLone, "A Tale of *Dungeons & Dragons* and the Origins of the Game Platform," *Analog Game Studies* 6, no. 3 (2019), https://analoggamestudies .org/2019/09/a-tale-of-dungeons-dragons-and-the-origins-of-the-game-platform; Gerald A. Voorhees, Joshua Call, and Katie Whitlock, *Dungeons, Dragons, and Digital Denizens: The Digital Role-Playing Game* (New York: Bloomsbury, 2012); José P. Zagal and Sebastian Deterding, eds., *Role-Playing Game Studies: Transmedia Foundations* (London: Routledge, 2018).

9. Aaron Trammell, "From Where Do Dungeons Come?" *Analog Game Studies* 1, no. 1 (2014), https://analoggamestudies.org/2014/08/from-where-do-dungeons-come/; Steven

Dashiell, "Rules Lawyering as Symbolic and Linguistic Capital," *Analog Game Studies* 4, no. 5 (2017), https://analoggamestudies.org/2017/11/rules-lawyering-as-symbolic-and -linguistic-capital/; Steven Dashiell, "'Rules as Written': Game Algorithms as Game Capital," *Analog Game Studies* 5, no. 3 (2018), https://analoggamestudies.org/2018/09/rules -as-written-analyzing-changes-in-reliance-on-game-system-algorithms-as-shifts-in-game -capital/.

10. Michael Witwer, *Empire of Imagination: Gary Gygax and the Birth of Dungeons & Dragons* (Bloomsbury, 2015); Aaron Trammell and Nikki Crenshaw, "The Damsel and the Courtesan: Quantifying Consent in Early *Dungeons & Dragons*," *International Journal of Role-Playing* no. 10 (2020): 10–25, https://doi.org/10.33063/ijrp.vi10.273

11. LaLone, "Tale of *Dungeons & Dragons.*"

12. William J. White, *Tabletop RPG Design in Theory and Practice at the Forge, 2001– 2012* (Springer, 2020).

13. For example, Alex Chalk, "A Chronology of *Dungeons & Dragons* in Popular Media," *Analog Game Studies* 6, no. 1 (2018), https://analoggamestudies.org/2018/06 /telling-stories-of-dungeons-dragons-a-chronology-of-representations-of-dd-play/; Premeet Sidhu and Marcus Carter, "The *Critical Role* of Media Representations, Reduced Stigma and Increased Access in *D&D*'s Resurgence," in *DiGRA '20: Proceedings of the 2020 DiGRA International Conference—Play Everywhere* (2020), 1–20, http://www.digra .org/wp-content/uploads/digital-library/DiGRA_2020_paper_223.pdf; Ryan Stanton and Mark R. Johnson, "The Audiences of *The Adventure Zone*: Analysing Actual Play as Inclusive Gaming Media," in *Proceedings of DiGRA Australia 2021*, online due to COVID-19 (2021), 1–4, https://digraa.org/wp-content/uploads/2021/02/DiGRAA2021 _paper_12.pdf.

14. Shelly Jones, *Watch Us Roll: Essays on Actual Play and Performance in Tabletop Role-Playing Games* (McFarland, 2021); Stephanie Hedge and Jennifer Grouling, *Role-Playing Games in the Digital Age: Essays on Transmedia Storytelling, Tabletop RPGs, and Fandom* (McFarland, 2021).

15. For example, Joseph P. Laycock, *Dangerous Games: What the Moral Panic over Role-Playing Games Says about Play, Religion, and Imagined Worlds* (University of California Press, 2015), 101–136; Sidhu and Carter, "*Critical Role* of Media," 3–4.

16. Laycock, *Dangerous Games.*

17. Peter Bebergal, *Appendix N: The Eldritch Roots of Dungeons & Dragons* (Strange Attractor Press, 2021); Curtis Carbonell, "Tabletop Role-Playing Games, the Modern Fantastic, and Analog 'Realized' Worlds," in "2016 Role-Playing Game Summit," ed. Evan Torner, special issue, *Analog Game Studies* (2016), https://analoggamestudies .org/2016/11/tabletop-role-playing-games-the-modern-fantastic-and-analog-realized -worlds.

18. Antero Garcia, "Gaming Literacies: Spatiality, Materiality, and Analog Learning in a Digital Age," *Reading Research Quarterly* 55, no. 1 (2020): 9–27, https://doi.org /10.1002/rrq.260; Adric Polkinghorne, Jane Turner, Manuela Taboada, and Jeremy Kerr, "Critical Fail: Addressing Problematic Designs in Table-Top Role-Playing Games for Narrative Therapy and Community Wellbeing," in *Proceedings of DiGRA Australia*

2021, online due to COVID-19 (2021), 1–5, https://digraa.org/wp-content/uploads /2021/02/DiGRAA2021_paper_22.pdf; Premeet Sidhu and Marcus Carter, "Exploring the Resurgence and Educative Potential of *Dungeons & Dragons*," *Scan* 40, no. 6 (2021): 12–16, https://issuu.com/scannswdoe/docs/scan_40_6_july2021_issuu; Enrique Uribe-Jongbloed, "Playing with Translation: Translanguaging Role-Playing Games in Colombia in the 1990s," in "Analog Games and Translation," ed. Jonathan Evans, special issue, *Analog Game Studies* (2020), https://analoggamestudies.org/2020/03/playing -with-translation-translanguaging-role-playing-games-in-colombia-in-the-1990s/.

19. Daniel Mackay, *The Fantasy Role-Playing Game: A New Performing Art* (McFarland, 2001).

20. For example, Eleanor Beidatsch, "In Dungeons and Dragons You Can Be Almost Anything You Want, So Why the Backlash over a Combat Wheelchair?" *ABC Australia*, May 1, 2021, https://www.abc.net.au/news/2021-05-02/dungeons-and-dragons -disability-in-tabletop-gaming/100068926; Amanda Cote, *Gaming Sexism: Gender and Identity in the Era of Casual Video Games* (New York: New York University Press, 2020), 190–197; Shelly Jones, "Blinded by the Roll: The Critical Fail of Disability in *D&D*," *Analog Game Studies* 5, no. 1 (2018), https://analoggamestudies.org/2018 /03/blinded-by-the-roll-the-critical-fail-of-disability-in-dd/; Shelly Jones and Tanya Pobuda, "An Analysis of Gender-Inclusive Language and Imagery in Top-Ranked Board Game Rulebooks," *Analog Game Studies* 7, no. 2 (2020), https://analoggamestudies .org/2020/12/an-analysis-of-gender-inclusive-language-and-imagery-in-top-ranked -board-game-rulebooks/; Sarah Stang and Aaron Trammell, "The Ludic Bestiary: Misogynistic Tropes of Female Monstrosity in *Dungeons & Dragons*," *Games and Culture* 15, no. 6 (2019): 730–747, https://doi.org/10.1177/1555412019850059; Michael Stokes, "Access to the Page: Queer and Disabled Characters in *Dungeons & Dragons*," *Analog Game Studies* 4, no. 3 (2017), https://analoggamestudies.org/2017/05/access -to-the-page-queer-and-disabled-characters-in-dungeons-dragons/; Aaron Trammell, "Misogyny and the Female Body in *Dungeons & Dragons*," *Analog Game Studies* 1, no. 3 (2014), https://analoggamestudies.org/2014/10/constructing-the-female-body-in -role-playing-games/.

21. D&D Beyond, "Moving On from 'Race' in One D&D," 2022, https://www .dndbeyond.com/posts/1393-moving-on-from-race-in-one-d-d.

22. Jodi Byrd, "Beast of America: Sovereignty and the Wildness of Objects," *South Atlantic Quarterly* 11, no. 3 (2018): 599–615.; Naithan Lagace, "Indigenous Representations and the Impacts of Video Game Media on Indigenous Identity" (MA thesis, University of Manitoba, 2018), http://hdl.handle.net/1993/33700; Beth Aileen Lameman, "The Good, the Bad, and the Sultry: Indigenous Women in Video Games," 2010, May 2, 2022, https://www.abtec.org/docs/IndigenousWomenInVideoGames.pdf.

23. Wizards of the Coast, *Tasha's Cauldron of Everything* (Renton, WA: Wizards of the Coast, 2020); *Van Richten's Guide to Ravenloft* (Renton, WA: Wizards of the Coast, 2021).

24. Sarah Albom, "The Killing Roll: The Prevalence of Violence in *Dungeons & Dragons*," *International Journal of Role-Playing* 11 (2021): 6–24, https://doi.org/10.33063/ijrp .vi11.281

25. Jones, "Blinded by the Roll."

INTRODUCTION TO DESIGNER VIGNETTES

Sam Mannell
Writer and Designer for MCDM and Ghostfire Gaming

As a nonacademic, I was honored to be invited to help work on this book and celebrate the fifty-year milestone of the game that's got its teeth into all of us somehow. The chapters here have been produced by scholars and writers of incredible caliber, and the work they have produced is exceptional, though you hardly need me to tell you that.

While I can't offer an academic inquiry, I hope instead to offer something else: to be a conduit. You may be thinking, who is this, and why do I care? Well, no one, and you don't need to care. Suffice to say, I love the game, and have played it, and created with it, and worked on it, and tried my best to share what I love about it with others. And ultimately that's the point: others. When you play the game, especially when you run it, it's about entertaining your friends—creating places and people that the table will savor.

I spoke to many other designers who are professionally involved in *D&D* today (or have been previously), and short excerpts from these interviews appear at the start of each part of the book. You may know some of them. You may not; that's also the point. It's my honor to introduce them to you, so that the voices of those who have been deeply involved with the community are here for others to find at its fiftieth anniversary.

A party of adventurers descends a staircase in a forest fantasy setting; an ambush awaits.
C Liersch, *Forest Ambush*, 2023. Pen and ink on paper.

FIFTY YEARS OF *DUNGEONS & DRAGONS*

Designer Vignettes I

I was running *D&D* at a video game company I was working at with people who grew up with video games. [*D&D*] was an entirely new experience for them. . . . It was unspoken, but there was this skepticism. People don't expect it to hook them. We had just started playing, and we were in a scenario where there was a tower infested with goblins, and the players were trying to clear it out. There was a player—they were a ranger—who had an ability that said, "When you attack somebody, you can shift them five feet." The player asks me: "Can I wait for the goblin to come to the edge of the tower, and before he turns around and goes back, could I shoot him with my arrow, and have him move five feet *this* way . . . so he falls off the tower?" The player had constructed this model in his head of what could happen, and it did not, in his mind, make any literal sense in the world of the game, but it made sense according to his power. According to the power, it was legal, but he couldn't imagine it. Well, that was my job. I said, "Sure, go ahead, give it a shot." He hits, and I describe the arrow hitting the goblin in the shoulder and spinning the goblin around, so that the goblin's off-balance, and that's why he falls. And the light went on in his head. He was like . . . "I can do anything. Anything I can think of, I can try, and Matt [the DM] is gonna come up with a way for it to make sense." . . . The fact he had to roll the dice, and the fact he had the rules to inspire action, and he had to interpret them and come up with a nonstandard use for them, that grants everything that's happening a sense

(*continued*)

Designer Vignettes I (continued)

of realism. And that's, I think, the hook for most people. "I understand the game, I predict the outcome of my plan, I execute the plan and wait to see if it works." Every game that is fun has that in it. In *D&D*, that's where the dice come in. Everyone in *D&D* has that experience of uncertainty. We have a plan, but will it work? As soon as the dice leave our hand, we hold our breath. And in that moment, and *only* in that moment, *all futures are possible*. And then the dice lands, and many worlds collapse into one result. And when you roll a 20, you're like, "Ahhh! I did it!" There are very few things that happen at the table that are truly universal, but everyone has that experience.

—Matt Colville
Owner of MCDM; previously lead writer for Turtle Rock Games;
creator of the *Running the Game* YouTube series

There's that ongoing argument, "Why hack *D&D* to do this when another system can do it better?" but that argument exists in the first place because *D&D can* be modified so much. And that's a big contributor to why a lot of people stay with it.

—Alison Huang
Award-winning adventure designer;
worked on *Candlekeep Mysteries*

Why *D&D* versus another game? Marketing. *D&D* is Xerox. *D&D* is Coke. *D&D* is Photoshop. *D&D* is basically the word that is synonymous with RPG. I don't think it means *D&D* is better. It is definitely better promoted. It definitely has inertia. But if the mechanics are just a framework for the bulk of the play, and you can change them to fit your needs, then promotion and inertia may be all you need.

—Mikaela Sims
Worked for Beadle & Grimm's; helped promote Dragonlance
for TSR in 1996; owned a hobby shop in 1997;
helped build White Wolf community from around 1998

2

FANTASY GAMES AT FIFTY: AN ACADEMIC MEMOIR

Gary Alan Fine

Back in 1977 when I began my research on fantasy role-playing games, I had no idea that there would eventually be a legitimate, expansive, and admired academic field of "game studies." My book, published in 1983, *Shared Fantasy: Role-Playing Games as Social Worlds*, was the first extended academic study of this community of gamers.[1] Looking back, I am both impressed and amazed at how this odd slice of leisure has grown. My research began before the rise of MMORPGs and LARPs (massively multiplayer online role-playing games and live-action role-playing games). People participated in this world in person; it was called "tabletop gaming," as that was the space of play. Fantasy role-play gaming was in its infancy, and the creators, men such as Gary Gygax and Dave Arneson, were still in the community. TSR (Tactical Studies Rules) was the leading publisher of these gaming materials. By 1977, when my research began, although *Dungeons & Dragons* (*D&D*) was prominent, other gaming systems, such as *Chivalry & Sorcery* (1977), *Empire of the Petal Throne* (M. A. R. Barker's remarkable universe, 1975), and *Traveller* (based on science fiction themes, 1977), were popular in the Twin Cities (Minneapolis–Saint Paul, Minnesota), where I conducted the bulk of my research.[2]

At the time of the study, I was a young assistant professor of sociology at the University of Minnesota. I had recently received my PhD in social psychology from Harvard University. As a small-group researcher, I was particularly intrigued with how groups produced culture and the way in which cultural themes shaped collective identity and shared action. This topic, linking culture, structure, and interaction, has been the focus of my research over a half century in studies of restaurant cooks, high school debaters, mushroom collectors, government meteorologists, chess players, senior citizen political activists, Civil War buffs, and other work and leisure communities. Over the years, I have taught at the University of Minnesota, University of Georgia, and now Northwestern University; I have studied groups in each community.

To understand the genesis of my fantasy gaming project, I return to my first ethnographic project, a study of Little League Baseball teams.[3] While I was in graduate school, much of my research involved laboratory studies of group behavior, but I was looking for a field site where I could find groups in situ that were oriented both to achieving a goal (instrumental culture) and to providing emotional satisfaction (expressive culture). Little League players wanted to win games and to have fun. I conducted this research for three years in Massachusetts, Rhode Island, and Minnesota, observing ten teams and hanging out with preadolescents before and after games. The publications from this study provided me with a certain prominence in sociology.

However, by the end of the project, I realized that there was a limitation to what I could claim. Little League teams each had a local culture, but the culture was thin. The boys—almost all were boys—spent only a few hours each week with their teammates, and most of that time was focused on the sport itself. Although nicknames and rituals were created and jokes were shared, the team was not a central feature of the lives of these suburban preadolescents. I hoped to find a community in which the culture was more salient.

One evening, my wife and I were invited to the home of a more senior colleague in my department. As we discussed my research on youth baseball, he explained that his teenage son had recently started to spend time with friends playing a game that centered on medieval fantasy, *D&D*. This boy and his friends were creating an imaginary universe in which they took on the role of characters and went on imaginary adventures. I was fascinated. This seemed like the cultural world-building that I had not found with my young baseball players. His son invited me to join him the next Friday evening. It is perhaps of some interest that he and his father were Native Americans, but he was eager to embrace medieval European mythologies (similar experiences are explored by Daniel Heath Justice in chap. 16 of this collection). For many teenagers, the world of J. R. R. Tolkien seemed universal. In our dreams, we were all hobbits, elves, and dwarves.

And so, in late 1977, I began to attend Friday night sessions of this Minneapolis gaming group that I labeled the "Golden Brigade." The event was held in the community room of a Minneapolis police station. Few police officers entered the room, and we appeared uninterested in their activities. Perhaps because of the locale, drugs or alcohol were not in evidence among the players. Anywhere from ten to fifty players would attend, sitting around different tables, most with about a half-dozen players. Players also hung out at a local gaming store, close to the police station. At that time in role-playing gaming, almost all the players were young men (typically aged thirteen to twenty-five). I was in my late twenties and not so different in age from the older players, many of whom belonged to science fiction subcultures. The few women who played were the girlfriends (the term used then) of the male players, and they were treated as not being serious about the activity. A few mildly rude remarks were made at their expense. The games were not as inclusive as they later became.

Typically, the evening began at 7:00 p.m. but could last until 3:00 or 4:00 a.m., particularly for those who had access to transportation or whose parents would pick them up. Most younger players left by midnight, and the games would become somewhat rowdier. At the start of the evening, as we broke into groups, each table would decide which game to play (*Chivalry & Sorcery* was particularly popular) and would decide if new characters would be created or previous ones used again. Would the story be continued, or would a new adventure begin? I was startled at first at the amount of time that it took to organize a game and to create characters. Often games did not begin until 9:00 p.m., two hours after gamers arrived. Creating and re-creating player characters was as much fun as actually role-playing. Of course, the person who was the dungeon master (DM), game master (GM), or referee controlled the pace of the activity. It was known that certain of the older and more experienced players would serve as the DM, and each had their own style, sense of humor, and narrative facility. What one's dice read mattered far less than what the DM interpreted the result to mean. They were storytellers. What was crucial was that the action continued, that player characters were not killed off, and that there were enough trophies and gold to spread around.

When I first attended, I knew nothing of the game, but after two years, I had become one of the more knowledgeable participants, occasionally asked to be the DM. And, in time, I was asked to join private groups. I joined two, including one run by M. A. R. "Phil" Barker, another faculty member at the University of Minnesota, who had a gaming group based on his fantasy game, *Empire of the Petal Throne* (1975).[4] As I became involved in these worlds, I read deeply in fantasy and science fiction. This was a genre that was sometimes labeled "boy's literature," although today many of the most prominent authors are women, and many fantasy worlds have feminist themes. These imaginary worlds have changed much over the past half century.

In addition to the observations in Minnesota, I also attended gaming gatherings, notably the early Gen Con conventions that were then held at the Parkside Campus of the University of Wisconsin in Kenosha. Hundreds of gamers descended on the campus for several days, engaging in role-playing games all night. Eventually the event, which had started at the TSR headquarters in Lake Geneva, took over the convention center in Milwaukee. My younger son attended several decades after my research had ended. Gen Con is now held in Indianapolis. Attending was an opportunity for me to meet gamers from around the region.

As part of my research, I gathered copies of printed magazines like TSR's house organ *The Dragon* (1976–2013), as well as the more informal zines—often mimeographed sheets that one or several gamers would compile every so often. Perhaps not surprisingly, some were more literate than others. Aside from reading these documents, I interviewed several gamers and game creators, including Gary Gygax and Dave Arneson, and learned something of the disputes about who created what and debates over intellectual property. It was a yeasty time.

By the end of the research, there were stirrings that *D&D* and other fantasy games led players to Satanism or suicide. While nature religions (Wiccan communities) have certainly grown over the decades, Satanism has not been a growth culture, despite the fears of some parents. Suicides were trickier. There were certainly young men, active gamers, who committed suicide. A few players seem to have become depressed because of what happened to their characters or because of rejection by their friends. One anecdotal claim pointed to seventy suicides, and these were certainly tragic moments for families understandably looking to find meaning and to assign responsibility. I never denied that some of these deaths might have been brought about by events in fantasy gaming groups. The point that I would always make is that it is impossible to know how many suicides were prevented. Many of these teenagers and young adults were searching for a community to belong to, and fantasy gaming might have provided a caring escape from isolation. While not wishing to weigh suicides against prevented suicides, I suspect that the latter group was larger. Our group in the Minneapolis police station was welcoming to most who wished to join.

After two and a half years, I felt that I had learned what I was going to learn, and it was time to leave the scene. I was a sociologist—a professor—and not a gamer. Over a short period of time, I left the scene and never returned, except a decade later to serve as a DM for my younger son and his friends for a few months.

However, my final testimony was my book (along with an essay about the *D&D* panic).[5] I had contacted the University of Chicago Press sociology editor, Marlie Wasserman, early in the research process, and she was interested in the project and asked to review the manuscript. When the manuscript was completed in 1981, she had left for Rutgers University Press, where she became press director. She was replaced by Douglas Mitchell at the University of Chicago Press, a beloved sociology editor. Doug proved to be as supportive of the project as Marlie. The manuscript was eventually sent to two reviewers, who both believed that the manuscript should be published. But there was a problem. When this manuscript on the sociology of fantasy gaming was sent to the faculty board at the press, there was concern whether the august University of Chicago Press should be publishing a scholarly treatise about—shudder!—a child's game. Back then, few academics examined popular culture. The world has changed substantially in forty years. So the faculty board made a decision. They asked for one additional review, and that had to be from a high-status reviewer who had high standards. Needless to say, I was nervous. But, fortunately, the happy ending of this fantasy was that the reviewer liked the manuscript, perhaps more than the original reviewers, and the manuscript was published. However, it was only published in hardback (until 2003), which limited the number of teenagers who purchased the work. But the book remains available for all who want a copy.

Although well over forty years have passed since my research began, I have great fondness for this project. I know that I could never last until 4:00 a.m. these days, but those long evenings spent gaming were thrilling times.

All during the course of the research, I believed that I was observing a rare shard of social interaction, never imagining the way in which fantasy gaming would become part of American—and global—culture.

NOTES

1. Gary Alan Fine, *Shared Fantasy: Role-Playing Games as Social Worlds* (Chicago: University of Chicago Press, 1983).

2. Edward E. Simbalist and Wilf K. Backhaus, *Chivalry & Sorcery*, 1st ed. (Fantasy Games Unlimited, 1977); M. A. R. Barker, *Empire of the Petal Throne* (TSR, 1975); Marc Miller, Frank Chadwick, John Harshman, and Loren Wiseman, *Traveller* (Game Designers' Workshop, 1977).

3. Gary Alan Fine, *With the Boys: Little League Baseball and Preadolescent Culture* (Chicago: University of Chicago Press, 1987).

4. Barker, *Empire of the Petal Throne*, 1975.

5. Daniel Martin and Gary Alan Fine, "Satanic Cults, Satanic Play: Is 'Dungeons & Dragons' a Breeding Ground for the Devil?" in *The Satanism Scare*, ed. James Richardson, David Bromley, and Joel Best (New York: Aldine de Gruyter, 1991), 107–123.

3

EXPLORATION AND EXPERIENCE: THE GAME CHANGERS

Jon Peterson

With the half-century anniversary of *Dungeons & Dragons* (*D&D*) at hand, what is so compelling about the game that it has survived so long and inspired so much? It is high time for a detailed historical investigation of two of its most influential design properties: exploration and experience (E&E).

When Gary Gygax first played a Blackmoor session with Dave Arneson,[1] Gygax found "the idea of measured progression (experience points) and the addition of games taking place in a dungeon maze as being very desirable."[2] This chapter leverages primary sources to chart the evolution of E&E systems through precursors in the tradition of wargames and commercial board games, paying special attention to areas where the Blackmoor approach proved particularly innovative. To this end, it covers

- *limited-intelligence* wargames, which simulated the ignorance of the tactical situation that commanders faced in historical battles;
- *veterancy* systems, which promoted wargame units for successful outcomes in combat;
- how those veterancy systems in turn merged with *victory point* mechanisms to result in the *experience point* mechanic in Blackmoor;
- and finally the fusion of that experience mechanic with the unique limited intelligence of dungeon exploration that fueled Blackmoor adventures.

D&D as published in 1974 popularized these concepts broadly but would not be the final word in the nature of experience or exploration. Many designers who, like Gygax, found these properties highly desirable would then tweak them to serve new purposes, especially as computers became available to handle the paperwork. The chapter concludes with some pointers to sources to further explore this tradition.

LIMITED INTELLIGENCE

The term "limited intelligence" applies to game systems in which one or more parties lack a real-time knowledge of the game situation, especially the position of opposing units. The term "fog of war" is also used for designs with this property. Sometimes game elements are obstructed from view by a physical barrier or are secretly recorded on paper until that information becomes available to players.

Limited intelligence is frequently leveraged by wargames, which are conflict simulation games that approximate the experience of command during warfare. The earliest tabletop games of this form broke off from chess—a game in which two competing players enjoy a commanding perspective on the same board, where the position of every piece is always visible to both.[3] This little resembles the situation in actual war—especially in the premodern era—where commanders ordered their troops to move based on imperfect intelligence reports of enemy positions received from the field, allowing them only a loosely coherent picture of the tactical situation. We might say that wargames truly came into their own when they attempted to recapture that property on the tabletop. The early nineteenth-century *Kriegsspiel* of the Reiswitz family departed from chesslike games by giving players only the sorts of written reports they would receive on the battlefield of the time, and allowing them to "move" only by writing orders to their troops. A third-party referee—sometimes called a "judge" or "umpire"—who secretly maintained an omniscient view of the terrain and troop positions would craft field dispatches from scouts and interpret how troops might respond to the orders that players issued. Players with any hope of victory had to maintain their own maps with the inferred position of troops to keep track of events.

Hobby wargames using miniature figurines were popularized in the Anglo-American world by H. G. Wells's *Little Wars* (1913).[4] Wells envisioned his game transpiring on a lawn reminiscent of *Tristram Shandy*, or perhaps the floor of a nursery, with his players moving their infantry, cavalry, and artillery with their own hands, and even aiming toy cannons to shoot wooden dowels at visible enemy ranks. But the principle of employing a neutral third-party referee to guard limited intelligence would reverberate through American hobby wargames that nominally followed the tradition of Wells.

Naval battle games would inspire a great deal of work on limited-intelligence systems. *Salvo* (1931),[5] the ancestor of the familiar children's game *Battleship*, was a pen-and-paper game in which both players would secretly record the location of their ships on a paper grid and then mark off the locations of bombardment hits and misses as they attempted to guess how their opponents' fleet was arranged. Unlike a traditional board game, the "moves" in *Salvo* took place in a dialogue, a conversation where players by trial and error propose where bombs will drop, after which their opponents report back verbally whether a hit was scored.[6]

Fletcher Pratt's Naval Wargame (1940) recommended an open floor space for positioning waterline models of warships that would be visible to all players.[7] But accounting for underwater vessels required a different approach: a "player handling a fully submerged submarine is sent out of the room and marks his moves on a sheet of paper."[8] Only when "the referee gets a submarine's maneuver sheet, showing the firing of torpedoes," will the floor space be marked to show the projectile, from which opposing commanders might infer the submarine's location.

Limited-intelligence mechanics became common in the naval wargames of the 1960s published by Avalon Hill. Following *Fletcher Pratt*, any naval wargame that involved submarines typically relied on some means of concealing their location from opposing players, starting with Avalon Hill's *U-Boat* (1961). *Bismarck* (1962) pioneered the distinction between a "search board," inspired by *Salvo*, which is used by the British player to locate the *Bismarck*, and a "battle board" representing the section of ocean where tactical combat between ships would be staged when the *Bismarck* is found.

The emergence of play-by-mail *Diplomacy* (1959) variants,[9] pioneered by John Boardman in 1963, opened new possibilities for third-party referees keeping game information secret from players. In-person tabletop *Diplomacy* required its seven players to simultaneously reveal written moves for each turn; when playing by mail, players would post their moves to a neutral third-party "gamesmaster" to reconcile everyone's actions. Once *Diplomacy* had adopted this refereed format, it began to resemble the written-order *Kriegsspiel* of the Reiswitz family. Each postal *Diplomacy* player had to maintain a paper copy of the map showing the position of their own and enemy forces based on the move results published by the referee.

When postal *Diplomacy* variants in the 1960s began to incorporate science fiction and fantasy themes, they replaced the traditional board with novel systems of exploration. Stellar-empire games in particular opened up new ways of thinking about an unexplored space where conflict takes place. *War of the Empires* (1967) turned the "search board" of *Bismarck* into a "sector map" of the galaxy and used the "battle board" for tactical ship combat that might arise during the course of play.[10] *Xeno* (1967) instead favored a cubical coordinate grid with 3,375 sectors.[11] To discover enemies, players must scout unfamiliar sectors to learn of the presence of planets and civilizations. These space wargames thus explicitly focused on the exploration of unfamiliar territory.

Gygax was an early player of space games like *War of the Empires*, which he personally revised in a 1969 edition.[12] Perhaps the most successful of these games was Philip N. Pritchard's *Lensman* (1969). When the International Federation of Wargaming started a fanzine called *Interplanetary Communicator* dedicated to this game,[13] we can see among its original subscribers both Gygax and Arneson, in addition to other members of their circles in the Twin Cities and Lake Geneva. *Lensman* was explicitly advertised as a game with "hidden movement, limited intelligence, battles on a separate hex board."[14] The space-empire game tradition, together with *Fletcher Pratt* and the various Avalon Hill naval games, shows the prevalence of limited intelligence in games leading up to *D&D*.

When fantasy themes began to enter *Diplomacy* variants, they too leveraged the neutral gamesmaster to manage limited intelligence. Most Tolkien-inspired variants had a rule for the One Ring: for example, *Mordor vs. the World II* explained that "the Ring is invisible. Its location must always be reported to the Gamesmaster."[15] A game might be set in an environment familiar from fantastic literature, or in an entirely novel imaginary world. The Midgard family of games, a spin-off of postal *Diplomacy* fandom, relied on a gamesmaster to manage a totally secret world map that players could only learn by exploring it.[16]

Gygax entered the commercial market for miniature wargame rules with the release of *Chainmail* (1971), coauthored by Jeff Perren.[17] *Chainmail* adapted the tradition of Wells's miniature wargames to the medieval setting. As such, it was largely a game where two competing players surveyed the same battlefield and could always see the positions of units. But as with *Fletcher Pratt*'s submarines, there were medieval battle situations where troops might disappear from view: namely, the construction of tunnels during sieges to undermine castle walls. Since opposing commanders would be unable to determine the location of each other's mining and countermining attempts, *Chainmail* stipulated that "these operations are only possible to conduct on paper. A third party is necessary to act as judge of the various attempts."[18] Limited information about underground activities was thus a part of the *Chainmail* system.

Chainmail is less remembered today for its medieval rules than for its famous "Fantasy Supplement," which detailed how the battles of Tolkien and Robert E. Howard might be re-created on a tabletop. To that end, the supplement systematized Heroes, Super-Heroes, Wizards, and various fantastic creatures from elves and dwarves to orcs and balrogs. As Gygax had involved Arneson in the mythical world known as the "Great Kingdom" of his Castle & Crusade Society, Arneson picked up *Chainmail* and began running fantastic adventures using its system as "the basis for all our combat" in his own allocated section of the Great Kingdom, which Arneson called Blackmoor.[19] But Arneson quickly began to develop new rules to suit a unique mode of play that emerged in his group.

"The big change was laying out the dungeon for explorations and the like combined with a maze that you have to map as you go along, thus offering the possibility of getting lost," Arneson would write to Gygax.[20] By taking his adventuring underground, Arneson created a unique new form of the fog of war. Even in a space wargame like *Xeno*, players had an open coordinate grid that showed them all of the potential areas of the map that they could explore. A mazelike dungeon, however, admitted of no bird's-eye view, no ostensible terrain map. Players only learned where it was possible to go by exploring, corridor by corridor, room by room, the confines and extent of the dungeon. A neutral third-party referee needed to prepare a dungeon map in advance and then tell players only what they would see at the particular location in the dungeon where they currently stood. This maze-driven style of play has little direct precedent in prior games and is probably best understood as an adaptation of fantasy literature sources. This use of limited information carried over aboveground as well, as "the terrain beyond the immediate surroundings of the dungeon area should be unknown to all but the referee."[21]

Moreover, the dungeon did not exist solely as a maze to be navigated; it was a venue where players would hunt through the underworld for monsters to defeat and prizes to recover. When Arneson conceived of the Blackmoor dungeon, he envisioned each room of the dungeon as a potential skirmish wargame to be fought by an exploring party against a set of defenders. Not every room in the dungeon would be occupied, but Arneson stipulated that the percentage of occupation would increase as you descended, so that "on the 1st level it was 1/6, on the 3rd level it was 1/3, and after the 6th level it was 50%."[22] But each defeated adversary in Blackmoor could help to make an adventurer more ready for further challenges, a concept that had its own roots in wargaming history.

VETERANCY

The early hobby wargamers in the 1950s intuited that some units should just be better than others. Tony Bath, then among the foremost wargamers in Britain, had already in 1956 devised a system for "Champions" in his game who were "elevated above the common warrior" and "given a numerical value in proportion to its importance."[23] That number reflected the superiority of one Champion over another, and the likelihood of prevailing in combat with another Champion. But Bath's Champions had a fixed numerical value that did not improve with combat experience.

Bath's circa-1960 "generalship" system ranked leaders on a scale from A to D and allowed that "promotion or demotion" could be applied if "either the winner has fought an outstanding battle, or that the loser has made an utter mess of it."[24] A success-driven rank increase could theoretically promote any sort of wargame unit: around the same time, Jack Scruby devised a system for "increased fighting value" that granted troops a bonus to performance if they won battles. After a victory, an infantry unit with a starting fighting value of 1 receives an incremental bonus: "In the next melee it fights in, its combat points will be counted at 1½ point per man. If it should win this melee, it then is given another IFV of ½ point, and thus becomes a 2 point regiment."[25] The loose cluster of practices that modeled improvement with combat experience had no accepted name at the time, so we shall refer to them here as "veterancy" systems.

While it is difficult to generalize about the multitude of veterancy systems proposed or used during this time of tremendous innovation in wargame system design, these systems attempted to model factors like "experience, training and discipline."[26] The least experienced troops might be called "recruits" or "green" or "militia." Troops who at least had undergone military training for their era might be called "line" or "regulars" or simply "normal." Don Featherstone, cataloging such systems in 1970, describes a four-tiered system from untried to tried to veterans to guards, where "as the campaign progresses so will units more rapidly rise in status as they acquire battle experience."[27]

These ideas began to enter board wargames in the late 1960s. Lou Zocchi's *The Battle of Britain* (1968) contains a section on "Veterans," which stipulated: "All aircraft which fought and survived one week of combat are classified as veterans. When these units enter combat, add one point to the die roll for combat results."[28] Joe Morschauser in 1966 proposed tracking even individual soldiers "in human terms," quantifying eyesight, toughness, and "staying power."[29] His green troops would have a low staying power, but "if the recruit does well in an action or two, survives, his staying power may be increased."

It was into this environment that the Twin Cities gamers began to develop veterancy systems for Napoleonic-era wargaming. As Dave Wesely worked toward his *Strategos N* rules in 1968, he developed a range of eliteness ranks for soldiers of the era. When Arneson used *Strategos* rules for his own campaigns, he integrated a veterancy system that showed how troops might improve from conscripts to regulars "after one-two battles," and with further success they might become experienced, then veterans,

Irregular troops	Cannot improve	
Conscripts	Can improve	
Regulars	two points (ADD ONE)	after one-two battles
Experienced	add one point	after 3-4 battles
Veterns	add one point	after 6 battles
Elites	add one point	after 8 battles
Guards	add one point	after 10 battles

3.1 Excerpt from *Corner of the Table*, January 1970, showing the number of victories needed to progress in veterancy.

then elites, and finally guards after some ten battles.[30] Systems with similar veterancy properties became prevalent in the Twin Cities: the *Strategos A* rules that Arneson coauthored with Randy Hoffa in 1969 show the same six-rank progression of veterancy from conscripts to guards.

The term "experience" became the general name Arneson used to describe the process of veterancy. In his Napoleonic Simulation Campaign, Arneson tabulated the experience of the units his players commanded. He ruled early in 1970 that "troops will be credited for gaining experience in a battle only if a battle report is submitted citing the units involved and the nature of the action."[31] Gary Gygax played in that campaign, and the concept of experience moved over into the set of naval rules Gygax and Arneson collaborated on for it: *Don't Give Up the Ship*. The 1971 draft of the game published through *International Wargamer* includes text like "with actual combat experience crews gain confidence if they won (if they lost then they aren't around) so for every successful boarding and capture raise the Crew Factor value by 1%."[32] Incremental systems of this kind coexisted with strict rank-based systems that awarded jumps for every battle or two.

A similar veterancy system could also be found at the time in *Tractics*, a modern-era miniature wargame designed by Gygax with members of his local group. The game's "morale" system positions troops on a continuum from green to veteran and regular to elite. As an example of this progression, the rules describe how, during World War II, "the U.S. 2nd Armored Division was a Green Regular unit when it landed in North Africa. By the end of the Tunis Campaign, it had become a Regular unit. After Sicily the 2nd was a Veteran division."[33]

Thus veterancy systems existed in quite a few wargames before *D&D*—though by no means all. Gygax's *Chainmail* loosely ranks its fantasy units by their efficacy: the class of Heroes in its "Fantasy Supplement" is specified as four times as powerful as the base medieval unit they are drawn from, which "can range from Light Foot to Heavy Horse." Similarly, the Super Hero is "about twice as powerful" as the Hero. The class of Wizards is defined to include Sorcerers and Warlocks; an addendum to *Chainmail* separated Wizards into strata of "four classes of persons endowed with magical ability."[34] The *Chainmail* rules do not, however, have any concept of veterancy, any way to become a more powerful Hero or Wizard. Perhaps the most significant innovation of Blackmoor was its progression mechanism, which had its origins in wargame point systems.

POINT SYSTEMS

Tabulating points to decide the victor of a hobby wargame became crucial to a number of innovations on the path to experience points in *D&D*. The idea goes back to Wells's *Little Wars* and his notion that a wargame campaign would encompass a series of battles, with no individual encounter deciding the course of the campaign. Campaigns placed battles in a strategic context, which allowed "scoring the results of each game [i.e., battle] and counting the points towards the decision of a campaign."[35] After settling on a target point total for the campaign, players "scored a hundred for each battle won, and in addition 1 each for each infantry-man, 1½ for each cavalry-man, 10 for each gun," with additional stipulations for prisoners. Wells drew inspiration for his system from the scoring of the card game whist, and once the hobby wargame community began adapting this system in the late 1950s, point systems became a key indicator of victory.

Wells, furthermore, stipulated that point values for units could allow opposing wargamers to balance customized armies for a fair contest. This idea became popular with later wargamers: for example, Larry Brom introduced "Sharpshooters" (similar to Bath's "Champions") worth two points each, assigned cavalry a value of three points, and proposed that "each player then builds up a 150 point army using any combination of forces according to their point value."[36] The basic idea of a point-buy system for balancing opposing armies would reach a wide audience through Morschauser, who showed a five-hundred-point game.[37]

Board wargames published by Avalon Hill in the 1960s focused on preconstructed battle scenarios in which the forces available to opposing players followed historical precedent, rather than on customizable armies. The most prevalent early victory conditions involved eliminating the opposing force or capturing a particular terrain position. But Avalon Hill games soon began to incorporate victory points. *Bismarck* in 1962 put it succinctly: "The player who has accumulated the most points when the game ends is declared the winner."[38] Points would be earned by sinking enemy vessels; the more hits required to sink them, the more points scored. Similar rules appeared in *Midway* (1964), and that game featured a direct correspondence between the number of hits required to sink a vessel and the number of points scored by sinking it. It was not until later in the decade, in Avalon Hill games like *1914* (1968), that the explicit term "victory points" was used to characterize these systems.[39]

Many space wargames of the 1960s followed the Avalon Hill precedent for victory points. The 1969 text of Phil Pritchard's *Lensman* incorporates a point tally system based on the destruction of enemy units, with the simple legend "High score wins." In Gygax's 1969 edition of *War of the Empires*, ships were similarly assigned point values "used in computing points gained by destruction of enemy ships."[40] These points translated into a currency called "credits," and in *War of the Empires*, "the winner of the game is the player who accumulates the largest number of credits." Credits can be used to purchase more ships, and thus to field larger armies for the conquest of the galaxy.

The budgeting of *War of the Empires* reflects the influence of economic board games on victory point systems. Accumulating money in such games would be familiar to anyone growing up in the 1960s thanks to the popularity of board games like *Monopoly*. Space wargames in particular drew on *Diplomacy*, which had as its original victory condition fielding the largest army, which in turn required controlling the majority of the thirty-four "supply centers" on the board, each of which allowed its controller to field a single military unit. But not long after postal *Diplomacy* games emerged, there followed economic variants of *Diplomacy*, where supply centers grant ten "chips" per turn in upkeep, and supporting an army

**Fold forward on dotted line and
write SUCCESS FORMULA under flap.**

| MONEY | FAME | HAPPINESS |

$ __10_,000 + __25_ ★s + __25_ ♥s = 60 pts.

OCCUPATION RECORD				SALARY LEVEL	★	♥
Check:	1st	2nd	3rd	0__	16	2
Farming				$1000_✓	10	4
Business				2000_✓	2	4
Sea	✓			3000_✓	6	10
Politics				4000_✓	10	4
Hollywood	✓			5000_✓		6
Uranium	✓			6000_✓	44	
Moon	✓	✓		7000__		30
				8000__		
				9000__		
COLLEGE EDUCATION				10,000__		
				11,000__		
Law				12,000__		
				13,C00__		
Medicine				14,000__		
Engineering				15,000__	Money score (cash-on-hand) at end of game:	
				16,000__		
Science	✓			17,000__		
				18,000__	$____,000	
College Degree				19,000__	©	

3.2 *Careers* (Parker Brothers, 1955) used a "Success Formula" scoring sheet, which folds over at the top to conceal secret goals from competing players.

costs around eight chips.[41] Numerous similar variants ensued, with complex budgetary allocation systems. When Arneson used a *Diplomacy* variant as a baseline for strategic-level actions in his Napoleonic Simulation Campaign in 1969, he implemented economic budgets for each of the participating nations to determine what sort of armies they could field. In the naval arena of Arneson's campaign, you could grow your fleet by taking "prize" ships from an enemy, which could also be converted into cash. Economic systems from the Napoleonic Simulation Campaign would be repurposed for the strategic-level medieval wargame transpiring in Arneson's region of the Great Kingdom, as forces like the Egg of Coot, the Duchy of Ten, and so on, contended for the Blackmoor area.

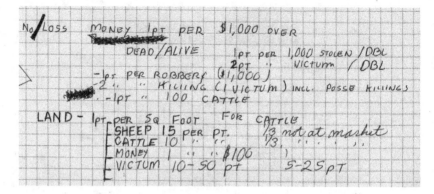

3.3 Point-scoring notes from Brownstone (ca. 1971).

Victory point systems exerted a decisive influence on Blackmoor through the "Braunstein" tradition of games pioneered by Dave Wesely. While the Braunstein games are largely remembered for the role-playing antics that they unleashed, Wesely planned a system for them that "spelled out how each player could score points and how to decide who won (highest score, 'obviously')."[42] For that aspect, Wesely was "inspired by *Careers* (each player sets their own secret victory conditions)." The Parker Brothers game *Careers* (1955) offers an important example of how victory points manifested in mainstream board games as well as wargames: in *Careers*, players must accrue sixty points to win, but before the game starts, each player secretly records target amounts of happiness, fame, and money points—adding up to sixty—that they need to secure.

Unfortunately, only very fragmentary documents from Wesely's early Braunstein games are known to have survived, but we have more direct insight into the point scoring of the Brownstone variant run in the Twin Cities by Duane Jenkins in the immediate run-up to Blackmoor. Brownstone's Old West setting encompasses gunslingers, bandits, law enforcement, ranchers, and various other staples of the genre, each of whom could score points by acquiring or protecting assets (land, cattle, cash) or by defeating various adversaries. A surviving sheet of notes from Brownstone shows, for example, getting one point per $1,000 retained, an exchange rate for cash into points familiar from *Careers*. It also shows a sort of bounty system, where killing an outlaw will give you one point per

$1,000 the outlaw stole—but if the outlaw is captured alive, your point take is doubled.

When Arneson announced to his local group the first session of what was to become Blackmoor, he called it a "medieval Braunstein."[43] While in retrospect we might take that construction to be synonymous with role-playing, we should not lose the connotation that it would be a game played for points, where players win points for their characters by accumulating money and defeating adversaries. It would be the fusion of such victory point systems with veterancy that would make Blackmoor unique among the games in its era.

TYING IT TOGETHER

Chainmail incorporated both point-buy and victory point wargame systems. To aid in setting up a battle, "a table of point values appears in these rules, and you will find it helpful in selecting balanced forces."[44] For medieval wargame units, *Chainmail* proposes that a light footman be worth 1 point, a light horse 3 points, a light catapult or cannon 15 points, and so on. Point values of troops can also be used to determine victory, "keeping count of gains and losses for a set number of turns, the winner being the side with the greatest number of accumulated points."[45]

The *Chainmail* "Fantasy Supplement" furthermore assigned point values to the creatures from Tolkien and sword-and-sorcery fiction. By its reckoning, an orc is worth 2 points, a hero 20 points, and a dragon 100 points. By the second edition of *Chainmail* in 1972, wizards had been divided into four levels of stratification, so that a lowly "Magician" has a point value of 70, whereas the highest "Wizard" goes for 100.

With that, we can begin to link Arneson's Blackmoor dungeon adventures to the system of *Chainmail*. Each occupied room of the Blackmoor dungeon was assigned a "protection point" value. While the exact system used likely varied over time, the system Arneson documented in *The First Fantasy Campaign* allowed rolling up to 50 protection points for rooms on the first level of the dungeon, 150 for the second and third levels, 250 on the fourth level, and so on. For allotting creatures from these protection points, Arneson reported that "the point values given in 1st edition

Chainmail formed the basis for my system."[46] For example, on the seventh level of Blackmoor dungeon, recorded protection points for rooms are between 150 and 500 points; one 500-point room contains 250 dwarves, which in *Chainmail* have a point value of 2 each, whereas another 300-point room contains four true trolls, which in *Chainmail* have a point value of 75 each.[47]

Just as *Chainmail* recommended "keeping count of gains and losses," so adventurers in Blackmoor would record the point values of adversaries they defeated in its dungeon. A surviving character record created by Dave Megarry for Blackmoor shows one of his adventurers, the "Earl's Scholar," defeating a 20-point Anti-Hero, which is the same value as given in *Chainmail*, as well as a 1-point Light Foot. However, Arneson quickly began to alter the point value system in *Chainmail*, in part to implement his hit-point system. *Chainmail* already had a rudimentary concept of fantastic units requiring a cumulative number of hits to defeat in ordinary combat, where, for example, "Ogres are killed when they have taken an accumulation of six missile or melee hits in normal combat."[48] Arneson modified this system by loosely coupling the number of hits taken by a creature with its point value, though he also introduced some randomness through the creation of his "hit die" system. So, for example, in *The First Fantasy Campaign*, Arneson notes Ogres "are worth 18 pts (or hits) with variations,"[49] whereas the point value of Ogres in *Chainmail* is 15. His "variations" often spanned a considerable range: his Giants, for example, take 12 to 72 hits, which is only tenuously anchored to the *Chainmail* point value of 50. Thus the kill record of the "Earl's Scholar" begins with a 57-point Lycanthrope, which would in *Chainmail* have a point value of 20. Ultimately, the notion that you score a number of points upon defeating a creature equal to the number of hits required to kill it reflects the victory point system of games like Avalon Hill's *Midway*.

In a crucial innovation, Arneson's Blackmoor campaign fused this record of points scored by victory in battle with its veterancy system, creating a mobility between strata of characters based on passing certain experience point thresholds. Within the Twin Cities gaming circle, these concepts developed in parallel with similar rank-based progression in point scoring games connected to Mike Carr's aerial wargame *Fight in the Skies*—but otherwise they have little obvious precedent.[50] Scant indication of such mobility existed previously in *Chainmail*: between its first and second editions, Gygax had stipulated that players should "treat normal figures armed with magical swords as Heroes."[51] The idea that material gain could lead to veterancy seemed to comfortably coexist with victory point systems in Blackmoor. Greg Svenson, one of the players in the Blackmoor campaign, handwrote into his copy of *Chainmail* a description of how a starting character would "become hero if possess magic equipment or survived several expeditions or become super hero if you kill 1,000 points of anything."[52] But it was that numerical "measured progression," when Gygax observed it early in 1973, that he immediately found compelling. Arneson had already begun to stratify wizard characters by a numerical "level," and as Gygax and Arneson collaborated toward *D&D*, the progression system would normalize around the idea of "levels" for all the character classes. The 1973 draft rules would summarize: "As players beat monsters in mortal combat and capture various forms of prizes (magic items and treasure) they gain 'experience.' This adds to their Experience Point total, and in this manner players will eventually progress to higher levels."[53]

The real impact of Blackmoor resulted from the pairing of Arneson's "measured progression" system with his idea of dungeon exploration. The dungeon existed as a sort of hunting ground for monsters and treasure that players could explore, returning to the surface to rest and enjoy their spoils before the next expedition. Each gold piece worth of treasure found translated directly into an experience point, and in many dungeon environments, cash was more abundant than adversaries. Dungeons could be practically infinite sources of wealth and its guardians; with wandering monsters (inspired by the random encounters of *Outdoor Survival*), rooms that restocked their occupants over time, and the potential discovery of progressively deeper and deeper levels, they promised an effectively infinite venue for adventure.

The stark novelty of the Blackmoor system could not disguise the roots of its innovations from the early adopters of *D&D*. Ken St. Andre, author of the early *D&D* variant *Tunnels & Trolls*, would in 1975 compare the dungeon to a familiar limited-intelligence game: "The game is played something like *Battleship*. The individual players cannot see the board. Only the D.M. knows what is in the dungeon."[54] Similarly, the relationship between experience points and victory points was not lost on St. Andre; he would write in 1976 about the object of the game being "to pile up 'experience points' (analogous to victory points in other games)."[55] But Blackmoor thoroughly transformed those precedents, in a way that would have a profound influence not just on future games but on popular culture.

LEGACY

With the hindsight of a half century, the clearest sign of the import of exploration and experience systems has been the inspiration they have provided to countless later games—and nongame practices—since the publication of *D&D*. It would be difficult to enumerate all the games that have embraced E&E mechanics, of which *Tunnels & Trolls* and TSR's *Empire of the Petal Throne* (1975) were only the earliest to hit the market; encyclopedic catalogs of such tabletop games have appeared in *Heroic Worlds* (1991) and *Designers & Dragons* (2013).[56] *D&D*, moreover, first appeared at the cusp of the personal microcomputer revolution, and its influence loomed large over the first computer games sold to consumers; the use of a graphical computer to selectively reveal a dungeon map offered a compelling alternative to reliance on a dialogue with a referee, and a computer could easily tabulate experience point accumulation and level advancement. *Dungeons & Desktops* (2019) enumerates the many games in this tradition.[57] Moreover, early tabletop systems for procedural generation of dungeons and their inhabitants would find their ultimate expression on computers.[58]

In the fifty years of revisions to *D&D* itself that followed, its E&E mechanics have remained more or less unchanged (a notable exception would be the recent vogue for story-driven "milestone" level progression), and the game now enjoys a renaissance of popularity following its fifth edition release in 2014. Its reward system of experience points and levels underlies the "gamification" that has permeated twenty-first-century commerce and culture.[59] Because, as Jane McGonigal said, "leveling up is one of the most satisfying kinds of feedback ever designed,"[60] the reward system of acquiring experience points and rising in level can be detached from games as such and connected to all sorts of ranked progressions. This is perhaps most apparent in social media or internet boards that track participation and, at certain thresholds, reward participants with anything from cosmetic titles to actual privileges. Similar systems are used in commercial loyalty programs, though this "gamification" strategy has been criticized in the game studies community as "exploitationware."[61]

It was in the Blackmoor system developed in the Twin Cities that E&E concepts took their initial shape. The very idea of "role-playing" itself is difficult to disentangle from E&E mechanics, which place players in the uncertain position of their characters and allow them to vicariously feel their characters' growth. Arneson himself would say, "RPG is, I feel, a game where the individual character can enhance his ability and station within the game through the characters used in play. . . . That's what I feel a[n] RPG should have as its very heart."[62] Not every game that markets itself as a "role-playing game" embraces E&E mechanics, but exploring worlds and leveling up are now so pervasive in games that their emergence warranted an investigation separate from how the more nebulous concept of "role-playing" took shape.

NOTES

1. Blackmoor is Dave Arneson's personal RPG campaign setting, which originated in the early 1970s. It was a setting for wargames and an early testing ground for what would later become *D&D*. Blackmoor was most thoroughly detailed in Arneson's *The First Fantasy Campaign* (Decatur, IL: Judges Guild, 1977).

2. Gary Gygax, "The Origins of D&D," *The Dragon*, no. 7 (June 1977). *The Dragon* was edited by Tim Kask (and others). It was published in Lake Geneva, WI, and the first issue appeared in June 1976.

3. Jon Peterson, "A Game Out of All Proportions," in *Zones of Control*, ed. Pat Harrigan and Matthew G. Kirschenbaum (Cambridge, MA: MIT Press, 2015).

4. H. G. Wells, *Little Wars: A Game for Boys from Twelve Years of Age to One Hundred and Fifty and for That More Intelligent Sort of Girl Who Likes Boys' Games and Books* (London: Frank Palmer, 1913).

5. *Salvo* (Starex Novelty Company, 1931).

6. See also pen-and-paper variants like "Patterns II" in Sid Sackson, *Gamut of Games* (New York: Random House, 1969).

7. Fletcher Pratt, *Fletcher Pratt's Naval Wargame* (New York: Harrison-Hilton, 1940).

8. Pratt, *Naval Wargame*, rule 6.

9. Alan Calhamer, *Diplomacy* (Cambridge, MA, 1959).

10. Tullio Proni, *War of the Empires* (1967), revised by Gary Gygax in 1969.

11. Jon Peterson, "Per Aspera ad Astra: The Material Culture of Early Space Empire Games," *ROMchip* 1, no. 1 (July 2019), https://romchip.org/index.php/romchip-journal /article/view/58.

12. Gary Gygax and Tullio Proni, *War of the Empires* (1969).

13. Sam Ferris, ed., *Interplanetary Communicator* 1, no. 1, first published in spring 1970.

14. Phil Pritchard, ed., *Galaxian* 2, no. 2 (Tucson, AZ). The first issue of *Galaxian* was published July 1, 1968.

15. Don Miller, "Mordor vs. the World II," *Thangorodim* 1 (1969), originally published in *Diplomania*, no. 8 (1966). *Thangorodim* was edited by Bill Duffie and published in Nyack, NY. The first issue appeared June 21, 1969.

16. Jon Peterson, *Playing at the World* (San Diego: Unreason Press, 2012), 451.

17. Gary Gygax and Jeff Perren, *Chainmail* (Evansville, IN: Guidon Games, 1971). A second edition was published in 1972.

18. Gygax and Perren, *Chainmail*, 29. These rules in turn draw on Jack Scruby's medieval mine/countermine rules in Jack Scruby, *Table Top Talk* 4, no. 2 (1965).

19. Arneson, *The First Fantasy Campaign*, 64.

20. Dave Arneson, letter to Gary Gygax, December 15 (misdated 12), 1972.

21. Gary Gygax and Dave Arneson, *Dungeons & Dragons* (Lake Geneva, WI: Tactical Studies Rules, 1974), vol. 1, 15. Also in draft 1973.

22. Arneson, *The First Fantasy Campaign*, 44.

23. Tony Bath, letter in *British Model Soldier Society*, no. 8 (October 1956).

24. Tony Bath, *War Game Digest* 4, no. 3 (1960). *War Game Digest* was edited by Jack Scruby, and later by Tony Bath and Don Featherstone. It was published in Visalia, CA, and Southampton, UK, and the first issue appeared in March 1957.

25. Jack Scruby, *War Game Digest* 4, no. 4 (1960).

26. A. H. Mitchell, *War Gamer's Newletter* , no. 54 (1966). *Wargamer's Newsletter* was edited by Don Featherstone. It was published in Southampton, UK, and the first issue appeared in April 1962.

27. Don Featherstone, *War Game Campaigns* (London: Stanley Paul, 1970), 35.

28. Lou Zocchi, *The Battle of Britain* (Mineola, NY: Gamescience, 1968), 12.

29. Joseph Morschauser, *Table Top Talk* 5, no. 2. *Table Top Talk* was edited by Jack Scruby. It was published in Visalia, CA, and the first issue appeared in January 1962.

30. Dave Arneson, *Corner of the Table* 3, no. 1 (1970).

31. Dave Arneson, *Ramsey Diplomat* 2, no. 4 (1970). *Ramsey Diplomat* was edited by Pete Gaylord. It was published in Roseville, MN, and the first issue appeared in November 1969.

32. Dave Arneson and Gary Gygax, *International Wargamer* 4, no. 10 (1971). *International Wargamer* was edited by John Bobek (and others). It was published in Chicago, and the first issue appeared in January 1968 (as *Spartan*).

33. Leon Tucker, Mike Reese and Gary Gygax, *Tractics* (Evansville, IN: Guidon Games, 1971), vol. 2, 28.

34. Gary Gygax, *International Wargamer* 5, no. 1 (1972).

35. Wells, *Little Wars*, 34.

36. Larry Brom, *War Gamer's Digest* 3, no. 2 (1959).

37. Joseph Morschauser, *How to Play War Games in Miniature* (New York: Walker and Company, 1962), 77. For later examples, see Peter Young and James Philip Lawford, *Charge!* (Morgan-Grampian, 1967), 99; Donald Featherstone, *War Game Campaigns* (Sport Shelf, 1970), 45; Charles Grant, *The War Game* (A. & C. Black, 1971), 171.

38. Avalon Hill Games, *Bismarck* (1962).

39. Avalon Hill probably borrowed this term from small-press wargames like *Confrontation* (Gamescience, 1967), designed by Phil Orbanes Sr.

40. Gygax and Proni, *War of the Empires*, 13.

41. Jerry Pournelle and Dan Alderson, "Economic Diplomacy," *APA-L*, no. 405 (1965). *APA-L* is the Amateur Press Association of Los Angeles, produced by LASFS (Los Angeles Science Fiction Society). Published in Los Angeles, the first issue appeared in October 1964.

42. David Wesely, Acaeum post, September 25, 2006, https://www.acaeum.com /forum/viewtopic.php?f=10&t=3888&start=20.

43. Dave Arneson, "Upcoming Club Events," *Corner of the Table* 3, no. 4 (April 1971).

44. Gygax and Perren, *Chainmail*, 3.

45. Gygax and Perren, 4.

46. Arneson, *The First Fantasy Campaign*, 44.

47. Arneson, 48. I use the seventh-level dungeon here because, as Arneson explains, the key for the original first six levels was lost, but the seventh through ninth levels "are the originals used in our game" (42).

48. Gygax and Perren, *Chainmail*, 1971, 41.

49. Arneson, *The First Fantasy Campaign*, 91.

50. In the fanzine *Aerodrome*, point-based progression systems had been documented for *Fight in the Skies* as early as November 1970 (issue #17); by the summer of 1973 (*Aerodrome* #38) we see "experience levels" resulting from the accumulation of "experience points." The player base of Blackmoor and *Fight in the Skies* overlapped significantly, so it is difficult to say which influenced which, and best to describe them as parallel.

51. Gary Gygax, "*Chainmail* Additions," *International Wargamer* 5, no. 1 (1972): 12–14.

52. Dan Boggs, "On the Creation and Evolution of Hit Points, Hit Dice, and Experience Points," *Hidden in Shadows* (blog), August 27, 2014, http://boggswood.blogspot.com/2014/08/on-creation-and-evolution-of-hit-points.html.

53. Gygax and Arneson, *Dungeons & Dragons* (1973 draft), 18.

54. Ken St. Andre, *Tunnels & Trolls* (Phoenix, AZ, 1975), 3. Later editions were published by Flying Buffalo.

55. Ken St. Andre, *Monsters! Monsters!* (Austin, TX: Metagaming, 1976), 18.

56. Lawrence Schick, *Heroic Worlds* (Buffalo, NY: Prometheus Press, 1991); Shannon Appelcline, *Designers & Dragons*, 4 vols. (Silver Springs, MD: Evil Hat Productions, 2013).

57. Matt Barton and Shane Stacks, *Dungeons & Desktops* (A. K. Peters, 2019).

58. Gary Gygax, "Solo Dungeon Adventures," *Strategic Review* 1, no. 1 (1975). *Strategic Review* was published by Tactical Studies Rules and edited by Gary Gygax and subsequently Tim Kask. It was published in Lake Geneva, WI, and the first issue appeared in January 1975. It was discontinued (to be replaced by *The Dragon*) in April 1976.

59. Sebastian Deterding, Rilla Khaled, Lennart E. Nacke, and Dan Dixon, "Gamification: Toward a Definition," in *CHI 2011*, May 7–12, 2011, Vancouver, BC, Canada, http://gamification-research.org/wp-content/uploads/2011/04/02-Deterding-Khaled-Nacke-Dixon.pdf.

60. Jane McGonigal, *Reality Is Broken* (New York: Penguin, 2011).

61. Ian Bogost, "Persuasive Games: Exploitationware," *Gamasutra*, May 3, 2011, https://www.gamasutra.com/view/feature/134735/persuasive_games_exploitationware.php.

62. Arneson, "My Life and Role Playing 3," *Different Worlds* 3 (1979).

4

COMBAT IN *DUNGEONS & DRAGONS*: A SHORT HISTORY OF DESIGN TRAJECTORIES

Evan Torner

"Roll for initiative!" Across all editions of *Dungeons & Dragons* (*D&D*), that iconic phrase means two things. The first meaning is *procedural*: players roll a d20, add or subtract ability modifiers from the result, and declare the final number to the caller or dungeon master (DM), who determines which order the player characters (PCs) and their foes will act. The second meaning is *liminal*: PCs enter the "magic circle" of combat, in which special rules governing time, space, fictional bodies, player behavior, and abstraction itself now apply. No longer is the game paced mostly by the players' conversation; now it proceeds at the rate at which player characters can mechanically overcome the combat obstacles—including the monsters' very bodies—that stand before them.

Combat is central to *D&D's play experience*. "A trip to the dungeon," writes Jon Peterson, "continually flip-flops between exploration and combat until, as the rules prophesize, 'the party leaves the dungeons or, are killed therein.'"[1] Fighting often takes up the bulk of many game sessions. Yet both the game's text itself and secondary literature about *D&D* focus more on players' imagination,[2] representation,[3] and simulation.[4] Character and world-building,[5] or even ethical dilemmas posed by the game,[6] dominate *D&D* discourse, despite the importance of (1) building and advancing a character that can survive and end combat encounters sooner rather than later, and (2) maintaining the necessary emotional, strategic, and attentional investment in those encounters when they come up. For example, I once played in a convention session using the 1977 *D&D Basic Set* and felt as if I had stepped into another world. There were eleven players, one of whom was our "caller," who would collect all our actions and dice results to report to the DM. This hierarchy, I was assured, was a time-saving measure. The DM would record the actions and numbers in their notes and respond with statements such as "Claw, claw, bite, miss, hit Tyrin for 6 damage, miss." The conversation was highly structured and regulated, with role-playing discouraged for efficiency's sake. The lineage between tabletop role-playing games (TTRPGs) and computer role-playing games (CRPGs) becomes painfully clear in these moments: the DM is best served by behaving like a computer program responding to player inputs; the computer in a CRPG becoming an algorithmic DM. PCs must then save characters in which they are emotionally invested from the churning grind of a battle.

Gary Gygax, one of *D&D*'s creators, reportedly ran short combat rounds.[7] If a caller was not present to "gather" all the players' actions in a battle, Gygax would simply point at each player in initiative order to make their rolls. "Hit and a miss," he would say. "Roll damage on the hit." And then on to the next player. Scholars and players alike attribute great storytelling capacity to *D&D*,[8] such that the ritualized, perfunctory speech acts of *D&D* combat rounds seem an odd counterpoint. Where is the sweeping narration of epic battles? Or the rhythmic and performative combat found in various human rituals over the past millennia? Instead, clarity and computation are sovereign in *D&D* combat. Again, to quote Peterson, "*Dungeons & Dragons* was the strategic campaign rules which linked battles run under *Chainmail* tactical miniatures rules."[9] In other words, rules and wargame culture from the early 1970s have more or less dictated the standard terms for all physical conflict in *D&D*-style TTRPGs for the past fifty years.

Role-playing itself is simply a structured conversation in which we manage our group's consent to fictional events. This point was raised by Emily Care Boss, as well as Vincent and Meguey Baker, in the "Baker–Boss Principle":

The fictional events of play in a role playing game are dependent on the consensus of the players involved in order to be accepted as having occurred. All formal and informal rules, procedures, discussion, interactions and activities which form this consensus comprise the full system used in play.[10]

Combat in *D&D* constitutes a special form of conversation: highly structured, ritualized, and purposefully devoid of the chaos of real fighting. Yet it is also a moving, intense narrative experience; an emotional roller coaster of decisions, rolls, and outcomes. *D&D* combat quantifies the bodily integrity of all its participants through "hit points," with the role-playing conversation unable to proceed beyond combat itself until the enemies' hit points are reduced to zero.

None of the assumptions underlying this special form of conversation are inevitable: they emerge from deliberate design and established tradition. Moreover, they have shifted over the past fifty years. Whereas early editions of the game were caught in a genuine tension between realism and playability,[11] later ones have marked a design struggle between playability, supplement bloat, and player agency. A rich history of *D&D* combat encounters has meant that hundreds of designers grapple with basic dilemmas: Are the enemies numerically too difficult? Does the encounter last too long? Can one model this encounter with maps and miniatures, or are we using theater of the mind? Do the player characters have reasonably interesting choices, both in the situation and in the system itself?

This chapter explores how *D&D* combat has developed over time, and what *D&D* combat means. To accomplish this, I first describe its core mechanisms and what *D&D* combat encounters of today inherited from *Chainmail*, *D&D*'s predecessor system. Then I will traverse the winding terrain of *D&D*'s different editions and their various treatments of the combat encounter—always as an ongoing design problem—to demonstrate how shifting conceptions of the *D&D* player dictate how combat is to be resolved. Finally, I discuss some core values and assumptions of *D&D* combat and its meaning, in my interpretation. *D&D* combat intends to provide a thrilling narrative experience for the players, but ironically its design tradition means dropping a not necessarily consensual conversation into a shared role-playing game (RPG) narrative. Players are intended to be free to choose among many options, while often being deprived of the greatest option of all: to refuse to fight.

HOW *D&D* COMBAT WORKS

Role-play, exploration, and combat are *D&D*'s three pillars. Bernard Suits (1972) famously wrote that games are "the voluntary attempt to overcome unnecessary obstacles."[12] If experience points were tied to the amount of treasure discovered, as in early versions of *D&D*, then combat literally stood between the players and the very thing that let them level up. But that was the point: combat is the agreed-on "unnecessary obstacle" placed before in-game rewards. In every *D&D* book, pages listing weapons and armor visually dominate the equipment section. Stat blocks suture monsters of classic myth and writer fancy alike to the mechanical requirements of combat. Spell tables focus on the combat readiness of a given spell: precise measurements of distance for casting (range), how many units of combat space it can hit (area of effect), how long it lasts in combat turns and rounds (duration), how long it takes to cast and its necessary materials (components, casting time), and how to mechanically resist it (saving throw).

D&D emerged from wargaming, which had both an ethos of "anything can be attempted"[13] and a reality of player arbitration and "rules lawyering."[14] PCs are often extremely concerned about positional advantage. Combat procedure emerged in the *D&D* play culture as a kind of compromise within the agonistic relationship between the DMs and the PCs: PCs would follow the agreed-on procedures, and DMs would in turn make their best attempt to make fair rulings.

D&D combat works by making a number of different variables available for fair arbitration:

- Which of the combatants go first and in what order
- Where the combatants are positioned with respect to one another
- Whether or not combatants' attacks hit their targets
- What numerical hit-point damage value the successful attacks inflict
- What special effects and resistances (e.g., saving throws) need to be accounted for and their impact on the fight
- Whether or not a combatant is removed from the battle, usually after seeing its hit points reduced to zero
- Whether or not morale from either side of the fight has collapsed and they run away

Below is a table that compares the key features of *D&D* combat across various rule sets.

EDITION	INITIATIVE & ATTACKS	HIT POINTS	TO-HIT & ARMOR CLASS	SAVING THROWS	MORALE	DEATH RULES
Original _D&D_ (_OD&D_) / _Chainmail_ (1974)	Opponents roll opposing dice; higher roll wins OR simultaneous movement (with written orders) possible	Equivalent of unit strength which, when depleted, directly affects morale	Low armor class is good. Both players in a fight roll "To hit" dice and the defender's is subtracted from attacker's	Roll to partially or fully avoid certain damage/effects. DM has the tables based on attack form, character level, and class	Significant measure of victory. Add 2D6 and consult a chart after ⅓ of units are casualties. Also affected by PC charisma	Losing side falls back from melee into retreat and rout. Optional rules for prisoners taken. Combatants "dead" at 0 or negative hit points
_AD&D_ (1977)	Both sides declare intended actions, then roll opposing D6s—higher goes first	Introduction of hit points and hit dice for both PCs and monsters	Low armor class (AC) is good. "To hit" rolls largely based on weapon type, which are then compared with opponents' AC on a table	Roll to partially or fully avoid certain damage/effects. DM has the tables based on attack form, character level, and class	PCs do not need morale checks, but they may be required among henchlings, especially if they've been mistreated, etc.; largely the same as OD&D. Optional.	PC death occurs at −10 HP; 0 HP means unconsciousness
_AD&D_ 2e (1989)	Initiative a contested roll, but modified by combatant abilities and situation	Hit dice for PCs and monsters. PCs recover with at least 1 HP per day of rest, and 3 HP per day of bed rest.	Low armor class still good. The term "THAC0" (To hit armor class 0) is used. Attack roll a d20, modified by situational, armor, weapon-type, character class and level.	Roll to partially or fully avoid certain damage/effects. DM has the tables based on attack form, character level, and class. Ability checks are _also_ possible as Saving Throws	Only NPC allies and monsters check for morale. Base roll is 2D10 against morale rating, asked for when at least 25% of the group has fallen, someone is felled by magic, and additional circumstances	PC death technically occurs at 0 HP, but everyone used optional rule to say it occurred at −10 HP

(continued)

EDITION	INITIATIVE & ATTACKS	HIT POINTS	TO-HIT & ARMOR CLASS	SAVING THROWS	MORALE	DEATH RULES
D&D 3e (2000)	Contested d20 rolls; "Surprise round" added—Certain characters may act before combat begins; Improved Initiative Feat allows players to heavily modify initiative roll; Introduction of Attacks of Opportunity	Hit points based on class level and modified by Constitution. Characters recover HP at the rate of their level number for each day of rest.	High armor class is good, and attacks now include "attacks of opportunity" and other options. Combatants roll d20 + modifiers to beat the number of the opponent's AC	Saving throws directly tied to derivatives of the 6 core stats, namely Fortitude, Reflex, and Will. The DM sets a specific difficulty class (DC) for the saving throw and the PC rolls a d20 plus modifiers to meet or exceed the DC.	No longer any set rules for morale.	If HP drops to 0, a character is *disabled*. At −1 to −9, a character is unconscious and dying, losing 1 HP per round unless they roll a 10% stabilizing check. Death happens at −10 HP or below. A Healing check (DC 15) can be made by another PC to stop HP loss.
D&D 3.5e (2003)	Initiative Check is a Dexterity check with associated bonuses; Characters can Ready or Delay attacks; Surprise Rounds and Improved Initiative still apply	Same as D&D 3e.	Same as D&D 3e.	Same as D&D 3e.	No set rules for morale.	Same as D&D 3e.

D&D 4e (2008)	Determine "Surprise Round," establish character positions on the grid, then roll initiative for each character once for the rest of the fight	Characters start with maximum HP, but at half of their HP they are "bloodied." This allows PCs and DMs to communicate the battle state without directly stating HP values aloud	High armor class is good. Attack rolls are a Standard action, and one rolls a d20 and adds/subtracts the *attack's* own base to-hit bonuses, plus other modifiers. Character's defenses are "base" defense, AC, augmented by Fortitude, Reflexes, and Will. Critical hit on a d20.	Saving throws have no differentiation based on attack type, character level, or anything else. To save, a PC selects an ongoing effect and rolls a d20: lower than 10, the effect continues. Higher than 10, and it ends.	No set rules for morale.	Characters that are reduced to 0 HP are unconscious and are dying. If they take their "bloodied" HP in damage below 0, they are dead. While unconscious, they make a death save every round. Fail 3 saves and the PC is dead.
D&D 5e (2014)	Characters make a Dexterity check on a d20 for Initiative, all Monsters get one Initiative roll too	HP starts at maximum and is reduced to 0. There are no status effects before HP is reduced to 0.	Higher armor class is better. Roll a d20 to attack and add appropriate modifiers, including ability score and proficiency bonuses. A "1" automatically misses, a "20" is a critical hit and player rolls the damage dice twice.	Saving throws involve PCs rolling a d20 modified with a class' standard ability score against a chosen DC by the DM: easy, medium, hard, or very hard	No morale rules exist in the core books for PCs. Monsters roll morale on a table after losing 25% of their forces	PC falls unconscious at 0 HP. PCs roll death saves every round to see if they stabilize. 3 successes stabilizes; 3 results in death. Players can die instantly from massive damage (past their negative max HP)

These core uncertainties drive *D&D* combat sequences. The stat block—vital mechanical information a DM needs to make the monster a threat—is a game instrument geared toward combat. It tells the DM how hard a monster is to hit or affect with spells (armor class, magic resistance), how many would tend to be present in a battle (number appearing), how much time/effort it might take to kill them (hit dice), and, of course, how many attacks per round and their effectiveness (attacks per round, damage per attack). A DM must learn a unique form of reading and interpretation to see such stat blocks and recognize whether or not a monster would be a good match for PCs in a fight.

In 1977, Don Turnbull in *White Dwarf* issues 1–3 laid out what he called the "Monstermark system," which attempted to mathematically systematize this special form of stat block interpretation into easy-to-read monster-difficulty numbers. These became a complex series of equations printed in a fantasy gaming magazine. Turnbull weighs hit dice against attacks per round and attack strength, as well as the relative "value" of a range of special abilities—from fire breathing to being undead—to produce the Monstermark rating for each opponent. This would go on to become the modern-day challenge rating (CR) system in both *D&D* 3e onwards and all editions of *Pathfinder*.

A fight thus begins long before the potential combat situation, in the mind of the DM. Some DMs lean heavily on random encounter tables, but many DMs preplan major set pieces such as specific battles against specific foes. Often PCs have little choice as to whether or not to fight, paradoxically because a high-quality *D&D* combat session requires substantial preparation by the DM. Generally, a DM will already have established the precise location and terrain of the fight, the monsters in it (with assistance from the CR and stat blocks), and the circumstances in which the fight might begin: ambush, awakened camp, ranged skirmish, and so forth. High-quality combat sessions incorporate environmental circumstances, such as fog or knee-deep water, into mechanical outcomes for the PCs, but these effects often prolong the battle.

COMBAT'S SPECIAL TIME

Should communication with the enemy be "undesired or unsuccessful,"[15] then a fight begins. Special time units of turns, rounds, and segments are introduced. Rounds are five to seven seconds long in the fictional world, and since the sunsetting of *AD&D*, a "turn" is a PC's own set of actions within that timespan shared among the group and monsters. The DM has players roll initiative to determine who goes in which order, recording the numbers to maintain a set order. Then the DM describes the combat situation, often with a visual aid or map. If a caller is being used, the caller "collects" the actions of the PCs at the table to then tell the DM when their initiative number comes up. Without a caller, players describe their actions individually to the DM. Each time the enemy's initiative comes up, they may launch their own attacks, often as a group.

On a PC's turn, in theory, they may try to do anything of less than five to seven seconds in duration. To reduce the number of enemies and the time spent in combat, PCs are, in practice, encouraged to maneuver themselves into an optimal combat position in which they cannot be surrounded, and use melee, ranged, or spell attacks on the enemies with the perceived least number of hit points to kill or disable them. Attacking with a spell such as "Magic Missile" does not require a to-hit roll, but all other attacks require that the players roll above a certain number on a d20 to bypass the target's armor class. A miss nullifies most attacks; nothing happens. A hit allows the PC to make a roll "for damage," which shows the DM how many hit points are reduced on the monster's tally. The enemies' attacks against the players follow the same formula: some combination of movement, rolling to hit, rolling damage, and players rolling saving throws against special effects.

Should all the PCs die in a fight, it becomes a "TPK," or "total party kill"—an often socially awkward situation when the DM annihilates the PCs, in whom players have much labor and emotion invested.[16] *D&D* is often played as an ongoing campaign; combat has serious and long-term consequences. One "consents" to a TPK, however, because the default power position of a *D&D* game is that a DM can end the life of a PC at any time, without appeal. The three main mechanisms that PCs have to stave off this arbitrary death are saving throws, hit points, and armor class.[17] If TTRPGs are a conversation, then the DM can always say "I kill you," but the PCs have limited ways to say "No, you don't!" Effectively, PCs interpose additional rolls in between other rolls, for their own protection.

But in a fight where anything may be attempted, must one always roll to attack and reduce hit points? Erick Wujcik famously argued, "If you are playing a dice-based role-playing game, you are already combining it with diceless role-playing."[18] PCs may try to cause a distraction, activate a hazard, or play on a battle leader's insecurities. This involves what the TTRPG community calls "fictional positioning,"[19] or PC manipulation of their own strategic position in the narration to achieve advantage. The game of swinging and missing, of attacks of opportunity, of hit-point attrition and enemy removal, turns out to be only one among several options for conducting *D&D* combat. In fact, reliance on those brute-force hitting-and-missing-and-damage subsystems over, say, the morale subsystem shows how *D&D* combat's roots in *Chainmail* have become distinctly misunderstood and forgotten.

CHAINMAIL

To appreciate how combat has changed over the decades, one should start with *D&D*'s progenitor, *Chainmail*, by Gygax and Jeff Perren. Wargaming coalesced in the 1950s and 1960s around Avalon Hill's *Tactics* (1954) board game, the war miniatures tradition of the British Model Soldier Society, and Allan Calhamer's coalition-building wargame *Diplomacy* (1959).[20] *Chainmail* was a game for those particular players. Gygax emerged from the *Diplomacy* and wargame fanzine community to build his own rules for fantasy miniatures battles with Perren, published as *Chainmail* in 1971. Dave Arneson would quickly use *Chainmail* to run his influential Blackmoor campaign in the Twin Cities,[21] and Gygax grew interested in Arneson's grid-based dungeon-crawl model. The rest is well-known gaming history.

   Chainmail makes the claim that "the following rules will . . . simulate what would have happened if the battle had just been fought in reality."[22] The game offers a torrent of rules, many of which have survived throughout various editions of *D&D*. For example, an infantry unit wielding a heavy crossbow in *Chainmail* may fire only every other turn.[23] This rule reflects the relative slowness of reloading a heavy crossbow versus a light crossbow, and the heavy crossbow deals correspondingly more damage. However, when a heavy crossbowman rolls to hit and misses, they would thus offer the enemy a minimum of two whole turns in which they have done zero damage. Despite the relative uselessness of the heavy crossbow as rendered through this "simulation" of medieval reality, this fire rate is carried from *Chainmail* through all editions of *D&D* until the present. *D&D* 5e at least permits PCs to improve their attack roll with a proficiency bonus, but the weapon is otherwise inaccessible to most classes and not much better than a longbow, which can fire every round. Many vestigial, even actively confusing aspects of *D&D* combat resolution design exist because they are simply carryovers from *Chainmail* without reflecting what that system was intended to do.

Chainmail's morale system serves as a counterweight. Veteran *D&D* players are frequently aware of morale rules but have rarely used them. Calculating and rolling morale compounds the administrative gameplay time of a combat round. For example, the "Post Melee Morale" rules require calculation of the "positive difference"[24] of losses sustained by the side with fewer casualties, then multiplied by a dice roll and compared to a chart that then documents progress toward surrender. Optional morale rules for taking prisoners, "excess casualties," or even the fairly obscure "Swiss/Landsknechte Pike Charge"[25] are all part of *Chainmail*. Morale collapse can end conflict without having to annihilate all the bodies of those who stand before you. But *Chainmail* also made morale calculations tedious and decidedly un-fun. Morale would perhaps be crucial in making *D&D* combat less genocidal and aggressively acquisitive, but it is sidelined in the play culture.

DIFFERENT EDITIONS, DIFFERENT WARS

D&D has had more than ten editions since 1974. Describing *D&D*'s combat shifts over time tells us what values did change, despite its *Chainmail* core. *Chainmail* had no DM; all editions of *D&D* have required at least one. *Chainmail* required miniatures; *D&D* transferred notions of combat space to the imagination and theater of the mind. *Chainmail* was about squad combat and attainment of battle victory conditions; *D&D* turned to individuals and their acquisition of treasure, experience, and magical equipment as they traversed, puzzle solved, and battled their way through various dungeons, castles, caves, ruins, and even wilderness sites. Mechanically speaking, combat in *Chainmail* relied on players rolling six-sided dice, consulting tables, and tabulating effects of troop deaths on squad units (including morale). *D&D* kept the tables but introduced (thanks to the Bristol Wargames Society and Lou Zocchi) various polyhedral dice to roll to hit (the d20) and to roll separately for damage (the d4, d6, d8, d10, and d12). Damage in *D&D* was calculated not in troop losses but in the personal bodily abstraction of "hit points."

The innovations of hit points, experience points, and differentiated to-hit/damage dice rolls alone let *D&D* completely and irrevocably change the design of fantasy wargaming and TTRPGs. *D&D* stressed the individual combatant's bodily integrity, damage-dealing potential, and overall improvement over time. Morale, which focuses on the collective over the individual, would still be in play but was overtly downplayed in favor of the ever-stimulating nature of life-and-death struggle. We must keep this tension between tactical simulation and individual heroics (and death) in mind as we examine fifty years of combat procedures.

Because original *D&D* (*OD&D*) is preoccupied with the simulation of medieval violence, a discomforting level of complexity is introduced around armor and armor class. The baseline of the game is to roll a die and then consult the right table. In *AD&D*, a low armor class (even in the negative numbers!) was good, making one harder to hit. In *AD&D* 2e (as well as in the *OD&D Dungeon Masters Guide*), early armor to-hit tables were substituted out with the "To Hit Armor Class 0" (THAC0) stat on a PC's sheet, which saved time but confused beginners. Issue 74 of *The Dragon* magazine even introduced a spinning-wheel "combat computer," permitting quicker tabulation of all the variables in a single attack at a game session. Wargaming's reliance on tables for modeling conflict lies at the center of this design. Individual heroics were not prioritized in this simulation at first but would become more pronounced as TSR produced ever-widening sets of rules.

AD&D 2e combat unintentionally metastasized. Supplement after supplement, including books such as *The Complete Fighter's Handbook* (1989) and the *Arms and Equipment Guide* (1991), expanded the player's options in preparing for fights. This included taking prestige classes such as the "cavalier" that afforded extra attacks, and introduced all the optional rules that made combat last even longer: called hit-location shots, held attacks, fighting styles, unique weapon rules, and more. Although these supplements made revenue for TSR, *D&D*'s publisher at the time, DMs had difficulties in accounting for all the variables and player options in a given fight, rendering late-1990s *AD&D* combat largely unplayable with the introduction of even one or two optional rules from supplements.

Tasked to overhaul *D&D* for its new owners at Wizards of the Coast and Hasbro, Monte Cook and Jonathan Tweet created *D&D* 3e (subsequently revised as 3.5e and then as *Pathfinder*) to simplify and declutter the whole system. Here, saving throws transform from the specific threat titles such as "Breath Weapon" to "checks" made against a PC's stats and a difficulty class number. Cook and Tweet also made armor class something one would want more of, translating complicated armor and to-hit tables into an easy-to-use set of stacking bonuses added to a d20 roll against a reasonably determined value. "Feats" were added to give characters special abilities. *D&D* 3e and 3.5e bear the influence of Eurogame-style elegant design: that the terminology and choices in the game should be immediately intelligible to all who might play it. Players understanding the game itself got more agency over their PCs' fate.

D&D 4e (2008) sought balance over that particular form of agency. Made in the shadow of *World of Warcraft* (2004–) and other competing fantasy products, *D&D* 4e was a purely combat-based miniatures game that afforded each character comparable advantages on the battlefield. This meant a standardization of various components of character building. Classes are described purely by their combat function—controller, defender, leader, or striker—and each gets a reasonable assortment of combat "powers," which are based on how often one can use them: at will, per encounter, or daily. Fourth edition improved *D&D* as a tactical combat game by providing PCs clear options in every fight, and a range of options beyond standard sword swinging for ten to fifteen rounds.

But *D&D* 4e wasn't successful despite its emphasis on game balance. *D&D* 5e showed the video game cultural shift from *World of Warcraft* to *Dark Souls* (2011). *Dark Souls* is unconcerned with encounter balance, preferring player dexterity and ingenuity for difficult enemy encounters. Player intelligence, coupled with fictional positioning, would intervene to rebalance the game in the players' favor. Consequently, combat balance was discarded: the dice will not go in your favor, so try to use your own wits as a player to seek ways of not rolling them. Combat in *D&D* 5e returned to an endless procession of rounds, which take up the majority of a session.

CORE ASSUMPTIONS AND VALUES OF *D&D* COMBAT

On February 19, 2022, Misha Panarin wrote on Twitter, while subtweeting the head *D&D* designer Ray Winninger:

The weirdest thing about [*D&D*] fans (and, apparently, head designers) is that the self-evident truth that *D&D* is a game whose core gameplay loop and reward structure is combat puts them on the defensive instead of going "yeah and I like it that way" or "yeah but whatever."[26]

Panarin highlights a noticeable anxiety within *D&D* fandom about how much combat dominates both the *D&D* books and the game itself. For context, Winninger had repeated a standard line of accepted *D&D* discourse that although the combat system is paramount to the *D&D* experience, he doesn't use it very much. Such a contradiction between inscribed rules intention and actual player usage could be chalked up to brand marketing—*D&D* sells better as a vehicle for exploration and storytelling than as a repackaged wargame and dice roll-off—but is nevertheless interesting to pursue.

In *AD&D* 1e (1977), Gygax writes: "Combat occurs when communication and negotiation are undesired or unsuccessful. The clever character does not attack first and ask questions (of self or monster) later, but every adventure will be likely to have combat for him or her at some point."[27] Yet combat in *D&D* is inevitable. As Panarin pointed out, one could simply acknowledge enjoyment of this game rhythm. *D&D* 4e indeed tried to address this issue by at least balancing different characters' effectiveness in combat so that all PCs could contribute strategically to a fight. However, such balance was not necessarily desired by *D&D*'s player base. For example, the Australian TTRPG critic Merric Blackman comments on the pacing and difficulty of *D&D* combat:

When people want "balanced" combat in Dungeons & Dragons, they don't want combat that is a 50/50 chance of either side winning. They want combat that the PCs will almost always win, but *feels* like they might lose. As you might expect, this is a bit tricky to pull off![28]

Thus one chimera of fifty years of *D&D* combat history comes into focus: whether player agency and true randomness are important, or rather player emotion and weighted randomness. Give players a "fair" fight, and they may perceive that the deck is stacked against them anyway. Make a fight too easy, and the players lose interest in the overall challenge of fighting. Make the fight too hard, and the players can neither advance the plotline nor enjoy themselves in a straightforward fashion. *D&D* both shackles the "anything can be attempted" freedom of a TTRPG or refereed wargame to a dense set of variables (e.g., PC abilities, monster stat blocks, and the rules themselves) and then asks the DM to not-so-obviously weight a difficult encounter in the PCs' favor. DMs can "fudge," or directly alter, dice roll outcomes to let the gameplay meet player expectations when the system fails to perform.

IDEOLOGY AND COMBAT

D&D combat remains thus a mild embarrassment for *D&D* enthusiasts, as well as a long-term problem seeking endless correction in its design. Thoughtful players admit this and frequently accept the uneven foundations of *D&D* combat so that they might still participate in a rich play culture and shared fantasy imaginary. But as Mary Flanagan and Helen Nissenbaum remind us, even in complex games, one can "[locate] the values that are relevant to a given project and [define] those values within the context of the game."[29] These combat systems are not value neutral and deserve further examination.

Modern wargaming itself emerged in reaction to World War I, "not only [providing] a harmless setting in which human beings could face some of war's challenges without destroying lives, property, or nature, but also taught something of the reality of [the] Great War to those not familiar with its practice."[30] However, this granted a kind of sacred ritual space to combat. Combat takes up its own "special" time in the gameplay[31] and has its own logic for space, bodies, potentialities, and basic math. Nineteenth-century wargame traditions let Prussian officers attempt anything to win a wargame scenario, whereas in the mid-twentieth century, the Cold War brought about the quantification of everything, a world mapped in "targets and numbers."[32] *D&D*'s unique combat system emerged from these two trends. As I have previously written, "a combat system usually arbitrates three major dimensions of a diegesis: time, space and the body, often described in that order within TRPG combat rules. Separate rules arbitrating these dimensions delineate combat from other contests, conflicts, and methods of resolution."[33]

With the discarding of morale, hit points become the primary counter for *D&D* combat time. A player should want to minimize their time in combat, for it will then reduce the possibility of something in the fight killing their PC. This means the best choices for a player during character creation and beyond would be those that let them hit in combat as often as possible for as much damage as possible. Certain forms of min-maxing behavior can be linked not to player dysfunction but to a genuine urge to maximize one's effectiveness against potential elongation and complication of future combat. One must transform one's character into a killing machine, often because one is otherwise at the mercy of the DM and the *D&D* combat round structure. Even the tiny "optional" morale section in the *D&D* 5e *Dungeon Master's Guide* remarks that a "failed saving throw isn't always to the adventurers' benefit. For example, an ogre that flees from combat might put the rest of the dungeon on alert or run off with treasure."[34] Killing the ogre, as the text implies, will actually ensure a smoother time for the adventurers.

This brings us to the narratives of warfare that *D&D* combat tells. When a monster is reduced to zero hit points, it is removed from the fight; it is ambiguously "dead." "Looting" the body is often a standard practice.[35] Here the annihilation of "humanoid" monsters in *D&D* combat is cleansed through rules and abstractions. Grant Piper writes of how "extremely brutal" medieval warfare actually was, and how "many people take the heroics from these times without taking the necessary reality that these battles produced."[36] *D&D* combat lets modern abstractions dominate both the realm of myth and legend and the realm of medieval warfare, cleansed of smell and moral turpitude. It is simply difficult to imagine medieval genocidal warfare, so one chooses to "master" it through the *D&D* combat metaphor.

In its design, *D&D* combat translates the fantastical into the mechanical and tactical. This moment of numerical diminution, of giving even gods "armor class" and "hit points," shows how *D&D* renders all beings intelligible: as potential participants in a fight. Without many alternatives to fighting, *D&D* in general does not give PCs good tools to de-escalate a conflict, or to suffer an enemy to live. The stories *D&D* tells would be much different if the lives of NPCs and monsters had any value, if they weren't just bodies of hit points standing between the players and the next chapter of the story.

CONCLUSION

In this chapter, I have briefly examined the contours of *D&D* combat and its potential interpretations. The combat subsystem began by simulating medieval warfare à la *Chainmail* but now takes up its own special time and space within most *D&D* sessions. The system over time has evolved neither toward realism nor toward playability. As Peter Perla argues:

The key to realistic wargaming lies in balancing the player's experience in [their] decision-making role with as accurate a representation as possible of the physical outcomes of his own decisions, his opponent's decisions, and the objective dynamics of combat.[37]

Instead of this model, a *D&D* fight emphasizes its own substantial length (including all the saving throws and armor class benefits that prolong it) and the reduction of an opponent's hit points to zero. Those who seek to play, run, or design in the *D&D* space will discover that, more than exploring a dungeon or negotiating character relationships, combat dominates runtime play. Roll for initiative.

NOTES

1. Jon Peterson, *Playing at the World* (San Diego: Unreason Press, 2021), 321.

2. Nicholas J. Mizer, *Tabletop Role-Playing Games and the Experience of Imagined Worlds* (Palgrave, 2019).

3. Aaron Trammell, "Representation and Discrimination in Role-Playing Games," in *Role-Playing Game Studies: Transmedia Foundations*, ed. José P. Zagal and Sebastian Deterding (Routledge, 2018), 440–447.

4. Peterson, *Playing at the World*.

5. Kat Schrier, Evan Torner, and Jessica Hammer, "Worldbuilding in Role-Playing Games," in *Role-Playing Game Studies: Transmedia Foundations*, ed. José P. Zagal and Sebastian Deterding (Routledge, 2018), 349–363.

6. Christopher Robichaud and William Irwin, *Dungeons & Dragons and Philosophy: Read and Gain Advantage on All Wisdom Checks* (Wiley-Blackwell, 2014).

7. Ernest Gary Gygax, "Letters," *White Dwarf*, no. 7 (1978).

8. See Stephen Cloete, *Gaming between Places and Identities: An Investigation of Table-Top Role-Playing Games as Liminoid Phenomena* (MA thesis, University of Witwatersrand, 2010); Jennifer Ann Grouling, *The Creation of Narrative in Tabletop Role-Playing Games* (McFarland, 2010).

9. Peterson, *Playing at the World*, 321n199.

10. Emily Care Boss, "Lumpley Principle (or Baker–Care Principle or Baker–Boss)," Black and Green Games, 2021, http://www.blackgreengames.com/terms#.

11. Peterson, *Playing at the World*.

12. Bernard Suits, *The Grasshopper: Games, Life, and Utopia* (Broadview Press, 1978), 54–55.

13. Peterson, *Playing at the World*.

14. Steven Dashiell, "Rules Lawyering as Symbolic and Linguistic Capital," *Analog Game Studies* 4, no. 5 (2017), https://analoggamestudies.org/2017/11/rules-lawyering-as-symbolic-and-linguistic-capital/.

15. Gary Gygax, *Players Handbook* (*AD&D* 1e) (Lake Geneva, WI: TSR/Random House, 1978), 104.

16. Nicholas St. Jacques and Samuel Tobin, "Death Rules: A Survey and Analysis of PC Death in Tabletop Role-Playing Games," *Journal of Japanese Analog Role-Playing Game Studies* 1 (2020): 20–27.

17. Peterson, *Playing at the World*, 321.

18. Erick Wujcik, "Dice and Diceless: One Designer's Radical Opinion," *The Forge*, 2003, http://www.indie-rpgs.com/articles/24/.

19. Chris Chinn, "Fictional Positioning 101," *Deeper in the Game*, March 8, 2008, https://bankuei.wordpress.com/2008/03/08/fictional-positioning-101/Ch.

20. For further information, see Peterson's chapter in this collection (chap. 3) and his book *Playing at the World* (2012).

21. D. H. Boggs, "Blackmoor as a CHAINMAIL Campaign," *Hidden in Shadows* (blog), July 20, 2017, https://boggswood.blogspot.com/2017/07/blackmoor-as-chainmail-campaign.html?m=1.

22. Gary Gygax and Jeff Perren, *Chainmail* 2e (Evansville, IN: Guidon Games, 1971), 7.

23. Gygax and Perren, *Chainmail* 2e, 11.

24. Gygax and Perren, 15.

25. Gygax and Perren, 18.

26. Misha Panarin, "The weirdest thing . . . ," Twitter, February 19, 2022, https://twitter.com/panarin_misha/status/1495189895702327296?s=21.

27. Gary Gygax, *Players Handbook* (*AD&D* 1e) (Lake Geneva, WI: TSR Games, 1978), 104.

28. Merric Blackman, "When people want . . ." Twitter, November 19, 2021, https://twitter.com/merricb/status/1461795945390264329?s=21.

29. Mary Flanagan and Helen Nissenbaum, *Values at Play in Digital Games* (Cambridge, MA: MIT Press, 2014), 75.

30. Peter Perla, *Peter Perla's The Art of Wargaming* (Bristol, UK: History of Wargaming Project, 2011), 169.

31. Evan Torner, "Bodies and Time in Tabletop Role-Playing Game Combat Systems," In *WyrdCon Companion Book 2015*, ed. Sarah Lynne Bowman (Los Angeles: WyrdCon, 2015), 160–176.

32. Adam Curtis, dir., *The Trap* (BBC, 2007).

33. Torner, "Bodies and Time," 164.

34. Mike Mearls, Jeremy Crawford, et al., *Dungeon Master's Guide* (*D&D* 5e) (Renton, WA: Wizards of the Coast, 2014), 273.

35. Esther MacCallum-Stewart, Jaakko Stenros, and Staffan Björk, "The Impact of Role-Playing Games on Culture," in *Role-Playing Game Studies: Transmedia Foundations*, ed. José P. Zagal and Sebastian Deterding (New York: Routledge), 174.

36. Grant Piper, "The Inhumanity of Ancient and Medieval Warfare Cannot Be Understated," Medium, September 14, 2021, https://medium.com/war-stories/the -inhumanity-of-ancient-and-medieval-warfare-cannot-be-understated-1c74db96b010.

37. Perla, *Art of Wargaming*, 264.

5

"DOCTOR HOLMES, I PRESUME?": HOW A CALIFORNIA NEUROLOGY PROFESSOR PENNED THE FIRST *DUNGEONS & DRAGONS BASIC SET*

Tony A. Rowe and Zach Howard[*]

When Gary Gygax and Dave Arneson wrote the three "little brown books" of the original *Dungeons & Dragons* (*D&D*), their intended target audience was fellow miniature wargame enthusiasts much like themselves.[1] Gygax's company, Tactical Studies Rules (later renamed TSR), spread word about the new game through wargaming associations, periodicals, and conventions, mostly in the American Midwest around TSR's headquarters in Lake Geneva, Wisconsin.[2] Many of TSR's early creative employees hailed from nearby wargaming groups, such as those in Carbondale, Illinois (Tom Wham, Tim Kask, and Gary "Jake" Jacquet),[3] and Arneson's home of Minneapolis–Saint Paul (Dave Megarry, Mike Carr, and David Sutherland).[4] TSR was making games by wargamers, for wargamers.

However, *D&D* quickly spread beyond this wargamer audience, and Gygax realized that the game had a twofold problem: he had rushed to get the game to market, so that "the [original] rules were slammed together, virtually non-edited," and "they were written in a way that a hard core military miniaturist could probably understand . . . but most of the people [who bought the game] didn't play military miniatures, so we got into trouble."[5]

---

[*]Special thanks to the Science Fiction Oral History Association.

Gygax would solve the first problem by leading the development of a new edition of the game and what became his magnum opus, the first three rule books of *Advanced Dungeons & Dragons* (*AD&D* 1e): the *Monster Manual, Players Handbook,* and *Dungeon Masters Guide* (*DMG*).[6] This project occupied Gygax for years as he and other TSR employees revised, organized, and expanded the core *D&D* rules.

In the meantime, the second problem would require "a simplified, clarified, introductory piece" to explain the game to a broad audience. This was a task for a nonwargamer, which meant someone outside of TSR. Gygax's prayers were suddenly answered when, "as if by divine inspiration, J. Eric Holmes got in touch with us and actually volunteered his services for just such an undertaking."[7]

Unlike TSR's employees, Dr. John Eric Holmes was a "professor, author, and . . . respected neurologist" from California who had no experience with miniature wargaming or game design. How did "the Good Doctor," as Gygax called him, become the first to write a major revision of the original *D&D* rules?[8]

"THE GOOD DOCTOR"

Holmes was a *D&D* player and fan of the same authors of fantasy literature and speculative fiction that inspired Gygax's famed "Appendix N: Inspirational and Educational Reading" list in the original *DMG*.[9] Holmes's fandom began when he discovered Edgar Rice Burroughs's Tarzan adventures at age eight[10] and later met the author, who autographed his copy of *Tarzan and the Leopard Men*.[11] Holmes matured into a voracious reader of works by other Appendix N authors, like Lord Dunsany, H. P. Lovecraft,[12] L. Sprague de Camp, Fritz Leiber, Jack Williamson,[13] and Andre Norton.[14] Holmes and Gygax could connect over a shared literary background of the same pulp novels, fantasy, and science fiction stories.

When Holmes was a youth, his father, Captain Wilfred J. Holmes, skippered the USS *S-30* submarine and later served as a naval intelligence officer during World War II. He became known for writing naval-themed adventure stories under the pen name Alec Hudson.[15] The younger Holmes inherited his father's writing talent and adopted his own pen name of Sidney Leland to publish his first science fiction story, "Beachhead on the Moon,"[16] while studying psychology at Stanford University.[17]

Over the next twenty-five years, Holmes served as a first lieutenant in the Marine Corps during the Korean War, attended medical school, started a family in Los Angeles, and joined the University of Southern California Medical School faculty to teach neurology and perform research. He published articles, book reviews, and letters in numerous medical and scientific journals and wrote popular science articles for *Analog* magazine.[18]

Holmes returned to fiction writing after reading the entirety of Burroughs's "hollow earth" books, set in the imaginary land of Pellucidar, to his two sons. When the boys asked for one more story, Holmes penned his own Pellucidar pastiche.[19] He contacted the Burroughs estate, which authorized this new sequel to be published by Ace Books. Holmes was surprised and delighted when he first spied his own *Mahars of Pellucidar* for sale during a weekly visit to *A Change of Hobbit* bookstore,[20] a nexus for the science fiction fan community in Los Angeles.[21]

THE CALIFORNIA SCENE

Not long before *Mahars* was published, Holmes learned how to play roleplaying games (RPGs) in the unique California gaming scene,[22] which in turn influenced his manuscript for the *Dungeons & Dragons Basic Set*.[23]

The Golden State was a major hub for early *D&D* adopters (Gygax estimates that Californians purchased half of *D&D*'s initial print run).[24] Whereas the game spread through the midwestern United States through wargame groups, *D&D* took hold in California through science fiction fan clubs and the historical reenactment group the Society for Creative Anachronism (SCA). These communities proved to be ideal audiences for this imaginative game, but confusion about how to play and a lack of familiarity with wargame terminology spawned many varied "California" ways to play *D&D* as each play group interpreted the rules in different ways.

Science fiction fan clubs and the SCA alike featured significant numbers of active female members in these predominantly male groups. As they started playing *D&D*, many of these women had a voice, through amateur publications, to write and share their own designs with the do-it-yourself attitude that defined the California scene. This was in stark contrast to the almost complete lack of women in wargaming clubs or employed as creators at TSR during the mid-1970s.[25]

The San Francisco–area game designer and writer Jon Freeman provided a critical viewpoint on this scene. To him, the poorly edited *D&D* rules were "a primer why good grammar, correct punctuation, and clear antecedents are necessary for proper communication,"[26] and blamed them for causing "campaigns to diverge widely."[27] Put simply, "what passes for D&D in Mountain View, California only vaguely resembles what passes for D&D in Lake Geneva, Wisconsin."[28]

Southern California supported a strong speculative fiction fan community through the Los Angeles Science Fantasy Society (LASFS). Mark Swanson was one "LASFSian" who learned to play *D&D* through his wargaming circles (Swanson was a former member of the International Federation of Wargaming, which was cofounded by Gygax himself).[29] Swanson described the strange new game in the LASFS Amateur Press Association distribution, or *APA-L*, in October 1974.[30] Soon other *APA-L* contributors, such as Lee Gold,[31] learned to play and then wrote about their own role-playing experiences. *D&D* discussion threatened to overshadow the publication's amateur fiction content,[32] so in June 1975 Gold founded a separate monthly APA zine, *Alarums & Excursions (A&E)*, focusing solely on *D&D*.

A&E's early discussion forums often centered on *D&D*'s confusing and contradictory rules, arguing about how an elf gains experience points in two classes and the limits of a *Charm Person* spell.[33] As Holmes describes it, "Beleaguered Dungeon Masters made up their own systems for handling these ambiguities. . . . Within a few years of its appearance, D&D had generated many more pages of commentary and revision than were contained in the original little rule books."[34] Players shared their "house rule" solutions in *A&E*, where other members gave feedback or adopted those rules in their own campaigns.

For example, players often overlooked or misunderstood *D&D*'s unclear spell memorization rule. Many players assumed magic-users could lob *Sleep* and *Fireball* spells at will. Lee Gold and others designed magic systems using spell points to put a limit on overpowered spellcasters.[35] Gygax wrote to *A&E* and clarified that a magic-user immediately forgets a spell once it is cast,[36] but many gamers preferred their own spell rules, leading to Freeman's hyperbolic declaration that spell points were used in "probably 99 percent of what are nominally termed D&D campaigns."[37]

As Freeman put it, *D&D* is "less a game than a game system, and in practice it's less *that* than a system for designing a game system."[38] Players created many different variations on the *D&D* formula and shared their designs through *A&E*. Steve Perrin, the SCA cofounder who would later design *RuneQuest* for Chaosium, codified his group's house rules into *The Perrin Conventions*[39] and wrote about his campaign in "Tuesday Morning Report" for *A&E*.[40] Dave Hargrave published his extensive *D&D* variant as *The Arduin Grimoire* and contributed installments of "The Arduin Chronicles" to *A&E*.[41] Lee Gold's Los Angeles group played with their "Gold Standard" rules.[42] Caltech (California Institute of Technology) students in Pasadena popularized high-power gaming and lethal critical hit charts with their own variant, dubbed "Dungeons & Beavers" (named for the Caltech mascot) by Gold's group.[43] Sometimes games used "open universe" rules where characters could travel between campaigns.[44] However, the Gold and Pasadena campaigns were wildly different, and it was agreed that these universes were "closed" to each other.[45]

One California innovation was integrated into TSR's official game rules mere months after the original *D&D* set was published in January 1974. Gary Switzer, owner of the Aero Hobbies game store in Santa Monica and a contributor to *APA-L*, played in the "Aurania" campaign. His group designed rules for a character with "box man" skills in lockpicking and disarming traps.[46] Switzer discussed the new "thief" class over the telephone with Gygax, who expanded the idea with subterfuge abilities and a percentile skill system. Gygax then distributed "The Thief Addition" (crediting Switzer as "Gary Schweitzer" from "sunny California") in May 1974.[47] Gygax further refined the class for the first *D&D* supplement, *Greyhawk*, with no credit given to Switzer.[48] The thief joined the fighting-man, magic-user, and cleric to become one of the four core character classes that would define the game. This was the first major *D&D* development to originate from outside of TSR or Gygax and Arneson's gaming circles. Switzer's group later compiled and self-published their other variant classes, reincarnation rules, and monsters in *The Manual of Aurania*, and they never shared their ideas with Gygax again.[49]

"HOW TO PLAY *D&D* WITHOUT PLAYING *D&D?*"

In August 1975, the Pasadena rules were published in *Spartan* magazine as *Warlock* with the cheeky subtitle "or How to Play D and D Without Playing D and D?"[50] The game featured a detailed combat system, a spell point system and expanded spell lists, additional player characteristics, critical hit charts, and a thief character class more customizable than the one published in *Greyhawk*.

Holmes's eldest son, Jeff, invited his father and younger brother to learn to play *Warlock* with his school friends in autumn 1975. Holmes was immediately hooked and trekked to Aero Hobbies the next day for copies of the *D&D* rules, *Greyhawk*, *Chainmail*, and *Warlock*.[51] One week later, Holmes began hosting game sessions with his own custom-made dungeon adventure, inviting his medical students and his sons' friends to join.[52]

Holmes wrote dramatized versions of his early adventures as short stories published both in *A&E* and in TSR's *The Dragon* magazine. Many of these tales featured Zereth the dark elf and Boinger the halfling, two characters rolled up by Chris Holmes when he first learned to play.[53] The dour Zereth and charismatic Boinger were an unlikely duo, and their roguish misadventures featured equal measures of derring-do and humor. The elder Holmes wrote the novella *The Maze of Peril* to serve as a record of his group's first dungeon expedition.[54]

Holmes wasn't exactly playing *D&D* at first. He ran game sessions with *Warlock*'s characters, combat, and magic systems along with *Aurania*'s samurai and Beorning character classes. He only used *D&D* rules for treasure, magic items, and monsters.[55] As Holmes admits, "I used [*Warlock*'s] combat table when I first began playing D&D because I could not understand the one in the original [*D&D*] books."[56] Even to an educated and well-read expert on fantasy fiction like Holmes, the *D&D* rules were perplexing without a background in miniatures wargaming. "They were intended to guide people who were already *playing* the game. As a guide to *learning* the game, they were incomprehensible."[57]

At first, Holmes felt angry about *D&D*'s opaqueness.[58] Then he decided to act on the situation. He wrote directly to Gygax and stated that "the original D&D rules needed revision" and he was "the person to rewrite them."[59] He proposed to edit what he called "Dungeons and Dragons for Beginners,"[60] later renamed as the *Dungeons & Dragons Basic Set*.[61]

Gygax was delighted.[62] "Dr. Holmes was kind enough to volunteer. I got to talking with him and [Eric] and I arrived at a very happy agreement."[63] TSR was short on cash, so in lieu of monetary payment, Gygax offered to send Holmes free TSR products for the rest of his life.[64] Gygax struck a bargain that "cost the company nary a red cent."[65]

"*DUNGEONS & DRAGONS* FOR BEGINNERS"

Holmes focused on adapting text from "the three original books and the first two supplements" (*Greyhawk* and *Blackmoor*)[66] while preparing his manuscript.[67] He preserved "the original words of the two game creators,"[68] including the "Byzantine D&D flavor of phrases like 'loathsome trolls are tough and rubbery and have the ability to regenerate.'"[69] He reduced the scope to a single forty-eight-page rule book by only including rules for the first three levels of play, a limitation retained throughout the following decade in later editions of the *Basic Set*.

Holmes organized and divided the book into four "vital parts" that make up the core elements of RPG rules: character generation (including character advancement), magic ("or, in a science fiction game, high technology, which is the same thing"), "the encounter" (including rules on interactions like combat, movement, and negotiations), and a section for the dungeon master (DM) (with monsters, treasures, magical items, and "guidelines for setting up and conducting adventures . . . with several examples").[70] Holmes tackled this last part with gusto, crafting a section that he titled "Dungeon Mastering as a Fine Art." He exceeded his duty as editor, adding his own advice on running games, a step-by-step example of play, and an introductory dungeon adventure, colloquially named "The Tower of Zenopus." This was the first TSR adventure written specifically for novice players on their first adventure. Contrast this with Arneson's high-powered "Temple of the Frog" adventure published in *Blackmoor*, where players may face off against dozens or even hundreds of enemies in a single encounter.[71] Holmes also included a brief, evocative background for the Zenopus dungeon and its neighboring trade city of Portown, a setting that shares similarities with H. P. Lovecraft's fictional settlement of Kingsport.[72]

Holmes adapted rules from other game systems into sections where the original *D&D* rules were lacking, such as combat. The only hint at how to

determine who strikes first in battle was a note about dexterity representing "speed with actions such as firing first, getting off a spell, etc."[73] In a
new section titled "Who Gets the First Blow?" Holmes's *Basic Set* unam-
biguously states that "the character with the highest dexterity strikes first."
He also clearly defined a combat round as lasting ten seconds. The initiative rule and ten-second combat round were adapted either from *Warlock*
or from similar guidelines in TSR's *Metamorphosis Alpha*.[74] *Warlock*'s order of
combat actions (movement, magic, archery, and melee) is mirrored in *Basic
D&D* (magic, missile fire, and melee), where no such rule existed in earlier
D&D books. Holmes incorporated rules from *D&D*'s miniature wargame
predecessor, *Chainmail*, for guidance on parrying, taking cover from missile fire, and treating a giant's thrown rock like one fired from a catapult.[75]

Holmes enjoyed letting players create "dragons, centaurs, samurai, and
witch doctors" for their characters and listed many of these nonstandard
options in the "Additional Character Classes" section.[76] Two examples
were nods to the Californian-designed classes he used from *Aurania*: the
Beorning (as a "lawful werebear") and the samurai (as a "Japanese Samurai fighting man").

Holmes completed his final draft by February 1977,[77] before Gygax took
"charge of the manuscript" for final edits and several notable changes.[78]
Holmes wrote the book as an introduction to the original *D&D* rules,
but by the time of publication, TSR was supplanting the original game
with the forthcoming *AD&D* rules. Wherever the manuscript directed
the reader to the original *D&D* or *Greyhawk* rules, the published version
instead referred to *AD&D*. In the *Basic Set*, *D&D*'s original three-part alignment system (lawful, neutral, and chaotic) was expanded to a five-part
system by adding a secondary axis of good and evil for lawful and chaotic
creatures, the same alignment system used in the *Monster Manual*, but
different from the nine-part system seen in later *AD&D* books. TSR also
added more spells, variable damage for monster attacks, rules for encum-
brance, and other miscellaneous changes to the *Basic Set*. The infamous
"broken" rule allowing dagger-wielding characters to attack twice per
round arose from TSR's changes before publication and does not match
Holmes's original manuscript.[79]

Despite these alterations, the published rule book is closer to the original *D&D* rules than *AD&D*, which uses a different armor class scale and

combat tables. Holmes's combat adaptations, noted earlier, were left intact, despite their differences from *AD&D*. Some of Holmes's innovations, such as the ten-second combat round, became standard rules carried forward in later *D&D Basic Set* editions.

RECEPTION

TSR unveiled the *Dungeons & Dragons Basic Set* at the Origins III convention in July 1977. The rules were sold in a box with a set of low-quality dice (Holmes described them as "small, hard to read [and] really ugly") and accessories for designing dungeons filled with monsters and treasure.[80] In 1978 these accessories were replaced by Mike Carr's *In Search of the Unknown*,[81] TSR's first stand-alone "dungeon module" for novice DMs. This was supplanted in 1980 by Gygax's own novice adventure *The Keep on the Borderlands*,[82] which included a civilized outpost, the titular keep, where characters may rest and resupply between sojourns to a monster-filled dungeon.

Holmes's fellow Californians generally gave favorable reviews of the *Basic Set*. Jon Freeman stated that the rules "give you a fighting chance to learn the game" and was thankful that the rule book "was written ('edited,' if you prefer) by someone outside the TSR establishment who knew a noun from a verb."[83] He felt that learning from another player was the best way to start, but "if you must venture into RPG country without a guide, this is the first place to visit."[84]

A&E contributor Bill Seligman bought a copy at Origins III and complimented Holmes directly for the good writing, organization, and clear examples: "Kudos to you, sir, at least future DMs will not have to struggle with what we had."[85] Lee Gold was less enthusiastic, and she described the set as "very pretty if you care for such things (I don't)." She admitted that some of the new rules were "useful," and while the organization was "spotty," at least it was "better than the original set."[86] The limited *Basic Set* was not immediately valuable to an experienced player like Gold, who had spent years deciphering and interpreting the original rules: "All in all, I don't consider it a very worthwhile investment."[87]

TSR's sales of *D&D Basic Set* grew year over year. Gygax estimates that *Basic Set* sales exceeded 100,000 units in 1978 and 250,000 units in

1979.[88] Holmes's work solved TSR's "second problem" and opened *D&D* to a vast audience of new players.

TSR's Tom Moldvay edited a revised *D&D Basic Set* that launched in early 1981 along with the new *D&D Expert Set*, featuring rules for characters up to level fourteen.[89] Holmes had envisioned the *Basic Set* as an introduction to the original *D&D* rules. These new *D&D Basic* and *Expert* sets (colloquially known as B/X) instead evolved into a separate game system produced in parallel to *AD&D*. B/X preserved the original *D&D*'s core, along with Holmes's *Basic Set* clarifications, and served as a counterpoint to *AD&D*'s dense rules. Two years later, Frank Mentzer directed a re-revision and expansion of the *D&D* rules, starting with *D&D Basic Rules Set* for beginner characters from levels one through three (just as Holmes had originally proposed), with later rules sets that covered high-level play like mass combat, ruling over dominions, and finally the *Immortals* rules for characters who transcend level-based play.[90]

BEYOND BASIC

Holmes hosted game sessions at Gen Con conventions and helped design *D&D* rules for the "Cthulhu Mythos,"[91] but did little other work with TSR. He served as an educated RPG ambassador to journalists with questions about the new hobby,[92] authored magazine articles about RPGs,[93] and penned a comprehensive book about the hobby, *Fantasy Role Playing Games*.[94] The *Basic Set* remains his crowning achievement in games, one that introduced the hobby to millions of new players. "I'm proud of the original *Basic Set* and I like to think I did a good job of describing . . . Dungeons & Dragons . . . so that everyone could enjoy it. The nicest compliment I ever got for it was from a game store manager who said, 'That's made a lot of people happy.'"[95]

Dr. Holmes passed away on March 20, 2010, at the age of eighty, survived by his wife, four children, and two grandchildren.[96] The do-it-yourself attitude and clearly written, simple rules of his *Basic Set* continue to inspire RPG designers today.

NOTES

1. Gary Gygax and Dave Arneson, *Dungeons & Dragons*, 1st ed., 3 vols. (Lake Geneva, WI: Tactical Studies Rules, January 1974).

2. Jon Peterson, *Playing at the World: A History of Simulating Wars, People and Fantastic Adventures, from Chess to Role-Playing Games* (San Diego, CA: Unreason Press, 2012), 459–460, 64–69.

3. Tim Kask, "Interview with Tim Kask," Save or Die! podcast audio, August 2, 2010, http://saveordie.info/?p=53.

4. Shannon Appelcline, *Designers & Dragons: The '70s*, ed. John Adamus (Silver Spring, MD: Evil Hat Productions, 2014), 22.

5. Rudy Kraft, "The Wizard of TSR: An Interview with Gary Gygax," *Gryphon*, Summer 1980.

6. Gary Gygax, *Monster Manual* (Lake Geneva, WI: TSR Games, December 1977); *Players Handbook* (June 1978); *Dungeon Masters Guide* (August 1979).]

7. Gary Gygax, "Sorcerer's Scroll," *The Dragon*, no. 35 (March 1980): 13.

8. Gary Gygax, "From the Sorcerer's Scroll," *The Dragon*, no. 14 (May 1978): 20.

9. Gygax, *Dungeon Masters Guide*, 224.

10. John Eric Holmes, *Martian Twilight* (Running Dinosaur Press, 1991), short story, outside back cover.

11. John Martin, "In the Burroughs Tradition: John Eric Holmes and *The Mahars of Pellucidar*," *Paperback Parade*, May 1995, 34.

12. John Eric Holmes, letter to editor, *Famous Fantastic Mysteries*, April 1946, 128.

13. John Eric Holmes, "Letter from Lt. John E. Holmes to P. Schuyler Miller, 1952," box 9, Papers of P. Schuyler Miller, University of Kansas, fol. 14, Kenneth Spencer Research Library Archival Collections, https://archives.lib.ku.edu/repositories/3/archival_objects/249039.

14. John Eric Holmes, "'Books' and 'Authors' Lists by Dr. J. E. Holmes, 1966," box 12, Papers of P. Schuyler Miller, University of Kansas, fol. 316, Kenneth Spencer Research Library Archival Collections, https://archives.lib.ku.edu/repositories/3/archival_objects/249341.

15. "Who's Who in This Issue," *Blue Book*, June 1950, 1.

16. John Eric Holmes [Sidney Leland Holmes, pseud.], "Beachhead on the Moon" (short story), *Blue Book*, February 1951.

17. "Who's Who in This Issue," *Blue Book*, February 1951, inside back cover.

18. John Eric Holmes, "Brain Waves and Thought Patterns," *Analog*, July 1962; "The Educated Flatworm," *Analog*, November 1962; "The Split Brain," *Analog*, August 1974.

19. Martin, "In the Burroughs Tradition," 34.

20. John Eric Holmes, *Mahars of Pellucidar* (New York: Ace Books, 1976).

21. Martin, "In the Burroughs Tradition," 36.

22. Appelcline, *Designers & Dragons: The '70s*, 317.

23. Gary Gygax and Dave Arneson, *Dungeons & Dragons Basic Set*, 1st ed., ed. John Eric Holmes (Lake Geneva, WI: TSR Hobbies, 1977).

24. Ed Goto, "Game Brings 'Sci-Fi' to Life," *Independent Press-Telegram* (Long Beach, CA), June 16, 1978, morning, A-22.

25. Jon Peterson, "The First Female Gamers," Medium, October 5, 2014, https://medium.com/@increment/the-first-female-gamers-c784fbe3ff37; Jon Peterson, *The Elusive Shift: How Role-Playing Games Forged Their Identity* (Cambridge, MA: MIT Press, 2020).

26. Jon Freeman, *The Playboy Winner's Guide to Board Games* (Chicago: Playboy Press, October 1979), 269.

27. Jon Freeman, *The Complete Book of Wargames* (New York: Simon & Schuster, 1980), 251–252.

28. Freeman, *Winner's Guide*, 270.

29. "New Members for February–March 1970," *International Wargamer Supplement*, March 1970.

30. Mark Swanson, "Myth Interstellar Bulletin #34," *APA-L*, October 24, 1974.

31. Lee Gold, "Haplography," *APA-L*, February 6, 1975.

32. Lee Gold, "APA-L & Roleplaying," unpublished MS, 2016.

33. Lee Gold, "Melee Mayday," *Alarums & Excursions*, June 1975.

34. John Eric Holmes, *Fantasy Role Playing Games* (New York: Hippocrene Books, 1981), 65.

35. Lee Gold, "Tantivy," *Alarums & Excursions*, June 1975.

36. Gary Gygax, letter to the editor, *Alarums & Excursions*, July 1975.

37. Freeman, *Winner's Guide*, 270.

38. Freeman, *Complete Book*, 243.

39. Appelcline, *Designers & Dragons*, 250–251, 317.

40. Steve Perrin, "Tuesday Morning Report," *Alarums & Excursions*, June 12, 1976.

41. David Hargrave, *The Arduin Grimoire* (Richmond, CA: David Hargrave, February 1977); "The Arduin Chronicles," *Alarums & Excursions*, August 16, 1977.

42. Jack Harness, "Reviews and Honorable Mentions," *Alarums & Excursions*, October 1975.

43. Gold, "Tantivy."

44. Jon Freeman, "*Dungeons & Dragons*: All Things Are Possible in the Most Popular Fantasy Game of the Decade," *Games*, September–October 1979, 11.

45. Harness, "Reviews and Honorable Mentions."

46. D. Daniel Wagner, "Manual of Aurania / Q&A with D. Daniel Wagner," OD&D Discussion, September 26, 2013, *https://odd74.proboards.com/post/128013*.

47. Gary Gygax, "The Thief Addition," *Great Plains Games Players Newsletter*, July 1, 1974.

48. Gary Gygax, *Supplement I: Greyhawk* (Lake Geneva, WI: Tactical Studies Rules, March 1975), 4–5, 9–12.

49. Hugh K. Singh, D. Daniel Wagner, and Larry E. Stehle, *The Manual of Aurania*, 1st ed., ed. Hugh K. Singh (Santa Monica, CA, May 1976).

50. Robert Cowan et al., "Warlock, or How to Play D and D without Playing D and D?" *Spartan Simulation Gaming Journal*, August 1975.

51. Chris Holmes, "Afterword," in *Tales of Peril: The Complete Boinger & Zereth Stories of John Eric Holmes*, ed. Allan T. Grohe (Wichita, KS: Black Blade Publishing, 2017), 328.

52. Eric M. Frasier, "My Time as Murray," in *Tales of Peril: The Complete Boinger & Zereth Stories of John Eric Holmes*, ed. Allan T. Grohe (Wichita, KS: Black Blade Publishing, 2017), 299–302.

53. Holmes, "Afterword," 328.

54. John Eric Holmes, *The Maze of Peril* (New York: Space and Time, 1986); Frasier, "My Time as Murray," 305.

55. Frasier, 303.

56. Holmes, *Fantasy RPGs*, 65.

57. John Eric Holmes and Tom Moldvay, "Basic D&D Points of View," *Dragon*, no. 52 (August 1981): 14.

58. Beth Ann Krier, "Fantasy Life in a Game without End," *Los Angeles Times*, July 11, 1979.

59. Holmes, *Fantasy RPGs*, 68.

60. John Eric Holmes, Gary Gygax, and Dave Arneson, "Dungeons and Dragons for Beginners," 3rd manuscript for *Dungeons & Dragons Basic Set* rule book, February 4, 1977, private collection, unpublished.

61. Gygax and Arneson, *Basic Set*.

62. Gary Gygax, "Q&A with Gary Gygax," reply to post on EN World Forum, September 26, 2003, https://www.enworld.org/threads/q-a-with-gary-gygax.22566/page-78#post-1141497.

63. Kraft, "Wizard of TSR."

64. David Carson, "Interview with J. Eric Holmes Who Wrote the Definitive Guide to *Dungeons & Dragons*," *Science Fiction Radio Show*, audio cassette, Science Fiction Oral History Association Archives (1982).

65. Gary Gygax, "Q&A with Tim Kask," reply to post on Dragonsfoot Forums, May 27, 2007, https://www.dragonsfoot.org/forums/viewtopic.php?p=434903#p434903.

66. Gygax, *Greyhawk*; Dave Arneson, *Supplement II: Blackmoor* (Lake Geneva, WI: Tactical Studies Rules, December 1975).

67. Holmes, *Fantasy RPGs*, 68.

68. Holmes, 68.

69. Krier, "Fantasy Life."

70. Holmes and Moldvay, "Points of View," 14.

71. Arneson, *Blackmoor*, 27–47.

72. Zach Howard, "How Zenopus Met His Doom," *Zenopus Archives*, October 31, 2012, http://zenopusarchives.blogspot.com/2012/10/how-zenopus-met-his-doom.html.

73. Gary Gygax and Dave Arneson, *Dungeons & Dragons Volume 1: Men & Magic* (Lake Geneva, WI: Tactical Studies Rules, January 1974), 11.

74. Cowan et al., "Warlock," 5; James M. Ward, *Metamorphosis Alpha*, ed. Mike Carr and David Sutherland (Lake Geneva, WI: TSR Rules, 1976), 10, 20.

75. Gary Gygax and Jeff Perren, *Chainmail* (3e) (Lake Geneva, WI: TSR, 1975), 12, 26, 35.

76. Holmes and Moldvay, "Points of View," 16.

77. Holmes, Gygax, and Arneson, "Dungeons and Dragons for Beginners."

78. Gary Gygax, "Q&A with Gary Gygax," reply post on EN World Forum, February 22, 2005, https://www.enworld.org/threads/q-a-with-gary-gygax.22566/page-136 #post-2051688.

79. Zach Howard, "Part 16: 'An Exchange of Two Blows with Ordinary Weapons,'" *Zenopus Archives*, January 9, 2014, https://zenopusarchives.blogspot.com/2014/01 /part-16-exchange-of-two-blows-with.html.

80. Holmes and Moldvay, "Points of View," 17.

81. Mike Carr, *In Search of the Unknown* (Lake Geneva, WI: TSR Games, November 1978).

82. Gary Gygax, *The Keep on the Borderlands* (Lake Geneva, WI: TSR Games, 1980).

83. Freeman, *Winner's Guide*, 270.

84. Freeman, *Complete Book*, 252.

85. Bill Seligman, "I Would Have Made a Great Platinum Dragon #10," *Alarums & Excursions*, August 16, 1977.

86. Lee Gold, "Archilowe," *Lords of Chaos*, December 1, 1977.

87. Lee Gold, "Tantivy," *Alarums & Excursions*, October 16, 1977.

88. Moira Johnston, "It's Only a Game . . . or Is It?" *New West*, August 25, 1980.

89. Gary Gygax and Dave Arneson, *Dungeons & Dragons Basic Set*, 2nd ed., ed. Tom Moldvay (Lake Geneva, WI: TSR Hobbies, January 1981); Gary Gygax and Dave Arneson, *Dungeons & Dragons Expert Set*, ed. David Cook and Steve Marsh (Lake Geneva, WI: TSR Hobbies, January 1981).

90. Gary Gygax and Dave Arneson, *Dungeons & Dragons Basic Rules Set 1*, 3rd ed., 2 vols., ed. Frank Mentzer (Lake Geneva, WI: TSR Hobbies, May 1983); Frank Mentzer, *Dungeons & Dragons Set 5: Immortals Rules*, 2 vols., ed. Anne Gray McCready (Lake Geneva, WI: TSR, June 1986).

91. Rob Kuntz and John Eric Holmes, "The Lovecraftian Mythos in *Dungeons & Dragons*," *The Dragon*, no. 12 (February 1978).

92. Krier, "Fantasy Life"; Martha Hewson, "A Game That Casts a Spell," *McCall's*, October 1980; Holmes, *Fantasy RPGs*, 67; Carson, "Interview with J. Eric Holmes."

93. John Eric Holmes, "Confessions of a Dungeon Master," *Psychology Today*, November 1980; John Eric Holmes, "The Psychopathology of Wargamers," *Space Gamer*, January–February 1980; John Eric Holmes, "Science Fiction and Fantasy Games," *Locus: The Newspaper of the Science Fiction Field*, December 1981; John Eric Holmes, "*Dungeons & Dragons*: Dangerous to Your Health?" *Beyond*, Winter 1982.

94. Holmes, *Fantasy RPGs*.

95. Holmes and Moldvay, "Points of View," 17.

96. "Obituaries—September/October 2010," *Stanford Magazine*, 2010, https://stanfordmag.org/contents/obituaries-6130.

6

REFLECTIONS ON THE OPEN GAME LICENSE: AN INTERVIEW WITH RYAN DANCEY

Michael Iantorno

Spearheaded by Ryan Dancey and developed alongside the third edition of *Dungeons & Dragons* (*D&D*; 2000), the Open Game License (OGL) Version 1.0a is a public copyright license created by Wizards of the Coast (WotC) that, upon its introduction, drastically altered how third-party content could be created for the popular tabletop role-playing game (TTRPG).[1] While players and other stakeholders have been influential in the design of *D&D* since its inception—contributing to industry publications, sharing resources at conventions, and forming vibrant communities on the internet—TSR generally maintained tight control over who could publish materials for the game. Representing a major shift in approach to the brand's intellectual property (IP), the OGL formalized a system where anyone could modify, copy, and redistribute aspects of *D&D* without procuring permission or paying licensing fees to WotC. The license primarily allows for use of the game's core rules and mechanics, encapsulated and presented in the publicly accessible System Reference Document (SRD), while certain narrative aspects (referred to as the Product Identity) remain under the control of the original publisher (Wizards of the Coast, 2000). The OGL has spawned a multitude of materials over the past twenty-five years, including one-off adventure modules, expansive rule supplements, and even fully stand-alone products such as the *Pathfinder Roleplaying Game*—a multimillion-dollar tabletop franchise that, for a period, eclipsed the sales of its predecessor.[2] Although the OGL was put aside in favor of the Game System License (GSL) for the fourth edition of *D&D*, it returned to prominence with the release of the fifth edition of the game. And, as WotC's tumultuous efforts to revise the OGL in 2023 made clear, countless content creators still rely on the license for both livelihood and leisure.

Ryan Dancey became professionally involved with *D&D* at a pivotal moment in its history, when TSR's finances were in disarray and plans for a third edition of the game were taking shape. As vice president of product development at Five Rings Publishing, Dancey helped orchestrate WotC's acquisition of both TSR and Five Rings and eventually found himself tasked with managing TSR's role-playing properties. It was at this time that Dancey pushed for the creation of the OGL as part of a broader strategy to make *D&D* profitable again. Inspired by the open-source software movement and looking for ways to diffuse a potential "edition war" between second and third edition, the OGL was designed to let players and third-party publishers create droves of diverse content for the game while WotC focused on its core product line.

A veteran of the role-playing, collectible card game, and video game industries, Dancey possesses unique insights into the business and legal histories of *D&D*. He joined Michael Iantorno for an interview in July 2021, where the two discussed topics ranging from the legal ramifications of the OGL to the transformation of the role-playing industry at the turn of the century.

INTERVIEW

MICHAEL IANTORNO: Shortly after WotC's acquisition of TSR, you were tasked with managing various role-playing properties, including the launch of the third edition of *D&D*. What initial changes were planned for the brand?

RYAN DANCEY: In the early stages of planning, we decided that we were going to stop developing campaign settings the way that TSR had been doing them. We also knew that we weren't going to create a bunch of "edge case" rule books—materials that were far outside of the mainstream of what we believed people were doing with *D&D*.

However, we also knew that there was a large audience of players entrenched in second edition who had invested in different campaign settings and rule books. If we asked those people to give all of that up and only play the core, high-fantasy version of *D&D* that we were going to make, there was a substantial risk that a large number of second edition players would never become third edition players. The market research and data analysis we had been doing—going all the way back to the eighties from TSR's old archives—was pretty clear that one of the big problems with second edition was that TSR hadn't gotten as many first edition players to convert as they could have. I wanted to avoid making that same mistake.

I would tell people all the time that our biggest competitor was not some other company—not White Wolf, not FASA, not Steve Jackson—it's us! We had to make something for players so it would be worth the pain to convert to a new rule set. We had to at least offer them a road map to that world. However, we weren't going to make those edge case products ourselves because we know they don't make any money. We also didn't want to be in the licensing business, as we couldn't have a team of people that reviewed and approved third-party products. It would be impossibly complicated, and it would expose us to a lot of bizarre legal issues we didn't want to be a part of.

MI: So you were faced with the issue of not wanting to publish certain types of content for *D&D*, but still wanting that content to be available for players. How did discussions of the OGL emerge from this?

RD: Well, in the late nineties, open-source software was all the rage. There were tech people everywhere in Seattle, and I'm a technical person—my background is in computer software. Also, somewhat weirdly, long before *Magic: The Gathering*, WotC had tried to create a thing called *Envoy*. The idea behind *Envoy* was that it would serve as a free mechanism to allow role-playing game publishers to make content that was compatible with other game systems. And this was driven by the fact that WotC's very first product was a book called *Primal Order*, which wasn't a role-playing game in and of itself but was designed to be used with other role-playing games. So the DNA of this idea was already in the company from long before it was a trading card game company.

I made a proposal to Peter Adkison—the CEO of WotC at the time—that we should consider adopting the idea of open source to make open gaming. Peter then sits up in his chair and is like: "This is not as far-fetched as people might think! I had this idea seven years ago and I love it."

MI: Even though you had the CEO on your side, was there any contention within WotC regarding the OGL?

RD: Oh, yeah! Well, it wasn't really a fight. What it was, really, was a bunch of people—specifically in R&D—thinking that the OGL was a horrible idea that was going to absolutely destroy the company. They went around the building telling other people how bad they thought it was going to be, politically maneuvering in an attempt to kill the OGL. It wasn't like we had a big meeting with the "pros" on one side and the "cons" on the other side. Instead we had a big meeting where I said we were doing it, and then for weeks afterwards people walked into Peter's office telling him that "if you let Ryan do this, you're going to destroy *Dungeons & Dragons!*" If Peter hadn't been a champion for the idea, it would not have been done, and then who knows what would have happened with third edition?

Weirdly, the legal team at the company looked at the OGL as a fun challenge. How do we create a license that does what we want it to do but doesn't destroy our business? One that doesn't just give away the family tools.

MI: Was it difficult to determine what elements of *D&D* you *could* protect under the OGL?

RD: Here's the real truth: very little can be legally protected in role-playing games. Lawyers know this, and WotC's lawyers certainly were aware as well. The industry operates under a legal theory which is not correct, which is that you cannot make products that are compatible with a person's role-playing game unless you have their permission first. There have been lawsuits, and although some of them have actually gone to court, most of them never do. Although that legal theory doesn't withstand much scrutiny, it is the default way the industry operates, as the fear of being sued sufficiently deters 99.9 percent of all attempts. For tiny companies especially, the legal jeopardy of just paying for a lawyer stops them from doing something they could probably legally do—that is, make materials that are compatible with other people's games.

We were lucky in that WotC's lawyers weren't coming from the position of thinking that 100 percent of our IP was protected and that we were giving up some of that protection. They were approaching it from the novel perspective that it is very difficult to protect any of that IP to begin with. In fact, they viewed the license as removing the issue of whether or not material can be copyrighted, and instead placing it into a new domain that binds users to certain terms and obligations. It's optional to opt-in, but if you do, you've entered into certain legal obligations and responsibilities. What you give up is mostly theoretical, but what you gain is the ability to make really cool stuff that is compatible with *D&D*.

MI: Was there any hesitance from third-party publishers to adopt the license?

RD: After we started talking publicly about the OGL, I spent most of my time in the ensuing six months trying to convince my peers at other companies that this was not a plan to screw them. Most people in the industry started from the proposition that WotC was going to entice them to do all this really cool stuff and then slam the door on them once they figured out what worked (or didn't work). They feared that WotC would take all the best stuff, make it their own, and then cut out the creators who invested their time and energy—leaving them with nothing and maybe even suing them. They didn't really want to be a part of it.

My goal was to fix the problem of second edition legacy content by having a lot of really cool stuff out there that WotC didn't have to make. I really wanted my peers to see this as a great opportunity. The more cool stuff, the better!

MI: How does that change WotC's publishing strategy, then? Were you essentially using OGL content as a way to drive people toward the system and your core products?

RD: Yeah, in fact, it's a weirdly theoretical argument. We were telling second edition players: "we know we're only making the core high fantasy *Dungeons & Dragons*, but we're sure that every conceivable option is going to be arriving shortly from third parties." Not only did we say that other people were going to do it, but also that they could do it too—anyone could become a publisher! That idea was a sufficient bridge to get a lot of people to accept the idea of third edition, many of whom would have been reluctant if there hadn't been a road map to get them back to status quo.

I am 100 percent convinced that the OGL made third edition succeed. If there had been no OGL, third edition would have lost players like second edition did. Instead of being a fraction of the size of second edition, it was multiples of the size of second edition, and the OGL was the bridge that got people from the old to the new.

MI: One criticism of the OGL was that the deluge of material eventually led to brand dilution and quality decay. Do you think that is a valid critique?

RD: I don't. If you go into any bookstore, there's a lot of crap on their shelves. Sturgeon's law is that 80 percent of everything is crap, but that doesn't stop great products from finding a market and being very successful. And there were definitely great products that were produced in the first wave of D20 products that found a market and were very successful.

I think a lot of people who make that criticism aren't really aware of the data. Prior to the release of third edition, role-playing game publishing was very small. There were only four or five profitable companies, at least profitable enough to pay a salary, and there were a very small number of people working in the field as freelancers, maybe ten. Most of the products that were produced in that era were splatbooks such as second edition campaign settings and support materials. Although the overall business was small, proportionally, it generated a ton of really bad products that people really didn't like. After the OGL, the whole world was different. There were a bunch more companies publishing role-playing games, hundreds of people working as freelancers, and the amount of money being spent in retail stores on role-playing games went way up. Retailers were the gatekeepers of our business—especially in 2000, in the middle of the internet transition—and if they didn't stock a product, it was really hard for a consumer to find it. If anything, the worst of the worst stuff mostly didn't even get distributed. Nobody ever saw the really bad, childish, awful stuff. You had to at least have the ability to get your thing into a printable format with a cover and a piece of art to get it on the shelf, so there was a certain bar that had to be met to get into retail stores.

Pathfinder found success, in part, because it was a great mix of game design and art and was created by people who knew what they were doing and how to build a business. It didn't matter how many other people produced games. When Lisa Stevens and her team created *Pathfinder*, they made a winner.

MI: With the OGL, *D&D* became something anyone could design for, and a lot of people feared it would dominate the RPG market and squeeze out smaller systems. How did it change the publication and design space for role-playing games of all types, not just *D&D*?

RD: The OGL was designed intentionally to collapse the design space of role-playing games. Specifically, it was devised to get people to stop making "*Dungeons & Dragons*, but with a twist" games and just make content for *D&D*. Before the edition transition, there were numerous games being made that didn't actually have a lot of value in terms of design. They were being made because people wanted to make something that was like *D&D*, but they couldn't do that outside TSR, so they had to do their own thing. The canonical example I always point to is *Palladium*. That game has no reason to exist. If Kevin Siembieda could have made a *D&D* clone and enhanced it with his own ideas, I'm sure that he would have just done that. The only reason he had to make a whole game was because he wasn't legally allowed to use *D&D* as the foundation. So the Open Game License didn't destroy the market for variant role-playing games; what it really destroyed was the market for variant *D&D*.

MI: In earlier interviews, you mentioned that the OGL would allow for a new talent pipeline to emerge, as anyone could design for *D&D*. Did that actually manifest during your time at the company?

RD: That's Mike Mearls! That's his story. He started off as a D20 guy and is now running *D&D*.

MI: To flip things the other way: was there a fear that designers would leave WotC because the license allowed them to develop *D&D* content on their own terms?

RD: At the very beginning, I would have said no, because why would you give up a wonderful salary and benefits package at WotC? It was more money than people would make anywhere else in the industry by a *lot*.

And then Chris Pramas went and did it, and a lot of people looked at Green Ronin Publishing and thought what he was doing was really cool! He has his own publishing company; he gets to make all his own decisions and nobody can tell him no. He can publish the stuff he wants to, and apparently he's making pretty good money. After Chris did it, it wasn't that long until Monte Cook did it, and soon there was a whole pipeline of folks who worked at WotC and then went off to do their own thing. But you'll notice there haven't been a lot of people that have done it lately. It's *really* hard to start a successful tabletop role-playing game publishing company. You have to be more than just somebody who's good at designing role-playing games; you have to be a business person. A lot of people tried it, and I think they discovered they didn't like it, or they couldn't do it, or it just wasn't their thing. They were great at being creative designers, but they weren't so good at running a company.

I think it's much less of a threat than it once was, and I don't suspect that anybody at WotC right now really views it as a problem. The people that are there today are probably super happy to be working at WotC and don't want to leave, but those people that did leave took a risk and went for it.

MI: We've been talking about the OGL as a success, yet it was eventually discarded in favor of the GSL for fourth edition. Even though you weren't involved with WotC at the time, do you have any insight as to why that change might have occurred?

RD: There was a big turnover at WotC. Peter Adkison left, I left, a bunch of founding people left, and the business was substantially downsized after the Hasbro acquisition. There were a lot of changes made in the way that WotC was going to operate, and shortly after the turnover, I believe there were a lot of people at the company who just *hated* the OGL. They didn't like the fact that there was all this content being produced that they didn't have control over. Where we started from the position of "this business is in absolute crisis and is dying, what can we do to save it?" they started from "we have a really good business, so what can we do to protect it?"

Fourth edition is probably a textbook case on what not to do with a brand like *Dungeons & Dragons*. However, personally, I don't think they made a lot of theoretical mistakes. They had a good strategy for making a game, and they recognized that their biggest competition at the time was *World of Warcraft*. By the time the fourth edition came out, MMOs [massively multiplayer online games] were degrading the tabletop role-playing network, and people were quitting their games in droves to go play. WotC had a lot of data, and they also had a good analysis of what they needed to do, but I know some of the people that were at the company at the time, and I can see the road map for them adopting a new licensing regime . . . wanting people to ask permission first, being able to stop the development of unwanted products, and putting up a bunch of barriers to entry, right? Apparently they succeeded in putting up so many barriers to entry that nobody entered! There was almost nothing meaningful produced that used the GSL or any of the other licensing approaches they adopted.

The fourth edition business cratered catastrophically, and a good argument can be made that the reason *Pathfinder* was so successful is because of fourth edition's shortcomings. Not only did WotC end up with a damaged brand, but they accidentally created their worst enemy: a game that was more successful than *D&D*. I believe that the success of *Pathfinder* and the failure of fourth edition both inform a lot of the decisions they made for fifth edition.

MI: You mentioned the publishers were initially worried about WotC pulling out the rug from under them, but one intriguing part about the OGL is that it's irrevocable. We've talked about ideas of corporate success, but I wonder if you think the permanency of the OGL is ultimately good for the hobby in general?

RD: The most important thing the OGL did wasn't about the OGL; it was about *D&D*. The release of the SRD under the OGL means that the game is now immortal. Nothing can be done at the corporate level to take *D&D* away from humanity. It can exist in some legal way, no matter what happens at WotC, Hasbro, or anywhere else in the future.

When I looked at the situation that TSR was in when they were acquired, I knew there was a very good chance that *D&D* would cease to exist because TSR had pledged its intellectual property against loans that they couldn't repay to different lenders. Had the company gone into bankruptcy, those lenders would have gone to bankruptcy court and fought over who controlled TSR's IP. If that happened, there's a very good chance we would have ended up with a situation where nobody controlled enough of *D&D* to do anything with it, and it would have just stopped existing. The OGL, with the System Reference Document, means *D&D* is immortal. That's the most important thing, and I think that's valuable to everybody.

CONCLUSION

While it is too early to confirm Dancey's claim of *D&D*'s immortality, it is easy to see the OGL's ongoing influence on how the game is developed, distributed, and played. Its rules are now embedded in diverse online systems, from sprawling fan wikis that catalog decades-long rule histories to virtual tabletops that allow users to play *D&D* with each other from halfway around the world. The *Pathfinder Roleplaying Game* and numerous other TTRPGs have built on third edition's design lineage, extending its life span far beyond its officially supported window and dispelling the idea of clean breaks between editions. And platforms such as Dungeon Masters Guild have furthered the notion that anyone can design for *D&D*, leveraging online marketplaces to create an approachable digital publishing ecosystem. Although the OGL is not solely responsible for any these outcomes—for example, in chapter 7 of this collection, Mateusz Felczak will elaborate on how digital games have helped popularize *D&D*'s rules and community-driven design philosophies—it plays an important role by establishing clear rules of engagement for the TTRPG. Still, it appears that many of the hesitations that publishers initially held toward the OGL may have been merited. In 2023, leaked internal communications revealed that WotC was contemplating changes that would revoke the existing OGL and replace it with a new version that would force creators to pay royalties, share earnings reports, and allow WotC to freely use third-party content for their own products. While WotC later abandoned these prospective alterations, they still raised doubts about the long-term outlook for the OGL. With licensed works still playing an enormous role in the success and popularity of *D&D*, even a small change to the OGL could significantly transform the TTRPG landscape.

NOTES

1. Wizards of the Coast, "Open Game License," 2000, https://media.wizards.com /2016/downloads/SRD-OGL_V1.1.pdf.

2. Scott Thorne, "Rolling for Initiative—Some Observations from Free RPG Day," *ICv2: The Business of Geek Culture* (blog), June 26, 2011, https://icv2.com/articles /columns/view/20425/rolling-initiative-some-observations-free-rpg-day.

7

PLAYING CUSTOM: A CURIOUS HISTORY OF *DUNGEONS & DRAGONS*–BASED DIGITAL GAMES MODIFICATIONS

Mateusz Felczak

Modifying a game to one's liking has a long tradition in both digital and tabletop franchises. Exploring different gameplay scenarios by adjusting the rules to particular needs is directly encouraged in the fifth edition (5e) *Dungeon Master's Guide* (*DMG*), where chapter 1 is titled "A World of Your Own." In the context of *Dungeons & Dragons* (*D&D*), such practices can arguably be traced back to the postcard sent by Gary Gygax to Dave Arneson in 1972, where possible modifications of *Chainmail* are mentioned, including "fantasy heroes and dungeon exploration."[1] In terms of digital games, the breakthrough happened in 2000, when Wizards of the Coast (WotC) provided the Open Game License Version 1.0a (OGL) to any designer who wished to use the basic *D&D* rules to create their own product. However, the last decade of computer games history can hardly be considered the heyday of digital *D&D*-based gaming, with only the latest efforts by both indie/small-scale (*Solasta: Crown of the Magister*, by Tactical Adventures) and well-established (*Baldur's Gate III*, by Larian Studios) companies successfully capitalizing on the resurgence of interest in collective dice rolling and fantasy dungeoning. Modding, on the other hand, has consistently been a driving force behind digital games exploring the *D&D* rule set and aesthetics. It has provided a platform for collective discussions on the intricacies of the subsequent *D&D* editions as well as ways of enriching the gaming experience beyond its official, systemic constraints. Defined as "player-made alterations and additions to pre-existing games,"[2] modifications (or mods) encompass "various ways of extending and altering officially released computer games, their graphics, sounds and characters, with custom-produced content."[3]

This chapter takes a closer look at computer role-playing games (CRPGs) only. As noted by game studies scholars, the term "role-playing games" refers to different forms (both digital and nondigital) across different media,[4] and the notion of "role-playing" does not necessarily mean exclusive focus on narrative, story-driven experience enacted by the players. This diversity is mirrored in the historical development of digital *D&D* games modding: the scope, goals, styles, and even aesthetics of fan-made modifications developed in the 1990s can be strikingly dissimilar to mods dedicated to the same titles, but designed and launched closer to the present times.

The following research is limited to juxtaposing mods and titles dedicated to various personal computer platforms, with particular titles selected on the basis of their popularity, relevance to the *D&D* franchise, and impact on the modding scene. The analyzed modifications will be put into three groups representing the three main eras of the digital *D&D* games: Gold Box games, Infinity Engine games, and Aurora and Electron Engines titles. Other games, such as the *Dark Sun* series and titles based on the System Reference Document (SRD) or full 5e license will serve as supplementary source material. With each of these three groups, I introduce two distinct categories or types of mods that act as an overarching framework for an in-depth analysis of selected examples of modding.

In the Gold Box games era, I first look at *Forgotten Realms: Unlimited Adventures* and *Dungeon Craft*, projects that provided toolsets and platforms for numerous fan-made adventures and modules. Then I discuss the *Gold Box Companion*, a tool designed to make engagement with the early-1990s digital *D&D* gaming a more streamlined experience. SSI, which produced the Gold Box games, was the first company to acquire the official *Advanced Dungeons & Dragons* (*AD&D* 1e) license, and multiple titles that shipped between the end of 1980 and the first half of 1990s established a blueprint for conversion of pen-and-paper (PnP) rules into a digital format.

Moving from the Gold Box–era *AD&D* rule set to the *AD&D* second edition (*AD&D* 2e) rule set, I delve into the realm of Infinity Engine games, which dominated the *D&D* CRPG market from 1998 to 2001. In this section, I identify the two most influential groups of mods: difficulty-based modifications and romance/companion-focused works.

The final of the three main sections focuses on the first and the second iterations of *Neverwinter Nights*, games that used the Aurora and Electron engines, respectively. This part offers an overview of persistent worlds designed to be multiplayer experiences.

Afterward, I move to discuss self-contained modules and re-creations of older *D&D* games with the use of the Aurora and Electron toolboxes. Although it has been noted that CRPGs shifted over time from being just vehicles for rules automation to providing more emphasis on story and nonmechanical components of gameplay,[5] I would argue that this process has not been a linear one. The pushback from modders at various stages of the genre's history is a testament to the fluctuation of design strategies.

My key research question reads as follows: to what extent have the *D&D* digital games been used, played, and altered by the community according to their (stated) narrative and mechanical source material? In general, I wish to investigate how the authors of mods and various communities of players approached digital CRPG games as *D&D* products. To this end, I analyze the actual content of the mods and explore the works of online fan communities that keep the modding of *D&D*-based games relevant and accessible, even if their digital source material is nowadays hard to obtain or even unplayable due to technological issues.

Theoretical context for this chapter is provided by fan studies[6] and works on digital fandom archives.[7] For the sake of space and argumentative stringency, I have omitted some crucial issues concerning the preservation of mods as integral parts of cultural digital heritage,[8] which deserve a separate study also in the context of *D&D* history. Besides building on already well-established studies on digital game modding from the perspectives of fans' productivity, motivations, precarity, and gender issues,[9] this study includes materials from four semistructured, written interviews conducted with modders to assess their experience with providing authorial content within the frameworks of the narrative and mechanical scaffoldings of the *D&D* system. Although the sample is by no means representative, I use it as supplementary data to illustrate key arguments.

The overarching premise of this chapter is connected with the titular idea of *playing custom* in its double meaning: *customs* understood as playing conventions and traditions established over time by particular modding communities and players, and the notion of *customization*—the creative drive behind modifying the experience of play beyond the constraints of imposed systemic boundaries.

GOLD BOX ERA: CRAFTING DUNGEONS

The so-called Gold Box games include a series of titles using the *AD&D* license, released from 1988 to 1992. All of them are based on the same engine, and their legacy is still very much alive in the modern *D&D* modding scene.

Gold Box, or SSI titles (from the name of their parenting company, Strategic Simulations Inc.), emerged on multiple platforms, from Apple II and Amiga to DOS and Commodore 64. Acting as a developer and sometimes doubling as a publisher, SSI introduced a variety of *D&D* settings to the digital market. To name just a few titles, *Curse of the Azure Bonds* (1989) remained in the Forgotten Realms, but *Champions of Krynn* (1990) and *Spelljammer: Pirates of Realmspace* (1992) used Dragonlance and Spelljammer settings, respectively. Another prominent title, the postapocalyptic *Dark Sun: Shattered Lands* (1993), suffered from development issues and switched from a Gold Box first-person to a top-down perspective, ultimately becoming subject to fan-made patches and alterations. It is worth noting that this initial wave of digital *D&D*-based games provided an unprecedented variety of settings, but not so much in the way of play styles. The Gold Box era remained rather conservative in its dungeon crawl formula, with encounter design closely tied to the architecture of the in-game spaces to accommodate a demanding mixture of combat and environmental puzzles. *Dark Sun* saw a slight shift toward a more role-playing approach, although in the late 1980s and early 1990s, digital *D&D* gamers were usually pitted against a ruthless dungeon master (DM) embedded in the strict system of rules, similar to the approach noted by

Jon Peterson in the context of wargaming communities that "had long granted the referee total authority over the execution of the system."[10] In the Gold Box games, the referee would translate into a digital, systemic simulation of a DM, albeit with all the limitations regarding its scripted reactivity patterns. Modifying the Gold Box games shortly after their release was not a common practice, and powergame-oriented play remained a default mode of enjoying the digital dungeon crawls.[11]

The available choice of play styles when it comes to digital *D&D* gaming improved dramatically with the release of *Forgotten Realms: Unlimited Adventures* (1993), a tool kit and a dungeon editor based on a modified version of the Gold Box engine, which (crucially) did not include the engine source code at the time of its release. Often acronymized as *FRUA*, it boasts a healthy modding community to this day. Some notable fan-based projects include re-creating copyrighted adventures and dungeon modules, thus keeping some of the early edition's *D&D* content alive and available in a playable, digital form. Many of the most elaborate works were made with *Dungeon Craft*, a stand-alone program heavily inspired by *FRUA*. *Dungeon Craft* is unique in its scope in a way that transgresses the boundaries of not only *AD&D* but also *D&D* in general. The self-contained adventures developed with the help of this editor encompass everything from the historic Roman Empire to *Call of Cthulhu* and *Cyberpunk* settings. Nowadays, adventure makers can also download and use the so-called hacks that enable modifications of the previously unchangeable rules and assets. For example, the original *FRUA* enforced discrepancies between the maximum strength ability scores of female and male characters, which were congruent with the *AD&D* rules. One of the most popular changes to *FRUA*, the *Unlimited Adventures Science Fiction Hack*, removes these limits altogether. It is informative to compare the rationale behind this alteration with the comments made by Gary Gygax, who later admitted regretting the introduction of gender inequality in the first edition of *AD&D* (1e).[12] In the aforementioned *SciFi Hack*, the changes were made to let modders introduce characters "that can apply to a variety of settings."[13]

GOLD BOX ERA: A MODERN-DAY COMPANION

Mods designed to work with Gold Box games predominantly addressed the moment-to-moment gameplay, focusing on attempts at streamlining the rule set and later on providing a number of ease-of-use changes. Even a cursory look at the most popular modding package dedicated to the products of that era, the *Gold Box Companion*, reveals the overall nature of the changes desired by the community of players. Here the convenience changes take precedence over drastic rule set overhauls: the customizable tool allows for adding a world map and combat views. *Gold Box Companion* also expands the amount of information displayed on the screen. The Save Game Editor paired with mild cheats—examples include an optional auto-identification of items and a "magical" refill of the replenished ammo—makes the gameplay definitely less tedious than it used to be at the time of the games' initial release.

Gold Box Companion takes the principle of the automated rule set that guided the design of the Gold Box games and applies it to elements that require not the DM's but the player's attention. In *Eye of the Beholder* (1990), players were expected to draw their own maps to navigate the in-game dungeons. At its initial release, even in the first Infinity Engine game, *Baldur's Gate* (1998), the in-game journal was practically devoid of features that might have turned it into a convenient quest tracker. Navigating mazes filled with traps, managing scant resources, and negotiating the power levels of combat encounters are made easier by enabling key features of the *Companion*. Notably, an option also exists to personalize the in-game audio features. It is hard to argue with the words of one of the *Gold Box Classics* reviewers: "Where the original games were strict interpretations of the rules as written, having the Companion is like playing *D&D* with a Dungeon Master who skips the boring stuff and ignores the more unfair rules, which actually brings it closer to the real experience of playing *D&D*."[14] In 2022, a collection of games called *Gold Box Classics* appeared on the popular digital distribution platform Steam, providing a chance for both the games and their dedicated modding tools to reach new, modern-day audiences. SNEG, the publisher of the collection, took some liberties in determining which titles do or do not belong to the Gold Box name, but access to the pioneering batch of digital *D&D* games has never been so easy, be it through Steam or other platforms such as GOG.

As argued by the scholar Tomasz Majkowski, modding culture has been shaped by the changing modes of production of video games, along with the need to distinguish between the work of professional developers and the products of fans' labor.[15] Before these two worlds were (briefly) joined again in the fan-made but commercially distributed modules for *Neverwinter Nights*, the next big step in digital *D&D* modding came with the introduction of the Infinity Engine.

INFINITY ENGINE: MAKING LIFE MORE DIFFICULT SINCE 1998

The somehow unexpected success of *Baldur's Gate*, a CRPG set in the Forgotten Realms setting, heralded a new era of digital *D&D* gaming. Titles based on the subsequent versions of this first Infinity Engine installment all share key features: a player-controlled party of up to six characters, real-time-with-pause combat, a pseudo-isometric point of view, and a distinct aesthetic of hand-painted interiors and map backgrounds. Coming after a few years' gap since the last official *D&D*-based game, these titles nevertheless retained the core design premises of their predecessors. Josh Sawyer, the designer behind numerous *D&D* digital games, offers a particularly telling comment concerning the first iteration of *Icewind Dale* (2000):

> I assumed everyone who picked up the game was as conversant as me in AD&D 2nd Ed/Forgotten Realms rules and lore, had played hundreds of hours of it in tabletop with similarly aggressive psychogamers, and had weathered fair but diabolically brutal DMs whose scenarios demanded quick thinking and ruthless min-maxing tactics.[16]

Such an explicit insight is a testament to the radical approach applied to digital *D&D* games for the large portion of their history. Only modern titles, like *Baldur's Gate III*, show efforts to communicate their rule set in a way that does not put players unfamiliar with *D&D* at an immediate disadvantage. One of the biggest and most recommended modifications for the original *Baldur's Gate* series (1998–2001), which is also compatible with the series' *Enhanced Editions* (2012–2013), is called *Sword Coast Stratagems* (*SCS*). It offers an extremely high degree of customization, with most options covering difficulty increase through altering plot-critical encounters. Although the key component of *SCS* drastically increases the quality of the opponent's artificial intelligence, this mod offers a possibility to tune both narrative and combat encounters to the level suitable for very experienced players. The majority of difficult fights in the *Baldur's Gate* series involve magic, and *SCS* rewards players who meticulously read item and spell descriptions and know how to counter the arcane and divine onslaughts unleashed on the party at the most inconvenient moments. As a DM, *SCS* is designed for those who have already played through a particular campaign. The challenge and the fun lie in overcoming the almost impossible odds and barely surviving to see what the next challenge has to offer. Such an approach has its downsides: the major story beats are gated behind demanding encounters, and the mods installation process and the in-game difficulty slider remain the only ways to adjust the ruthless digital DM to a player's liking.

It is probably safe to assume that, throughout the 1990s and early 2000s, a substantial degree of familiarity with the tactical intricacies of the system was expected of the digital *D&D*-based games players. However, rules changed over time, and mods for games using the already antiquated versions of *D&D* are still being made and actively played. This situation creates an interesting conundrum. On the one hand, modding offers a unique opportunity to (re)visit the "legacy" iterations of *D&D* through experiencing modern-day content created by dedicated fans of a given digital game franchise. On the other hand, taking a closer look at the lists of popular Infinity Engine mods reveals that systemic constraints are usually treated as an obstacle to overcome rather than a chance to immerse oneself in worlds governed by the now-derelict editions of *D&D*. For example, one of the biggest mods offering optional rule changes for Infinity Engine games, *The Tweaks Anthology*, evokes PnP authority mostly to justify adjustments that simply make the game easier. When asked about the importance of the official PnP rules and guidelines in their modding practice, one of my respondents offered a telling statement: "When it comes to the official rules I'm aware of, I follow them when it's convenient, and I bend them when it's not" (Anon2). Such sentiment was prevalent among all my interlocutors, thus highlighting the common practice of tabletop and digital *D&D* players of adjusting the systemic rules to the particular gameplay goals.

INFINITY ENGINE: FLESHING OUT YOUR PARTY

Providing an exhaustively nuanced account of all the modding repositories for the Infinity Engine (IE) is perhaps impossible, but even cursory
queries reveal an abundance of companion-related and romance-focused
mods. Without delving too deep into the technical intricacies of modding, it is important to note that most of the available tools allowed for a
fair amount of creative leeway, albeit inevitably constrained by the engine
limitations. One of my interviewees named IE a "grandpa" but also noted:

> Nevertheless, such a grandpa can deliver an interesting story, and that's why,
> even after several years, I didn't abandon making Infinity Engine mods. Even
> building on something that is far from ideal opens up creative possibilities and
> gives an opportunity to tell a moving, interesting, chilling or even risqué story.
> (Anon1)

This response suggests that the appeal of IE modding does not reside
solely in the realm of tactical encounters. Engine limitations for *D&D*
games from that era stimulate storytelling that relies heavily on the written word, but some mods managed to balance out narrative and combat
encounters. One of the most well-received modifications that achieved
narrative complexity while still offering demanding fights is the *Solaufein
Romance Modification Pack* by Westley Weimer. It allows *Baldur's Gate II*
players to recruit a new drow elf companion, who will, apart from citing
passages from W. H. Auden and Robert Frost, also "attempt to romance
the PC [player character] regardless of race, gender or other loved ones."[17]
Modeled after the Forgotten Realms hero Drizzt Do'Urden, *Solaufein* con-
veniently defies the racial stereotypes ingrained in *AD&D* 2e (see chap. 15
by Amanda Cote and Emily Saidel in this collection). However, reaching pivotal moments of his romance requires defeating at least three
challenging encounters, in which some enemies actually "cheat" by the
AD&D 2e standards, having too many free-to-use abilities and hit points
or using "illegal" tactics. Testing the assumption of heroic fantasy underpinnings of *AD&D* 2e and quest design of IE games set in the Forgotten
Realms seemed to be the goal of *Valen NPC Mod*, another work by Weimer.
Here players who welcomed a titular female vampire among their ranks
must face unprecedented outbursts of Valen's visceral violence, a moral
(and mechanical, given the difficulty of the fights that players are pushed
into) challenge rarely seen in the digital adaptations of *D&D*.

Mods' FAQs (frequently asked questions) contain some evidence of their authors' motivations for experimenting with certain elements of the *D&D* rule set. Perhaps the most straightforward ones concern the joinable nonplayer characters (NPCs)—characters that players can add to their party. In the documentation for *Fade*, one of the popular NPC mods for *Baldur's Gate II*, the author provides a simple reason behind including a romance option for this particular character: "because I love the idea of the Fey'ri and my DM wouldn't let me play one in Real Life Sunday™ roleplaying."[18] This tongue-in-cheek statement is an example of a common rationale behind modifications of the *D&D*-based digital games. The NPCs category in major mod repositories such as Spellhold Studios, the Sorcerer's Place, and The Gibberlings Three contributes to a large portion of overall downloads, and the option to tie emotional, friendship, or romantic bonds with the joinable characters becomes a major selling point for potential players, visibly highlighted in the FAQs and forum discussions on particular mods. Out of twenty-one NPCs (spanning nineteen separate mods) listed on the main Spellhold Studios web page, only five did not include any "romance" path, although these options are not necessarily focused on the PC (player's main character—the protagonist of the Bhaalspawn saga). The information concerning romantic development of a relationship with an NPC is usually included in the FAQ section, and one can assume that such content is expected by the community. Omitting this component is more often than not a deliberate design choice, sometimes playfully commented on by a mod's author(s) in the documentation. For example, the Yeslick FAQ answers the question "Is he romanceable?" by stating: "Absolutely, if you have a vivid imagination and don't mind having no references to it in the game whatsoever."[19] Such remarks are not uncommon in the materials concerning mods for the IE and pre-IE *D&D* digital games, which can be considered as a type of metacommentary referring to the necessity of players' involvement in paratextual activities, needed to fill in the narrative and mechanical gaps in the source material.

The Infinity Engine games—and *Baldur's Gate II* in particular—in fact instigated and popularized the option to have meaningful interactions between the players and party members, which quickly became a staple of computer RPGs, contributing to the success of other BioWare hits like

Mass Effect and the *Dragon Age* series. The Infinity Engine games instigate interpersonal character development through extremely limited means: owing to the technical constraints, modders must resort to branching dialogue options rather than explicit graphical storytelling, which arguably does make their narrative solutions closer to the courtly love trope.[20] Ultimately, mods with romantic components marked an important milestone in the history of digital *D&D* games, although many of the most influential ones retained a combat-based component. These two interwoven paths of advancing the modding scene and testing the limits of creativity within the *D&D* framework changed their course quite radically with *Neverwinter Nights*, the then-upcoming 3D title that made mod makers reconsider the scope and goals of their projects.

AURORA AND ELECTRON: MULTIPLAYER GALORE

In 2002, just one year after the premiere of the *Baldur's Gate II* expansion, BioWare would introduce a dramatic shift in its approach. Despite retaining a lengthy story stretched across a campaign more than fifty hours long, *Neverwinter Nights*, the studio's next game based on the newer iteration of the *D&D* system, would be more of a tool kit rather than solely a single-player experience, crafted to accommodate the needs of multiplayer-focused online communities. Aiming for a bigger market than its famous Infinity Engine predecessors, BioWare saw potential in online and emergent gameplay. This shift was linked with changes in the gameplay formula: the pseudo-isometric perspective gave way to 3D models, and the party size was significantly reduced; the first iteration of the series effectively restricted the player's agency to one character only. The Aurora Toolset, released along with the main game, allowed users to create self-contained adventures (modules) that can be linked to a larger campaign. Some of the so-called premium modules have been adapted by BioWare into separate products sold in the manner of DLCs (downloadable content); this is perhaps the most straightforward example of a company capitalizing on the work of dedicated modders.[21] A special type of module is persistent worlds: fan-created game worlds that operate continuously in real time, providing a backdrop for any narrative developments within a separate digital realm curated by the hosts.

Among the differences between tabletop *D&D* and digital games based on *D&D*, perhaps the most pronounced are gameplay pace and number of encounters. In the digital medium, it is significantly easier to implement combat-heavy scenarios without the need to perform lengthy and sometimes cumbersome calculations, as the dice rolls and ability/attribute checks happen behind the scenes. At the same time, video games traditionally afford a certain degree of agency that must be maintained and exerted within the constraints of the medium. This is especially evident in the second important functionality of the Aurora and Electron engines: the ability not only to craft single-player-focused modules but also to design and maintain multiplayer servers with persistent digital worlds. Agency—understood as overcoming functional and emotional challenges through the means provided by the designers and other players—is a crucial element of the gameplay experience,[22] but even games focused on emergent, multiplayer gameplay require a significant degree of prestructuring the conditions that enable the enactment of certain scenarios. Thus, working with the *Neverwinter Nights* tool kit to craft a multiplayer campaign resembles the preparation of a tabletop DM only superficially; making a particular scenario work in the digital medium requires no less, but a different skill set from its PnP counterpart. When asked about the intricacies of their workflow, one of the modders commented: "Sketching area layouts on paper along with important NPCs is a good start, but often I would just play with the toolset to see what could be done, and use that to further lift the quality of the final experience" (Anon4). It is worth remembering that in multiplayer *D&D* games, players and DMs share the same digital version of the world, with all its spatial properties. Dedicated role-playing servers and modules allow a great variety of options, including custom kits and alternative rules, although some of the tools normally available for players under the PnP rule set are almost universally absent from the digital games. Examples include spells like "Teleport" or "Plane Shift": when used at players' discretion, they risk derailing the narrative experience, which in digital games is expressively and closely tied to the spatial and environmental storytelling conveyed through both the aesthetics and functional properties of the assets. Despite these limitations, the commercial success of the *Neverwinter Nights* series allowed long-running dedicated role-playing servers to thrive and offer their own version of a *D&D* experience, also for those who simply lack the opportunity to participate in tabletop sessions. The second iteration of the franchise changed both the engine (swapping Aurora for Electron) and the design philosophy. While *Neverwinter Nights 2* improved on the single-player campaign, its toolset has become less intuitive to use, thus, somewhat paradoxically, contributing to the longevity of the Aurora modding scene.

AURORA AND ELECTRON: SINGLE-PLAYER MODULES AND RE-CREATED ADVENTURES

Aurora Engine modding is strikingly dissimilar to previous *D&D* games modding in terms of its creative breadth and overall simplicity for those who wish to try the tool kit without any prior coding or script-writing knowledge. That being said, customizing scripts is one of the most powerful tools at the disposal of Aurora and Electron modding communities. HCR script mod (its acronym aptly translates as "hard-core rules") allows users to customize the in-game rules to align more with their *D&D* third edition (3e) counterparts. It is perhaps curious to see such labeling for a modification that does not introduce any new boss fights or tactical challenges, instead relying only on rigorous application of the PnP rules. To understand why PnP *D&D* may be considered "hard-core" when translated into digital game, it may be informative to consider one of the highly praised fan-made campaigns for *Neverwinter Nights*, the multichapter adventure *Swordflight*. It is notoriously problematic for non-melee characters and requires careful planning of the character build to achieve the desired narrative progress. While the original, single-player *Neverwinter Nights* campaign has been toned down in terms of encounter design, required levels of resource management, and reactivity to different character builds, *Swordflight* is anything but. The rules concerning resting and interacting with monsters, NPCs, and the environment have been taken extremely seriously, allowing players—just as a human DM might—to make their own mistakes and learn from them. BioWare game designers arguably could not risk alienating their audience by opting for such rigid PnP rules enforcement. The vanilla *Swordflight* single-player campaign was meant to encourage players to create their own modules, not to struggle to successfully conquer the campaign.

Neverwinter Nights extended the scope of possibilities associated with traditional tabletop *D&D*, but the structure of gameplay still arguably relied more on the conventions afforded by the digital medium of video games. One of the most experienced *Neverwinter* modders told me that the knowledge acquired by "20+ years of tabletop RPGs . . . definitely helps to understand the framework of how to make an engrossing module, though the methods vary considerably" (Anon4). *Neverwinter Nights* modding took a radically different approach from the previous *D&D*-based digital games also due to the possibility of designing modules: stand-alone adventures that share many similarities with their PnP counterparts. These types of mods are perhaps structurally the closest to campaigns crafted by DMs in tabletop *D&D*, albeit with an important caveat of enforcing the predesigned patterns of interactivity without the possibility of negotiating them, as is (theoretically) the case with human DMs. With the advent of *Neverwinter Nights Enhanced Edition*, some modules—usually previously accepted by BioWare—achieved the status of official DLCs. Because of the free-form format, modules may vary drastically in terms of length, narrative tone, and difficulty, the latter depending on the player's familiarity with a particular authorial take on the selected *D&D* rule set as well as on the preferred gameplay style.

Modules play a crucial role in digital content preservation. *Pool of Radiance* (1988), the first *D&D* title to be released on popular home computer platforms, has been meticulously re-created as a module for *Neverwinter Nights 1* and *2*. The original game, based on the *AD&D* 1e adventure module *Ruins of Adventure*, was a breakthrough effort to truly popularize *D&D* in the digital games medium, and the *Pool of Radiance Remastered* modules aim at bringing this experience to new players, though the conversion to the *D&D* third edition (3e) rules resulted in a number of discrepancies between the original game and its reintroduction using new assets and largely refurbished mechanics. Another example of a mod that provides an opportunity to revisit—or simply get to know for the first time—the classic dungeon-crawling experience of early digital *AD&D* adaptations is *Eye of the Beholder*, of which two parts have also been re-created as *Neverwinter Nights* modules. The modder's approach reveals important priorities of the design: "We stuck with the original map designs and plot, but added over 25 new side quests that build on the original story."[23]

CONCLUSION

The evolution from a rigid, rules-heavy dungeon-crawling approach implemented by the Gold Box–era games toward the quasi-MMO, community-driven design philosophy of *Neverwinter Nights* to some extent resembles the transformation of gameplay conventions of tabletop *D&D*. What once was a relatively niche pastime designed for a specific, rather narrow group of enthusiasts with previous wargaming experience turned into a much more accessible activity, with diverse narratives and personal stories becoming more important than ruthless min-maxing character optimization.

Examples of modifications and practices of modding analyzed in this chapter provoke questions concerning their intended audience. I would argue that all three eras of digital *D&D* games presented here offered at least two ways of making the content of these titles engaging for different audiences. One design philosophy addressed the ease-of-use changes and made narrative elements more diverse and attractive, while the other appealed to the already initiated. The latter group may not even be that familiar with the *D&D* rules, but acknowledged the quirks, uncanny gameplay solutions and metastrategies implemented in the particular digital games. The game studies scholar Tom Welch argues that modding as an activity affords the inclusion of identities, narratives, and rules underrepresented in the initial versions of games, and may in some instances "transform gaming into something affectively beneficial."[24] However, the changing dynamics of the present-day production cycle encourage designers to reach out to fans at the early stages of production,[25] which substantially changes the modding landscape. These shifts can be witnessed in the case of *Baldur's Gate III*: the game's early-access version, released more than a year before the planned premiere, has been open to modding activities from the beginning.

Each of the three periods of digital *D&D* gaming introduced a new element to the reception of both tabletop rule sets and the playful customization culture expressed by modding. The Gold Box titles, along with other SSI *D&D* games, defined the core implementation of turn-based combat as a staple that modern 5e digital games, like *Baldur's Gate III* or *Solasta*, can refine and build on. The IE titles initiated a long history of continuously supported, fan-made modding tools and an unprecedented variety of mods, placed on a spectrum from demanding combat challenges to romanceable NPCs with multiple branching dialogue options. Last but not least, the *Neverwinter Nights* series reintroduced the digital *D&D* experience to the mainstream gaming public while providing a relatively easy-to-use tool kit with possibilities of crafting individual modules as well as intricate, multiplayer worlds.

NOTES

1. Jon Peterson, *The Elusive Shift: How Role-Playing Games Forged Their Identity* (Cambridge, MA: MIT Press, 2020), 47.

2. Olli Sotamaa, "When the Game Is Not Enough: Motivations and Practices among Computer Game Modding Culture," *Games and Culture* 5, no. 3 (2010): 240.

3. Tanja Sihvonen, *Players Unleashed! Modding The Sims and the Culture of Gaming* (Amsterdam: Amsterdam University Press, 2011), 12.

4. José P. Zagal and Sebastian Deterding, eds., *Role-Playing Game Studies: Transmedia Foundations* (New York: Routledge, 2018).

5. Douglas Schules, Jon Peterson, and Martin Picard, "Single-Play Computer Role-Playing Games," in *Role-Playing Game Studies: Transmedia Foundations*, ed. José P. Zagal and Sebastian Deterding (New York: Routledge, 2018), 107.

6. Nicolle Lamerichs, *Productive Fandom: Intermediality and Affective Reception in Fan Cultures* (Amsterdam: Amsterdam University Press, 2018).

7. Melanie Swalwell, Helen Stuckey, and Angela Ndalianis, eds., *Fans and Videogames: Histories, Fandom, Archives* (New York: Routledge, 2017).

8. Niklas Nylund, Patrick Prax, and Olli Sotamaa, "Rethinking Game Heritage: Towards Reflexivity in Game Preservation," *International Journal of Heritage Studies* 27, no. 3 (2021): 268–280.

9. Sotamaa, "When the Game"; Nathaniel Poor, "Computer Game Modders' Motivations and Sense of Community: A Mixed-Methods Approach," *New Media and Society* 16, no. 8 (2014): 1249–1267; Julian Kücklich, "Precarious Playbour: Modders and the Digital Games Industry," *Fibreculture Journal*, no. 5 (2005), http://five.fibreculturejournal.org/fcj-025-precarious-playbour-modders-and-the-digital-games-industry; Bridget Whelan, ed., *Women and Video Game Modding: Essays on Gender and the Digital Community* (Jefferson, NC: McFarland, 2020).

10. Peterson, *The Elusive Shift*, 7.

11. T. L. Taylor, "Power Gamers Just Want to Have Fun? Instrumental Play in a MMOG," in *Proceedings of DiGRA 2003*, 301–311, http://www.digra.org/wp-content/uploads/digital-library/05163.32071.pdf.

12. Gary Gygax, "Q&A with Gary Gygax," EN World, February 23, 2005, 136, https://www.enworld.org/threads/q-a-with-gary-gygax.22566/page-136#post -2054939.

13. Jon Marshall, "Unlimited Adventures Science Fiction Hack V 1.0," http://frua .rosedragon.org/pc/hacks/scifiua.txt.

14. Jody Macgregor, "The Classic Gold Box D&D Games Are on Steam, but What's Special about Them?" *PC Gamer*, 2022, https://www.pcgamer.com/the-classic-gold -box-dandd-games-are-on-steam-but-whats-special-about-them/.

15. Tomasz Majkowski, "Erotyka w Fanowskich Modyfikacjach Gier Cyfrowych: Przypadek SexLab," *Teksty Drugie*, no. 5 (2019): 102.

16. Josh Sawyer, "Balance in Single-Player CRPGs," Tumblr, May 31 2017, https:// jesawyer.tumblr.com/post/161302725596/balance-in-single-player-crpgs.

17. Westley Weimer, "Baldur's Gate II: Slaufein Romance Modification Pack," https://weidu.org/solarom/README-SolaRomance.txt.

18. Mistress Elysia, "Fade F.A.Q.," Spellhold Studios forum, May 2014, http://www .shsforums.net/topic/23426-fade-faq/.

19. Pixel Kaiser, "Yeslick NPC," https://spellholdstudios.github.io/readmes/yeslicknpc -readme-english.html.

20. Magdalena Bednorz and Joanna Kucharska, "Only If for a Knight: Romantic Sub-plots in CRPGs in the Light of Courtly Love Trope," in *DiGRA/FDG '16: Abstract Proceedings of the First International Joint Conference of DiGRA and FDG* 13, no. 2 (August 2016). http://www.digra.org/wp-content/uploads/digital-library/paper_338.pdf.

21. Kücklich, "Precarious Playbour"; Hector Postigo, "Of Mods and Modders: Chasing Down the Value of Fan-Based Digital Game Modifications," *Games and Culture* 2, no. 4 (2007): 300–313.

22. Tom Cole and Marco Gillies, "Thinking and Doing: Challenge, Agency, and the Eudaimonic Experience in Video Games," *Games and Culture* 16, no. 2 (2021): 201.

23. Jay Watamanuik, "The Eye of the Beholder Project," Internet Archive, https:// web.archive.org/web/20090331110524/http://nwn.bioware.com/players/profile_eye ofthebeholder.html.

24. Tom Welch, "The Affectively Necessary Labour of Queer Mods," *Game Studies* 18, no. 3 (2018), http://gamestudies.org/1803/articles/welch.

25. Aphra Kerr, *Global Games: Production, Circulation and Policy in the Networked Era* (New York: Routledge, 2017).

8

A RETURN TO THE MAGIC CIRCLE: *DUNGEONS & DRAGONS* AND FRIENDSHIP & MAGIC FIFTY YEARS ON

Stephen Webley

On behalf of the Accidental Tourists: Gnome Chomsky (Steve Webley), Dianthus Dryas (Deborah Fleming), Red Creeper Jones (Tim Winters), Ianhorn D'Burglar (Ryan Foster), Mon'Ki (Gavin Foster), Zoot (Mat Hicks), Bayleaf (Jez Thomas), and Lord Tony (Tony "Dungeon Master" Woodall)

This is the story of "the Accidental Tourists": eight aged adventurers in their fifties who during the pandemic rediscovered *D&D* and each other after decades lost in the wilderness of our working lives. It is a story that could have existed only because of the sudden change to our collective normativity. Whilst authority imploded, issuing conflicting instructions, whilst the world erupted in rage over the murder of George Floyd, whilst banks pumped trillions of dollars into collapsing economies, a small group of protesters in Minneapolis daubed graffiti on an underpass wall: "Another End of the World Is Possible." Watching protests unfold into racial conflict and the emergence of a new generation of graffiti—it was so different from the slogans we painted on the classroom walls of our youth in the 1970s and 1980s, such as "Never Work" or "Ban the Bomb"—we sat stunned. Our angst was due to the realization that our day had passed, that, since the end of the Cold War, we had been overly complacent. Should we have never worked, and just played games?

In crisis, our group reached out to one another after a four-decade adjournment from *D&D*. It became a story of a hermetic gnome wizard, a feminist dwarven gunslinger, a drunken bard and his no-nonsense girl-friend, a sociopathic thief (chaotic stupid), an obsessional monk, and a cleric who could not tell the truth. Oh, and let us not forget—it is also a story of a dungeon master (DM), who not only had to navigate the perils of remote play but had to bring the gang back together. This is a story of how the vitalism of *D&D* had always changed our realities and had always enabled us to deal with the anxiety-inducing experience of reality.

We had all started playing *Advanced Dungeons & Dragons* first edition (*AD&D* 1e) together in 1981. It was the usual story of rushing home from school and avoiding homework, instead preparing for weekend gaming sessions. We read widely, painted figures, and rolled characters. We learned that the stories we tell about our reality and identities are collaborative acts of imagination; the view of the "other" and the opinion of the "other" mattered. How we interpret and accept our differences is part of the story we tell about who we are as a community, how we are aligned with social authority. However, what influenced us the most was the very fact that we delved into the foundations of how *AD&D* 1e was created; the list of books and authors in Appendix N of the *Dungeon Masters Guide* under the heading "Inspirational and Educational Reading."[1] *AD&D* 1e was a brutal world; progression was slow. It took many sessions of cooperative play to reach the level and success needed for domain play—that elusive level of play when you finally have the social power to afford a castle of your own, or the followers you needed to maintain your farmstead so that you could afford to venture into the special series of dungeons created by Gygax himself, such as the legendary Tomb of Horrors (ToH).[2]

ToH represented a revolution in tabletop role-playing games (TTRPGs): it was the first of the North American published modules that did not require the genocide of a dungeon population but instead fostered lateral thinking and problem-solving, involving puzzles and traps set across multiple maps.[3] For a group of teenagers who would not usually flinch at the prospect of swaths of dead orc children in modules such as *The Keep on the Borderlands*,[4] ToH was a nasty but pleasant surprise. ToH was a battle against Acererak, a demilich, an undead wizard kept in existence by pure desire, who built the deadliest dungeon ever known. It was a sudden change that brought the sheer vitalism of Gygax's imagination into the lives of millions of players. Gygax seamlessly blended tropes from science fiction, horror, and fantasy, creating a stunningly original interactive form of weird fiction.

AD&D 1e drew on the magical power of ideology from Robert E. Howard's Conan stories. It was founded on the cosmic weirdness of H. P. Lovecraft. Its system of magic involved rites, rituals, and secret knowledge learned by the postapocalyptic survivors of Jack Vance's Dying Earth stories.[5] It created a unique alignment system from the works of Poul Anderson, and the social realism and ethics of "othering" of Michael Moorcock. It drew on the vertiginous dreamscapes and pantheons of Lord Dunsany. And it threw itself headlong into the romanticism of Edgar Rice Burroughs. It did not shy away from the impact that faith and religion had on society, as did Tolkien.[6] Moreover, *AD&D* 1e required pure inventiveness on behalf of its players, who could find themselves transported across planes and cosmic realities with little warning. *AD&D* 1e was without genre boundaries, a world where the Tolkienesque and modern genre fantasy held little influential sway.[7] It was a cultural artifact that was seen as radical and subversive. ToH changed our perspectives from the colonialist power fantasies of generations of previous fiction to that of the potential of transgressive daydreams. Gygax's new world empowered us to radically question social normativity and what we considered the power and right of authority. Survival meant cooperation, not domination.

The journalist David M. Ewalt considers ToH to be the deadliest game module ever devised and the apex of game design.[8] The dungeon's sudden changes in space, temporality, and social cohesion exemplified why *AD&D* 1e was such a magical experience. To survive ToH, the metagame mattered; plans took days of discussion, and friendship mattered as much as character alignments. Plans came to fruition during late-night phone calls hidden from parents; we feared the dreaded scroll of owing arriving from the utility provider. Handwritten notes were passed around classrooms. Reality was changed, distorted by Acererak as his vitalism—his immortal desire—invaded our everyday lives. What we found occurring in our lives was what the play scholar Johan Huizinga called the "magic circle."[9] At its heart was a vitalism that occurred in a social dialectic of time and space, transgressing boundaries, reconceptualizing normativity.

AD&D 1e was a unique product of its sociopolitical era. Gygax was influenced by the comic books of his youth, such as the Entertainment

Comics (EC) horror titles that had a genre-bending mix of high adventure, humor, and radical social critique. Such comics became contraband material in the United States and United Kingdom during the McCarthy era, not because of their overt horror but because they were ideologically destabilizing, promoting nonredemptive narratives, self-reflectiveness, and anticonsumerism.[10] *AD&D* 1e was a game where survival required social cohesion, life for the lone hero was brutish and short, and a social contract was foundational to survival. Gygax was metaphorically on the same page as early film luminaries such as George A. Romero, John Carpenter, Ridley Scott, and James Cameron when it came to the literary, artistic, and cinematic influences that augured the early age of postmodernity. In a world of fractured images and individual consumers, communities were undermined and authority suspect.

Society was at a loss how to react to Gygax's success. To the ideology of Reaganomics, *D&D* was simultaneously play, thus the opposite of work and unimportant, but also dangerous, subversive, satanic. We reveled in the stigma of being players. We were just playing the game, and the world of Greyhawk became as important as our own. Greyhawk was a world like ours, one of perpetual conflict. Although a patriot, Gygax was disillusioned, and with a vast knowledge of military history, his fear of the Cold War seeped into our world of play. By 1984 the Cold War was hot once again, and everybody was asking serious questions about what it meant to live in a psychosocial reality when the threat of nuclear destruction was a daily news staple. In Greyhawk, remnants of collapsed societies and ruins were everywhere; we sought out adventure in the vestiges of long-lost cultures, seeking secret knowledge from their past. We were playing with what Susan Sontag called the imagination of disaster; caught between the forced choice of destruction or the mundanity of a life of consumerism, we played with the images of destruction.[11] Our own narratives became nonredemptive; there was no "good" end to these adventures, as there was no end to the ethical conundrums we found ourselves in. Authority, just as in the reality of the eighties, burgeoned into endless self-referential questions. Gygax saw his world as trapped in a tension between morality and ethics. In Greyhawk, each country, civilization, and region had its own alignment. Paralleling the very real Cold War, it was a world divided ideologically. What did it mean to be a lawful good adventurer in a chaotic evil land? What did it mean to be a subject of a realm that did not share your ethical subjectivity? The message was clear: difference mattered. The magic circle we found ourselves in was one of vitalism, jeopardy, and the promise of rewards that stretched from the mechanics of leveling to learning something about ourselves. *AD&D* 1e was born out of the unrest, violence, and optimism and disillusionment of the 1960s. The collapse of the civil rights movement, the disillusionment of the Vietnam War, the great spectacle of the Apollo moon landings—all were subtexts of Gygax's creation. We were submerged in this imaginary world of conflicting influences.

As the threat of the Cold War faded with the collapse of the Soviet Union, our games, like our rapidly digitized society, became more codified by the rigidity of realism. We had complex charts for critical hits, multiple tables for damage to specific body parts, complex rules for falling damage. The magical nature of thieves' abilities in *AD&D* 1e (originating from Fritz Leiber's *Fafhrd and the Gray Mouser* pulp fantasies) were nerfed—or reduced/balanced. The established role of religion was changed to suit more modern sensibilities. Reality was pushing its own fantasy agendas onto our gaming imaginations. We were now gaming firmly in the wake of the huge success of the *Star Wars* trilogy. Everything was increasingly focused on the notion of Joseph Campbell's "hero's journey."[12] We strove now to be the individual hero who leaves home on a perilous journey, has epic adventures, and returns to change society, if not the world. *AD&D* 1e was changing from a world of social cohesion to a world where everybody desired to be exceptional. Computer games had taught us to seek immediate gratification, quick leveling, insta-healing, and endless streams of fireballs. Lateral thinking had taken a back seat. Slowly fading into the distance were the countercultural and subversive elements that had sparkled in the Gygaxian world.

However, our true gaming revolution came unexpectedly in our mature lives under the lockdown of the pandemic. It started when our DM decided to get the gang back together. We faced two hard choices: how to play and what to play. We chose fifth edition (5e), not because it was more accessible than *AD&D* 1e, not because it was more streamlined, more commercialized, but because it was prebuilt into the online role-playing tabletop simulator Fantasy Grounds (FG).[13] Initially the results were mixed; FG has a steep learning curve for players and DMs. It became integral to our play but also the hardest part to manage—we just had to learn to live with a user interface (UI) designed to serve a multiplicity of RPGs. In-game communication began with Skype and later switched to the much more versatile Discord; we all got webcams, and we all looked old!

Older maybe, but we fell straight back into the same magic circle. Some of us had not spoken to each other for decades, yet within the first session we were back in the same place, as if time had never passed. Locked down, we yearned for game night, to find a new sense of normativity in friendship and magic we thought was long lost. The organization needed to run a remote game came easy; during lockdown we had no social lives. Despite the anxiety of the pandemic, the new normal of lockdown was good. The metagame slipped seamlessly from crumpled notes passed around classrooms to voluminous conversations on WhatsApp. The working week became a blend of mundane remote working and intricate plan making.

D&D was our tillerman; it was our port in a storm.[14] It was another end to our world that we had control over. Rules became secondary, the edition we played didn't matter because we returned to our original type of play; what mattered most was the subversive vitalism of Gygax's vision. Playing our characters, not the game, became more important. Instead of being murderous conquerors (there were still odd mishaps), we came up with guileful plans to defeat our opponents with administrative tasks, the threats of tax and health and safety audits. With complex subterfuges, we used the normative mundanity of life that had frustrated us prepandemic as playthings to defeat opponents. We tried to ingratiate ourselves into Saltmarsh society—by getting a mortgage to buy a seafront property. And because in real life we couldn't, we did an awful lot of shopping.

Now in our fifties, coping with the COVID-19 pandemic lockdown, we may have turned our game into a Kafkaesque dystopia. But that is just our game: uncannily reminiscent of Will McLean's much beloved cartoon in the *AD&D* 1e *Dungeon Masters Guide* of a party of adventurers in Grey-hawk playing at being workers in an industrialized society. Your game will be whatever you wish; just take responsibility for it. Our game is still running, and hopefully we will still be playing at *D&D*'s sixtieth anniversary. It may be more important than ever that we are still playing in a decade's

"It's a great new fantasy role-playing game. We pretend we're workers and students in an industrialized and technological society."

8.1 Who is playing what? "Papers & Paychecks," by Will McLean, 1979. In *Advanced Dungeons & Dragons Dungeon Masters Guide*, by Gary Gygax (Lake Geneva, WI: TSR, 1979).

time. We will all be older, and the world may be an even more unsettling place. The graffiti that so perturbed us at the start of the pandemic is a reference to climate change activism. It's a call to grieve now, get it over with, accept that there will be a new normal far beyond what we can allow ourselves to imagine. The ethos is to "play at the world," learn to die often as if in a game. In our youth, we changed our world to escape both mundanity and the horror of extinction. But we became mundane; as adults we forgot the importance of magical transformation, of earning experience in the world in favor of earning paychecks to consume stuff. Now we are ready to play again, to earn experience by living modestly, disabusing ourselves of complacency, teaching others our mistakes. Living cooperatively, growing, building, making. Shopping in Greyhawk is far more fun than it is at the mall. What has play taught us yet again? Try being average; ditch your exceptionalism in favor of being the subject of exceptional circumstances. Because if you play enough, we can collectively start rebuilding; out of repetition comes the new, the unique, the difference that will truly matter.[15] What we relearned is how vitalist the world can be if you allow yourself to believe in magic. Imagine, just for an instant, if everybody you knew allowed themselves to believe they lived in a world where absolutely everything was possible. It is all in Gygax's vision of how the game could be played. Find another end to this world!

NOTES

1. Gary Gygax, *Dungeon Masters Guide* (Lake Geneva, WI: TSR Games, 1979), 224.

2. Gary Gygax, *The Tomb of Horrors: An Adventure for Character Levels 10–14, Dungeon Module S1* (Lake Geneva, WI: TSR Hobbies, 1978).

3. Wayne MacLaurin, "Return to the Tomb of Horrors," *SF Site Reviews, SF Site: The Home Page for Science Fiction and Fantasy*, 2019, https://www.sfsite.com/03b/ret53 .htm.

4. Gary Gygax, *The Keep on the Borderlands* (Lake Geneva, WI: TSR Games, 1980).

5. A. VenderMeer, "Afterword," in *Appendix N*, ed. P. Bebergal (London: Strange Attractor Press, 2020), 327–330.

6. Jeffro Johnson, *Appendix N: The Literary History of Dungeons and Dragons* (Kouvola, Finland: Castalia House, 2015).

7. Johnson, *Appendix N*.

8. David M. Ewalt, *Of Dice and Men: The Story of Dungeons & Dragons and the People Who Play It* (London: Scribner, 2013), 140–145.

9. Johan Huizinga, *Homo Ludens: A Study of the Play-Element in Culture* (London: Routledge & Kegan Paul, 1949).

10. D. Hajdu, *The Ten-Cent Plague: The Great Comic-Book Scare and How It Changed America* (New York: Picador, 2008).

11. Susan Sontag, "The Imagination of Disaster," in *Against Interpretation and Other Essays* (1966; New York: Picador, 1990), 209–225.

12. Johnson, *Appendix N*.

13. *Fantasy Grounds* (SmiteWorks, 2004–2021).

14. I am indebted for this point to Professor David Webb of Staffordshire University, an expert reader of Canguilhem, for our friendly conversations throughout the pandemic.

15. J. Halstead, *Another End of the World Is Possible* (Durham, NC: Self-published, 2020).

A *D&D* playing group gathered around a table. The players have costumes and props that resemble their in-game characters. The increasingly hybrid and digital nature of modern *D&D* play is represented in the digital tools present at the table, such as computers, phones, digital character trackers, etc. C Liersch, *D&D Session*, 2023. Pen and ink on paper.

INFLUENCING *DUNGEONS & DRAGONS*

Designer Vignettes II

Most kids pick up games right away. Adults are further removed from playing pretend. Most kids are already sort of playing a role-playing game. They don't always have shame, whereas adults are less able to put themselves out there; they think, "What if I don't do a good job?" [Kid's aren't really] worried about doing a good job, they're worried about having fun, which is how you do a good job in role-playing games! I have a distinct memory of the summer after fourth grade. When I woke up, what was important to me was what was happening in *D&D*. *Titanic* came out that summer. I recall a friend doing a sinking boat scenario, and I swear to you I could taste the water going into my lungs as that ship went down.

—James Introcaso
Lead designer for MCDM; contributor to many official *D&D* books; designer of *Burn Bryte*; host of *Table Top Babble*

As an adult, you know, there's definitely less "this is real, and if I believe hard enough, I'll get to be a part of it," but I think that's what makes *D&D* so fascinating. Being swept away is a choice. There have been moments where my character has been afraid or furious and I've felt my heart pounding. . . .

(continued)

Designer Vignettes II (continued)

While there's always a sort of background knowledge for me of "I have to roll this die to see how the story goes" that keeps me anchored in reality, there are also moments where that world is very, very real.

—**Sadie Lowry**
Writer and designer for *Light of Xaryxis* and *Call of the Netherdeep*;
regular writer and editor of MCDM's *Arcadia* magazine

In fantasy there's horses, and swords, and a blacksmith. Science fiction doesn't have this. I say we're gonna play a sci-fi game, and you have no idea if there's FTL [faster-than-light speeds], if it's cyberpunk. Is it on Earth? Are there robots? There's no shared tapestry that we all take for granted. That's one of the reasons *D&D* succeeds. It doesn't have to explain its tropes.

—**Matt Colville**
Owner of MCDM; previously lead writer for Turtle Rock Games;
creator of the *Running the Game* YouTube series

I was really into monsters. What does it eat? How does it behave? I was really into *The Spiderwick Chronicles*; I had no idea that Tony DiTerlizzi had already done all of that art for Planescape. And there was that field guide, right? That idea that this stuff is out there but you can't see it, but if you have this book, you can see it. You can see what adults don't. The idea that each page [in the *Monster Manual*] is waterlogged is a huge clue. It's supposed to look like something you've discovered in a fantasy world. You look at Richard Whitter's concept sketches; they're behind the other artwork, but it looks like someone saw the creature and made a field sketch! And there's notes from experts! It's like, here's something that exists already, what do you want to do with it?

—**Justice Ramin Arman**
Senior game designer for *Dungeons & Dragons*;
previously worked as a prolific freelancer and for Beadle & Grimm's

9

"YOU'RE GOING TO BE AMAZING": THE MERCER EFFECT AND PERFORMATIVE PLAY IN *DUNGEONS & DRAGONS*

Esther MacCallum-Stewart

This chapter examines how spectated games of *D&D* have affected modern play styles. I discuss how new ways of consuming *D&D* have provided a perspective that suggests a highly active mode of play that focuses on imaginative acting more than number crunching and the minutiae of rules. This has arisen not only from the popularity of games viewed by the incoming player base but also through a persistent clash between the rules of the game and *D&D*'s emphasis on imaginative play, which is uniquely enacted in every game.

By comparing how *D&D* rule books have framed the game as a played experience, I discuss how the conflict between rules and imagination has resulted in an indistinct perception of how *D&D* can be played and how spectated instances of the game have continued this blurring effect. By using the "actual-play" example of *Critical Role* (2015–present),[1] this chapter demonstrates how playing *D&D* is now understood via popular media, and why these modes of playfulness have risen to the fore. This recentering is partly a result of the massive growth in younger players, who learn to play by consuming visual media rather than reading rule books. In turning initially to transmedial artifacts such as actual-play playthroughs and shows, commentary, live streams, and instructional videos on sites such as Twitch and YouTube, prospective players therefore experience *D&D* first as a spectated performance, with rule book second.

Actual-plays of tabletop role-playing games (TTRPGs) are currently extremely popular. Of these, although by no means the first, *Critical Role* is undoubtedly the most successful, garnering millions of viewers for each show, and becoming the most popular on the live-streaming channel Twitch. The show runs weekly, with seven regular players taking part in an extended *D&D* campaign run by dungeon master (DM) Matthew (Matt) Mercer. An episode is usually between three and a half hours and five hours long, with a section in the middle (while the players take a break) showcasing fan art and advertising other shows on the channel. A data breach in 2021 estimated that *Critical Role* had earned nearly US$10 million in live-streaming revenue, not including revenue from sponsorships, merchandise, and other publications.[2]

Actual-plays present a TTRPG play style that privileges theatrical performance and extensive in-character role-play. The shows, which are predominantly either live-streamed or prerecorded podcasts, are largely unedited in terms of player interaction but contain high-level production values, including dioramas and miniatures made by skilled artists, editing that adds Foley and other effects to rebroadcasts, and skilled players and DMs with encyclopedic knowledge of the rules for each game. Although the players on the show are clear that they are presenting their own personal style of play, the popularity and ubiquitous style of actual plays have led to a perception that this is how all *D&D* games will be run when players first pick up their dice. This is especially true because actual-play players often appear in the first instance as new to *D&D*, thus seeming to pick up the game immediately, or are alternatively formed of groups who are already familiar with each other and have strong interpersonal bonds, allowing for effective social cohesion. Most of these players and game masters (GMs) are additionally performers—voice actors, podcasters, and nerd culture enthusiasts. Considerable frustration—and a little jealousy—has been leveled against actual-plays, as they require high levels of performative ability and group cohesion, as well as avoiding more systemic forms of play common to TTRPGs, such as getting bogged down in rule book decision-making, arguing over a technicality in the rules, or agonizing over the next turn. Most frequently, the participants of an actual-play remain in character almost entirely throughout the show, and the DM is skilled at switching between highly flavorful descriptions of the role-play world, NPCs who interact with the players as equally nuanced personalities, and rules explanations that are both accurate and obeyed by the players. Much of this is due to the nature of the show; for example, quibbling over rules is boring to watch and breaks the flow of a game, so it is easier to simply agree and move along, and vibrant acting of a character makes for a faster narrative, but this is rarely presented as extraordinary or, indeed, difficult to accomplish. Actual-plays are additionally seen as breaking the theoretical precepts of earlier TTRPG studies, most notably those contained in Gary Alan Fine's *Shared Fantasy: Role-Playing Games as Social Worlds* (1983),[3] as they have reconfigured playthroughs of TTRPGs in a public domain.[4]

Thus viewers witness a style of play known as "the Mercer Effect"—named for *Critical Role*'s DM Matt Mercer. Whereas most viewers are aware that they are watching a performative version of a TTRPG, the play style encouraged by this medium is frequently emulated by groups trying out the games for the first time. However, *D&D* is a difficult, complex game, with skilled role-playing taking many other forms beyond heavy role-play of characters, and this is not always possible to do "out of the gate."

This chapter examines how the Mercer Effect has changed from a term initially used to describe an aspirational form of play to a description of a style of play in and of itself, and how this change in perception has also affected how *D&D* is understood as a played experience. Playing the game in this way cements the current iteration of played *D&D* as an imaginative experience rather than a systemic one, but it is perhaps more flexible than critics might like to suggest, with the predominance of "homebrew" systems still happily carving their own played pathways. I suggest that the Mercer Effect as a play style or methodology of play is also a result of the game itself becoming an uncontrollable ludic experience. Each subsequent edition lays down rules and practices for play, but these have moved away from a closely controlled experience by each DM to a collaborative act of imagination by the entire player group. Although the Mercer Effect is certainly not the only way to play, it lies at the far end of a creative direction that *D&D* has been steadily moving toward, one that is inevitable as playful creativity replaces the rule-based structure of the game as a primary focus.

THE MERCER EFFECT

On December 24, 2018, a post by Mister-builder on the r/DMAcademy forum of Reddit—a forum for DMs to solicit advice about running their games—first identified the Mercer Effect. The post appealed to readers for advice about managing a new party with too high expectations. Titled "How do I beat the Matt Mercer effect," the post read in full:

I'm running a campaign for a lot of first-timers, and I'm dealing with a lot of first-timer problems (the one who never speaks up, the one who needs to be railroaded, the NG[5] character being played CN and the CN character being played CE). Lately, however, there's a new situation I'm dealing with. A third of my group first got interested in D&D because of Critical Role. I like Matt Mercer as much as the next guy, but these guys watched 30+ hours of the show before they ever picked up a D20. The Dwarf thinks that all Dwarves have Irish accents, and the Dragonborn sounds exactly like the one from the show (which is fine, until they meet NPCs that are played differently from how it's done on the show). I've been approached by half the group and asked how I planned to handle resurrection. When I told them I'd decide when we got there, they told me how Matt does it. Our WhatsApp is filled with Geek and Sundry videos about how to play RPGs better. There's nothing wrong with how they do it on the show, but I'm not Matt Mercer and they're not Vox Machina. At some point, the unrealistic expectations are going to clash with reality. How do you guys deal with players who've had past DMs they swear by?

TL;DR Critical Role has become the prototype for how my players think D&D works. How do I push my own way of doing things without letting them down?[6]

The post received a huge amount of attention, with other posters commenting on the sudden prevalence of this behavior in players and DMs, making judgments about the show (favorable and unfavorable), giving advice, and containing a response from Matt Mercer himself, who apologized, sent an encouraging message to the DM to "abandon expectations and just have fun together as friends,"[7] and gave advice on how to speak to the players about the issue. Finally, Mercer pointed out that the people at the *Critical Role* table were both experienced and professional voice actors:

We are a table of professional actors, and I have been DMing for well over 20 years. We have spent our lives training in particular skills that allow us to get as immersed in the characters as we enjoy doing. Anyone can jump in as deeply, should they wish to, but EXPECTING that immediate level of comfort and interest is unfair and absurd.[8]

"WE CAN'T ALL BE SCANLAN SHORTHALT":
HOW TO PLAY *D&D* "CORRECTLY"

To understand the frustration of DMs and players at the Mercer Effect, as well as how *Critical Role* and its contemporaries have changed the way the game is played, it is important to first interrogate how the act of playing *D&D* has been presented to players via the rule books. The opening sections of every *Players/Player's Handbook*, bar original *D&D* (*OD&D*), contain a short welcome and a description of what to expect from play. Encoded in this description are tenets for each iteration, encapsulating the ethos of play. These shifting, often contradictory introductions help explain why no default version of playing *D&D* exists, and frame why this assumption is problematized. Fifty years after the first edition, *D&D*'s rule books have created a game that has no fixed way to play—like the earth, its core is lava.

For example, the *AD&D* 1e *Players Handbook*, published in 1978, contains notable elisions that one would expect as a default today. Shannon Appelcline notes:

What's astonishing is what's not in this book. For example, you won't find rules about how to actually roll your abilities! The *Dungeon Masters Guide* (1979) has that! Similarly, there are no rules for combat or even saving throws! Instead the player only got summaries of what the rules systems were like—not the actual systems![9]

Appelcline and Jon Peterson both agree that in the early iterations of *D&D*, instructions on how to play were not initially described to players, an approach that seems absolutely bizarre, given the complexity of the game, even in its early stages.[10] Rather, this was the domain of the DM, who kept the rules secret from the players and revealed them either via verbal description or as play went along. Peterson suggests that this is perhaps because the first rule books assumed that one of the authors would be present to explain rules at the table—after all, the early version of *D&D* was an alternative to miniature wargames, designed to be played at small events and conventions, where the authors would be present to take the DM role. Subsequent writing about *D&D* in related fanzines encouraged DM autonomy and "invisible systems" of rules.[11] These discussions, suggestions, and sometimes arguments clearly suggest that a unilateral understanding of the game did not exist. This is understandable if we see the game as designed to be played at conventions as an alternative to wargames, rather than a retailable product, and one that spread quickly among university societies that did not necessarily communicate directly with one another (for further discussion of this topic, see chap. 5 by Tony A. Rowe and Zach Howard in this collection).

Adaption by players in gaming societies around the United States demonstrates that *D&D* almost immediately started to grow beyond its confines. Jon Peterson identifies a number of reasons for this trend, notably that the leveling system did not extend beyond a certain point. I would argue beyond Peterson that the game provoked the imagination, and the imagination "broke" Gygax's original game of dice, paper, and numbers, turning it almost immediately into something new. Peterson's discussion of fan behavior shows that the clash of players versus rules quickly became almost ideological in form—but this in itself is an act of imagination, as DMs and players tried to reconfigure the game to work for their own small groups, all with different needs and goals.

Mary Flanagan argues in *Critical Play* that "games carry beliefs within their representation systems and mechanics . . . a careful examination of social, cultural, political, or even personal themes."[12] In this case, *D&D* inadvertently provided all of these as an aspect of play—a game based in a fantasy world with limitless opportunities to build stories around the "kill monsters in a dungeon" premise. The game almost demands, by its very nature, that players imagine what is going on within a fantastical universe. Characters have exciting, dramatic roles such as "cleric" or "wizard." Acting out the personae of these individuals must have seemed almost instinctual or needed, especially given the plethora of supporting fantasy literature, art, and other writing that was becoming increasingly popular in tandem with the game (see chap. 11 by Dimitra Nikolaidou in this collection). Expanding this world according to an individual group's cultural influences or storytelling desires therefore became an embedded element of play as characters, scenarios, and mythos quickly escaped the limitations of the manuals. At the same time, even if groups were still playing a technical "dungeon crawl" version of the game, it contained so many vibrant, imaginative elements that players could not help but want to expand more. Surrounded by a boom in fantasy writing, elements of play seemed all around them, brought to life by the authors they were reading at the same time that they played.

Gygax's attempt to rein in this adventurism is apparent in the preface of the *AD&D* 1e *Players Handbook*, where he awkwardly welcomes players to the game but also tries to lay down some ground rules:

There is a need for a certain amount of uniformity from campaign to campaign in *D&D*. . . . No individual can actually dictate the actual operations of a campaign, however, for that is the prerogative of the Dungeon Master.[13]

Jon Peterson sees this preface as an attempt by Gygax to put the genie back in the bottle. Gygax tries to reiterate that the DM has ultimate control, and that through that person, rules dictate play. This is something he persistently argued in fanzines as the game rapidly spiraled beyond his ludic control.[14] Perhaps more aptly, Gygax seems to be snapping shut his version of Pandora's box so that hope remains for his version of the game. By providing "all the truly essential information," he tries to retain the essence of the *D&D* that he wanted to play. However, in a very real sense, the death of the author had already come at the cost of the birth of the player. The game had already developed far beyond these rules in an imaginative context, birthing multiple forms and escaping proper workings of "hard rules." Quickly moving beyond the impracticality of a closed-system game toward emergent play and rules,[15] *D&D* was already regarded as a "design-a-game" kit by the majority of its players.[16] And, on a personal level, I can testify to this. *AD&D* 1e was my first introduction to the game. I was too young to take in all the rules, even though I read the manuals exhaustively, and I had no friends who wanted to play with me. *AD&D* 1e for me was largely an imaginative practice, supported by the art in the rule books more than the vast amount of rules that surrounded them. I played a lot of *AD&D* 1e, but it was all in my head, on boring walks in the rain around nature reserves where I became the brave elf forging her way through the wilds in search of treasure. I had one set of dice,[17] and the d12 got lost somewhere,[18] and there was no one else to play with, so my dungeons were entirely in my head, not a piece of square paper or miniature in sight.

This type of patterning becomes typical for the *Player's Handbook* introductions. Each edition of the game lays down precepts for play, attempting to dictate the ideological conditions that reflect each subsequent set of rules, but whether players entirely adopted them is moot at best. Despite Gygax's wishes, one can see an obvious movement from a tabletop game with some role-playing, to a role-playing game that partially takes part on a table and places "imagination" before dice. By *D&D*'s revised third edition (3.5e), this is very much in place. The second sentence of the *D&D* 3.5e *Player's Handbook* reads: "D&D is a game of imagination in which you participate in thrilling adventures and dangerous quests by taking on the role of a hero—a character you create."[19] The possessive apostrophe used for "player's" in the rule book's title emphasizes that the game truly belongs to the players, rather than being directed toward them only after the GM has created their world. Not only are the players in command, but they are playing imaginatively.

Fourth edition *D&D* (4e) tried to flip back toward ludic play, with dice, miniatures, and "form and structure" coming before pesky "imagination" in the opening salvo of the manuals; however, this edition was notoriously unsuccessful (see chap. 6 by Michael Iantorno in this collection for more detail).[20] Wizards of the Coast (WotC) misread its developing audience, tying players too closely to combat, miniature play, and statistical streamlining. *The Player's Handbook* (subtitled *Arcane, Divine, and Martial Heroes*) emphasizes rather meanly how *D&D* is a step above a children's game of make-believe, made so by its use of more rigorous ludic elements. Imagination takes a firm second place:

A roleplaying game is a storytelling game that has elements of the games of make-believe that many of us played as children. However, a roleplaying game such as D&D provides form and structure, with robust gameplay and endless possibilities. . . . While the D&D game uses dice and miniatures, the action takes place in your imagination.[21]

Graeme Barber summarizes this misstep in his analysis of the game:

4ed D&D was getting back to the "roots" of D&D, which excited a lot of players. It shouldn't have, though, because what Dungeons & Dragons, as a cultural institution, had become to many players was not . . . close to its roots at all.[22]

I will return to the disjoint between player expectation and play style— but the important thing here is that *D&D* had become such a sprawling game (already twenty-five years after its initial version) that players did not realize how systemically orientated the "roots" of *D&D* really were, and were angry to discover that the imaginative aspect was so reduced. Barber additionally argues that much of the time spent by players world-building, refining, and re-creating the *D&D* environment and worldscape to make it a more welcoming place was thoughtlessly removed in 4e in favor of more rigid, outdated representations of the world, its races, and history:

The world I'd known and loved had been trashed in a racist orgy of destruction that disproportionately affected the non-white parts of the world.[23]

Fourth edition demonstrated clearly that despite attempts to rework a more rules-heavy version of the game, imaginative processes were in ascendency, including players rebuilding worlds to combat less palatable aspects seen in earlier versions or starting to build alternative game worlds that varied dramatically from the fantasy setting of Faerûn. The success of *Pathfinder*,[24] initially a spin-off version of 3.5e that heavily favored role-play, flexible character development, and combat that allowed characters to demonstrate flair and prowess, was heavily predicated on the publisher, Paizo, being clear that players could build their own worlds, and giving them the flexibility to do so.

Fifth edition *D&D* (5e) rescinds much of the rules-heavy, prescriptive play of 4e.[25] Instead, it crystallizes the importance of imaginative play and creating unique worlds. Fifth edition embraces the player as an imaginative agent, beginning with the opening description of play in the *Player's Handbook*:

The *Dungeons & Dragons* roleplaying game is about storytelling in worlds of swords and sorcery. It shares elements with childhood games of make-believe. Like those games, *D&D* is driven by imagination.[26]

Alongside this more open form of play, WotC has taken a number of steps to allow greater player autonomy, many of which were removed in 4e. The developers addressed some of the problematic restrictions in the game so as to welcome all players and create diverse worlds. This includes making the canon more open, allowing problematic aspects of lore to change or be removed, and acknowledging that lore cannot possibly be cohesive, given the vast power of player and DM agency to reform the world:

Key to our approach is the belief that the story belongs to the DM and the players, not us. We make a conscious effort to preserve as many opportunities as possible for DMs to play with their own ideas. That's why we don't produce sourcebooks that spool out a ton of backstory. The DM or player remains the ultimate arbiter of what's true in their expressions of D&D.[27]

By returning the game to a less restrictive OGL (Open Game License), WotC also enabled players once again to make and publish their own worlds. Often these are wildly different from the original content—for example, *Dimension 20*'s "Tiny Heist"[28] repurposes the *D&D* world as one of fairies, bugs, and toys living in the backyard of an American family. This focus on imagination and player agency continues throughout the official 5e expansions. *Tasha's Cauldron of Everything* includes rules on removing racial attributes for characters and holding an initial "session zero" with players before a game begins to establish "hard and soft limits for play."[29] "Imagination is a strange and wonderful thing," writes Matt Mercer in his preface to *Explorer's Guide to Wildemount*,[30] emphasizing that the world he has created is there to be reinterpreted.

All these changes are a huge step away from the early versions of highly prescriptive guidance for play. *D&D*'s rules are now constructed to accommodate a vast audience, rather than the more closed early groups of convention or university play. The rule books and wider public face of WotC acknowledge and encourage the varieties of play available to players and DMs, very deliberately opening up the systems available, rather than closing them. As a result, there are a huge number of rules, but while the core remains the same—most notably in the three main rule books, *Player's Handbook*, *Dungeon Master's Guide*, and *Monster Manual*—the play around them differs wildly. It is this aspect that is key to why the Mercer Effect is often viewed unfavorably, despite its huge influence over the ways that gamers consume the text and plays the game.

LOOSEY-GOOSEY

In the fiftieth second of the first episode of *Critical Role*, Matt Mercer says to the camera/audience, "Do note, for all you hard-core gamers out there, a lot of this is house-ruled, kind of loosey-goosey, having a good time, so all you number crunchers, stop paying attention there, just have fun with it."[31] Thus virtually the first moment of the show is an assertion that the game being played by *Critical Role* differs from the rule books, and it uses two TTRPG slang terms to do so: "house rules," meaning that the game is built apart from the rules in some way and uses its own world or ludic elements, and "loosey-goosey," meaning that even these are subject to change, depending on the situation.

As the first few episodes also make clear, the game has been adapted from *Pathfinder*, which the group had been playing offscreen for two years before the show began.[32] This is not a usual game; it is not running to usual rules. Importantly, Mercer points this out immediately to avoid criticism that the game is not being played "correctly," but his comment also uses familiar terminology from within the *D&D* community to indicate a familiar type of change.

Critical Role's location as a broadcast is also an important aspect of both its popularity and the audiences it reached. The show was initially broadcast on Twitch by Geek & Sundry, a YouTube channel expanding into live streaming. Geek & Sundry (2012–2019) was part of YouTube's initial channel-building initiative. After early success with the board game playthrough show *Tabletop* (2012–2017) and comedy series *The Guild* (2012–2013), the channel produced geek-related content through regular shows highlighting interviews, playthroughs, discussions, and hangouts. The channel was personality driven, with creators Felicia Day and Wil Wheaton becoming nerd celebrities in their own right and inviting many of their friends and coworkers onto the various shows as guests. However, in 2015, like many YouTube channels, Geek & Sundry was starting to lose viewers to Twitch, a platform that provided the immediacy of live streams and allowed viewers to not only experience play in real time but also potentially interact directly with the people they were viewing.

As the in-house advertising of the early shows demonstrates, *Critical Role* was only one of several new, experimental shows being rolled out on Twitch by Geek & Sundry. Twitch's revenue model meant that its success depended on subscriber numbers to ensure its continuance, with early shows privileging viewer input to draw people in. Recordings of the show placed on YouTube after the live broadcasts include a box showing the chat channel from Twitch in the first few episodes (it is mercifully removed from episode 33 onward). However, a vital aspect of *Critical Role*'s initial transmission was that Geek & Sundry was not a dedicated role-playing channel. Instead the channel addressed a more general audience from twenty-something geek culture. Returning to Mercer's opening words in episode 1, this context shows him to be reassuring the viewer. *Critical Role*, he implies, is a show that will be easy to watch and understand, divorced from heavy rules, dice, and schematics. It is "a fantastical fantasy adventure" with "likely nerdy and enjoyable voice actors"—thus easy and fun to watch, substituting storytelling for the density of numbers and dice rolling.

"BIG MONEY, NO WHAMMIES": *CRITICAL ROLE* AND 5E

Critical Role rapidly became the flagship of Geek & Sundry on Twitch. The cast members were personable and laid-back; many reviews and discussions mention the obvious friendship between the players, and it is a central note in the tableside book created about the show.[33] The cast ("cast," not "players") focused on acting and storytelling, playing the game in character, with Mercer directing play via colorful and interesting NPC characters. Although the system was a homebrew, Mercer's knowledge and explanation of 5e rules, when needed, were clear and effective. Players did what they were told and didn't cheat or metagame (the one member who did was removed from the series), and overall the series demystified the processes of playing *D&D* by having rules and systems play second fiddle to the story line. Despite the group having already been together for two years, the players frequently asked questions or needed explanations, most likely because they had switched systems from *Pathfinder* to 5e, but also serving to emphasize a lack of gatekeeping (it was okay to ask for clarification or forget one of *D&D*'s endless intricacies), and there was a relaxed, forgiving attitude by everyone if things weren't played exactly by the book—players often confess making mistakes and account for them, or forgive each other for accidentally doing things more powerfully than they should. Mercer's ability to DM without constantly referring back to the rule book made playing the game seem easy.

Critical Role became a hit because it was watchable, not because it provided viewers with an exhaustive breakdown of how to play *D&D*. Early comments on the Twitch chat demonstrate that for many, the game was regarded as extraordinary—most especially the skills of Mercer as a DM and his ability to role-play the various NPCs, or of individual moments where players did something extraordinary, like sing their spells or act out something in a particularly amusing way. Tweets and responses also suggested that players and DMs were starting to adopt *Critical Role*'s play style in their own games. This was not always positive. During the chat in an early episode, a DM reported that his bard player decided to change class after they demanded she sing all her spellcasts. While the commenter seems proud of this swap, it is an early indication that adopting the *Critical Role* style of play was both difficult to do and off-putting to some players.

Critical Role's success came at a point where *D&D* as a game was becoming popular again—and it is difficult to separate the rapid escalation in *D&D*'s popularity from the high profile that actual-plays gave the game. Whereas 4e tried to appeal to MMORPG players and missed by overproviding on detail, 5e created a more relaxed entry point for nerds rather than experienced gamers. It supported this with easy-access publications like the 5e *Starter Set*,[34] providing a stripped-down version of the rules, pregenerated characters, and a short adventure. Marketing emphasized the imaginative context of the game, not the rules. Finally, actual-plays and rules explanations became part of *D&D*'s social media and marketing, and WotC's allowance of second-party shows like *Critical Role* pushed the game back into the spotlight.[35]

Although the accessibility of 5e definitely helped the game become popular, *Critical Role* is also responsible for a massive increase in players of *D&D*. In 2019, 40 percent of *D&D* players were under the age of twenty-four.[36] The same WotC report states that 4.3 billion minutes of *D&D* have been watched online—and although it is unclear whether this is solely from WotC's supported channels, or whether it includes others like *Critical Role*, the inclusion of this statistic draws a clear parallel between the watching of actual-play shows and the growth in new players. The essential extrapolation one can make from these statistics is that the *D&D* community is new, and it has come to the game not via the rule books but via actual-plays such as *Critical Role*. Thus a new player's experience of play is initially that of an actual-play, and not in a more direct manner through a play session they have experienced themselves. This is where the key split of people deriding the Mercer Effect conflicts with those who have come to the game directly through *Critical Role* and the shows like it.

"CRITTERS": FANDOM AND THE MERCER EFFECT

Fandom has always been a little about taking part in creating something to do out of your favorite text, but there's a difference between crafting the perfect fanfiction and insisting your fanfiction become what happens on the big screen.[37]

The fan base of *Critical Role* has largely been portrayed as a positive, welcoming community,[38] although more recently splits have been seen between the fans on Reddit (who interpret the show as is and focus on the episode as played) and fans on Tumblr (who produce artistic and creative responses, including fan art and stories). By supporting and encouraging their fans (the breaks in each show are bookended by a lengthy reel of fan art, for example), *Critical Role* created an environment where fans were consuming the playing of the game, not 5e itself. This is important, as a by-product of watching the show over playing the game was a perception that the play style within it was a default mode, without really acknowledging that it was one of many options available. This was reinforced by eliding the issue and not providing a place for it to be discussed within the show; *Critical Role* was about playing, not explaining, the game. Thus DMs and players who did not follow this method of play sometimes found themselves in similar situations to that of the Reddit user Mister-builder: having to live up to exceptionally high standards via a play style that they might not particularly enjoy; or simply not being able to develop play in their own ways, forced instead to access the extremely high bar of in-character role-playing that happens in the show; or dealing with the misassumptions that some of the house rules in *Critical Role* were canonical forms of play.

It's clear from Mercer's response to Mister-builder about the original "Mercer Effect" post that he was unhappy players were making demands of how a *D&D* game should run, and he did not recommend the adoption of a play style that was difficult for a DM to implement, especially when the players needed to learn and understand the game first. The object of any game is most often to have fun, after all. However, discussion around the creation of the Mercer Effect tends to ignore this in favor of condemning the show for creating a restrictive mode of play. Here I'd like to return to my discussion of *D&D*'s rules and how they developed to examine why this discussion is rather reductive. In short, the move toward "imagination" in the written introductions to the rules means that, quite simply, there is absolutely no one way to play the game. It is supported by actions such as WotC's statements about canon, which emphasize individualism and difference in play. In addition, the randomization of dice rolling and the rule books' encouragement of players to describe and react to a largely imaginative environment mean that there can never ever be one game played in the same way as another.

There is a conflict here, because *Critical Role* is a performed show, and this is a nuance that is held up by both supporters and detractors of actual-play games. By creating entertainment, the Mercer Effect is often regarded as being less about play than it is about spinning a good yarn and making something interesting to spectate. It cannot, however, be held against a "correct" way to play, because such a thing simply does not exist. There is no correct way to play *D&D*, and harkening back to the rule books to find this simply underscores this ethos.

I do not wish to be rude to fans at this point. I am a fan myself, of many things, and I fully acknowledge that my fandoms might not be for everyone. However, fandom can often form cohorts, which both become closed systems and appear to enforce a prescriptive reading of a specific text. Schisms inside the *Critical Role* fandom demonstrate that the show is divisive, even to its own admirers, in itself a fairly common aspect of extremely large fandoms containing many disparate voices. At the center of this is *Critical Role's* introduction of *D&D* to new players, inadvertently creating a highly specific mode of play, and inducting a sizable block of players into the game while doing so. It is understandable that more seasoned DMs might find this frustrating or even threatening. It's also clear that there's a certain amount of jealousy amongst detractors; for example, some DMs simply can't re-create these playful circumstances. Others do not want to. The simple assertion that these differences are absolutely fine does, however, seem to miss many people. However, overall, the Mercer Effect stands at a crisis point at which an established community is challenged by a huge new influx of people. For many, this change is threatening.

CONCLUSION

The cast of *Critical Role* is extremely good at entertaining, and their games are incredibly fun to watch. The show has spawned multiple emulations, thus establishing itself as a key determinant of how *D&D* is conveyed through played media to other fans and players. The show has also come to represent a key moment in the cultural development of *D&D*, presenting a user-friendly, entertaining version of the game to a wide audience, and having reciprocal influence on how *D&D* is played and understood as a cultural artifact. I have used aspects of *Critical Role*'s play style in my own games—and I believe it has enhanced them. It is not the only way to play, nor does it set itself out to be a definitive "how-to." "The Mercer Effect" was a term coined by, and then discussed by, fans. It is not named in, or presented by, the show as a methodology—and this includes spin-off shows in which the cast discuss play and give tips and tricks. Yet the Mercer Effect is a technique that has encouraged people to explore and have fun with what is ultimately an incredibly complex game with a high barrier to entry. By stating that their system is "loosey-goosey," *Critical Role* also reinforces a pathway—one that is supported by WotC—that it's okay to use the rule books as a guideline rather than a definitive text. Though this had been going on for years in *D&D* groups, it may not have been so obvious to outsiders.

As a result, the Mercer Effect is the epitome of a conflict arising through the popularization of a game and a vastly expanding player base. As a community grows, so its central tenets become less clear. The Mercer Effect also demonstrates how far *D&D* has changed ideologically, from a restrictive mode of gaming to one that not only is free-form in nature but also promotes creativity over rules. Its central contradiction—the highly complicated rules, systems, and worldscapes versus the ideology of individual imaginations—is by its very nature unresolvable, yet this is also a central joy of *D&D*, potentially what brings many players to the game. The everything-and-nothing configuration of play within *D&D*, initially created with secret rules governed only by the DM, is now firmly in the hands of all players at the table. The Mercer Effect is a methodology for play—a very good one—but recognizing that is often less easy among the endless fan debate, discussion, and reinterpretation of the text. It is, however, difficult and specific to implement, requiring many things that players may not possess (expertly crafted dioramas, and the ability to adopt many different voices or sustain in-character activity for at least three hours). It is also rather too complex to delve into here, where the examination of play has been about the conflicts between play styles, not the creation of a new mode in which to do so. Fan behavior, assumptions, and opposition to the series (it's okay not to like something, which appears to be something fans frequently forget) have also clouded the argument, making it appear that players have to take a binary stand, "use the Mercer Effect or don't." In reality, the game and the play style are far different—unique every time, and governed by both the circumstances of the game and the world existing around it—and this is in itself the essence of what makes *D&D* such a fascinating game. While there is no real answer to whether the Mercer Effect is "good" or "bad"—and nor should there be—the reality is that it has been hugely responsible for a grassroots change in the ways that the game is played, and while players may not want to adopt this play style in their own games, it has regardless had a positive effect on the perception and playing of *D&D*.

NOTES

1. *Critical Role*, https://critrole.com, Twitch stream, 2015–present.

2. Maya Hutchinson, "Twitch Leaks: Critical Role Earns $9.6M," WePC, 2021, https://www.wepc.com/news/twitch-leaks-critical-role-earnings-payout/.

3. Gary Alan Fine, *Shared Fantasy: Role-Playing Games as Social Worlds* (Chicago: University of Chicago Press, 1983).

4. Premeet Sidhu and Marcus Carter, "The Critical Role of Media Representations, Reduced Stigma and Increased Access in *D&D*'s Resurgence," in *DiGRA '20: Proceedings of the 2020 DiGRA International Conference—Play Everywhere* (2020), http://www.digra.org/wp-content/uploads/digital-library/DiGRA_2020_paper_223.pdf; Shelly Jones, ed., *Watch Us Roll: Essays on Actual Play and Performance in Tabletop Role-Playing Games* (Jefferson, NC: McFarland, 2021).

5. These acronyms refer to a character's "alignment," a system in *D&D* rules whereby a character's actions are ascribed across two axes, good–evil and lawful–chaotic. NG = "neutral good," CN = "chaotic neutral," CE = "chaotic evil." The *Player's Handbook* encourages players to use these nine alignments to determine the behavior of a character and allows DMs to penalize characters who do not role-play accordingly; however, alignment is increasingly not used in many games owing to the complexities of adhering to it as a role-played action and a more general perception by players that these criteria have become increasingly fuzzy definitions that are difficult to determine collectively.

6. Mister-builder, "How do I beat the Matt Mercer effect?" post on r/DMAacademy, Reddit, December 24, 2018, https://www.reddit.com/r/DMAcademy/comments/a999sd/how_do_i_beat_the_matt_mercer_effect/.

7. Matt Mercer, "How do I beat the Matt Mercer effect," reply to post on r/DMAacademy, Reddit, December 24, 2018, https://www.reddit.com/r/DMAcademy/comments/a999sd/comment/eclht66/.

8. Mercer, reply to "Matt Mercer effect."

9. Shannon Appelcline, quoted in Charlie Hall, "D&D's Original Player Handbook Finally Available as a PDF," July 8, 2015, Polygon, https://www.polygon.com/2015/7/8/8913529/dungeons-and-dragons-1e-phb-pdf.

10. Jon Peterson, *The Elusive Shift: How Role-Playing Games Forged Their Identity* (Cambridge, MA: MIT Press, 2020).

11. Peterson, *The Elusive Shift*, 246–253.

12. Mary Flanagan, *Critical Play: Radical Game Design* (Cambridge, MA: MIT Press, 2009), 2.

13. Gary Gygax, *Advanced Dungeons & Dragons Players Handbook* (Lake Geneva, WI: TSR / Random House, 1978), 6.

14. Peterson, *The Elusive Shift*.

15. Joan Soler-Adillion, "The Open, the Closed and the Emergent: Theorizing Emergence for Videogames Studies," *Game Studies* 19, no. 2 (2019), http://gamestudies.org/1902/articles/soleradillon#_edn1.

16. Peterson, *The Elusive Shift*, 223.

17. Rest assured I have a LOT more now.

18. I mean what are d12s useful for anyway?

19. Wizards of the Coast, *Player's Handbook Core Rulebook 1*, 3.5e (Renton, WA: Wizards of the Coast, 2003), 4.

20. Wizards of the Coast, *Player's Handbook: Arcane, Divine, and Martial Heroes*, 4e (Renton, WA: Wizards of the Coast, (2008).

21. *Player's Handbook* 4e, 3.

22. Graeme Barber, "4E D&D, the After Action Review," *POC Gamer*, December 30, 2017, https://pocgamer.com/2017/12/30/4e-dd-the-after-action-review/.

23. Graeme Barber, "The POC Gamer Story," *POC Gamer*, 2019, https://pocgamer.com/the-pocgamer-story/.

24. Paizo, *Pathfinder* (Redmond, WA: Paizo, 2009).

25. Wizards of the Coast, *Player's Handbook*, 5e (Renton, WA: Wizards of the Coast, 2014).

26. *Player's Handbook* 5e, 5.

27. Chris Perkins, "D&D Canon," *D&D Studio Blog*, Wizards of the Coast, July 29, 2021, https://dnd.wizards.com/dndstudioblog/dnd-canon.

28. Brennan Lee Mulligan, "Tiny Heist," *Dimension 20* (Dropout TV, 2019).

29. Wizards of the Coast, *Tasha's Cauldron of Everything* (Renton, WA: Wizards of the Coast, 2020), 7, 139–141.

30. Matt Mercer and Wizards of the Coast, *Explorer's Guide to Wildemount* (Renton, WA: Wizards of the Coast, 2020), 3.

31. Matt Mercer, "Arrival at Kraghammer," *Critical Role*, season 1, episode 1, July 24, 2015, https://www.youtube.com/watch?v=i-p9lWIhcLQ.

32. Liz Marsham and the cast of Critical Role, *The World of Critical Role: The History behind the Epic Fantasy* (London: Del Rey, 2020), 17.

33. Marsham et al., *The World of Critical Role.*

34. Wizards of the Coast, *Dungeons & Dragons Starter Set* (Renton, WA: Wizards of the Coast, 2014).

35. See Sidhu and Carter, "Critical Role of Media," for a more in-depth discussion.

36. Wizards of the Coast, "A History Check on 2019, D&D's Best Year Ever" (Renton, WA: Wizards of the Coast, 2020), https://drive.google.com/drive/folders/1OetQ_ -Vrm6DhTrhhRrwHut29hLqfeR75.

37. Kate Gardner, "Spider-Suits and Luke Skywalker: How Entitlement Is Messing Up Fandom," *The Mary Sue*, December 21, 2018, https://www.themarysue.com/fan -entitlement-last-jedi-spider-man/.

38. Marsham et al., *The World of Critical Role.*

10

THE OTHER *D&D*: RELIGION(S) IN *DUNGEONS & DRAGONS* FROM *DEITIES & DEMIGODS* TO TODAY

Adrian Hermann

Representations of religion(s) and mythologies are deeply woven into the history and present of *Dungeons & Dragons* (*D&D*) through all its editions since 1974. In fact, an almost endless amount of detail exists to be explored regarding these topics across the copious publications from Tactical Studies Rules (TSR) and Wizards of the Coast (WotC) over five decades. Much could (and hopefully still will) be written about the ways in which various elements of historical religion(s) and mythologies were integrated into the game through the imaginations of Dave Arneson and Gary Gygax, as well as some of the other early contributors to the original edition of *Dungeons & Dragons* (*OD&D*) and the first edition of *Advanced Dungeons & Dragons* (*AD&D* 1e) (like Robert J. Kuntz and James M. Ward). This legacy was then built on and transformed over the following decades by writers and designers like Frank Mentzer, David "Zeb" Cook, Aaron Allston, Julia Martin, Colin McComb, James Wyatt, Rich Redman, Skip Williams, and Christopher Perkins.[1] While I explore some aspects of this history here, this chapter cannot attempt to present a detailed reconstruction of all aspects of religion(s) in the many instantiations of the "granddaddy of all role-playing games."[2] Rather, I concentrate on an overview of two aspects of how these topics were treated over the last fifty years: regarding their relevance for *player characters* (focusing on the cleric class and its history) and *theologically* regarding the role of deities and other "ultra-powerful being[s]" in the game.[3]

Introduced already in *OD&D*'s three little brown booklets in 1974 as the third choice next to fighting-men and magic-users, the cleric character class can be considered *D&D*'s single most influential contribution to the treatment of religion not only in (fantasy) role-playing but arguably in fantasy literature and other media (like computer games and comics) more generally. Before *OD&D*, the figure of a fighting healer, imbued with divine magic but clearly distinct from a wizard, was not common. The term "cleric" was rarely found in fantasy literature up to this point.[4] Since a figure similar to the cleric was not yet present in *OD&D*'s wargaming precursor *Chainmail* (1971),[5] aspects of the class might have been partly inspired by developments in the early play culture of Arneson's Blackmoor campaign in the early 1970s, where a village-priest-turned-bishop[6] fought a vampire named "Sir Fang" (who earlier had been another player's character). This "first *D&D* cleric"[7] was seemingly influenced by the vampire hunter Dr. Van Helsing from the mid-twentieth-century B-horror films of Hammer Film Productions, as well as by the 1960s gothic soap opera *Dark Shadows*.[8] In preparing the *OD&D* rules for publication, Gygax seemed to have added overtones of medieval templar knights and, famously, a prohibition from using sharp weapons. This was allegedly based on a medieval tapestry picturing Odo of Bayeux with a mace-like weapon. Still, what we get in *OD&D* are "priests entirely without religion,"[9] as there is little descriptive text, and the cleric's characterization (just like the other existing classes) is solely through the rules itself. We learn about clerics' ability to turn away undead monsters as well as heal and support the adventuring party through spells like "Cure Light Wounds," "Protection from Evil," and "Bless." The "silver cross" and "holy water" on the list of available equipment,[10] as well as the specific biblical overtones of some of the other clerical spells like "Turn Sticks to Snakes" and "Insect Plague," hint at the Christian background of this figure,[11] which is generalized into a more common "holy man." In addition to these more mechanical elements, the most details about the implied inspirations for the class can be glanced from its level titles: Acolyte, Adept, Village Priest, Vicar, Curate, Bishop, Lama, Patriarch.[12] A few years later, the 1977 *D&D Holmes Basic Set*[13] describes clerics as "humans who have dedicated themselves to one or more of the gods,"[14] while the *AD&D* first edition (*AD&D* 1e) *Players Handbook* (1978) mentions that the class "bears a certain resemblance to

religious orders of knighthood of medieval times." *AD&D* 1e adds that
the cleric is "dedicated to a deity, or deities, and at the same time [is] a
skilled combatant at arms."[15] *AD&D* second edition (*AD&D* 2e) in 1989
sees the "priest" as a "believer and advocate of a god from a particular
mythos,"[16] with clerics (next to druids) as their most common type. In
D&D third edition (3e) the cleric is presented in the *Player's Handbook*
(2000) as a "master of divine magic and a capable warrior."[17] Fourth edition (4e) clerics in 2008 are described as "holy warriors and healers" that
are "courageous and devout."[18] As "divinely inspired warrior[s]," they
"have been invested with the authority to wield divine power on behalf
of a deity, faith, or philosophy."[19] Finally, the fifth edition (5e) *Player's
Handbook* (2014) introduces the cleric as a "priestly champion who wields
divine magic in service of a higher power."[20] As "intermediaries between
the mortal world and the distant planes of the gods," they serve these
powers not as ordinary priests but as "healers and warriors," "imbued
with divine magic."[21]

Throughout the last fifty years, the cleric class has become one of the
iconic elements of *D&D*. However, the class has mostly implied a "Chris-
tianized" model of a "playable polytheism."[22] Rather than being based on
what we know about how polytheistic religious practice served primarily
as a strategic "competence and creativity in dealing with everyday problems,"[23] the cleric represents a kind of individualized and systematized
version of polytheistic worship, presupposing a fixed "ritual system with
a stable pantheon of gods and a rigid system of beliefs."[24]

Another aspect closely connected to the cleric class is the distinction
between arcane and divine magic, which since *OD&D* has been deeply
baked into the rules of the game. By adopting this distinction, *D&D*
partakes in a reception history of late-nineteenth- and early twentieth-
century ethnographic and anthropological academic discourse in which
"magic" is clearly distinguished from "religion."[25] While the game also
subverts this distinction by treating both arcane and divine power as
magic, their contrast at least partly implies modern understandings of religion as "private, intellectual, spiritualized" and devoid of social power.[26]
In some ways, by adopting this modern binary, the magical worlds of
D&D still share in the sensibilities of our capitalist, secular modernity,
where religion is an individual affair and clearly distinct from magic.[27]

Who (or what) are the deities that clerics serve? What is the *theology* of *D&D*? The three booklets of *OD&D* contain no descriptions of gods or deities. Nevertheless, the two campaigns out of which the game emerged, Arneson's Blackmoor and Gygax's Greyhawk, did include (semi)fictional deities (like "St. Cuthbert of the Cudgel" and the "Church of the Facts of Life").[28] *OD&D* supplement IV (*Gods, Demi-Gods & Heroes*, 1976)[29] and the famous *Deities & Demigods* cyclopedia for *AD&D* 1e (1980)[30] then offered dungeon masters (DMs) and players copious deities from numerous historical (and some fictional) contexts—each one described as a particular "mythos."[31] In the following years, campaign-setting publications like the *World of Greyhawk Fantasy Game Setting* (1983) and the *Forgotten Realms Campaign Set* (1987) also began to introduce fictional pantheons.[32] Later editions revised *Deities & Demigods* (or *Legends & Lore*, as the book was retitled for a few years) and detailed the fictional pantheons of the *D&D* multiverse in countless supplements—providing complex fictional theologies and descriptions of the nature and activities of these gods.[33] The fourth and fifth editions finally began to include suggested fictional (and, in the case of 5e, also historical) pantheons already in the core books (the *Player's Handbook* and *Dungeon Master's Guide*). Gradually however, as deities and religion(s) became, over the course of the editions, clearly established as a central aspect of the game—to make a long story short—the many references to historical deities and religious traditions of earlier editions were mostly replaced by a focus on the fictional pantheons of the various *D&D* campaign worlds. In the current fifth edition of the game, the only remains of the *Deities & Demigods* tradition are tables of Celtic, Greek, Norse, and Egyptian deities in Appendix B of the *Player's Handbook*, as well as some scattered references to these gods throughout the core books. These tables are described as presenting "fantasy-historical pantheons" that provide "fantasy interpretations of historical religions from our world's ancient times."[34]

THE CLERIC CHARACTER CLASS: WORSHIP OF THE GODS IN *D&D* ACROSS THE EDITIONS

As already mentioned, the cleric was one of the three original character classes in *OD&D*. In the beginning, the class was limited to humans as player characters. *AD&D* 1e later allowed nonplayer character (NPC) clerics of other races and mostly got rid of this restriction in *Unearthed Arcana* in 1985.[35] Beyond the information gleaned from scattered rules—like the mentioning of fanatically loyal "faithful men" that a cleric's stronghold attracts—the class's description in *OD&D* is almost completely devoid of any concrete information about possible religious backgrounds. In 1975, *Supplement I: Greyhawk* introduced the "paladin" as an always lawful variant of the fighter class, and *Supplement II: Blackmoor* described the "monk" as a cleric subclass seeking "physical and mental superiority in a religious atmosphere."[36] Both of these classes have since been included in all editions of the game in some form or another. *Greyhawk* also introduces "druids" as a monster, and *Supplement III: Eldritch Wizardry* (1976) expands the druid into a second cleric subclass "closely attuned to Nature, serving as its priests rather than serving some other deity."[37] In the 1977 *D&D Basic Set,*[38] the "pious clerics" (5) are described as having "dedicated themselves to one or more of the gods." Using spells, the cleric can heal others (from second level onward) while being "forbidden by his religion from the drawing of blood" (6). In addition, "evil cleric spells" (reversed from the good cleric ones, for example, "Cause Light Wounds" or "Contaminate Food and Water") are specifically mentioned (18). The *AD&D* 1e *Players Handbook* in 1978 describes clerics as bearing "a certain resemblance to religious orders of knighthood of medieval times."[39] They are "dedicated to a deity, or deities" (20). In addition, druids, as a "sub-class" of the cleric but "more effective in wilderness situations" (18), are characterized as "the only absolute neutrals" and "priests of nature" (20). Half-elven and half-orc clerics can now also be played, and elven, dwarven, and gnome clerics appear in the game only as NPCs; halflings only have druids (14). *AD&D* 2e's *Player's Handbook* (1989) sees the introduction of the grouping "priest," which encompasses the classes of "cleric" and "druid," the second of which serving as an example of what are called "priests of specific mythoi."[40] Later these were also known as "specialty priests," a term introduced in 1990 in *Forgotten Realms Adventures.*[41] While dwarves still cannot be magic users, they can now be clerics, as can all other races. A "priest" is generally described as a "believer and advocate of a god from a particular mythos" (32). Priest spells in *AD&D* 2e are "divided into 16 categories called *spheres of influence*." These include "All, Animal, Astral, Charm,

Combat, Creation, Divination, Elemental, Guardian, Healing, Necroman-
tic, Plant, Protection, Summoning, Sun, and Weather" (33). The *Player's
Handbook* for 3e (2000) describes the cleric as a "master of divine magic
and a capable warrior."[42] They are the intermediaries through which the
gods work, and are distinguished between good and evil clerics (29). Taking on missions from their "church" or "ecclesiastical superiors," clerics
are mostly devoted to a particular deity or alternatively "to a cause or a
source of divine power" (30). While clerics and other classes are able to cast
divine spells (e.g., druids, monks), they are no longer grouped together
as "priest classes" as they were in *AD&D* 2e's *Faiths & Avatars*.[43] The later
published *Deities & Demigods* supplement for 3e does include a taxonomy
in which clerics and druids are described as "priestly characters."[44] Most
importantly, the introduction in 3e of "prestige classes" as specific spe-
cialization options introduced a large variety of options for clerics (see
Defenders of the Faith).[45] In 4e, clerics are described as "holy warriors and
healers" that are "courageous and devout" (15) and "invested with the
authority to wield divine power on behalf of a deity, faith, or philosophy" (60).[46] "Paragon paths" replace the "prestige classes" of the earlier
edition, with specific options available for clerics like "Angelic Avenger,"
"Divine Oracle," or the classic "Warpriest" (72–74). Finally, in 2014, 5e
presents the cleric as a "priestly champion who wields divine magic in
service of a higher power" (45).[47] Clerics are "intermediaries between the
mortal world and the distant planes of the gods" whom they serve, not as
ordinary priests but as "imbued with divine magic" (56). The most important aspect of character creation, then, is "which deity to serve and what
principles . . . to embody" (57). In this newest edition, clerics must also
choose a "divine domain," with the *Player's Handbook* offering a choice
between "Knowledge, Life, Light, Nature, Tempest, Trickery, or War" (58),
and later sourcebooks providing additional domains (e.g., Death, Forge,
Peace).

In summary, then, what is apparent throughout most of the history of
the cleric class is a model of "playable polytheism." Similarly, playing a
cleric in *D&D* implies fundamentally drawing on a distinction between
divine and arcane magic. This raises the question of what future versions
of this class could look like that move beyond these two established ideas.
While such variations have already been explored (e.g., in the Dark Sun

and Eberron campaign settings), a more radical critique of the "Christian" and "Western" premises of the concept of religion—the result of the last twenty years of critical scholarship in the study of religion[48]—could lead to new and innovative ways of thinking about religion(s) in *D&D* over the next decades of the game's existence.

DEITIES & DEMIGODS: THEOLOGIES IN *D&D* ACROSS THE EDITIONS

Although the three *OD&D* booklets do not contain any explicit discussions of gods and religious entities, the play cultures out of which the game developed in the early 1970s already had their cast of godly and religious characters. Gygax's Greyhawk campaign, where "gods sometimes intervene[d]," early on featured "St. Cuthbert of the Cudgel" or a "Church of Crom, Scientist."[49] Arneson's Blackmoor had "Bishop Carr," who ran a "Church of the Facts of Life" and was "administrator of the Doctrines of Whatever and the interpreter of the Great Commentaries of Wishy-Washiness."[50] In the early campaigns and play tests, religion was present but was often treated only half-seriously.[51] In this spirit, *OD&D*'s *Greyhawk* (1975) mentions "Odin, Crom, Set, Cthulhu, the Shining One, a demi-god, or whatever"[52] as examples of the "ultra-powerful" beings whom the "Gate" spell could bring to the material plane. This indicates how both historical and fictional deities could become part of the game, and in the end it did not seem to matter much what gods a DM would include in their game.[53] Still, the *Greyhawk* and *Blackmoor* supplements, despite their titles, do not describe any of the deities that Gygax, Arneson, and their players had come up with. Like the dungeons and the wider worlds surrounding them, which *OD&D* expected each DM to create on their own, the deities that would appear in campaigns would also have to be determined by each playing group.

Only with the publication of the final *OD&D Supplement IV: Gods, Demi-Gods & Heroes* (1976) did the game first receive detailed information on such entities, whose existence in the game world had been taken for granted until then.[54] However, this supplement does not detail fictional deities from the ongoing Greyhawk and Blackmoor campaigns. Rather, it offers lists and brief game statistics for historical real-world deities and pantheons (for example, "Egyptian Mythology," "Gods of India," "Greek Mythology," and "The Celtic Mythos") as well as fictional entities from Robert E. Howard's Conan stories and Michael Moorcock's Elric of Melniboné saga.

AD&D 1e expanded on this treatment of deities and religion(s) through the comprehensive *Deities & Demigods* cyclopedia published in 1980.[55] It offers many additional and enlarged entries on historical and real-world pantheons while replacing Howard's Hyborea with Fritz Leiber's "Nehwon Mythos." In addition, the first two printings also include the "Cthulhu Mythos," based on H. P. Lovecraft's writings.[56] The book also features a section titled "Nonhumans' Deities." The early format for the treatment of religion(s) in the game was established by these two publications and can be seen in the presentation of gods and mythological figures in game terms with the respective stat blocks (i.e., "armor class" and "hit points"), as well as short descriptions.[57] *Deities & Demigods* also for the first time presented instructions on "Dungeon Mastering Divine Beings" and other topics that relate to "making religion playable" like "Clerics and Deities," "Omens," "Divine Ascension," and "Mortality and Immortality."

Like the three *OD&D* booklets, the 1978 *AD&D* 1e *Players Handbook* also does not contain any references to concrete deities, speaking about such entities only in the abstract, with the exception of a reference to druids as "medieval cousins of . . . the ancient Celtic sect."[58] Nevertheless, the *AD&D* 1e *Dungeon Masters Guide* (1979) states that "serving some deity is an integral part of *AD&D*."[59] At this point, Gygax's own campaign seems to have included "9 demigods, 3 demon lords, and a handful of Norse and other gods."[60] In his foreword to *Deities & Demigods*, he is extremely critical of how deities were apparently treated by many players and DMs, being either mostly ignored or appearing "at the slightest whim of player characters" to rescue them.[61] As it provides the resources for a different treatment of the topic, Gygax describes *Deities & Demigods* as "an indispensable part of the whole of *AD&D*" and "integral to Dungeon Mastering a true *AD&D* campaign."[62]

While the *AD&D* 2e *Player's Handbook* (1989) only speaks of deities in the abstract ("deities of wisdom and knowledge"),[63] and the *AD&D* 2e *Dungeon Master's Guide* (1989) only mentions "self-proclaimed gods, goddesses, and demi-gods,"[64] *AD&D* 2e's *Legends & Lore* (1990)[65] is a completely revised version of the earlier supplements on religion(s). While a new introduction was added and some mythologies were excised (like the Babylonian and Finnish chapters), the general format remained the same. The presentation of deities and mythological figures from real-life cultures (as well as from Arthurian legend and Fritz Leiber's Nehwon stories) changed focus, away from "game mechanics and weapons" and toward "role-playing and using the gods," with an emphasis on "the society and civilization of the people who worshiped the pantheon in question" (4). *AD&D* 2e's *Legends & Lore* therefore does not give stats for the gods themselves but rather generalizes the concept of "avatar" (already previously described in the "Indian Mythos" section of *Deities & Demigods*). Gods, according to the book, cannot enter the Prime Material Plane but rather must send an avatar (6). Each god's avatar is thus given stats, while the powers of the gods themselves are "impossible to quantify" (7), despite the description of various "Divine Abilities" (for example, "all gods automatically receive the initiative," "all greater gods . . . automatically make all saving throws" [7]). The taxonomy in which these abilities are organized separates the deities into "Greater Gods," "Intermediate Gods," "Lesser Gods," "Demigods," and "Heroes" (7).

The most interesting supplement for *AD&D* 2e that deals with religion and deities, however, is *On Hallowed Ground* (1996) for the *Planescape* setting.[66] For the first time, this book spends a substantial number of words on a detailed theoretical exploration of religion, a sort of "theory of religion" in game form. Closely oriented toward the language and perspective of *Planescape*, *On Hallowed Ground* describes a complex theology in which "primers" (those born on one of the worlds of the Prime Material Plane) and "planars" (those born on the Inner or Outer Planes of existence) have very different relationships to the gods (called "powers" in the setting). The primers have "faith" in the gods, as they have not had any direct contact with them, while the planars worship gods because they have experienced and seen the "powers" (12). "Priests" are described as especially important, with "clerics" worshipping a whole pantheon (even if they might be focused on one deity) and "specialty priests" following and upholding "the tenets of only *one* power" (11–12). Only on page 60 does the book then begin to detail a large variety of "pantheons," both historical (Sumerian, Finnish, Greek, Chinese, etc.) and fictional (dwarven, elvish, monstrous powers, etc.). Even if the book's status as a *Planescape* supplement puts it at odds with some of *AD&D* 2e's core rules (and there is much in it that was not picked up by the future development of *D&D*), in its treatment of religion, *On Hallowed Ground* simultaneously stands in the tradition that began with *OD&D's Gods, Demigods & Heroes* while also breaking much new ground. Eight years later, 3e's *Deities & Demigods*, written by Rich Redman, Skip Williams, and James Wyatt and published in 2002,[67] can be considered the pinnacle so far of this kind of intellectual and philosophical exploration of religion(s) in *D&D*.

Third edition consolidated efforts into a single line of the game (now just called *Dungeons & Dragons*) and finally offered some information on deities and religion(s) already in the core rule books. The 3e *Player's Handbook* (2000) names example deities from Greyhawk (this edition's standard setting) for each race and class and, in a three-page section on "Religion,"[68] gives a short description of nineteen of the most common deities of this world. The 3e *Dungeon Master's Guide* (2000) limits its discussion of the subject to two pages,[69] leading with the claim that "no force affects society more strongly than religion,"[70] and offering suggestions on how the deities mentioned in the *Player's Handbook* fit into their societal contexts. These still very limited treatments of religion are then supplemented by the 2001 book *Defenders of the Faith* and a revised *Deities & Demigods* for 3e, which shares little beyond the name with the original 1980 book.

Deities & Demigods (2002)[71] is the most important and most detailed treatise on religion(s) in *D&D's* fifty-year history and represents an intriguing combination of all the prior ways of treating the topic.[72] Especially the first chapter written by James Wyatt (who has a degree in religion from Oberlin College and a master of divinity from Union Theological Seminary) contains much more detailed theoretical reflections on making religion playable in a *D&D* game than were available before. In a long section titled "The Nature of Religion," the book first introduces different models of religion—"pantheons, monotheism, dualism, animism, mystery cults, and nondeist beliefs (forces and philosophies)" (5)—including the concept of "tight" and "loose" pantheons, a novel description that can still be found in 5e. Second, it discusses the "nature of the gods," providing various options for the deities' involvement in a campaign world, their relationship to their worshippers, and whether or not the gods can die (5). This material forms the basis for instructions on how to build one's own pantheon. The other chapters introduce the idea of "divine ranks" (from 0 to 21+), basically a form of "level" for deities, and further detail for the "*D&D* pantheon" of the Greyhawk setting. The book then provides examples of "tight" pantheons inspired by the Greek, Egyptian, and Nordic traditions, presented in ways that are "divorced from their historical context" and oriented toward the needs of the game (99). Unlike their treatment in *AD&D* 2e's *Legends & Lore*, both the gods and their avatars are given game stats in the second chapter, which deals with "the game mechanics that make deities work" (25). In this way, 3e's *Deities & Demigods* exemplifies the tension inherent in *D&D*'s treatment of gods and deities from *Supplement IV* onward: are deities ultrapowerful "spiritual beings" beyond the game's normal rules, which should be used sparingly (if at all) in the game, or are they "just some *really* powerful monsters" (4)? Giving the gods the most detailed statistics in any of the publications in the "other *D&D*" tradition of *Deities & Demigods*, this book sticks to the latter answer (or leaves the choice to players and DMs) (4). In this way, 3e also represents the pinnacle of what Evan Torner describes as the main way in which *D&D* "renders all beings intelligible: as potential participants in a fight" (see chap. 4 by Evan Torner in this collection). In the rest of the second chapter, 3e's *Deities & Demigods* provides suggestions on how to roleplay a deity and incorporates the idea of "proxies" (who speak on behalf of a deity) and "petitioners" (spirits who become divine servants) from earlier *Planescape* publications. An interesting additional chapter at the end of the book discusses "Other Religions": fictional religions (reworked from Wyatt's own campaigns)[73] that go beyond the standard polytheistic models of most *D&D* worlds and instead use the monotheistic, dualistic, and mystery cult models. An appendix on "Divine Ascension" brings this classic aspect of *D&D* religion to 3e, providing players with rules on how to have their twentieth-level characters ascend to godhood.

How has religion featured in the game after this pivotal publication? In 4e, the *Player's Handbook* (2008) provides eleven deities regularly worshipped by player characters.[74] This list of "lawful good," "good," and "unaligned deities" from the *Player's Handbook* is supplemented in the 4e *Dungeon Master's Guide* (2008) with more detailed descriptions of the "evil" or "chaotic evil" "Malign Gods."[75] These gods and goddesses provided for

4e's *D&D* world were either taken from existing fictional *D&D* settings (Greyhawk and the Forgotten Realms), renamed and reworked from historical pantheons (Greek, Norse, and Egyptian), or created from scratch (the deities Ioun, Melora, and Torog).[76] This new pantheon, created for what became known as 4e's "Points of Light" setting (named for the settlements among the darkness and wilderness of the assumed world),[77] was part of a new creation myth based on a war between the "primordials" of the Elemental Chaos and the gods of the Astral Sea that formed part of the reworking of *D&D*'s planar cosmology for 4e. The conflict was given the name "Dawn War" in later supplements like *The Plane Above: Secrets of the Astral Sea* (2010).[78] As a list of "Dawn War Deities," this pantheon is also included as a sample pantheon in 5e's *Dungeon Master's Guide*. The 4e *Dungeon Master's Guide* also has a short section on religion in the context of describing "organizations" found in the *D&D* world.[79] "Temples and religious orders" are seen as powerful organizations, which are especially important for characters who draw on divine power, like clerics and paladins. Still, even temples dedicated to the same god might differ greatly from city to city, as the worship of the gods is not organized in centralized, worldwide hierarchies, and most temples are places where more than one of the gods is worshipped.[80]

No book similar to *Deities & Demigods* was published for 4e. What comes closest is 2010's *The Plane Above: Secrets of the Astral Sea*, which details the "divine dominions" where the gods and goddesses of 4e's world live, and describes the "Dawn War" they fought against the primordials. What is missing from the 4e core books, therefore, are instructions on how to design one's own deities and pantheon. As all other editions of *D&D* had explicitly foregrounded—or at least implicitly hinted at—this possibility and had often supported it with "pick-and-choose" publications in the *Deities & Demigods* tradition, this marked a significant change.

The importance of creating one's own fictional pantheon—often stressed until 3e—also corresponds to the increasing focus on fictional pantheons in published campaign settings over the years. While 1980's *World of Greyhawk* folio,[81] the first detailed setting published by TSR, did not include any information on deities, the boxed-set edition in 1983 finally lists sixty gods and demigods and describes twenty-two of them in detail.[82] In the second half of the 1980s, for example, with the *Forgotten Realms Campaign Set*

(1987) and *Dragonlance Adventures* (1987),[83] the inclusion of fictional deities and pantheons, as well as separate books on religion(s) in the respective settings (*Faiths & Avatars*, 1996; *Powers & Pantheons*, 1997),[84] became
the standard.[85] This continued in 3e with books like *Faiths & Pantheons*
(Forgotten Realms, 2002), *Holy Orders of the Stars* (Dragonlance, 2005), and
Faiths of Eberron (2006), in addition to the information already provided in
the respective campaign setting publications.[86] The 4e *Campaign Guides* for
the Forgotten Realms and Eberron include detailed sections on religion(s)
and deities, and 5e's *Sword Coast Adventurer's Guide* (2015) equally presents
compact information on religion and the gods of the continent of Faerûn.[87]
Other 5e setting books, like *Eberron: Rising from the Last War* (2019) and
Explorer's Guide to Wildemount (2020), also contain such details.[88]

   Since *AD&D* 2e, then, the inclusion of detailed fictional pantheons has
become standard for published *D&D* campaign settings. In a certain sense,
this increasing focus on fictional deities and religions represents a shift
and at least a partial abandonment of the tradition (which started with
OD&D's Gods, Demigods & Heroes and *AD&D* 1e's *Deities & Demigods* cyclopedia) of using only slightly fictionalized versions of real-world historical
deities and the publication of detailed general books on religion(s). While
in 3e this "other *D&D*" tradition still had a strong presence in parallel to
the fictional deities and religions of the campaign settings, in 4e this idea
was basically absent. In 5e its only remnants are the short descriptions
and tables of "historical" Celtic, Egyptian, Greek, and Norse pantheons in
Appendix B, "Gods of the Multiverse," of the *Player's Handbook* (2014).[89]
Gods from these pantheons are also mentioned in the descriptions of
the cleric's divine domains as possible deities to be affiliated with.[90] The
5e *Dungeon Master's Guide* (2014) contains a short section titled "Gods
of Your World."[91] It presents basic information on different types of religions and how to include them in a campaign world. These few pages,
then, while still containing much helpful information for players and
DMs about how to present religion(s) in their game, are what remains (so
far) of an extensive treatment of the subject in *AD&D* 1e and 2e, as well
as in *D&D* 3e—which had culminated in the publication of a fully revised
Deities & Demigods in 2002.

   As I have tried to show, the *Deities & Demigods* tradition—the "other
D&D" of the last fifty years—has very much been a part of what makes

D&D what it is. The figure of the cleric and the theologies of *D&D*, in combination with the planar cosmology (a third aspect of how religion and
mythology have been included in each edition that I have not been able
to explore here), have contributed a lot to making the various worlds of
the game's multiverse feel like *D&D*. As 5e pushes forward into the Astral
Plane in *Spelljammer: Adventures in Space* (2022) and visits the mists of the
Ethereal Plane in *Journeys through the Radiant Citadel* (2022),[92] and with
glimpses of *One D&D* on the horizon, it remains to be seen if religion(s)
in the future will once more receive the attention that merits a revised
version of *Deities & Demigods* for the next iteration of the game.

NOTES

1. As this list of names indicates, there is a dire need to examine what contributions
to the treatment of religion(s) and mythologies in *D&D* were provided by those who
are not white, cis men. I hope this preliminary overview will offer some starting
points for such further explorations.

2. Gary Gygax, *Players Handbook* (*AD&D* 1e) (Lake Geneva, WI: TSR Games, 1978), 2.

3. Gary Gygax and Robert J. Kuntz, *Dungeons & Dragons Supplement I: Greyhawk*
(*OD&D*) (Lake Geneva, WI: Tactical Studies Rules, 1975), 28.

4. Jon Peterson, *Playing at the World: A History of Simulating Wars, People, and Fantastic Adventures, from Chess to Role-Playing Games* (San Diego: Unreason Press, 2012),
172–179; Joseph P. Laycock, *Dangerous Games: What the Moral Panic over Role-Playing
Games Says about Play, Religion, and Imagined Worlds* (Berkeley: University of California Press, 2015), 61.

5. Gary Gygax and Jeff Perren, *Chainmail* (Lake Geneva, WI: Tactical Studies Rules,
1971).

6. In *The Elusive Shift: How Role-Playing Games Forged Their Identity* (Cambridge, MA:
MIT Press, 2020), 18–19, Jon Peterson writes: "Mike Carr, who belonged to Arneson's
Twin Cities group, played a preacher in the Brownstone setting. . . . [He], following his religious calling in Brownstone, became the 'village priest' of Blackmoor." In
Arneson's Blackmoor campaign notes published in *The First Fantasy Campaign*, this
figure is then described as "Bishop Carr." Dave Arneson, *The First Fantasy Campaign*
(1977; 3rd printing, Decatur, IL: Judges Guild, 1980), 29.

7. Havard, "[Characters] Bishop Carr—First D&D Cleric," *Havard's Blackmoor Blog*,
January 22, 2011, http://blackmoormystara.blogspot.com/2011/01/bishop-carr-first
-d-cleric.html.

8. This claim is discussed in Peterson, *Playing at the World*, 179, as well as in the following blog posts: James Maliszewski, "The Original Cleric," *Grognardia*, July 15, 2010,
http://grognardia.blogspot.com/2010/07/original-cleric.html; Havard, "Bishop Carr";

Demos Sachlas, "OD&D Clerics," *OSR Grimoire*, May 2, 2020, https://osrgrimoire.blog spot.com/2020/05/od-clerics.html. This context seems also to have provided the cleric's important skill of turning the undead.

9. Peterson, *Playing at the World*, 173.

10. Gary Gygax and Dave Arneson, *Dungeons & Dragons Volume 1: Men & Magic* (*OD&D*) (Lake Geneva, WI: Tactical Studies Rules, 1974), 14.

11. James Maliszewski, "The Implicit Christianity of Early Gaming," *Grognardia*, December 23, 2008, http://grognardia.blogspot.com/2008/12/implicit-christianity-of -early-gaming.html.

12. Gygax and Arneson, *Men & Magic*, 16. The odd inclusion of "Lama" among a list of Christian titles is puzzling (see also Justin Alexander, "Reactions to OD&D: Gods & Clerics," *The Alexandrian*, December 31, 2020, https://thealexandrian.net /wordpress/45687/roleplaying-games/reactions-to-odd-gods-clerics). It seems to be the result of a Gygaxian insertion replacing "Abbë" in an earlier version of the list (Jon Peterson, "The Dalluhn Manuscript: A Pre-publication Edition of *Dungeons & Dragons*," 2015, https://www.dropbox.com/s/b8js9zz8lp0qwzw/DalluhnManuscript -12.2015-Peterson.pdf, 18), but more research is needed on this issue.

13. John Eric Holmes, ed., Gary Gygax, and Dave Arneson, *Dungeons & Dragons Basic Set* (Lake Geneva, WI: TSR Hobbies, 1977).

14. Holmes, Gygax, and Arneson, *Basic Set*, 6.

15. Gygax, *Players Handbook* (1e), 20.

16. David "Zeb" Cook et al., *Player's Handbook* (*AD&D* 2e) (Lake Geneva, WI: TSR, 1989), 32.

17. Monte Cook, Jonathan Tweet, Skip Williams, et al., *Player's Handbook* (*D&D* 3e) (Renton, WA: Wizards of the Coast, 2000), 21.

18. Rob Heinsoo, Andy Collins, James Wyatt, et al., *Player's Handbook 1* (*D&D* 4e) (Renton, WA: Wizards of the Coast, 2008), 15.

19. Heinsoo et al., *Player's Handbook 1* (4e), 52, 60.

20. Mike Mearls, Jeremy Crawford, et al., *Player's Handbook* (*D&D* 5e) (Renton, WA: Wizards of the Coast, 2014), 45.

21. Mearls et al., *Player's Handbook* (5e), 56.

22. While Maliszewski ("Implicit Christianity," 2008) only detects an "implicit Christianity" in *D&D*, in the present collection Daniel Heath Justice (chap. 16) describes the "Christian triumphalism" and "dualistic Christo-colonial cosmologies of *D&D*" as a central aspect of how racist tropes are embedded in the game.

23. Jörg Rüpke, *Pantheon: A New History of Roman Religion*, trans. David M. B. Richardson (Princeton, NJ: Princeton University Press, 2018), 9; see also Jörg Rüpke, "Wie funktioniert Polytheismus? Götter, Bilder, Reflexionen," *Mediterraneo Antico* 15, nos. 1–2 (2012): 233–246.

24. Rüpke, *Pantheon*, 10.

25. Hans G. Kippenberg, *Discovering Religious History in the Modern Age*, trans. Barbara Harshav (Princeton, NJ: Princeton University Press, 2002), 81–97; Randall Styers, *Making Magic: Religion, Magic, and Science in the Modern World* (Princeton, NJ: Princeton University Press, 2004).

26. Styers, *Making Magic*, 224.

27. See Styers, 224.

28. Gygax and Kuntz, *Supplement I: Greyhawk*.

29. Robert Kuntz and James M. Ward, *Dungeons & Dragons Supplement IV: Gods, Demigods & Heroes* (*OD&D*) (Lake Geneva, WI: TSR Rules, 1976).

30. James M. Ward, with Robert J. Kuntz et al., *Deities & Demigods* (*AD&D* 1e) (Lake Geneva, WI: TSR, 1980).

31. *Gods, Demi-Gods & Heroes* (1976) uses this term in its introduction (giving the plural as "mythos" instead of "mythoi") and in some, but not all, of the section titles (other terms used are "Mythology," "Gods," "Gods and Heroes"). In the premium edition of *OD&D* published in 2013, all section titles use "Mythology" instead. *AD&D* 1e's *Deities & Demigods* (1980) uses "Mythos" for all section titles (except for "Nonhumans' Deities"). The use of the term is likely related to the prominence in fantasy fandom of speaking of the "Cthulhu Mythos" as a shorthand for H. P. Lovecraft's works. See S. T. Joshi, *The Rise, Fall, and Rise of the Cthulhu Mythos* (New York: Hippocampus Press, 2015). Timothy J. Kask's foreword to *Gods, Demigods & Heroes* states that the booklet "will enable you to incorporate a number of various mythologies into your game/campaign. . . . Mythology is defined as 'a body of myths, especially: the myths dealing with the gods, demi-gods and heroes of a particular people, usually involving the supernatural.' Myth is defined as a legend." The quotation in this passage (and with it the title of the supplement), is taken from the *Merriam-Webster Dictionary*. As the seventh edition from 1963 (561) and the 1981 printing (755–756) provide the following text, it seems that Kask slightly adjusted his quotation from the entry on "mythology," which reads: "**b**: a body of myths; *esp*: the myths dealing with the gods, demigods, and legendary heroes of a particular people and usu. involving supernatural elements." *Merriam-Webster Dictionary*, 7th ed. (1963), 561. In any case, this reference established the title for *Deities & Demigods* and similar books all the way until 3e.

32. Gary Gygax et al., *World of Greyhawk Fantasy Game Setting* (*AD&D* 1e) (Lake Geneva, WI: TSR, 1983), 64–78; Ed Greenwood et al., *Forgotten Realms Campaign Set* (*AD&D* 1e) (Lake Geneva, WI: TSR, 1987).

33. James M. Ward, with Robert J. Kuntz et al., *Legends & Lore* (*AD&D* 1e) (Lake Geneva, WI: Tactical Studies Rules, 1984).

34. Mearls et al., *Player's Handbook* (5e), 297.

35. Gary Gygax et al., *Unearthed Arcana* (*AD&D* 1e) (Lake Geneva, WI: TSR, 1985).

36. Dave Arneson, *Dungeons & Dragons Supplement II: Blackmoor* (*OD&D*) (Lake Geneva, WI: Tactical Studies Rules, 1975), 1.

37. Gary Gygax and Brian Blume, *Dungeons & Dragons Supplement III: Eldritch Wizardry* (*OD&D*) (Lake Geneva, WI: Tactical Studies Rules, 1975), 1.

38. Holmes, Gygax, and Arneson, *Basic Set*.

39. Gygax, *Players Handbook* (1e), 20.

40. Cook et al., *Player's Handbook* (2e), 34.

41. Jeff Grubb, Ed Greenwood, et al., *Forgotten Realms Adventures* (*AD&D* 2e) (Lake Geneva, WI: TSR, 1990).

42. Cook et al., *Player's Handbook* (3e), 21.

43. Julia Martin, with Eric L. Boyd et al., *Faiths & Avatars* (*AD&D* 2e) (Lake Geneva, WI: TSR, 1996), 1.

44. Rich Redman, Skip Williams, James Wyatt, et al., *Deities & Demigods* (*D&D* 3e) (Renton, WA: Wizards of the Coast, 2002), 20.

45. Rich Redman, James Wyatt, et al., *Defenders of the Faith* (*D&D* 3e) (Renton, WA: Wizards of the Coast, 2001), 51–75.

46. Heinsoo et al., *Player's Handbook 1* (4e).

47. Mearls et al., *Player's Handbook* (5e).

48. See Jonathan Z. Smith, "Religion, Religions, Religious," in *Critical Terms for Religious Studies*, ed. Mark C. Taylor (Chicago: University of Chicago Press, 1998); Jason A. Josephson, *The Invention of Religion in Japan* (Chicago: University of Chicago Press, 2012); Adrian Hermann, "Distinctions of Religion: The Search for Equivalents of 'Religion' and the Challenge of Theorizing a 'Global Discourse of Religion,'" in *Making Religion: Theory and Practice in the Discursive Study of Religion*, ed. Frans Wijsen and Kocku von Stuckrad (Leiden: Brill, 2016), 97–124; Kevin Schilbrack, "The Concept of Religion," in *The Stanford Encyclopedia of Philosophy*, Summer 2022 edition, https://plato.stanford.edu/archives/sum2022/entries/concept-religion/.

49. See Gygax and Kuntz, *Supplement I: Greyhawk*.

50. Arneson, *The First Fantasy Campaign*, 17.

51. Also, early on, in his first letter to the fanzine *Alarums & Excursions*, no. 2 (1975), Gygax mentioned that religion was a "touchy area," which was, he claimed, why he did not include "existing religions" in Greyhawk. *Alarums & Excursions* was edited by Lee Gold. It was published in Los Angeles, and the first issue appeared in June 1975. Nevertheless, in his foreword to *Deities & Demigods*, Gygax praised the book, which was full of elements of historical religions, as "indispensable" and "integral" to the game (Ward et al., *Deities & Demigods*, 2). Later, in 2006, Gygax commented that he did "not advocate any use of actual religion in an RPG" and claimed that he "did not write Deities and Demigods, nor did I use it in my campaign." E. Gary Gygax, "Gary Gygax Q&A: Part XII," reply to post on EN World, August 23, 2006, https://web.archive.org/web/20121005102945/http://www.enworld.org/forum/archive-threads/171753-gary-gygax-q-part-xii-8.html#post3024755. Advice about avoiding offending players' personal beliefs is also repeatedly presented in Frank Mentzer's Basic/Expert/Companion/Master/Immortal (BECMI) *D&D* rule sets from the mid-1980s: the *Players Manual* and *Dungeon Masters Rulebook* in *Dungeons & Dragons Set 1: Basic Rules* (1983); *Dungeons & Dragons Set 3: Companion Rules* (1984); and *Dungeons & Dragons Set 4: Master Rules* (1985); all by Frank Mentzer, ed., Gary Gygax, and Dave Arneson, and published by TSR. A further exploration of Gygax's (and Arneson's)

own religiosity and its influence on the early development of the game—as well as on later editions, especially during the "Satanic Panic" of the 1980s—is beyond the scope of this chapter. Some preliminary information and discussions of some aspects of such influences can be found in Peterson, *Playing at the World*; and Laycock, *Dangerous Games*. In the present collection, Victor Raymond and Gary Alan Fine (chap. 19) touch on how deviance and alleged Satanism were connected to *D&D*'s early public reputation, and Sam Mannell (see Designer Vignettes) links the game's ability to provide moments of ekstasis and a sense of belonging in a community to role-playing games' similarities with religion.

52. Gygax and Kuntz, *Supplement I: Greyhawk*, 28.

53. See also Gerald Nachtwey, *Strictly Fantasy: The Cultural Roots of Tabletop Role-Playing Games* (Jefferson, NC: McFarland, 2021), 99.

54. Kuntz and Ward, *Gods, Demigods & Heroes*.

55. The best and most detailed exploration of the book and its representations of deities and religion(s) is James Holloway's *Patron Deities* podcast with over a hundred episodes, available on his Patreon page, https://www.patreon.com/monsterman.

56. Later editions of the book dropped the references to both Moorcock and Lovecraft for complex copyright reasons. See Jim Ward, "The Making and Breaking of *Deities & Demigods*," post on EN World, May 28, 2019, https://www.enworld.org/threads/the-making-and-breaking-of-deities-demigods.666377/.

57. It seems the format was at least partly created by Gygax himself, who in the foreword claims: "I informed both James Ward and Rob Kuntz of the direction which the overall work was to take. . . . The format used . . . was actually developed through close consultation with myself" (Ward et al., *Deities & Demigods* [1e], 2). Ward ("The Making and Breaking") equally remembers: "Gary gave me a format to use that was much like a monster manual listing. That was fine with me as it gave me an order and focus for each listing."

58. Gygax, *Players Handbook* (1e), 21. In the *Basic D&D* line that TSR published from the late 1970s to the early 1990s, explicit treatments of religion(s) and deities in the sense of *Deities & Demigods* played only a minor role. The *D&D Basic Set* prepared by Holmes (1977) only once mentions "Zeus, Crom, Cthulhu or whatever" in an allusion to *OD&D* (39). No specific deities or gods are described in Moldvay's and Cook's *Basic* and *Expert Rules*. Tom Moldvay, ed., Gary Gygax, and Dave Arneson, *Dungeons & Dragons Basic Rules* (Lake Geneva, WI: TSR, 1981); David "Zeb" Cook, ed., Gary Gygax, and Dave Arneson, *Dungeons & Dragons Expert Rules* (Lake Geneva, WI: TSR, 1981). Mentzer's *Basic Rules* (1984) avoid speaking about gods in the characterization of the cleric, who is described as "dedicated to serving a great and worthy cause" (*Players Manual*, 24), but suggest to the dungeon master that "mythological deities," "similar to the mythological gods and goddesses of days long past" (like "Zeus, Apollo, Poseidon, and so forth") could provide additional "flavor" to the game (*Dungeon Masters Rulebook*, 15). The *Companion Rules* (1984) and *Master Rules* (1985) also avoid any detailed references to specific historical or fictional deities, even while the latter describes the paths that player characters can take to become immortals themselves.

59. Gary Gygax, *Dungeon Masters Guide* (*AD&D* 1e) (Lake Geneva, WI: TSR, 1979), 111.

60. Gygax, *Dungeon Masters Guide* (1e), 112.

61. Ward et al., *Deities & Demigods* (1e), 2.

62. Ward et al., 2. However, Gygax later claimed he did not use *Deities & Demigods* himself; see n. 51.

63. Cook et al., *Player's Handbook* (2e), 34.

64. David "Zeb" Cook et al., *Dungeon Master's Guide* (*AD&D* 2e) (Lake Geneva, WI: TSR, 1989), 132.

65. James M. Ward, Troy Denning, et al., *Legends & Lore* (*AD&D* 2e) (Lake Geneva, WI: TSR, 1990).

66. Colin McComb et al., *On Hallowed Ground* (*AD&D* 2e) (Lake Geneva, WI: TSR, 1996).

67. Redman et al., *Deities & Demigods* (3e).

68. Cook et al., *Player's Handbook* (3e), 90–92.

69. Monte Cook, Jonathan Tweet, Skip Williams, et al., *Dungeon Master's Guide* (*D&D* 3e) (Renton, WA: Wizards of the Coast, 2000), 159–160.

70. Cook et al., *Dungeon Master's Guide* (3e), 159.

71. Redman et al., *Deities & Demigods* (3e).

72. As a gaming supplement, however, the book was not always well reviewed; see, e.g., the thread at https://www.enworld.org/threads/deities-and-demigods.118066/.

73. James Wyatt et al., "*Deities and Demigods* Design Team Interview with Rich Redman, Skip Williams, and James Wyatt," interview by Michael Ryan, Wizards .com, April 7, 2002, archived at http://rpg.nobl.ca/dnd.php?x=dnd/ps/ps20020407a.

74. Heinsoo, *Player's Handbook 1* (4e), 20–23.

75. James Wyatt et al., *Dungeon Master's Guide* (*D&D* 4e) (Renton, WA: Wizards of the Coast, 2008), 162–163.

76. See Mearls et al., *Dungeon Master's Guide* (5e), 11.

77. See Wyatt et al., *Dungeon Master's Guide* (4e), 148, 150.

78. Rob Heinsoo et al., *The Plane Above: Secrets of the Astral Sea* (*D&D* 4e) (Renton, WA: Wizards of the Coast, 2010).

79. Wyatt et al., *Dungeon Master's Guide* (4e), 155–156.

80. Wyatt et al., 155.

81. Gary Gygax et al., *The World of Greyhawk Fantasy World Setting* (*AD&D* 1e) (Lake Geneva, WI: TSR, 1980).

82. Gary Gygax et al., *World of Greyhawk* (1983), 64–78.

83. Greenwood et al., *Forgotten Realms Campaign Set*; Tracy Hickman, Margaret Weis, et al., *Dragonlance Adventures* (*AD&D* 1e) (Lake Geneva, WI: TSR, 1987).

84. Martin et al., *Faiths & Avatars*; Eric L. Boyd et al., *Powers & Pantheons* (*AD&D* 2e) (Lake Geneva, WI: TSR, 1997).

85. Dark Sun, a campaign setting first published for *AD&D* 2e in 1991 and last updated for 4e in 2010, is the most famous outlier, as the world of Athas is "a world without deities." Troy Denning, Timothy B. Brown, et al., *Dark Sun Rules Book* (*AD&D* 2e) (Lake Geneva, WI: TSR, 1991), 28. Clerics in the setting "worship one of the four elemental planes: earth, air, fire, or water" (29).

86. Eric L. Boyd, Erik Mona, et al., *Faiths & Pantheons* (*D&D* 3e) (Renton, WA: Wizards of the Coast, 2002); Sean Everette, Cam Banks, Chris Pierson, Trampas Whiteman, et al., *Holy Orders of the Stars* (*D&D* 3e) (Renton, WA: Wizards of the Coast, 2005); Jennifer Clarke Wilkes, Ari Marmell, C. A. Suleiman, et al., *Faiths of Eberron* (*D&D* 3e) (Renton, WA: Wizards of the Coast, 2006).

87. Steve Kenson et al., *Sword Coast Adventurer's Guide* (*D&D* 5e) (Renton, WA: Wizards of the Coast, 2015).

88. Jeremy Crawford, James Wyatt, Keith Baker, et al., *Eberron: Rising from the Last War* (*D&D* 5e) (Renton, WA: Wizards of the Coast, 2019); Matthew Mercer et al., *Explorer's Guide to Wildemount* (*D&D* 5e) (Renton, WA: Wizards of the Coast, 2020).

89. Mearls et al., *Player's Handbook* (5e), 297–299.

90. This move toward fully fictional pantheons or fictional treatments of historical religious traditions can also be seen in *Mythic Odysseys of Theros*, which acknowledges that the "roots of Theros lie in the myths of ancient Greece" (5), but then presents a pantheon of fifteen fictional gods, some of which are clearly versions of ancient Greek deities. F. Wesley Schneider, James Wyatt, et al., *Mythic Odysseys of Theros* (*D&D* 5e) (Renton, WA: Wizards of the Coast, 2020). Despite the inclusion of a "Greek" pantheon in 5e's *Player's Handbook* (2014), then, this fictional "Greek" pantheon in *Theros* continues the trend toward including religion(s) in *D&D* primarily in fictionalized forms.

91. Mike Mearls, Jeremy Crawford, et al., *Dungeon Master's Guide* (*D&D* 5e) (Renton, WA: Wizards of the Coast, 2014), 10–13.

92. Christopher Perkins et al., *Spelljammer: Adventures in Space* (*D&D* 5e) (Renton, WA: Wizards of the Coast, 2022); Ajit A. George, F. Wesley Schneider, et al., *Journeys through the Radiant Citadel* (*D&D* 5e) (Renton, WA: Wizards of the Coast, 2022).

11

SPELLING WITH DICE: THE ROLE OF *DUNGEONS & DRAGONS* IN CONTEMPORARY SPECULATIVE FICTION

Dimitra Nikolaidou

In 2015, right after receiving the prestigious World Fantasy Award for his novel *Bone Clocks*, David Mitchell stated the following in an interview with the online *Wired* magazine:

> I played *Dungeons & Dragons* as a kid. A lot of us did, actually, a lot of writers I know did. In the bars late at night at literary festivals, sometimes the conversation will get around to—with sort of a huddle of us in the corner, saying, "So, did you play *Dungeons & Dragons?*" And it's amazing how many say yes. So Gary Gygax has a lot to answer for. There's probably a Ph.D. thesis out there, in the realms of possible Ph.D. theses that someone could write somewhere, on Gary Gygax's influence on the 20th century novel. Because it would not be negligible.[1]

Mitchell's interview highlights two separate phenomena: the influence that *Dungeons & Dragons* (*D&D*) has had on literature, and the fact that this influence has long gone unrecognized. I argue that the game's roots in pulp narratives and wargaming, as well as the well-documented social stigma attached to early gamers, explains why *D&D* initially attracted little academic or literary attention. And yet, since its inception, it has been an important factor in shaping contemporary speculative fiction. Moreover, its multifaceted influence is becoming increasingly pronounced given the dissemination of *D&D* narratives in multiple media.

The aim of this chapter is to establish, through the dual lens of cultural studies and narrative theory, the processes through which the multiple narrative elements, tropes, and master plots which make up *D&D* have been seeded in speculative literature, heavily influencing the genre. Following that, I focus on specific instances where this influence was made manifest. Finally, I discuss the ways in which various *D&D* elements, particularly the problematic elements associated with the game's origins in pulp culture and wargaming, were negotiated in fiction. The conclusions suggest that the influence of *D&D* has shaped not only contemporary speculative fiction but also the culture of the fantastic in general, becoming a decisive factor in the evolution of the genre.

A RECIPROCAL RELATIONSHIP

The relationship between *D&D* and fiction has always been reciprocal; Gygax might have claimed pulp narratives among his inspirations, but his creation would go on to inspire new directions in speculative fiction and beyond.[2] I suggest that despite the difficulty of ascertaining the influences behind cultural artifacts and works of literature in particular, *D&D*'s manifold impact on fiction can be traced by focusing on two different yet interlocked issues: first, the narrative and cultural process through which *D&D* becomes a particularly decisive influence on the culture of the fantastic, informing both authors and consumers of speculative fiction; and second, the tracking of *D&D* tropes, narratives, and master plots frequently encountered in speculative fiction and beyond.

I begin by examining the process through which *D&D* influences the culture of the fantastic, with a focus on fantastic narratives. For that, we need to begin with the game's relationship with speculative fiction. In the *Advanced Dungeons & Dragons* first edition (*AD&D* 1e) *Dungeons Masters Guide* (1979), "Appendix N: Inspirational and Educational Reading"[3] lists the people[4] who influenced the game designers; the list includes pulp luminaries,[5] horror writers, and literary authors. While Gygax also credits comic books, genre movies, fairy tales, tales of fantasy, historical reference books, and medieval bestiaries, one could argue that speculative pulp fiction had already amalgamated these additional influences. *D&D* invited players to inhabit these pulp stories instead of passively consuming them. Indeed, the ability of the game to allow players to enter fantasy storyworlds, and narrate their own stories within, remains one of its most significant draws.

Despite *D&D* being play, scholars from multiple fields argue that narratives (of all types) yield significant transformative force and are crucial in shaping our identity, our culture, our shared beliefs, and our perception of ourselves and others.[6] *D&D* narratives in particular are not simply stories we consume, on par with movies or novels; instead they are particularly immersive stories we simultaneously create, consume, and enact. This strengthens their ability to influence participants at an even more fundamental level than other storytelling media. And while these participants, even when fully engrossed in the game, are capable of distinguishing between their experiences inside and outside the storyworld, their perception of the fantastic itself is deeply influenced by *D&D* narratives, given that these are bound to be much more immersive than other types of fantastic narratives they might consume.[7] As a result, participants' expectations of speculative[8] narratives are shaped by *D&D* to a great degree, not only in terms of setting and character archetypes but also in terms of plot, pacing, theme, and even ideological underpinnings (the good–evil dichotomy is a prime example).

The results of this deep-seated influence on participants who are also authors of speculative fiction are, of course, direct: scholars such as Paul Cobley, Paul Ricoeur, and Marie-Laure Ryan have highlighted how the preexisting narratives and narrative patterns that surround us inform and shape the narratives we ourselves produce, even if we choose to negotiate, subvert, or transgress those narratives.[9] However, it should be added that even those participants who will not go on to become creators are quite likely to be consumers of speculative narratives, and as such, their taste, often shaped by *D&D* (directly or, as shown hereafter, indirectly), also influences the shape of speculative fiction.[10]

The impact of *D&D* on fantasy narratives and fiction in particular was strengthened by other factors related to the game's subculture, its evolution, and its reach. To begin with, *D&D* itself was inspired by pulp culture, which is particularly open to evolution, permutation, and renewal,[11] thus offering itself up to a variety of transmedial interpretations. This quality was highlighted by the open, collaborative nature of early tabletop role-playing game (TTRPG) culture, which encouraged engagement with the material in a variety of forms, including the crafting of new narratives in the form of fiction, art, or even other games, at least in the beginning.[12]

Along with the existence of a fertile creative culture, *D&D* includes some inherent traits that further encouraged the dissemination of its narrative elements; games scholars Esther MacCallum-Stewart, Jaakko Stenros, and Staffan Björk attempt to summarize some of these. To begin with, they posit that the flexibility of the core role-playing game (RPG) elements, in terms of creating an underlying discourse, ensures that these elements are capable of flowing and mutating according to the demands of different media.[13] The authors provide several observations to support their claim, suggesting that "the formulaic nature of an RPG game—a diverse party of adventurers, a series of quests and trials and the potential for individual and group heroism (or failure) lends itself well to science fiction and fantasy writing, where this structure is an established formula."[14] Indeed, the structure of a *D&D* session, which typically includes the classic plot elements (exposition, rising action, climax, falling action, and denouement),[15] facilitates authors' attempts to transcribe and expand their experience into a written story. In addition, authors are likely to use transcriptions of campaigns, campaign notes, characters, and homebrew settings directly, in some cases making only slight changes to avoid copyright infringement. Essentially, much of the preparatory work required by a speculative fiction author, especially in terms of world-building and plot outline, has already been completed during a *D&D* campaign.

A final point of direct influence between *D&D* and the culture of the fantastic is the wide dissemination of *D&D* narrative elements into other media, since these elements will also influence authors who have not participated in a *D&D* game. Despite being considered a niche hobby for many decades, *D&D* has exerted an outsize influence in the culture of the fantastic, for various reasons. To begin with, by purposefully using the most familiar of fantastic tropes in an attempt to create a common denominator and facilitate understanding of the game, *D&D* summarized these tropes and then categorized them in an easily understood terminology that in many cases replaced previously used lingo,[16] thus reaching beyond the audience of fantastic literature. MacCallum-Stewart, Stenros, and Björk suggest that the migration of RPG developers in other media is responsible for the dissemination of "tropes, concepts, types of storytelling and stereotypes into broader culture."[17]

However, it was not only the migrating developers who contributed to this dissemination; *D&D* participants themselves also carried these elements over into other media, ensuring their prevalence in the culture of the fantastic. The strongest example is the genre of digital gaming, which was developed concurrently with *D&D* and, according to a number of scholars, owes its shape and form to *D&D*. In their introduction to *Dungeons & Dreamers*, Brad King and John Borland write: "Scratch almost any game developer who worked between the late 1970s and the early 2000s, and you're likely to find a vein of role-playing experience."[18] Further scholarship has detected a direct line of evolution linking tabletop role-playing games to digital games. Matt Barton posits that "'the holy grail' of early computer programming"[19] was the adaptation of the tabletop role-playing experience into digital form. He also notes the science-fiction-themed *Fallout* (1997) and *Knights of the Old Republic* (1998) as examples of the fantasy-themed *D&D* providing inspiration for digital RPGs of different genres. Indeed, it is easy to detect the tropes, themes, and mechanics of *D&D* in both single-player and massively multiplayer online role-playing games (MMORPGs).[20] As digital games became more and more popular, these *D&D* elements became further entrenched in the mainstream.

Additionally, and while digital games remain the most prominent example, I would argue that *D&D* has influenced many media, shaping the culture and narratives of the fantastic. Some of these media include webcomics, which in the first decades of the twenty-first century provided an outlet for many *D&D* participants who wanted to expand their gaming narratives, graphic novels, podcasts, and TV series and films. Popular film and TV creators (such as Dan Harmon, Wil Wheaton, Matt Groening, Joss Whedon, Jon Favreau, Noelle Stevenson, and Kevin Smith) have referred to the many ways in which the game has inspired their work; specifically, the actor Joe Manganiello has commented on the revival of *D&D* in an article by Keith Stuart published in *The Guardian*, and has said that "[a] lot of today's actors, directors and writers grew up playing *D&D* and you can see that in their shows."[21]

As a final addendum, the effects of *D&D* on the fantasy traditions beyond the Anglophone world should not be underestimated. The game was available in mainly Western, non-English-speaking countries, either in translation or simply sold at specialty stores, even when few fiction books were. As such, it influenced perceptions of the fantastic in these countries, further entrenching the hegemonic presence of Anglo-Saxon fantasy. The effect was particularly strong in countries that did not have an established local fantasy tradition, essentially shaping the work of future authors for whom the game provided an entry point to the genre.

These observations suggest that, apart from providing authors with inspiration and structure, D&D also permeates the culture of the fantastic in multiple ways, further influencing participants who attempt to write fiction, shaping consumer expectations, and even reaching nonparticipants who are still bound to encounter the tropes, stereotypes, and structures rooted in the game.

OF DICE AND PEN

This brings me to the second part of my argument: charting manifestations of D&D's influence in literature. While the results of the process—through which D&D elements inspire and in some cases prevail in the culture of the fantastic—cannot be quantified, some prominent examples showcase the game's reaching power. The obvious example, of course, is the many writers who directly claim TTRPGs as inspiration. David Mitchell's statement concerning the influence of D&D on his work is far from unique. Among the significant and influential authors who have been gamers, and in many cases still are TTRPG enthusiasts, are Raymond Feist, Elizabeth Moon, George R. R. Martin, Patrick Rothfuss, Ari Marmell, China Miéville, Scott Lynch, Junot Díaz, Jim Butcher, Brandon Sanderson, Dan Wells, Jen Williams, Howard Taylor, Miles Cameron, Steven Brust, James S. A. Corey, Steven Erikson, Nancy Kilpatrick, Edward McNally, N. S. Dolkart, Sharyn McCrumb, Cory Doctorow, Joe Abercrombie, Arturo Pérez-Reverte, and Sherman Alexie. In some of these cases, the influence is readily apparent to the reader. For example, the protagonists in works by Butcher, Martin, Abercrombie, Lynch, and Rothfuss, who have been vocal about their participation in the game, readily betray their roots. Other works such as Erikson and Esslemont's Malazan series are known for originating directly from campaign notes.[22] In some cases, such as the work of Mitchell and Miéville, the influence is less pronounced (interestingly, the less obvious the influence, the more likely the literary recognition of the work). Finally, while the majority of tie-in novels related to *D&D* are popular only among fans of the game, some became successful beyond gaming circles. Weis and Hickman's best-selling *Dragonlance* novels are the most well-known example, but Salvatore's Icewind Dale trilogy also falls under this category.

From the foregoing selection of authors, it should be clear that the influence of *D&D* is not limited to the type of narratives mentioned in Appendix N. Instead it reflects the various functions that the game has had for different participants. As an example of the diverse ways in which *D&D* can shape the process, the literary fantasist and academic China Miéville has cited the intense systemization of the fantastic along with the inspiring bestiary as inspiration for his award-winning novels.[23] Junot Díaz, whose novels focus on the immigrant experience, refers to *D&D* as a "storytelling apprenticeship" in which he "learned a lot of important essentials about storytelling, about giving the reader enough room to play."[24] The fantasy author Elizabeth Moon created her heroes to counter the image of paladins popularized in *D&D*. Sharyn McCrumb and Jennifer Egan have used *D&D* itself as a plot point;[25] Ethan Gilsdorf has referred to *D&D*'s ability to ignite creativity and lead toward self-actualization[26] (as a matter of fact, kindling the imagination and encouraging storytelling skills comes up often in interviews and scholarship alike).[27] The variety of these statements suggests that the influence of *D&D* goes beyond familiar tropes. At this point, I would add that *D&D* has been connected by scholars to the development of empathy, a necessary trait for an author.[28] Others, like René Schallegger, have focused on the challenge of constructing a single narrative out of differing visions colliding during a session, resulting in the creation of life-enriching narratives. In other words, *D&D* (as well as TTRPGs in general) is very likely to benefit authors—and by benefiting them, it strengthens its influence on the work they produce on multiple levels, even if these authors do not produce works of speculative fiction.

For the authors who do produce speculative fiction, however, this influence can be quite pronounced, sometimes to the point of shaping their work. While some aspects of this influence, such as character archetypes, plot, and pacing, are readily apparent, others concerning sociopolitical and ideological issues (and the inevitable reactions to those) often go unnoticed. One reason is that some of these aspects were already present in pulp fiction. However, *D&D* ensured their perpetuation and, in many cases, either strengthened them or mutated them to a form suitable for play, which was then once again disseminated into fiction through the processes I have discussed. To further support the second part of my argument, it is now useful to examine some of these aspects, as well as the way in which they were used, negotiated, and in many cases subverted by authors.

SPELLING WITH DICE

I argue that shifts both subtle and sweeping concerning plot, world-building, pacing, characters, and magic systems in speculative fiction can be traced back to the technical aspects of role-playing storytelling. *D&D* narratives, especially in the early days of the game, focused on adventure, exploration, combat, and treasure seeking as done by a group traversing a pseudomedieval world. While these plots and storyworlds were already abundant in fantasy and sword-and-sorcery fiction, *D&D* appears to have had two effects on the genre: first, it set stories similar to its gaming experience as the fantasy "standard" through the process described earlier; and second, it introduced subtle shifts in the dominant plots and storyworlds. These shifts almost always built on preexisting pulp themes concerning exploration, adventure, and treasure seeking. However, in terms of plot, *D&D* introduced the concept of level progression, highlighted the importance of "loot," and entrenched the idea of a grand battle as the inevitable culmination of the adventure.[29] The combat-centric nature of the game and the random encounter tables used by a dungeon master (DM) to create a game narrative also began to make their appearance in the work of fiction authors, building on the episodic nature of pulp narratives. The concept of "classes" also prioritized protagonists who were less versatile and more focused on a specific skill.[30] Magic systems overall tended toward the quantified and systematized.

The effect of *D&D* on storyworlds and world-building might have been more pronounced. While *D&D* encourages homebrew settings and races, these should still facilitate the rules of the game. Thus the limit is not only the imagination of the *D&D* participants-turned-authors (despite persistent claims encountered in *D&D* game texts); as Rebecca Borgstrom suggested, "Each datum provided by a role-playing game is a trade-off between lost possibility—the stories you can no longer tell—and structure, which helps tell the stories that remain."[31] Thus stories originating in campaigns often shared a recognizable style of world-building. In terms of spatial elements, the often-generic cities of pseudomedieval campaign settings, whose inbuilt familiarity might have been useful game-wise, were repurposed in fiction and resulted in derivative and often limited imagery. In terms of nonhuman races, *D&D* solidified a specific image of elves, dwarves, and gnomes (largely taken from Tolkien but modified to fit the need of the game), not as mythical creatures but as another variant of humanity, essentially removing them from their mythic, wondrous origins and steering them toward quantifiable characters complete with almost inescapable stereotypes (for example, the elven archer, the dour dwarf, the biracial outsider). Notably, when transcribing their campaigns into fiction, many authors chose to add minor deviations from the standard *D&D* races, magic, and topography while still staying close to the spirit of the game. Noticing some of these connections, MacCallum-Stewart, Stenros, and Björk have gone as far as to term all TTRPG-inspired fiction as derivative.[32] However, marked exceptions do exist, particularly when considering the intricate homebrew campaign settings (often so decidedly different as to eventually evolve into new TTRPGs).[33] It follows that *D&D*-inspired fiction also has the potential to evolve beyond an imitation of the game's narratives.

These examples suggest that *D&D* as inspiration has a dual function. While it is commonly accepted among authors that the game does provide them with inspiration, storytelling skills, and motive, it is also likely to narrow down their creative choices, especially given the previous discourse on the often prescriptive power of narrative. Often, to transcend these limitations, the author has to have a clear understanding of how deeply *D&D* (and the works it influenced) has shaped their perception of fantasy narratives. Without this process, the game's elements are likely to transfer themselves into a player's works of fiction even if they do not serve a function within. This connection might suggest a possible reason why works that are not as directly influenced by *D&D* campaigns often gain more critical recognition, as this departure signifies increased awareness of the authorial process and thus a more mature work. Thus, rather than stigma, this suggests a possible alternate explanation for why less obviously influenced fantasy has typically received more literary recognition.

However, other aspects of *D&D*'s influence on literature would soon attract particular attention, becoming a point of cultural conflict and negotiation. In particular, transcribing *D&D* elements in fiction often resulted in the perpetuation of either problematic stereotypes or problematic omissions. Race, gender, and sexuality in particular are among the most strongly contested issues in this regard, and thus their influence on speculative fiction merits particular attention.

RECLAIMING SPECULATIVE NARRATIVES

In terms of race, *D&D*'s roots in wargaming, Tolkien's *The Lord of the Rings*, and early works of pulp fantasy, as well as the game's focus on specific demographics,[34] resulted in various instances of "fantasy racism." As Helen Young notes in *Fantasy and Race*,[35] the genre's problematic relation with race has a dual aspect: on one hand, classic and pulp fantasy has always been Eurocentric, and on the other hand, it places racial conflict at its core. *D&D* expanded on these qualities. Its standard storyworlds were amalgamations of Western cultures and historical periods. Though these storyworlds were expanded on in various supplements focusing on Asian- and African-inspired settings, by the developers' own admission,[36] the main purpose of these supplements was to provide opportunities for adventure, not to accurately represent these cultures—a fact that resulted in the conscious perpetuation of negative stereotypes. Most importantly, however, in *D&D* race is presented as character, with certain races (usually dark-skinned ones) being inherently evil or intellectually inferior, and mixed-race individuals depicted as perpetual outsiders. The combat-centric narratives presented the annihilation of such races as the culmination of the plot. Players' demographics suggest that the game did not attract the attention of nonwhite audiences until much later, and as such the issue remained uncontested. On the contrary, in terms of gender, the problematic depictions and stereotyping of women and the

normalization of sexual assault are well documented. Articles and letters to the editor appeared early on in the *Dungeon* and *Dragon* magazines,
suggesting the issue was widely discussed both among the developers
and within the *D&D* subculture. Finally, while *D&D* game texts specified that genders, human races, and sexualities were equal within their
storyworlds, the actual narratives differed.[37] The "symbolic annihilation"
of homosexuality and alternative lifestyles,[38] as well the perpetuation
of patriarchal structures in game narratives, was the norm. Given that
D&D's influence in other technical elements of speculative fiction writing
is apparent, it stands to reason that the game has also contributed to the
perpetuation of these elements as well.

However, while the regressive elements of *D&D* have been widely discussed, its contribution to the evolution of speculative fiction in terms of
social issues has been underestimated. The fact still remains that *D&D* did
introduce progressive elements—such as gender-equal societies, female
fantasy heroes, non-Western heroes, and heroes of color—early on, long
before these elements were commonplace in fiction. Thus, participating
in a *D&D* game did bring future authors into contact with storyworlds
where these elements were canonical, despite the limitations and negative stereotyping I have discussed. One possible reason for these progressive elements is the nature of the medium: being a game, *D&D* needed
to cater directly to women gamers or gamers who desired to experience
non-Western narratives, and designers were more flexible and attuned to
the needs of the market than authors who write purely to express themselves.[39] Moreover, by creating and directing their own characters, participants were allowed to challenge stereotypes and tropes in a manner that
a reader is not able to do. The fact that, unlike authors, participants are
not constrained by marketability concerns further encourages narrative
experimentation. This leads to a further observation: *D&D* brought many
participants into contact with diverse narratives, given its nature as a collaborative storytelling game, two qualities that ensured, in different yet
interrelated ways, that the game would soon become a platform for the
negotiation of the fantasy genre.

These negotiations are a core element of the *D&D* experience. While
preexisting genre narratives, rule sets, and the game text itself can be
highly prescriptive factors, during actual play of the game, participants

are still free to subvert or even overturn the expected narrative. In fact, a number of unique *D&D* qualities do encourage subversion and negotiation. Paradoxically, one of these factors can be located in the game's reliance on pulp, since genre and pulp narratives are open to subversion and change as well as being particularly sensitive to cultural shifts. Two more factors that make it likely that participants will negotiate *D&D* narratives are immersion and agency. During the game's flow, players are less likely to adhere to textbook narratives or even their own initial inspiration, instead making personal choices that make the subversion and transgression of tropes and stereotypes more likely than the authorial process does. This process is helped by the fact that the gaming table is a place where (ideally) one shares one's story with friends and thus is safe to experiment, and players have no commercial or editorial demands made on their narrative. Moreover, the collaborative nature of the game means that all players are exposed to one another's narrative choices, including subversive ones. The introduction of one character transgressing the usual tropes transforms the entire game narrative into a transgressive one and also introduces concepts that an author working alone and being inspired solely by popular culture may not have considered. One indication that this process does take place is that *D&D* tie-in novels, such as the Dragonlance series, did include diverse characters even though the game texts were still restricted to stereotypical concepts at that time.

In summary, the game by default invites the negotiation of genre tropes, and as such, it disseminates the result of said negotiations in fiction. Even as the fifth edition of the game focused on eliminating socially problematic elements, it can be said that this process began as soon as the first players joined each other at the gaming table—directly and indirectly challenging previously established tropes and narratives.

CONCLUSIONS

Given the recent inclusion of speculative narratives across media into the mainstream, and the increased popularity of *D&D* in particular, the game's multilevel influence on literature is being discussed openly for the first time. It appears that the reciprocative relationship between *D&D* and creative work, particularly speculative fiction, is key to understanding not only the current culture of the fantastic but, given the increased popularity of the genre, modern popular culture in general. Interestingly, the discourse on representation, visibility, and cultural hegemony that dominates discussions of speculative fiction today appears to have been previously negotiated within gaming groups. This resulted in the gradual evolution of the game away from its more problematic elements, and more in alignment with wider cultural shifts. As such, the game is found to have provided an influence not only in terms of world-building, plot, and character, but also as a platform for the negotiation of fantastic narratives. Further research into the connection between specific *D&D* participants-turned-authors is likely to further illuminate the process as well as assist writers and game designers alike in their work.

NOTES

1. John Joseph Adams and David Barr Kirtley, "Genre Snobbery Is a Bizarre Act of 'Self-Mutilation,'" *Wired*, December 9, 2016, https://www.wired.com/2015/11/geeks -guide-david-mitchell/.

2. *Speculative fiction* is the umbrella term encompassing all genres and subgenres of the fantastic.

3. Gary Gygax, *Dungeon Masters Guide* (Lake Geneva, WI: TSR, 1979), 224.

4. These authors are Poul Anderson, John Bellairs, Leigh Brackett, Fredric Brown, Edgar Rice Burroughs, Lin Carter, L. Sprague de Camp, August Derleth, Lord Dunsany, Philip José Farmer, Gardner Fox, Robert E. Howard, Sterling Lanier, Fritz Leiber, H. P. Lovecraft, A. Merritt, Michael Moorcock, Andre Norton, Andrew J. Offutt, Fletcher Pratt, Fred Saberhagen, Margaret St. Clair, J. R. R. Tolkien, Jack Vance, Stanley Weinbaum, Manly Wade Wellman, Jack Williamson, and Roger Zelazny.

5. By "pulp" we usually refer to literature that is mass produced and of low literary value; however, speculative pulp narratives differ to a degree. In the United States, speculative fiction was initially published almost exclusively in zines and periodicals, yet these cheap magazines hosted authors who would go on to be considered classics of the genre, including Jack Vance, Michael Moorcock, Ray Bradbury, and others. In the late fifties and early sixties, when respected British authors such as Tolkien, Dunsany, and Lewis became popular in the United States and perception of the genre shifted, many of these so-called pulp stories were anthologized and found their way to the bookstores. For this reason, the already precarious distinction between "pulp fiction" and "high art," which many popular culture scholars already resist, is even more blurred in the case of speculative fiction. Literary merit aside, though, Gygax's inspirations can safely be categorized as adventure fiction. Jon Peterson, in particular, points out that Gygax's literary sources were first and foremost works of popular fiction. As such, we must carefully distinguish these

works from ancient legends or classic fantasy literature. See Jon Peterson, *Playing at the World: A History of Simulating Wars, People and Fantastic Adventures, from Chess to Role-Playing Games* (San Diego: Unreason Press, 2012), 84.

6. While this particular quality of narrative has been discussed by scholars of various disciplines, Troy Leaman's concept of "stealth persuasion" touches on game narratives in particular and thus is of particular interest. Troy Leaman, "Playing for Change: Free Market and the Rise of Serious Tabletop Role-Playing Games," in *The Role-Playing Society: Essays on the Cultural Influence of RPGs*, ed. Andrew Byers and Francesco Crocco (Jefferson, NC: McFarland, 2001), 184–207.

7. Experience among players might vary; however, scholarship has recently established how deeply influential tabletop role-playing games (TTRPGs) can be for participants. For an in-depth discussion of this process, see Leaman, "Playing for Change," 188; Sarah Lynne Bowman's discussion of how character creation allows for an exploration of identity in Bowman, *The Functions of Role-Playing Games: How Participants Create Community, Solve Problems and Explore Identity* (Jefferson, NC: McFarland, 2010); and René Reinhold Schallegger, *The Postmodern Joy of Role-Playing Games: Agency, Ritual and Meaning in the Medium* (Jefferson, NC: McFarland, 2018).

8. Although *D&D* is a fantasy game, it has always borrowed heavily from horror and science fiction; quite importantly, players also borrow from these genres to build their characters. Daniel Mackay's theory concerning the use of "fictive blocks" that players combine in character creation further illuminates how the game has always been interconnected with various subgenres of the fantastic. Mackay, *A New Performing Art: The Fantasy Role-Playing Game* (Jefferson, NC: McFarland, 2001).

9. See Paul Cobley, *Narrative*, 2nd ed. (Routledge, 2014); Marie-Laure Ryan, *Narrative across Media: The Languages of Storytelling* (University of Nebraska Press, 2004); and Paul Ricoeur, "The Concept of Narrative Identity," *Philosophy Today* 35, no.1 (1991): 73–81.

10. At this point, it should be noted that while many creatives participated in, and were inspired by, games other than *D&D*, most of these games themselves were heavily influenced by *D&D*. Erik Mona accurately calls the game the lingua franca of role-players and points out that most people's understanding of what a TTRPG is comes from *D&D*. Mona, "From the Basement to the Basic Set: The Early Years of *Dungeons & Dragons*," in *Second Person: Role-Playing and Story in Games and Playable Media*, ed. Pat Harrigan and Noah Wardrip-Fruin (Cambridge, MA: MIT Press, 2007), 25. Moreover, as Shannon Appelcline showcases throughout his exhaustive historical treatise *Designers & Dragons*, many of the TTRPGs that followed were created as either an answer or a complement to *D&D*. To quote Appelcline: "Though players felt empowered to create their own variants of *D&D* (1974), *D&D* was nonetheless the standard that nearly everyone was playing. It was so ubiquitous that players were able to move their characters from campaign to campaign to convention and back—all without even thinking about which game folks might be playing. Campaign worlds might even interact. . . . Despite the existence of early alternate FRPGs like *Empire of the Petal Throne* (1975) and *Tunnels & Trolls* (1975), *D&D* remained the gold standard." Shannon Appelcline, *Designers & Dragons: A History of the Roleplaying*

Game Industry (Silver Spring, MD: Evil Hat Productions, 2013), 349. It is also notable that even when games such as White Wolf's *World of Darkness* actively attempted to distance themselves from *D&D*, they still ended up negotiating its various elements, thus further establishing the game as influential. *D&D*'s influence on TTRPGs, and thus on any TTRPG-inspired product, cannot be overestimated.

11. For an in-depth discussion on the fluidity of pulp narratives, see Clive Bloom, *Cult Fiction: Popular Reading and Pulp Theory* (Palgrave Macmillan, 1998); Scott McCracken, *Pulp: Reading Popular Fiction* (Manchester University Press, 1998).

12. The degree to which *D&D* creators welcomed these derivative works varied, depending on the game's ownership; however, the culture remained welcoming. Although the creators of *D&D* and Gygax in particular became stricter as the game became more successful, the subculture itself remained participatory.

13. Esther MacCallum-Stewart, Jaakko Stenros, and Staffan Björk, "The Impact of Role-Playing Games on Culture," in *Role-Playing Game Studies: Transmedia Foundations*, ed. José P. Zagal and Sebastian Deterding (New York: Routledge, 2018), 177.

14. MacCallum-Stewart, Stenros, and Björk, "Impact of Role-Playing Games," 178.

15. The actual experience of a session might, of course, differ, as players might choose to take an entirely different route, but the common structure of published *D&D* adventures follows this pattern.

16. Examples include but are not limited to the broad categorization of agile, resourceful heroes as "rogues," the specification of gold pieces as standard fantasy coinage, the quantification of magic and spells, the exclusive use of robes and flowy clothing for spellcasters, the obligatory animal companions of nature-loving heroes, the raging ability of barbarians (which overcame even Robert E. Howard's depiction of Conan as a cunning, cold-blooded character), the fantasy tavern/inn as a starting point for adventures, and so on.

17. MacCallum-Stewart, Stenros, and Björk, "Impact of Role-Playing Games," 172.

18. Brad King and John Borland, *Dungeons & Dreamers: A Story of How Computer Games Created a Global Community*, 2nd ed. (Pittsburgh: ETC Press, 2014).

19. Matt Barton, "The History of Computer Role-Playing Games Part 1: The Early Years (1980–1983)," Gamasutra.com (now Game Developer), February 23, 2007, accessed February 7, 2020, https://www.gamedeveloper.com/design/the-history-of -computer-role-playing-games-part-1-the-early-years-1980-1983-.

20. Examples of *D&D* game mechanics include the existence of classes, races with their own abilities and moral alignment, quantified spellcasting systems, and skills.

21. Keith Stuart, "'It's Cool Now': Why *Dungeons & Dragons* Is Casting Its Spell Again," *The Guardian*, November 29, 2019, https://www.theguardian.com/games /2019/nov/29/gamers-back-under-dungeons-and-dragons-spell.

22. Malazan began as a *D&D* campaign before migrating to the *Generic Universal RolePlaying System* (*GURPS*).

23. Joan Gordon, "Revelling in Genre: An Interview with China Miéville," *Science Fiction Studies* 30, no. 3 (November 1993).

24. Ethan Gilsdorf, "A Game as Literary Tutorial," *New York Times*, July 13, 2014, https://www.nytimes.com/2014/07/14/books/dungeons-dragons-has-influenced-a-generation-of-writers.html.

25. Sharyn McCrumb, *Bimbos of the Death Sun* (TSR/Ballantine, 1987); Jennifer Egan, *The Keep* (Alfred A. Knopf, 2006).

26. Gilsdorf, "A Game as Literary Tutorial."

27. See Eric Silver, Amanda McLoughlin, Brandon Grugle, and Michael Fische, "Why All Writers Should Play Dungeons & Dragons," *Electric Literature*, October 2017, https://electricliterature.com/why-all-writers-should-play-dungeons-dragons/.

28. See Andreas Lieberoth and Jonas Tier-Knudsen, "Psychological Effects of Fantasy Games on Their Players: A Discourse-Based Look at the Evidence," in *The Role-Playing Society: Essays on the Cultural Influence of RPGs*, ed. Andrew Byers and Francesco Crocco (Jefferson, NC: McFarland, 2001), 48, for a summary of research on the connection between empathy and RPGs, as well as Schallegger, *Postmodern Joy*, for a discussion of the empathy-developing process.

29. While battles were a staple of high fantasy (e.g., *The Lord of the Rings*), sword and sorcery was as likely to rely on cunning heroes escaping a dangerous situation or tricking their enemies. However, the combat-centric nature of *D&D*, which derived from wargaming, appears to have influenced fantasy toward one type of resolution over another.

30. Before *D&D*, Fritz Leiber's heroes Fafhrd and the Grey Mouser, as well as Robert E. Howard's Conan, are examples of thieves who were also skilled warriors; Michael Moorcock's Elric is a sorcerer who is skilled with a sword. However, *D&D* put forward the concept of adventurers who focus on a specific skill set instead. To draw examples from the work of authors who have openly admitted to *D&D*'s influence, Scott Lynch's Locke Lamora is a rogue, Raymond Feist's Pug is a wizard, Elizabeth Moon's Paks is a paladin, and Patrick Rothfuss's Kvothe is a bard (who, like *D&D*'s bards, can also cast spells).

31. Rebecca Borgstrom, "Structure and Meaning in Role-Playing Game Design," in *Second Person: Role-Playing and Story in Games and Playable Media*, ed. Pat Harrigan and Noah Wardrip-Fruin (Cambridge, MA: MIT Press, 2004), 58.

32. MacCallum-Stewart, Stenros, and Björk, "Impact of Role-Playing Games," 177–178.

33. Appelcline's *Designers & Dragons* showcases the influence of *D&D* on games that belong to different genres from fantasy, such as *Traveller* and *Call of Cthulhu*. This observation suggests not only that *D&D* can be influential across genres and media, but also that it remains an influence even through the elements that do not resonate with players.

34. The sociologist Gary Alan Fine's treatise *Shared Fantasy: Role-Playing Games as Social Worlds* (Chicago: University of Chicago Press, 1983) found that *D&D* was primarily played by middle-class white males. Interestingly, political orientation did not play a role.

35. Helen Young, *Race and Popular Fantasy Fiction* (New York: Routledge, 2016).

36. For reference, see Gary Gygax, David "Zeb" Cook, and François Marcela-Froideval, *Oriental Adventures* (TSR, 1985), on the cultural amalgamation of Asia, and *Dragon*, no. 189 (1993) for the reasoning behind the representations of fantasy Africa as "savage."

37. The lack of racism between humans was discussed in the first edition, while gender equality was mentioned in the third edition. Sexuality was not mentioned until the fifth edition.

38. Gaye Tuchman, "The Symbolic Annihilation of Women by the Mass Media," in *Hearth and Home: Images of Women in the Mass Media*, ed. Gaye Tuchman, A. K. Daniels, and J. Benet (New York: Oxford University Press, 1978), 3–38.

39. While one reason for this flexibility is the desire for increased sales, it should be noted that designers were in direct contact with the player base due to the open and often collaborative nature of TTRPG subculture.

12

CLASSROOMS AND DRAGONS: LEARNING FROM *DUNGEONS & DRAGONS*

Premeet Sidhu

Dungeons & Dragons (*D&D*) is great for learning because it doesn't feel like you're learning. There aren't any rigid goals or assessments—at least not in the way we expect. *D&D* prioritizes player satisfaction above all else. The game's flexible rule set, safe play environment, and reliance on imagination give players greater control over the game, allowing for more personalized and enjoyable play experiences. Unsurprisingly, this versatility aligns with contemporary teaching and learning practices that are becoming more "student centered" and motivated by the learners. Through its adaptable design, *D&D* encourages players to learn more about themselves and the worlds around them just by playing and engaging with the game. Although *D&D*'s impact on game design is a large part of its legacy that is well documented,[1] its contribution to learning deserves similar celebration in light of the game's fiftieth anniversary.

This chapter explores what players learn in *D&D* and how those skills and experiences can be used to stimulate deeper enjoyment of the game. Supported by existing research, this chapter also highlights the benefits and challenges of directly targeting or creating learning experiences for players. The first part of the chapter focuses on describing the most common skills that players acquire naturally throughout their play of *D&D*, such as (1) literacy, (2) reflection, and (3) social development. The second part looks at how *D&D* can be used for learning in both formal and informal environments, such as (1) educational, (2) clinical, and (3) leisurely play contexts. Together, these discussions offer ideas on how *D&D* play can be enhanced and improved by providing players with considered learning opportunities. By investigating the most popular possibilities for learning in *D&D*, I hope to demonstrate the game's innate connection to learning—which I argue is a significant part of its current legacy and projected future.

WHAT DO *D&D* PLAYERS LEARN?

Alongside their rise in popularity, games are increasingly being valued for their potential use as positive teaching and learning tools.[2] This has led to increased interest in, and creation of, "serious games," or games that have a primary purpose other than entertainment.[3] More recently, scholars have explored what commercial or nonserious games can teach us when we play them.[4] While it may not have been Dave Arneson or Gary Gygax's intention to create an educational game, learning in *D&D* occurs in both formal and informal play contexts. Throughout their play experiences, *D&D* players meaningfully develop and learn more about their literacy, reflection, and social skills, which can positively influence their overall enjoyment of the game.

LITERACY

One of the key skills *D&D* players learn is literacy. Being able to comprehend language expressions and communicate in diverse ways is a fundamental part of playing the game. In the past, literacy was usually defined as being able to read and write, which dominated many educational approaches toward teaching literacy.[5] More recently though, our understanding of literacy has changed. We now consider literacy to include a range of language comprehension abilities such as identifying, understanding, interpreting, creating, and communicating in various ways, both individually and socially.[6] *D&D* leverages literacy development as a way for players to enjoy and succeed inside the game.

Players can expand their literacy abilities in a variety of ways. In their gameplay sessions, and beyond them as well, dungeon masters (DMs) and players read lexically dense game handbooks filled with tables of rules and jargon.[7] They consume—and sometimes even create—written, visual, and oral forms of *D&D*-related content.[8] They also modify and modulate their spoken language and physical expressions during gameplay depending on their audience and the character they are role-playing.[9] Echoing Nicholas Mizer, "As players define and re-define a game world, they must take apart some of its pieces, make new sense of them, and then communicate the new state to one another by reassembling the words and images used to conjure the world."[10] All *D&D* players engage their literacy capabilities in some way. Not because they *have* to—to achieve some learning outcome or demonstrate their competence—but because they *want* to. It adds greater meaning and value to their experience of *D&D*.

D&D's player's handbooks (*PHBs*) have long identified the necessity of critical and creative thinking in the game. The first edition *Advanced Dungeons & Dragons* (*AD&D* 1e) *PHB* notes that "imagination, intelligence, problem solving ability, and memory are all continually exercised by participants in the game."[11] Published thirty-six years later, the fifth edition *PHB* shares the sentiment that "D&D is a game that teaches you to look for the clever solution, share the sudden idea that can overcome a problem, and push yourself to imagine what could be, rather than simply accept what is."[12] Even Gygax himself claimed that "after all, the game's major appeal is to those persons with unusually active imagination and . . . intellect."[13] Though the rules, players, and context of *D&D* play have transformed over the years, the need to critically analyze and creatively solve problems in the game has not.

The link between *D&D*, literacy, and related skills such as critical thinking and creativity has been explored by educational researchers and practitioners. During the game's formative years, educator and librarian Joy C. Kennedy observed that "the game involves such intensive reading . . . to gain the skills and knowledge necessary to play."[14] Since then, we have seen that *D&D*'s ingrained literacy development has translated into many players' abilities to create and communicate their own engaging stories, characters, and content across different media such as books, films, and podcasts.[15] Modern research validates *D&D*'s ability to facilitate key literacy skills such as reading, writing, and verbal communication.[16] Notably, Antero Garcia collected twenty-six months' worth of ethnographic data from leisurely *D&D* players and identified three different spaces where literacies were being developed and sustained: (1) at the table, (2) in the game, and (3) beyond the table.[17] Garcia found that nondigital games like *D&D* allowed players to "maintain important, fluid relations with the materials and spaces that cultivate play and gaming culture."[18] Essentially, the multiple literacy practices enacted by players across various spaces and times with different materials let them unlock deeper meanings from their play. Extending Garcia's exploration of literacy learning in leisurely games, academics and educators continue to outline how *D&D* can be directly embedded or used to inspire teaching practices and literacy activities in formal learning environments like primary, secondary, and tertiary education classrooms.[19] For example, in a yearlong ethnographic study of a third-grade math class, primary school teacher Alexandra Carter demonstrated that *D&D* could improve students' literacy and enthusiasm toward class content. Motivated by their interest in the game, Carter's students designed and played *D&D* games, which reinforced concepts they had already covered in class throughout the year. She found that the player-led design and cooperative play of *D&D* offered "a plethora of opportunities for students to grow as creative, critical thinkers," and she noted her students' improvement in these areas outside of the game.[20]

As evidenced by these examples, current research into literacy learning and *D&D* shows that relevant literacy skills developed through *D&D* play can transfer into real-life applications and contexts. *D&D*'s flexible rule set and imaginative setting inspire players to improve their multimodal literacies so that they can derive more enjoyment out of their *D&D* experiences in ways that are personalized to their preferred styles of play. *D&D*'s mostly nondigital play format, combined with players' consistent negotiation of time, material, and space, during and after the game, presents exciting opportunities for future literacy research—particularly in nondigital learning contexts.

REFLECTION

D&D also teaches players to reflect on actions and their consequences through role-play. Our current understanding of reflection in learning is informed by John Dewey. He argued that reflection was not just the act of passively recalling something. Instead, he defined it as a deliberate and active thought process that encouraged learners to question the motivations behind their actions and speculate on other possibilities.[21] Although one of the enduring critiques of Dewey's definition highlights the lack of time that learners usually have to achieve *active* reflection,[22] activities incorporating reflective practices are still widely used in formal learning settings and are understood to benefit both educators and learners. As *D&D* is "infinitely flexible"[23] and often requires a significant time investment from players, it offers numerous opportunities for both active and passive reflection.

Reflection in *D&D* is experienced through role-play. Despite the game's many variables, creating or embodying a character is a consistent part of all play experiences. *D&D* players and DMs will have skills, personalities, perspectives, and life experiences that can be similar to, or different from, the characters that they role-play.[24] However, these points of similarity and contention provide a strong starting point for players to consciously and unconsciously reflect on how they, their characters, and others around them perceive and navigate the world.

Although each edition of the game has changed over the years, they all share the similar sentiment that *D&D* offers "endless possibilities and a multitude of choices."[25] The game also intends to provide a safe space for players to reflect on these possibilities and choices. Throughout their adventures, players, DMs, and their characters will be confronted by a variety of creatures, objects, and situations that they must deal with in some way. Noted by Jessica Hammer, Alexandra To, Karen Schrier, Sarah Lynne Bowman, and Geoff Kaufman, RPGs like *D&D* give players "the opportunity to practice, take risks, and learn effectively without the distraction of potential disaster."[26] Regardless of the choices you make, the safe game space of *D&D* and extended time spent role-playing characters encourage players to continually reflect on their experiences and actions—often building greater awareness of their empathetic understanding, morality, and personal perspectives.

The influence of reflection on players' morality, ethics, and self-awareness has been covered in diverse interdisciplinary research. Mikko Meriläinen collected accounts from players that suggest that *D&D* increases self-awareness and empathy. He argued that the dynamic and interactive nature of *D&D* "enables the player to constantly reflect on both in-game and off-game happenings and adjust themselves in relation to the game world, the other characters and the other players."[27] This is supported by Samantha Clarke, Sylvester Arnab, Luca Morini, and Lauren Heywood's game-based learning research,[28] which also determined that *D&D*'s flexible game mechanics and interactive multimodal feedback supported greater self-reflection in players. Thomas Duus Henriksen observed that "game-design at its best manages to implement the learning objective into the game mechanics, thereby encouraging a reflection-in-action process,"[29] which is clearly present in *D&D*. Focusing on reflection as a means to learn other skills, Jennifer Cole Wright, Daniel E. Weissglass, and Vanessa Casey examined *D&D*'s impact on young adult moral reasoning. They conducted preliminary empirical research with tertiary education students that required participants to play through six *D&D* games with social and moral dilemmas and then reflect on their experiences and relationships in weekly online journals. They observed that the game's imaginative role-play structure served as an "engaging, interactive, 'moral training ground' that promotes positive moral development,"[30] and emphasized how the game gave players the ability to see beyond their own perspectives. This is backed up by Stéphane Daniau's work, which investigates the transformative potential of tabletop role-playing games (TTRPGs) and notes that reflection is a tradition of many role-players because it lets them "explore the meaning of their practice, whether through informal feedback or, occasionally, via elaborate considerations about theory and practice."[31] Diverging from this, academics have also discussed how players are beginning to reflect on specific content and experiences they encounter in *D&D* that are representative of similar real-world examples. For instance, Samantha Noll questions whether it is ethical for *D&D* characters to summon other creatures to do their bidding. She argues that even in the real world there is "a big difference between befriending animals and forcefully controlling animals in order to make them fight by your side."[32] Likewise, research has found that experiences with failure in *D&D* were generative of deeper in-game and out-of-game player reflections, suggesting that failure created moments of positive learning that were used to inform future play of the game.[33]

From the foregoing research, it is clear that learning to reflect is a vital part of the *D&D* play experience, which also affects the development of related skills such as moral reasoning, empathetic understanding, and awareness of perspective. As Malte Brinkmann asserts: "Valuable transformation [in learning] is characterized by reflection on experience, opening of experience, and a widening of experience."[34] Through continued roleplay and *D&D*'s malleable design, players and DMs participate in many experiences that give them the chance to continually reflect on and learn about themselves, the game, and the wider worlds around them.

SOCIAL DEVELOPMENT

Opportunities for social interaction are another key motivator for *D&D* play. A common goal of many education curriculums worldwide is for learners to develop and enhance their social skills. As a result of the COVID-19 pandemic, during which physical proximity to others has been limited, the importance and value of social interactions have risen.

Games have always been considered as inherently social activities,[35] but success and enjoyment in *D&D* rely heavily on the social interactions between players and their characters. *D&D*'s collaborative nature and flexibility enable positive social development in both digital and nondigital play contexts. For younger players, this means that *D&D* is a constructive place to practice basic social skills like eye contact and awareness of body language. However, as players grow older and become more experienced, the social development possibilities of *D&D* become more pronounced as players encounter complex social scenarios such as overcoming disagreements and learning how to navigate disruptive ideas, actions, and people.

The first edition *AD&D PHB* emphasizes that "there is nothing quite like a successful *D&D* campaign, and its success is based upon the efforts of all participants."[36] More recently, the fifth edition *PHB* equally stressed the importance of positive social interactions, stating that "playing *D&D* is an exercise in collaborative creation. Your collective creativity will build stories that you will tell again and again, ranging from the utterly absurd to the stuff of legend."[37] David Amor, developer of the digital multiplayer quiz game *Buzz!*, described how "game design isn't about creating a game that is strategically deep as much as it is about making sure that the game . . . creates interesting interaction between players."[38] *D&D* excels in giving players autonomy and control over their play experiences, but because of the collaborative nature of the game, players must learn to negotiate their actions, responses, and expectations in consideration of others. With the release of *D&D*'s adventure campaign *The Wild beyond the Witchlight* (2021)—which removed the requirement for combat in the game (i.e., you'll never have to roll for initiative again if you don't want to!)—it is evident that a central part of modern *D&D* play is the social interaction that happens between players and their characters.

Since the game's creation, there has been significant research into the social dimensions of *D&D* in both serious and leisurely play contexts. In his ethnographic study of *D&D* players during the early 1980s, Gary Alan Fine observed the social and collaborative practices of the game and discovered that players constructed shared meanings and values during their gameplay and role-play experiences.[39] He summarized that "fantasy [in *D&D*] is constrained by the social expectations of players and of their world,"[40] confirming that all *D&D* play requires some level social negotiation from players. Aubrie Adams clarifies that "it is not the mere act of role-play which satisfies [social] needs; rather, it is through the act of communication. Table-top fantasy RPGs are guided entirely by talk and interaction."[41] Although not every *D&D* game is played in a shared physical or social environment—the key alternative being online campaigns conducted through platforms such as Roll20, Tabletop Simulator, Fantasy Grounds, or Zoom—contemporary game studies research from Premeet Sidhu and Marcus Carter showed that pivotal gameplay experiences like death are heightened by the physical proximity and social realities that *D&D* players are required to share.[42] Broader research into RPGs also recognizes that players of games like *D&D* are exposed to imaginary social situations that allow them to practice their problem-solving abilities and increase their social confidence in safe and supportive environments.[43] Scholars have argued that imaginative games like *D&D* allow players to experience social interactions that go beyond their normal range of experiences, such as large-scale diplomatic solutions, missions of mercy, and economic transactions.[44] Throughout their natural play of *D&D*, players "use, reveal, or develop several soft skills, including strategies for conflict resolution, diplomacy, teamwork, leadership, relationships, debating/speaking skills, and spontaneous problem-solving."[45] Interestingly, research has also mentioned the potential for enacting transgressive social interactions within the game. In particular, Joseph P. Laycock has suggested that the flexibility and role-playing nature of *D&D* permit players to vent and explore antisocial impulses as well as exalted ideals.[46] However, as reiterated throughout this section, players are only able to explore actions or experiences that are also deemed appropriate by others at the table due to *D&D*'s inherent sociality and shared play experiences.

As conveyed in the considerable research and discourse available, social interactions in *D&D* are a core part of the game's appeal and educational value. In addition to the game's ability to facilitate personal expression and self-reflection, a large part of what drives player engagement toward *D&D* is the promise of social connection and formation of deep relationships.

LEARNING FROM *D&D* IN DIFFERENT PLAY ENVIRONMENTS

The wonderful thing about learning from *D&D* is that it can happen in both formal and leisurely games and contexts. While *D&D* has been used in classrooms and clinics for more "serious" educational purposes, players and DMs are also learning from *D&D* play in their casual games. This flexibility is what makes *D&D* really exciting for learning in the future. Having recognized the game's ability to improve players' literacy, reflection, and social skills, I have outlined some ways that *D&D* games can be used for learning purposes in educational, clinical, and leisurely play settings.

EDUCATIONAL CONTEXTS

D&D's adaptable design, minimal resource requirements, and group participation make it an ideal learning tool for classroom environments. Existing research and applications by educators show how *D&D* has been used to inform teaching pedagogies, deliver content, and create interesting learning experiences for students. In primary and elementary school environments, research has found that *D&D*-inspired activities—both digital and nondigital—can enhance the literacy, reflective, and social capabilities of learners in various subject areas.[47] *D&D* play has also been successfully integrated into secondary school classrooms, with scholars providing guidelines for educators on how to best incorporate the game to suit the learners' needs.[48] Here the game can be designed to introduce, consolidate, or reaffirm certain themes, content, or experiences that learners will encounter in different subject areas. For example, researchers have leaned into the game's literary nature, and much of its educational application has been in English classrooms—exploring key elements of required reading texts[49] or increasing learners' enjoyment and enthusiasm toward the subject.[50] In addition to this, educators have found practical success in using the game to address the social, emotional, and literacy needs of certain students.[51] When incorporated into tertiary education settings, *D&D* has inspired the "storytelling" teaching approaches of lecturers[52] and has sponsored positive moral development in young adult learners.[53] However, while *D&D*'s flexibility, sociality, and imaginative celebration make it an ideal and engaging activity for formalized learning environments, adapting *D&D* games to effectively target specific content and relevant learning outcomes is time-consuming and difficult for educators who are unfamiliar with the game.[54] To minimize this obstacle, it is important for educators who are considering using *D&D* in the classroom to question why they want to use it. Is the game being used to achieve an explicit learning outcome, or is it being used to inform broader teaching approaches? Is learner engagement the priority? What value do *D&D*-based activities have for the diverse learners in the classroom? If educators can pinpoint and clarify the reasoning behind their use of *D&D*, it becomes easier to design and adapt the game for their goal.

CLINICAL CONTEXTS

D&D has immense potential for clinical application because the game's embodied role-play, flexible design, and social play increase players' self-awareness and reflective skills, which can complement other existing clinical therapies and practices. Previous investigations found *D&D* to have benefited some players diagnosed with clinical depression,[55] social anxiety disorders,[56] and obsessional schizoid personalities.[57] In conjunction with other play therapies, *D&D* has also been seen to facilitate social development in some gifted children and adolescents.[58] The game's fantasy role-play structure allows players to work through motivations, feelings, and any underlying personal fantasies or urges "in a safe, dis-placed way."[59] This can particularly benefit individuals who struggle to open up or explore their behaviors in traditional clinical settings and therapy sessions. Through consistent play of the game, people are able to naturally develop reflection skills that help them recognize and clarify deeper similarities and differences between their character's motivations, feelings, and actions, and their own.

Elsewhere, contemporary not-for-profit organizations like Game to Grow and the Bodhana Group have also used *D&D* to support individuals in social therapeutic contexts.[60] The game has also recently been used for online group therapy and socialization during COVID-19.[61] In these group settings, individual players are able to work toward alleviating any underlying social anxieties and practice social skills such as active listening, eye contact, and understanding of body language through continued play of the game. However, as clinical settings are highly sensitive, and individuals have various needs and goals, *D&D* may not be the right supplementary activity for each individual. Research also indicates the reluctance of clinical professionals like social workers and therapists to use *D&D* as a therapeutic intervention or tool. However, this hesitation stems mainly from the practitioners' unfamiliarity with the game before application.[62] Even though the research surrounding the effectiveness of *D&D* for therapeutic applications is limited to mainly anecdotal evidence,[63] *D&D*'s future in this space is promising, as the research we do have supports empirical evidence found in the broader discipline of role-playing therapy, which has historically been successful in addressing outcomes for learning.

LEISURELY PLAY CONTEXTS

D&D does not have to be applied or experienced in "serious" contexts for players to have learning experiences through the game. But what do players learn about when they don't *have* to learn? As most *D&D* play occurs in leisurely environments rather than educational ones, it is important to reiterate that learning is inevitable while playing the game. However, as signposted heavily throughout this chapter, DMs and players in leisurely play settings can enhance their learning in *D&D* simply by creating and participating in opportunities for personal expression, self-reflection, and collaboration. Taking this idea one step further, players and DMs can challenge themselves to take in-game actions that they normally would not. The leisurely context of *D&D* allows players to experience and grapple with dark, uncomfortable, and transgressive play situations and concepts that may not be available for them to explore safely in the real world. Throughout their casual play of *D&D*, most players will at some point experience heightened emotions related to death, betrayal, or frustration. Players will inevitably regret decisions or comments they have made in-game and will be forced to deal with the consequences that affect not only them but other players in their group. *D&D* affords players the opportunity to challenge boundaries and transgress expectations (from both themselves and others) with minimal real-life harm.

CONCLUSION

Throughout its history, *D&D* has demonstrated how leisurely games can provide players with organic opportunities for learning. When Dave Arneson and Gary Gygax cocreated *D&D* in 1974, they designed a tabletop role-playing game that offered players greater agency and control over their play, which allowed for more personalized and enjoyable game experiences. The combination of *D&D*'s flexible design, safe play environment, and reliance on imagination has made it an ideal game for players to learn from.

Supported by relevant literature and research, this chapter has reviewed how learning in *D&D* is commonly experienced—identifying *what* players are learning from *D&D* and *where* this learning can be facilitated. Opportunities for players to improve their literacy, reflection, and social skills emerge naturally from playing the game. While these specific skills have been targeted in more formal learning environments such as classrooms or therapy clinics, they can just as easily be encountered in leisurely play. By leaning into and using the game's most popular experiences of learning related to literacy, reflection, and socializing, all DMs and players can incorporate more meaningful experiences of learning into their games. In addition to the game's clear design influence and broad sociocultural impacts, *D&D*'s educational legacy and future are promising.

NOTES

1. For example, Jon-Paul Dyson, "The Influence of Dungeons and Dragons on Video Games," Strong National Museum of Play, May 6, 2011, accessed December 7, 2021, https://www.museumofplay.org/2011/05/06/the-influence-of-dungeons-and -dragons-on-video-games/; Esther MacCallum-Stewart, Jaakko Stenros, and Staffan Björk, "The Impact of Role-Playing Games on Culture," in *Role-Playing Game Studies: Transmedia Foundations*, ed. José P. Zagal and Sebastian Deterding (Routledge, 2018), 172–187; Jon Peterson, *The Elusive Shift: How Role-Playing Games Forged Their Identity* (Cambridge, MA: MIT Press, 2020); Wizards of the Coast, *Player's Handbook* (5e) (Renton, WA: Wizards of the Coast, 2014).

2. For example, Jonathan Belman and Mary Flanagan, "Designing Games to Foster Empathy," *International Journal of Cognitive Technology* 15, no. 1 (2010): 5–15, accessed December 9, 2021, https://tiltfactor.org/wp-content/uploads2/cog-tech-si -g4g-article-1-belman-and-flanagan-designing-games-to-foster-empathy.pdf; James Paul Gee, *What Video Games Have to Teach Us about Learning and Literacy* (New York: Palgrave Macmillan, 2003); Jessica Hammer, Alexandra To, Karen Schrier, Sarah Lynne Bowman, and Geoff Kaufman, "Learning and Role-Playing Games," in *Role-Playing Game Studies: Transmedia Foundations*, ed. José P. Zagal and Sebastian Deterding (Routledge, 2018), 283–299; Jon McFarland, "Leveling Up for the Teacher-Practitioner," *Schools* 17, no. 1 (2020): 115–135, https://doi.org/10.1086/708359; Jane McGonigal, *Reality is Broken: Why Games Make Us Better and How They Can Change the World* (London: Jonathan Cape, 2011); Jonathan Ostenson, "Exploring the Boundaries of Narrative: Video Games in the English Classroom," *English Journal* 10, no. 6 (2013): 71–78, https://www.jstor.org/stable/24484129; Jan L. Plass, Richard E. Mayer, and Bruce D. Homer, *Handbook of Game-Based Learning* (Cambridge, MA: MIT Press, 2020); Kat Schrier, *We the Gamers: How Games Teach Ethics and Civics* (Oxford University Press, 2021); Kurt Squire, *Videogames and Leaning: Teaching Participatory Culture in the Digital Age* (New York: Teachers College Press, 2011).

3. Clark C. Abt, *Serious Games* (University Press of America, 1987).

4. Weimin Toh and Fei Victor Lim, "Using Video Games for Learning: Developing a Metalanguage for Digital Play," *Games and Culture* 16, no. 1 (2021): 583–610, https://doi.org/10.1177/1555412020921339.

5. For example, Brian Cambourne, *The Whole Story: Natural Learning and the Acquisition of Literacy in the Classroom* (Auckland: Ashton Scholastic, 1988); Susan R. Copeland and Elizabeth B. Keefe, *Effective Literacy Instruction for Students with Moderate or Severe Disabilities* (Baltimore, MD: Brookes Publishing, 2007); William S. Gray, *The Teaching of Reading and Writing: An International Survey* (Paris: UNESCO, 1956).

6. For example, United Nations Educational Scientific and Cultural Organization (UNESCO), "Literacy," UNESCO, 2021, accessed January 5, 2022, https://en.unesco .org/themes/literacy.

7. Joy C. Kennedy, "Dungeons and Dragons," *Journal of Reading* 25 no. 6 (1982): 596, www.jstor.org/stable/40029125.

8. Antero Garcia, "Gaming Literacies: Spatiality, Materiality, and Analog Learning in a Digital Age," *Reading Research Quarterly* 55, no. 1 (2020): 20–21, https://doi.org/10.1002/rrq.260.

9. Tomáš Košt'ál, "The Language of Dungeons & Dragons: A Corpus-Stylistic Analysis" (BA thesis, Charles University, 2021), http://hdl.handle.net/20.500.11956/157387.

10. Nicholas J. Mizer, *Tabletop Role-Playing Games and the Experience of Imagined Worlds* (Palgrave Macmillan, 2019), 3.

11. Gary Gygax, *Advanced Dungeons & Dragons Players Handbook* (Lake Geneva, WI: TSR Hobbies, 1978), 7.

12. Mike Mearls, "Preface," in *Player's Handbook* (5e), by Wizards of the Coast (Wizards of the Coast, 2014), 4.

13. Gygax, *Players Handbook*, 5.

14. Kennedy, "Dungeons and Dragons," 596.

15. Mearls, "Preface," 4; Hannah Reich, "What Dungeons and Dragons Can Teach Writers about Collaboration and Crafting Narrative, Characters and Worlds," ABC News, accessed December 10, 2021, https://www.abc.net.au/news/2021-01-31/dungeons-and-dragons-writing-games-narrative/13082620.

16. For example, Garcia, "Gaming Literacies"; Olivia Haslett, "It Crits Different: Analysis of Dungeons & Dragons and Tabletop Roleplaying Games as an Oral, Collaborative, and Immersive Genre of Literacy" (honors thesis, University of Tennessee, 2021), https://scholar.utc.edu/honors-theses/291; Stefanie L. B. Kaylor, "Dungeons and Dragons and Literacy: The Role Tabletop Role-Playing Games Can Play in Developing Teenagers' Literacy Skills and Reading Interests" (MA thesis, University of Northern Iowa, 2017), https://scholarworks.uni.edu/grp/215/; Csenge Virág Zalka, "Adventures in the Classroom: Creating Role-Playing Games Based on Traditional Stories for the High School Curriculum" (MA thesis, East Tennessee State University, 2012), https://dc.etsu.edu/etd/1469/.

17. Garcia, "Gaming Literacies," 16–21.

18. Garcia, 23.

19. For example, Lewis Morgan and Ian Turner, "Can Playing Table-Top Role-Play Games Help Children Learn?" *Primary Science* 170 (2021): 30–32, https://www.ase.org.uk/resources/primary-science/issue-170/can-playing-table-top-role-play-games-help-children-learn-morgan; Premeet Sidhu and Marcus Carter, "Exploring the Resurgence and Educative Potential of *Dungeons & Dragons*," *Scan: The Journal for Educators* 40, no. 6 (2021): 12–16, https://search.informit.org/doi/pdf/10.3316/informit.961535866968944; Michael Smith and Alayna Cole, "Teacher as Game Master: Using Tabletop Role-Playing Games in the Classroom," in *Proceedings of DiGRA Australia 2019* (February 12–13, 2019), https://digraa.org/wp-content/uploads/2019/01/DIGRAA_2019_paper_3.pdf; Marcelo M. Valença, "Disciplinary Dungeon Master," in *Pedagogical Journeys through World Politics*, ed. Jamie Frueh (London: Palgrave Macmillan, 2020), 209–218.

20. Alexandra Carter, "Using *Dungeons and Dragons* to Integrate Curricula in an Elementary Classroom," in *Serious Games and Edutainment Applications*, ed. Minhua Ma, Andreas Oikonomou, and Lakhmi C. Jain (London: Springer, 2011), 346, https://doi.org/10.1007/978-1-4471-2161-9_17.

21. John Dewey, *How We Think* (Boston, MA: D. C. Heath, 2010), 6.

22. For example, Samantha Clarke, Sylvester Arnab, Luca Morini, and Lauren Heywood, "Dungeons and Dragons as a Tool for Developing Student Self-Reflection Skills," in *Proceedings of the International Conference on Games and Learning Alliance*, ed. Manuel Gentile, Mario Allegra, and Heinrich Söbke (Springer, 2019), 102–103, https://doi.org/10.1007/978-3-030-11548-7_10; Neville Hatton and David Smith, "Reflection in Teacher Education: Towards Definition and Implementation," *Teaching and Teacher Education* 11, no. 1 (1995): 34, https://doi.org/10.1016/0742-051X(94)00012-U.

23. WotC, *Player's Handbook* (5e), 5.

24. Hammer et al., "Learning and Role-Playing," 289.

25. Wizards of the Coast, *Player's Handbook* (3.5e) (Renton, WA: Wizards of the Coast, 2003), 4.

26. Hammer et al., "Learning and Role-Playing," 293.

27. Mikko Meriläinen, "The Self-Perceived Effects of the Roleplaying Hobby on Personal Development: A Survey Report," *International Journal of Roleplaying* 3, no. 3 (2012): 53, https://doi.org/10.33063/ijrp.vi3.224.

28. Clarke et al., "Dungeons and Dragons as a Tool."

29. Thomas Duus Henriksen, "Games and Creativity Learning," in *Role, Play, Art: Collected Experiences of Role-Playing*, ed. Thorbiörn Fritzon and Tobias Wrigstad (Stockholm, 2006), 12, http://jeepen.org/kpbook/kp-book-2006.pdf.

30. Jennifer Cole Wright, Daniel E. Weissglass, and Vanessa Casey, "Imaginative Role-Playing as a Medium for Moral Development: Dungeons & Dragons Provides Moral Training," *Journal of Humanistic Psychology* 60, no. 1 (2020): 99, https://doi.org/10.1177/0022167816686263.

31. Stéphane Daniau, "The Transformative Potential of Role-Playing Games: From Play Skills to Human Skills," *Simulation and Gaming* 47, no. 4 (2016): 424, https://doi.org/10.1177/1046878116650765.

32. Samantha Noll, "By Friendship or Force: Is It Ethical to Summon Animals to Fight by Your Side in *Dungeons & Dragons?*" in *Dungeons & Dragons and Philosophy: Read and Gain Advantage on All Wisdom Checks*, ed. Christopher Robichaud (Wiley, 2014), 170, https://doi.org/10.1002/9781118921166.ch12.

33. Premeet Sidhu, Marcus Carter, and Jen Scott Curwood, "Unlearning in Games: Deconstructing Failure in *Dungeons & Dragons*," in *Proceedings of DiGRA Australia 2021* (February 9–10, 2021), https://digraa.org/wp-content/uploads/2021/02/DiGRAA2021_paper_17.pdf, 1–4.

34. Malte Brinkmann, "Repetition and Transformation in Learning," in *Transformative Learning Meets Bildung: An International Exchange*, ed. Anna Laros, Thomas Fuhr, and Edward W. Taylor (Rotterdam: Sense Publishers, 2017), 81.

35. For example, Juho Hamari and Lauri Keronen, "Why Do People Play Games? A Meta-Analysis," *International Journal of Information Management* 37, no. 3 (2017): 136, https://doi.org/10.1016/j.ijinfomgt.2017.01.006; Kirsi Pauliina Kallio, Frans Mäyrä, and Kirsikka Kaipainen, "At Least Nine Ways to Play: Approaching Gamer Mentalities," *Games and Culture* 6, no. 4 (2011): 327–353, https://doi.org/10.1177 /1555412010391089; Castulus Kolo and Timo Baur, "Living a Virtual Life: Social Dynamics of Online Gaming," *Game Studies* 4, no. 1 (2004): 1–31, http://www .gamestudies.org/0401/kolo/; Lotte Vermeulen and Jan Van Looy, "Happy Together? A Gender-Comparative Study into Social Practices in Digital Gaming," in *Multiplayer: The Social Aspects of Digital Gaming*, ed. Sonja Kröger and Thorsten Quandt (Routledge, 2013), 59–69; Nick Yee, "Motivations for Play in Online Games," *CyberPsychology & Behavior* 9, no. 6 (2006): 772–775.

36. Mike Carr, "Foreword," in *Advanced Dungeons & Dragons Players Handbook*, by Gary Gygax (Lake Geneva, WI: TSR, 1978), 2.

37. Mearls, "Preface," 4.

38. David Amor, quoted in Jesper Juul, *A Casual Revolution: Reinventing Video Games and Their Players* (Cambridge, MA: MIT Press, 2010), 121.

39. Gary Alan Fine, *Shared Fantasy: Role-Playing Games as Social Worlds* (Chicago: University of Chicago Press, 1983), 194–200.

40. Fine, *Shared Fantasy*, 3.

41. Aubrie S. Adams, "Needs Met through Role-Playing Games: A Fantasy Theme Analysis of *Dungeons & Dragons*," *Kaleidoscope: A Graduate Journal of Qualitative Communication Research* 12, no. 6 (2013): 72, https://opensiuc.lib.siu.edu/kaleidoscope /vol12/iss1/6.

42. Premeet Sidhu and Marcus Carter, "Pivotal Play: Rethinking Meaningful Play in Games through Death in *Dungeons & Dragons*," *Games and Culture* 16, no. 8 (2021): 1044–1064, https://doi.org/10.1177/15554120211005231.

43. For example, Matthew S. Abbott, Kimberly A. Strauss, and Allen F. Burnett, "Table-Top Role-Playing Games as a Therapeutic Intervention with Adults to Increase Social Connectedness," *Social Work with Groups* 45, no. 1 (2021): 16–31, https://doi.org/10.1080/01609513.2021.1932014; Sarah Lynne Bowman, "The Psychological Power of the Role-Playing Experience," *Journal of Interactive Drama* 2, no. 1 (2007): 1–15, http://www.interactivedramas.info/archive/IDJ_2_1_2007_01.pdf; Raul Gutierrez, "Therapy & Dragons: A Look into the Possible Applications of Table Top Role Playing Games in Therapy with Adolescents" (MA thesis, California State University, San Bernadino, 2017), https://scholarworks.lib.csusb.edu/etd/527.

44. Wright, Weissglass, and Casey, "D&D Provides Moral Training," 102; Daniau, "Play Skills to Human Skills," 437.

45. Daniau, "Play Skills to Human Skills," 427.

46. Joseph P. Laycock, *Dangerous Games: What the Moral Panic over Role-Playing Games Says about Play, Religion, and Imagined Worlds* (University of California Press, 2015).

47. For example, Carter, "Using Dungeons and Dragons"; Morgan and Turner, "Can Playing TTRPGs Help"; Rosalba Spotorno, Marco Picone, and Manuel Gentile,

"Designing an Online *Dungeons & Dragons* Experience for Primary School Children," in *Proceedings of the International Conference on Games and Learning Alliance*, ed. Iza Marfisi-Schottman et al. (Springer, 2020), 207–217.

48. Sidhu and Carter, "Exploring the Resurgence"; Smith and Cole, "Teacher as Game Master."

49. Kip Glazer, "Imagining a Constructionist Game-Based Pedagogical Model: Using Tabletop Role-Playing Game Creation to Enhance Literature Education in High School English Classes" (PhD diss., Pepperdine University, 2015), https://digitalcommons.pepperdine.edu/etd/641.

50. Jenna Abbott, "Implementing Elements of *Dungeons and Dragons* to Increase Students' Enjoyment and Interest in the Subject of English," in *Through the Looking Glass: Reflective Research in Post Compulsory Education*, vol. 15, ed. Angela Brzeski et al. (University of Central Lancashire, 2020), 9–16, https://teachereducation.uclan.ac.uk/wp-content/uploads/2020/07/2020Through-the-Looking-Glass_Vol-15.pdf #page=9; Zalka, "Adventures in the Classroom."

51. Caitlin Jones, "*Dungeons and Dragons* as a Literacy Event in the Classroom," *Idiom* 41, no. 2 (2005): 58–65, https://search.informit.org/doi/10.3316/aeipt.148793.

52. Marcelo M. Valença, "Disciplinary Dungeon Master," in *Pedagogical Journeys through World Politics*, ed. Jamie Frueh (London: Palgrave Macmillan, 2020), 209–218.

53. Wright, Weissglass, and Casey, "D&D Provides Moral Training."

54. For example, Abbott, "Implementing Elements of *D&D*."

55. John Hughes, "Therapy Is Fantasy: Roleplaying, Healing, and the Construction of Symbolic Order," paper presented at *Anthropology IV Honours: Medical Anthropology Seminar* (Australian National University, 1988), accessed April 4, 2022, http://www.rpgstudies.net/hughes/therapy_is_fantasy.html.

56. For example, Abbott, "TTRPGs as a Therapeutic Intervention"; Cecilia D'Anastasio, "Therapists Are Using Dungeons & Dragons to Get Kids to Open Up," *Kotaku*, May 2, 2017, accessed April 4, 2022, https://www.kotaku.com.au/2017/05/therapists-are-using-dungeons-dragons-to-get-kids-to-open-up/.

57. Wayne D. Blackmon, "Dungeons and Dragons: The Use of a Fantasy Game in the Psychotherapeutic Treatment of a Young Adult," *American Journal of Psychotherapy* 48, no. 4 (1994): 624–632, https://doi.org/10.1176/appi.psychotherapy.1994.48.4.624.

58. Julien G. Rosselet and Sarah D. Stauffer, "Using Group Role-Playing Games with Gifted Children and Adolescents: A Psychosocial Intervention Model," *International Journal of Play Therapy* 22, no. 4 (2013): 173–192, https://doi.org/10.1037/a0034557.

59. Blackmon, "Use of a Fantasy Game," 628.

60. Game to Grow, "About," Game to Grow, accessed April 4, 2022, https://gametogrow.org/about/; Bodhana Group, "Home," Bodhana Group, accessed April 4, 2022, https://www.thebodhanagroup.org/.

61. Per Eisenman and Ally Bernstein, "Bridging the Isolation: Online Dungeons and Dragons as Group Therapy during the COVID-19 Pandemic," Counseling Service

of Addison County, March 31, 2021, accessed April 4, 2022, https://www.csac-vt
.org/who_we_are/csac-blog.html/article/2021/03/31/bridging-the-isolation-online
-dungeons-and-dragons-as-group-therapy-during-the-covid-19-pandemic.

62. For example, Eric Lis, Carl Chiniara, Robert Biskin, and Richard Montoro, "Psychiatrists' Perceptions of Role-Playing Games," *Psychiatric Quarterly* 86, no. 3 (2015): 381–384, https://doi.org/10.1007/s11126-015-9339-5; Ben-Ezra Menachem et al., "Social Workers' Perceptions of the Association between Role Playing Games and Psychopathology," *Psychiatric Quarterly* 89, no. 1 (2018): 213–218, https://doi.org/10.1007/s11126-017-9526-7.

63. Sören Henrich and Rachel Worthington, "Let Your Clients Fight Dragons: A Rapid Evidence Assessment Regarding the Therapeutic Utility of 'Dungeons & Dragons,'" *Journal of Creativity in Mental Health* (2021): 1–19, https://doi.org/10.1080/15401383.2021.1987367.

13

AN ENSEMBLE OF (ROLE-)PLAYERS? EXPLORING THE INFLUENCE OF PERFORMANCE ON *DUNGEONS & DRAGONS*

David Harris and Josiah Lulham

DAVID: A few years ago, walking around PAX AUS, I saw on sale a book called *Improv for Gamers* by Karen Twelves (2018). The book boasted on its back cover that it could improve players' and game masters' ability to generate environments and create compelling drama as part of their role-play. By the end of the day, it had sold out. This piqued my interest: I had learned improvisation skills as part of my theater practice over a number of years, and on reflection, they had been an invaluable set of skills for the way I subsequently facilitated *Dungeons & Dragons* games. This caused me to wonder: To what degree does my art practice factor into the play of *D&D*? And how do other people's practices factor into their play?

JOSIAH: Meanwhile, a friend of mine in an improvisational theater ensemble began streaming the *D&D* games they were playing with the rest of their ensemble. The company improvises new Shakespeare plays and would, as part of their games, improvise new soliloquies or deliver monologues in iambic pentameter to gain advantage on rolls. After watching a few of these games, an additional question formed for us both: to what degree has *D&D* influenced theatrical and other performance arts?

Dungeons & Dragons (*D&D*) has a unique capacity to generate stories through the live interactions of those playing. Over the fifty years of *D&D*, both the game and the way it is played have changed, growing the game's and its players' capacity to tell complex stories in a multitude of forms—from spaces such as the humble kitchen table, to the international online streaming stage (see Esther MacCallum-Stewart, chap. 9, in this collection). The game has had a profound and far-reaching effect on digital game design, with digital role-playing games (RPGs) taking many cues from the systems that Gary Gygax and Dave Arneson designed. As Dimitra Nikolaidou demonstrates, D&D play has even influenced the written novel (see chap. 11 in this collection). The influence that interests us, however, is the symbiotic influences of performance practice on D&D, such as the evident embrace of theatrical improvisation techniques implied or explicit in various D&D handbooks; and the influence of D&D and role-play on theatrical performance practices, as illustrated in Josiah's anecdote above. There is an art to playing D&D—a performance art, as Daniel Mackay suggests[1]—and it is this relationship between theatrical performance practices and tabletop role-play that we explore in this chapter.

Evidence suggests that D&D, when developed, was not intended to be performative. Gary Gygax was initially skeptical of RPGs that placed performance and "storytelling" above the gameplay:

"Storytelling" games are not RPGs. Neither are "diceless" games.
An RPG creates a story, [it] does not follow a script. That's a play, possibly improv theater.[2]

Gygax held various skepticisms of those who participated in role-play using the system he coauthored. Although Gygax was critical of "thespianism" in his game, he was also as critical of the indolent play of "seek and destroy missions, vacuous effort where the participants fight and kill some monster so as to gain more power and thus be able to look for yet more potent opponents."[3] For our discussion, though, we explore the thespianism that Gygax was so wary of, observing how D&D today has become a framework not solely for the imaginative play of battles and combat, but, as Mackay observes, the basis for the performance of improvised characters and stories and the authoring of shared narratives.[4]

To investigate the influence of D&D on performance practice, we interviewed twelve artists—performers, musicians, actors, writers, and theater makers—all of whom play primarily D&D fifth edition (5e). We asked them about the parallels they saw between their arts practice and their tabletop role-play, and in writing about their experiences here, we take an emic approach to their descriptions of their play experiences.[5] In other words, understandings of *D&D* play are largely framed in the words of our interviewees and drive our analysis.

Interviewees told us about the groups they played with, drawing parallels between the ways in which they collaborate with other artists and the play they share with others around the table. Tables of players develop over time their own conventions of play, as Fine observes with his examples of *idioculture*—the development of a "small-scale culture."[6] These idiocultures, as described by our interviewees, emerged through a shared commitment to playfully collaborate on the stories they tell. This commitment was enabled by a trusting collaboration between players, not dissimilar to the shared practice developed by ensembles of improvising musicians and theater performers.[7]

At the outset, it is worth asking: how did *D&D*—designed by a person publicly dubious of the "thespianism" of its play—come to generate gameplay that is so performance-like? In the following section, we consider this question by exploring the feedback loop between the designers of *D&D* and the player communities that define the way the game is played.

"THESPIANISM" SANCTIONED AS A FORM OF ROLE-PLAY IN *D&D*

D&D play has always been a creative practice. Everyone around the table is taking part in the conjuring of a world, the performance of characters, and the authoring of a story.[8] Despite Gygax's resistance to "thespianism," some communities of *D&D* players were less interested in the numerical wargaming origins from which *D&D* emerged, and more enthusiastic about both performance and creativity with the narratives they were enacting—which may have influenced the design of subsequent editions of *D&D*. Fans who played these games, as Evan Torner has shown,[9] became avid theorists of role-play and tabletop role-play gaming and expressed their theories and ideas initially in a mix of commercial magazines and fanzines, followed by discussions hosted on internet forums such as the Forge. Here players innovated with their role-play and with *D&D*, creating their own campaigns, adapting or changing the game mechanics,[10] and theorizing modes of play that fostered a greater degree of Gygax's dreaded "thespianism."

As one of our interviewees, Tilly, speculates, it may well have been discussions on the Forge forums that inspired Wizards of the Coast (WotC) to include directives in their handbook derived from improvisation techniques as they iterated on the game with the release of new editions:

> D&D took a look at how the story game community [on the Forge] was structuring their design. Fourth edition has skill challenges, but no way of structuring narrative, it is simulationist. [The] narrative structure[s players use] is more "post-Forge community," you pick the story you want to tell and then find a system to play it. D&D usually has a mechanic and you fit your story to it. D&D took some of those mechanics [from the Forge]. For example, [the more recent game mechanic] "inspiration" is something they've used. [The mechanic of] advantages comes from that improvisation in OSR [the Old School Renaissance, which privileges "classic" tabletop role-playing gameplay], rather than the simulation.

In other words, while early D&D rule sets may have provided the initial framework for what Daniel Mackay would come to define as a "new performing art,"[11] it was a process of feedback between RPG subcultures and D&D's publishers that resulted in the inclusion of gameplay suggestions regarding more improvisatory and performative play. In other words, how players played influenced the designers of D&D's systems.

In turn, this has nourished the emergence of texts that support this improvisational play. Karen Twelves's Improv for Gamers (2018) is one of a growing number of resources for players to "better" their skills in improvisation.[12] Many of the activities included in Twelves's book are themselves adapted from improvisational theater techniques that aid in creating worlds, characters, and stories collaboratively.

As WotC has continued to iterate with D&D 5e, the game mechanics have substantially altered to enable further improvisation by players and dungeon masters (DMs) alike. In an overview of D&D 5e by the comedian and D&D podcast host Griffin McElroy for Polygon, he notes that fourth edition's procedural rules for combat, use of miniatures, and reliance on game maps made "theater of the mind" styles of play almost impossible. He goes on to suggest that 5e enables players to imagine a greater deal of actions for their characters and encourages a greater degree of creativity and improvisation from both the players and their DM: "It's less mechanical, and more theatrical."[13] As mentioned earlier, for the artists and role-players we interviewed, the most commonly played edition of the game is D&D 5e.

PERFORMANCE AND THE ART OF *D&D*

Having looked at the influences of player preferences for more performance-like role-play on iterations of *D&D*, and considered how these preferences fed into iterations of *D&D* that supported more performance-like role-play, we now look at some of the ways in which role-play and arts practice influence each other. What emerges in our interviews with theater makers and performance artists who play *D&D* is a kind of symbiotic relationship between their play and their art. As we have observed, newer editions of *D&D* have embraced improvisation techniques. However, what our interviewees illustrate is that role-playing and *D&D*'s systems have also influenced theater and performance.

Danni, a member of an ensemble of performers who improvise long-form theater shows, explained how the group played *D&D* online during the various COVID-19 lockdowns that occurred across the world in 2020. They role-played as a way of learning and practicing additional skills of storytelling and world-building for their stage performances. "Marcus [one of our ensemble members] got interested in DMing and started running games during lockdown; and it was a training tool—a performative language of how we *do* [our improvisational performance] was kind of embedded in that from the start." Danni explains that Marcus, their DM, adapted the game mechanics to create extra opportunities for improvisations that would affect the game world or determine the outcomes of player actions in the game: "If there is a good character moment, Marcus will give us an advantage roll, or there'll be moments written into the game that allow one of our characters to do a soliloquy instead of a roll for intimidation or charm or something."

Actors we spoke to explained the similar relationships they had to the characters they played in *D&D* and the characters they played onstage. Terry, a theater actor and director, observed that he is "not very role-play-ey" in his playing of character Flip, nor is he a writer of extensive backstories. Terry suggested instead that the way he discovers his characters during the play of *D&D* is not dissimilar to the way he discovers his characters in a stage play he might be rehearsing for: "[Flip's] choices, and . . . how I'm discovering him is how I like to discover when I'm performing. Yes, I have an understanding about wants and needs [of a character], but as a performer, I feel I investigate 'on the floor' [rehearsing and running a scene with other actors] in response to everyone [during rehearsal and performance]. I'm definitely exploring them [a character in a play and my character in *D&D*] both as I would as performer and player." In other words, for both the play of *D&D* and the exploratory work of the performance rehearsal space, similar techniques of "discovering" characters are being employed.

Other aspects of arts practice, our interviewees reflected, also made their way into their role-playing—and from role-playing into arts practice. Another actor, Adelaide, explained that a key preparation technique she uses for film acting arises from her practice as a *D&D* player:

The show I worked on recently, I got the script a few weeks prior, [and then] you arrive on set, and you sit there, you get an hour, and I journal the given circumstances [of the character I'm playing in the film]—where is the character, what are they doing, what [are they doing] prior to this moment?—leading into what they do . . . I think I got that way of working from *D&D*, because I was playing before I worked in film, and I started seeing parallels between private [acting] practice with a character [and my *D&D* characters].

Adelaide went on to observe how *D&D* play had helped her ability to access emotion on set, often by transposing the connections she feels with her role-played characters to those she is playing on film: "I think, funnily enough, being open to emotion has been a real—has been spearheaded by playing *D&D*. . . . Like, if this was my *D&D* character: how could I be as emotionally invested with this scripted character as my *D&D* character?"

This emotional investment in character could be coupled with gesture and expressed in the way players sit at the table. Kelly described that because she was not proficient at speaking with different accents, it was difficult to give voice to her characters. However, she tended to use her body to distinguish the character she was role-playing from herself: "I lean back, or I hunch over. . . . I know that, yeah, character voices are something really easy to make a character distinct. But I have a raspy, monotone voice . . . so I have to give them a bit more personality." For Jack, an occasional player and committed DM, this labor of "doing character" is always visible. He can always see players endeavoring, to some extent, to *act out* or *perform* their characters: "Even if they're not putting on those characters in the way we expect, they're still performing; you're watching them go through the intellectual process of being someone else." Tilly describes "being someone else"—their character—with the metaphor of *inhabiting* their character: "Inhabiting is feeling the catharsis of your character's suffering. . . . You feel what your character feels, and you actively seek out the embodying process." For Tilly, being a character during a *D&D* game is a kind of *pursuit* of bodily intensity or feeling by the player as they play their character.

Where Tilly describes her pursuit of an affective experience of character with a kind of single-mindedness, Jim—a performance artist who works in hospitals doing therapeutic clown work with children—reflects on the way in which his performance work and his *D&D* play both demand a kind of flickering between different mindsets:

You have these three brains operating in tandem all the time. You have the clown embodiment which seems to be in control; you have a writer's brain considering the arc of the story of the performance; and a director's brain that is considering the scene and its relation with everything else. I flicker between these. And this is like *D&D*: I have myself as the character, my attention to the character sheet, my [character's] capacities; and I have the dice and the other people at the table.

Much of this resonates with the work of scholars like Fine, Mackay, and Waskul,[14] who investigate the fluidity of personification around the *D&D* table with reference to Erving Goffman's frame analysis. Fine, summarizing Goffman's frame analysis, suggests that interactions between individuals are fundamentally bounded by specific framings that limit available relevant *meaning* for that interaction, and interacting individuals move fluidly between these frames: "Central to this approach is the assertion that human beings reside in finite worlds of meaning and that individuals are skilled in juggling these worlds."[15] Waskul develops these ideas with reference to the way in which a role-player's identity shifts between frames of interaction as they participate in role-playing, and names three different frames of identity: person, player, and persona.[16] Each frame corresponds to different modes of interaction during a session of role-playing: in the frame of *persona*, one is, as Fine puts it, enacting a "fantasy self" as one plays a character and focuses on the character's goals;[17] in the frame of *player*, one is viewing one's character through the mechanics and rules of the game being played and must know how to "manipulate a vast system . . . that specifies what a fantasy persona can and cannot do";[18] and, in the frame of *person*, one interacts with others as some everyday identity outside of the realms of play, as "students, employees, adolescents, adults."[19] In Kelly's, Adelaide's, and Tilly's reflections on *D&D* role-play, all of them flicker between descriptions of their play experience in both a *player* and a *persona* frame.

In Waskul's formulation, however, the motivation to adopt and role-play a *persona* seems to arise from the requirements of being a *player* as dictated by the rules of the game. What motivates Adelaide, Kelly, and Tilly to pursue their character's embodiments through how they speak, how they sit, and how they pursue the feeling of *inhabiting* their characters, however, does not necessarily arise from the requirements of the game's rules; rather, as Jim suggests with reference to the "other people at the table," it emerges from the environment collaboratively enacted by participants around the table. Where players are motivated to inhabit their characters by what Fine calls their *engrossment* in the playing of the game,[20] as a performer there is, perhaps, an autotelic motivation to perform for the other performers around the table, thereby creating an idioculture of inhabiting characters and performing them.

Such a closeness experienced between performer and character, between player and persona, however, requires collaboration around the table. A focus on collaboration is often eschewed by those analyzing and theorizing about what it is we are doing when adopting a persona or performing a character—many theorists tend to focus on individual experiences of character,[21] paying less attention to the environment that role-playing games cultivate. In our interviews with performers and artists about their *D&D* play, what emerges as a key similarity is that both performance spaces and role-play spaces are spaces for *collaborative playfulness*, and spaces that enable *something* to be accessed that people cannot access alone. When asked to reflect on the games that were their favorite, interviewees would refer both to the content of the stories created and to the sense of comfort and trust they had around the table. This trust was important, we were told, because it enabled people to practice what Danni called their "instinctual improvisation abilities"; DMs and players alike engaged in the improvised creation of environments and situations based on the interests of those present around the tabletop.

In her reflections on trust and risk in musical and theatrical improvisation, the flautist and scholar Ellen Waterman observes that improvisation is necessarily social and demands that every individual take a risk in trusting those they play and work with to be deeply attentive to one another, and to be responsive to the contexts being enacted by the improvising group.[22] One of our interviewees, Nathaniel, echoes this sentiment when he talked about the trust shared around the table he game-mastered for, noting the incremental growth in trust that players developed together as they journeyed through the world Nathaniel presented to them:

Wacky and wild and wonderful things happen without too much consequence. But I can trust the players—and they have taken things seriously. They can drop the mood [becoming more serious] when needed. . . .

I think role-playing for me seems like, with a group like this, seems like a rolling stone sort of thing, [it] gathers momentum. If everyone trusts a little bit, it becomes a little bit bigger, and then people can trust each other with more important things, which could be character objectives, or game objectives, or secrets, or items, I guess. I think that, yeah, it's like an exponential sort of thing.

As players become more trusting, they also become more comfortable to try things with their group that would be risky in other contexts. Victor Raymond and Gary Alan Fine observe that the play of *D&D* allows for performances of deviance because of the safe conditions established by the community around the table (see chap. 19 in this collection). In this case, deviance can refer to the inhabiting and performance of another character. Kelly explains that she is able to more comfortably explore and enact performative moments with her *D&D* group than elsewhere, and this, she reflects, has made her a better role-player:

Performing is always a stressful experience, especially to an audience. And it's a situation where you're vulnerable, and you're in a position where people can tell you you're doing it wrong. But in *D&D* when you're in a good group it's much more of a safer space that can push you outside your comfort zone. Like, you can try an accent, and it might sound really bad, but you can try new things and are supported to do things, and it feels safe. You can keep doing that until you can do things better.

As a *D&D* player, the "getting better" that Kelly refers to was echoed by a number of interviewees, most of whom spoke of one group of *D&D* players they shared a table with that had a commitment to "better" play, be that becoming "better" role-players or collaborating on "better" stories together. In each case, room to experiment and "get better" was enabled by a trusting collaboration with other players. It is worth noting that "better" is understood here from the perspective of the people we interviewed, as opposed to some universal standard of "better" play. For our players, "getting better" usually meant leaning into a performative style of gameplay, as Kelly refers to earlier: putting on accents or adopting body language that denoted your character was often framed as something that made one's role-play "better."

Trust and comfort in playing and improvising together can also allow for a greater "intensity" of experience when playing and storytelling together. "Intensity," a word that often arose for our interviewees, might describe two things: the degree of attention players give to the game and its play, akin perhaps to "immersion as absorption" identified by Gordon Calleja;[23] and the affective experience of this play—referring to an intensity that manifests autonomically in the body before being qualified in language as a feeling.[24] Claudia described this intensity of role-play as a result of *being in the zone*: "The zone is being super focused on the story, really being in character and making decisions in character." This resembles what Keith Sawyer might describe as *group flow*. Sawyer distinguishes *group flow* from Mihaly Csikszentmihalyi's *flow states*, the latter being defined as an "individual's psychological experience."[25] For Sawyer, there is also the *flow* of playing together—whether playing music in an ensemble, improvising theater, or the seamless teamwork experienced by sports teams.[26] Similarly, the play theorist Bernie De Koven, with reference to Csikszentmihalyi, formulates group states of flow as *CoLiberation*—a state of flow available only among collaborators, a *special something* that can only be produced by the collaboration among a whole group: "CoLiberation is what happens when we work extraordinarily well together. Like on a basketball team or in an orchestra, when we actually experience ourselves sharing in something bigger than any one who is present."[27] For those we spoke to, these states—whether *group flow* or *CoLiberation*—became increasingly available to players the longer they played together, as they learned over time the kind of role-play and storytelling they wanted to engage in.

Thinking with De Koven, we might call each table of players a *play community*: a group of people who iteratively establish, through negotiation, discussion, compromise, and inspired suggestion, the conventions of their play.[28] We adopt the term *play community* here because De Koven is interested in the *phenomenological experience of play*. Where Fine's "idioculture" is concerned with the sociological bounds of *D&D* play, it cannot account for the *feeling* of playing and performing together, the frisson of inhabiting one's character and performing for friends around the table—play as CoLiberation. As role-players spend time together, they learn more about the kind of play they want to share in and tend toward a unique understanding of their collaborative play; "getting better," as Kelly put it, at this play over time. This leads to increasingly satisfying play experiences that are felt by those participating, as well as the adaptation of one's own gameplay to fit in with the group. As Jim observes of his playing with one group for approximately eight years, one starts to "embody" the expectations, norms, and play conventions enacted by those around the table over time. He draws a parallel between this and his therapeutic clown work with children in hospitals, which he tells us is responsive to both the audience and his collaborators:

What I really think audiences, no matter their age, need to experience is joy. As well as intensity. And I feel quite comfortable being able to be an option or a vehicle for delivering joy—and that for me is synonymous with play—especially as a clown. My video editing, my puppetry; it's all about play. And that involves things like identifying the game, consent to play, and messing with the rules. . . . I think play is . . . it's yourself or a group of people . . . I think it's an understanding of rules; or there's an idea of rules, and it's about finding joy through that. . . . Clowning is all about giving and taking offers. . . . [For me] it's taking the fool or the clown archetype into *D&D*, and it's been really joyful doing that. And hopefully causing joy for others at the table in our stories too.

What Jim illustrates here is that the way he plays *D&D* with this play community is not dissimilar to the way he improvises responsively to audiences and his clown collaborators when performing. In other words, *playfulness* becomes integral to both Jim's role-play and Jim's art practice. In both instances, we might say that Jim is making art—or, at the least, adopting a similar "imaginary" for both his role-play and performance improvisation practices. This resonates with a reflection of De Koven as he describes how he sees games: "I think of games as social fictions, performances, like works of art, which exist only as long as they are continuously created."[29]

Importantly, though, Jim is not making art alone. He follows his own playfulness while responding to the play of the group—both the group of clowns he works with, and the group of role-players he plays with. In

Chris's case, one of the *D&D* groups with which he plays regularly formed after their involvement in an immersive theater performance ensemble. Many of the play conventions of this group were, Chris suggests, indirectly informed by the group's shared history as a performance ensemble:

We [my *D&D* group] [have] all done immersive theater. In immersion there's less opportunity to *star*. The audience is never in one place [roaming around the immersive performance venue], you're often performing one-on-one or [to] a small group. You have to do your part, even though not everyone [in the audience] will see it. Also, they [my *D&D* group] [have] all played *D&D* a lot. I think they've moved past the point of wanting [their role-play] to be a solo show. Perhaps being dedicated to a character and *relationships* is more interesting.

In other words, Chris's performance ensemble became, perhaps, a kind of role-play ensemble, less interested in what each individual role-player could make, and more interested in what they could create together. For Chris, this collaborative ensemble of both immersive theater performers and *D&D* role-players is similar because of "the fact that they both achieve or like, um, nourish the same part of me." Such nourishment, for Chris, is only achievable as part of a group collaborating together, becoming what De Koven calls a "play community"[30]—or, as we invite you to consider it, a play ensemble.

A PLAYFUL ENSEMBLE

As we have illustrated, many similarities exist in the ways that artists orient themselves toward their practice and the ways that role-players orient themselves toward their play. Over time, they form tight-knit communities of collaborators, who share in the nourishing playfulness of performing characters and worlds with and for the others around them. *D&D*, then, is not only an example of a performance art medium, as Mackay and others have argued;[31] it is an example of a collaborative art form that can only be enacted by an ensemble of players. In theatrical terms, the ensemble is a wholly unique thing, an "exceptional . . . *melos*, the underlying sense of the whole. More extraordinary, even, than the individual performances or . . . the characters . . . [it is a] profound awareness of everything . . . going on within the group."[32]

As *D&D* has iterated across multiple editions, its rule sets have supported more performance-like play, partially in response to the preferences

of players also iterating on these systems. These games of role-play performance in turn influence performance practices in play, and vice versa. As
Terry suggests, the way that actors work with one another "on the floor"
can feed into how they work with one another at the D&D table. Viewing
D&D as a collaborative performance conducted by an ensemble of role-
players across months or years of play sessions invites us to reconsider the
place of D&D. We are not just role-players, but virtuosos of a performance
art for a small audience of friends. In other words, no matter how we play,
as role-players we find ourselves in a lineage of performance, creativity, and
art. We, the players, are artists.

NOTES

1. Daniel Mackay, *The Fantasy Role-Playing Game: A New Performing Art* (Jefferson, NC: McFarland, 2001).

2. Gary Gygax, "Q&A with Gary Gygax," EN World, December 16, 2003, accessed August 5, 2021, https://www.enworld.org/threads/q-a-with-gary-gygax.22566/page -87#post-1272407.

3. Gary Gygax, quoted in Harvey Smith, "The Dungeon Master: An Interview with Gary Gygax," Witchboy.net, n.d., accessed August 15, 2021, http://www.witchboy .net/articles/the-dungeon-master-an-interview-with-gary-gygax/.

4. Mackay, *New Performing Art*.

5. See Thomas Hylland Eriksen, *What Is Anthropology?*, 2nd ed. (London: Pluto Press, 2017), 56–57.

6. Gary Alan Fine, *Shared Fantasy: Role-Playing Games as Social Worlds* (Chicago: University of Chicago Press, 1983), 136–137.

7. See Ellen Waterman, "Improvised Trust: Opening Statements," in *The Improvisation Studies Reader: Spontaneous Acts*, ed. R. Caines and A. Heble (New York: Routledge, 2015).

8. Mackay, *New Performing Art*.

9. Evan Torner, "RPG Theorising by Designers and Players," in *Role-Playing Game Studies: Transmedia Foundations*, ed. José P. Zagal and Sebastian Deterding (New York: Routledge, 2018).

10. Torner, "RPG Theorising," 197–198.

11. Mackay, *New Performing Art*.

12. Karen Twelves, *Improv for Gamers* (Evil Hat Productions, 2018); see also Graham Walmsley, *Play Unsafe: How Improvisation Can Change the Way You Roleplay* (Scotts Valley, CA: CreateSpace Independent Publishing Platform, 2009); Martin Ralya, *Unframed: The Art of Improvisation for Game Masters* (Seattle, WA: Engine Publishing, 2014).

13. Griffin McElroy, "Here's How *Dungeons & Dragons* Is Changing for Its New Edition," Polygon, July 9, 2014, https://www.polygon.com/2014/7/9/5882143/roll-for-initiative-understanding-the-next-edition-of-dungeons-dragons.

14. Fine, *Shared Fantasy*; Mackay, *New Performing Art*; Dennis D. Waskul, "The Role-Playing Game and the Game of Role-Playing: Ludic Self and Everyday Life," in *Gaming as Culture: Essays on Reality, Identity and Experience in Fantasy Games*, ed. J. P. Williams, S. Q. Hendricks, and W. K. Winkler (Jefferson, NC: McFarland, 2006).

15. Fine, *Shared Fantasy*, 181.

16. Waskul, "Role-Playing Game."

17. Fine, *Shared Fantasy*, 4, in Waskul, "Role-Playing Game," 21.

18. Waskul, "Role-Playing Game," 21.

19. Waskul, 21.

20. Fine, *Shared Fantasy*, 196.

21. See Sarah Lynne Bowman, *The Functions of Role-Playing Games: How Participants Create Community, Solve Problems and Explore Identity* (Jefferson, NC: McFarland, 2010); Sarah Lynne Bowman and Andreas Lieberoth, "Psychology and Role-Playing Games," in *Role-Playing Game Studies: Transmedia Foundations*, ed. José P. Zagal and Sebastian Deterding (Routledge, 2018).

22. Waterman, "Improvised Trust."

23. Gordon Calleja, *In-Game: From Immersion to Incorporation* (Cambridge, MA: MIT Press, 2011).

24. Brian Massumi, *Parables for the Virtual: Movement, Affect, Sensation* (Durham, NH: Duke University Press, 2002), 24.

25. Mihaly Csikszentmihalyi, *Flow: The Psychology of Optimal Experience* (New York: HarperCollins, 1990).

26. Keith Sawyer, "Group Creativity: Musical Performance and Collaboration," in *The Improvisation Studies Reader: Spontaneous Acts*, ed. R. Caines and A. Heble (New York: Routledge, 2015).

27. Bernard De Koven, "CoLiberation," DeepFun, 1992, accessed December 8, 2021, https://www.deepfun.com/colib.htm.

28. Bernard De Koven, *The Well-Played Game: A Player's Philosophy* (1978; Cambridge, MA: MIT Press, 2013).

29. De Koven, *The Well-Played Game*, xiii.

30. De Koven.

31. Mackay, *New Performing Art*; see Sarah Hoover et al., "Performance Studies and Role Playing Games," in *Role-Playing Game Studies: Transmedia Foundations*, ed. José P. Zagal and Sebastian Deterding (New York: Routledge, 2018).

32. Simon Callow, "Introduction," in *Dodin and the Maly Drama Theatre: Process to Performance*, ed. M. Shevtsova (London: Routledge, 2004), xi.

14

FORGING FAMILY THROUGH QUEER *DUNGEONS & DRAGONS*

Jay Malouf-Grice

FINDING FAMILY

Late in 2017, I was at a *Game of Thrones* (*GOT*) viewing night in Sydney's (Australia) inner-west. At the time *GOT* was immensely popular and the object of equal parts appreciation and ridicule (with far more of the latter toward the conclusion of the show). Max, a white, queer, nonbinary person and close childhood friend of mine, had invited me to the showing at their share house full of fellow queer nerds. *Nerd* is a reclaimed insult turned into a term of endearment. The term conveyed a recognition of one's status as someone who actively and enthusiastically engages in activities deemed frivolous, childish, boring, or useless by the rest of society. Before the heckling of *GOT* began, Max introduced me to our Dungeon-Mum-to-be, Emory, who was also plonked down on the floor in Max's crowded lounge room. At this time, Emory identified as a bisexual woman and "big-time nerd."

Emory worked full-time in retail and balanced a weekly online *Dungeons & Dragons* (*D&D*) campaign and daily text-based role-playing with her partner at the time, who lived in the United States. She was looking for a particular group of people who would fulfill her requirements for her kind of role-play-focused style of play. A few days after this, Emory added Max, my partner El, me, and someone I had never met before named

Cerys, to a Facebook Messenger group chat. Cerys was one of Emory's coworkers and took on acting and directing jobs at this time. Over the next few days, the chat filled up with people's character descriptions.

My character is Romeo Squish, a frog-like humanoid from a marshland far away. I . . . worship the phases and tides of the moon. At the moment I'm looking at being a Druid . . . oh, also. I always wear a big floppy overcoat and a huuuuge blue-mage-esque floppy hat. They have the dual purpose of concealing my iden-tity and, as they are kept wet, they keep my fragile skin moist.

This is an excerpt taken from the chat thread, posted by Max, who would play Romeo, and quoted verbatim. Max's character introduction began the process of collaborative world-building, as Romeo was firmly anchored in this imagined world, with his moon worshipping and need for moisture. Max also drew on references, for example, "blue-mage-esque hat," which referenced the Blue Mage in *Final Fantasy*, which contained wizards with hats so large they obscured all their face. This description drew on the assemblage of play,[1] with its assortment of references and heavy use of imagery that tied the character to a world we did not know of yet—a world typed and talked into being.[2]

In Max's small introduction, they achieve "narrative truth" through "verisimilitude," or the appearance of truth, rather than "verifiability."[3] The insertion of the detail about Romeo's moisture requirements and physicality evoked a reality that could very easily be real. However, the sensorial imagery in this introduction was also employed to encourage other group members to commit to the fantasy. I chose to view *D&D* as just as much about offer and acceptance as it was about world-building. This was my first time introducing a character, so I followed suit and described my monk Cereza as "a leatherworker and trader of certain ser-vices at her mobile caravan business, 'Below the Belt.'" She was a leath-erworker by day and a sex worker by night; I hoped the synergy between these occupations would not go unappreciated. El sent his description next: "A stranger approaches with blue skin and strange markings, he is very pretty, very flamboyant and has a certain air about him, literally he's made of air, he's a genasi." A genasi is a humanoid that is descended from genies; genasi often have elemental affinities, and Enki's was air. Max had established a lighthearted tone but also made offers to continue build-ing the world through character description that was taken up by others in an effort to use the virtual space of the chat to start the creation of a world-building "generic space."[4]

Before long, we had our sixth member, Jace. He was Cerys's partner (now fiancé) at the time and had never played *D&D* before. When he was invited into the chat, we greeted him, and he responded with "Woo! Go team! Wait are we a team? I'm not sure. I've never played this before." Emory answered immediately, "Yes, we are a team!" A few moments passed before Emory followed up with "Well, you are all a team. I'm everything else." Not knowing when the role-play would traditionally begin, but wanting to test the limits, I framed my next response as if it was coming from my character by indicating it with quotations and my character's name, "Cereza: 'For now, love.'" Max followed suit and commented "Romeo: Not quite," in response to the idea that we were already a team. Emory answered us both with "Shhhh you're a team" and then said:

I will put you through terrifying trials and forge you into a ✳family✳

I included the use of the starry emojis around the word "family" because they are an important indicator of nuance. Marcel Danesi, in their study of emojis, suggested that emoji use is primarily "adjunctive," meaning that they are usually there to add additional meaning, rather than replace other forms of communication.[5] In a structural semantic analysis of emoji use, one must consider the "nuances" emojis lend to communication, while also considering the emojis' relationship to the ways the message is "constructed, framed, and presented."[6] Emory was both emphasizing the importance of the concept of family and distancing this particular usage of that concept from the standard notion of a family. The placement of the sparkle emojis around the word required a specific and conscious typing action. It demarcated "family" from the rest of the sentence to elevate its importance and also to highlight this particular usage of "family" as a concept to be sought after, a fitting reward to "terrifying trials."

Here Emory was drawing on the trope of the family of misfits who *earn* their familial status, as opposed to receiving it through birth or blood. This idea of family was rooted in her experiences listening to *D&D* podcasts and absorbing media about parties of unrelated people who accomplish great deeds together. These stories involved often dysfunctional but fiercely loyal groups of friends who lived in a fantasy world full of trials, who would do anything to help each other through them. Richard Page outlined the potential of games to become a "crucible" for the kind of selfhood people wanted to create.[7] *D&D* is also a crucible, a rite of passage deployed by Emory, that bonded the player characters in-game and the players outside of the game. Emory brought the "primary frame" and the "third frame" together in a conscious effort to set the foundations for group cohesion, even before we had met one another in person.[8] The primary frame is the world outside of the game, and the third frame is the shared fantasy, and by bridging this binary of the actual world and the virtual fantasy, Emory was channeling the uniting power she believed that *D&D* possessed.

This chapter will bring the concept of "fictive kinship" into a dialogue with *D&D* and, like Nelson, argue for the concept's continued relevance for urban social groups.[9] The *"D&D* family" was an emerging concept in the field, but the term has its roots in a long history of fictive kinship and forging bonds through sharing playable fantasies.[10] The fresh wave of work on *D&D* that heralds its capacity for queer utopias covers the innovative ideas of queer players in-game.[11] This chapter seeks to build on this work while also drawing attention to the *D&D* "way of thinking" that players deploy to reimagine their everyday relationships and lifeworlds.[12] It was adapted from my thesis, which explored the everyday impacts of *D&D* and video games in certain subsections of Sydney's queer communities. Through participant observation in both the virtual worlds cocreated in *D&D* and the virtual worlds coinhabited in video games, I saw how *D&D* offered an enticing tangible alternative to digital gaming,[13] an alternative for queers who did not see mainstream digital gaming worlds, or the spaces they generated, as applicable to their lives. I concluded that the flourishing of *D&D* in Sydney's queer communities was indeed partly about the experimentation, identity formation, and validation it encouraged.[14] *D&D's* popularity among my participants was also partially about resisting dominant narratives about fantasy being seen as a cis-hetero space.[15] But for the community I was researching, the specific type of role-playing that *D&D* encouraged developed a *D&D* way of thinking that shaped social lives, careers, kinship ties, and even how the players perceived Sydney itself.[16]

THE ROLE-PLAY SPACE

Max replied to Emory's prophetic statement about forging family with "RS: when *cough sniffle snort* when the tide is right." RS was Max's abbreviation for their character's full name, Romeo Squish. This comment received laugh reacts from everyone, in the form of laughter-face emojis. The text between the asterisks is the action performed by the character, in this case, Romeo was imagined as spluttering like a frog in the delivery of this line. Emory responded to this thread with "😭😭 you nerds are already RPing [role-playing] I love you so much." The placement of the crying faces, in this context, indicated uncontainable joy. Max responded to this with "Dungeon Master. More like Dungeon mum." "Dungeon Mum" stuck and became this group's version of a dungeon master, as it combined the tropes of an all-knowing world-maker with the conventions of the "mum-friend." A "mum-friend" is a social category that originated on Tumblr as a term for the friend who behaves in a way that can be interpreted as "motherly" to their other friends.

Emory, hereafter called Dungeon Mum, employed the reclaimed usage of "nerds" to bring the group together under a single expression of queerness. Nerdiness and queerness were undergoing a symbiotic popular renaissance at this time, which is even more present in popular media today.[17] Leigh Fine, who documented this phenomenon, wrote from a US context, so the interpretation of nerdy behavior and its queerness is somewhat different in the context of Australia. Australia's sport-obsessed culture provided a hegemonic counterpoint against which the idea of a nerd is constructed.[18] This surfaces earlier in the subtext of Jace's comment about being a team, which was accepted and then reformulated with the emotively weightier word "family." Fine's observation that nerdiness and queerness are never associated with societal success is a formative stereotype for the practical uniting of queerness and nerdiness.[19] The group's collective commitment to role-play, and Dungeon Mum's framing of this behavior as familial, began the process of generating a safe space for these kinds of alternative familial bonds to form. The assemblage of play, or the various references that frame the game, can be traced back to this small chat window, which would be continually referenced during in-person gatherings to grant those spaces this virtual quality.[20] This chat was an online generic space that fostered a united "queer sensibility"[21] that was less about being LGBTQIA+ and more about being a nerdy adult whose idea of a good time is pretending to be a bard or a frog.

Before our first gathering, Cerys messaged the chat: "Hey Friendos! Your local Tiefling Paladin and Human Barbarian will get to the bus just on 6! I'll jump on the barbarian's back to get us there faster!!" Her continuation of the role-play tone established in the chat marked her engagement with the world we were collectively building. Her mixing of the narrative, performative, and the actual world frames,[22] by talking about the characters in third person and first person, placed these fantasy characters within the urban environment of Sydney. It is humorous, but it is also an acceptance of the offer established by Max's original text-based display of role-play, and Dungeon Mum's encouragement of role-play. When both Jace and Cerys arrived, Max, El, Emory, and I were already at Emory's place, seated around a large table. Emory was positioned at the table's head, her various notes hidden behind her laptop screen. We greeted each other in person, some of us for the first time, and Cerys was the first to give voice to something that many people had apparently been thinking: "It's crazy seeing everyone's actual faces, I've been imagining everyone as their characters for so long." Although everyone had pictures of their faces on Facebook, the nature of the generative chat thread seemed to shift the virtual representations of the players.

On our first night playing, Dungeon Mum described the starting location of the campaign, which was a D&D classic: a busy pub. A few of our characters had prior connections to one another that had been established in the chat on Facebook Messenger, but, for the most part, we were strangers. Once Dungeon Mum had described our surroundings in detail, she asked, "What would you like to do?" This signaled the official beginning of the campaign. Helkis, played by Cerys, spoke first in her character voice, which was Scottish tinged, brash, and direct. The content is not as important as the affect, as each person discovered their character in the "moment of vocalization."[23] This moment of vocalization is characterized in Mackay's work as "when the player speaks, the character lives."[24] This is true, but even at this moment, everyone was referring to the assemblage of images they already had conjured about Helkis in their minds from the chat. While Cerys did not "share bodies" with Helkis, her body actualized Helkis's virtual existence.[25] As play continued, Cerys's

14.1   The party, drawn by Dungeon Mum and painted by Max. Helkis is in the middle; clockwise from top left are Fred, Enki, Cereza, and Romeo.

body and voice created Helkis, the purple-skinned tiefling paladin with the tail of an alligator.

A tiefling is a half devil, and a paladin is a holy knight with the powers to channel their god through their weapon. Cerys channeled Helkis through her body by drawing on her own repertoire of images, references, and generative stereotypes and perpetuated the kinds of affective space making that Dungeon Mum had started. The space thus shifted into a role-play space with the physical embodiment of the virtual characters. It was up to the other players to decide how they were going to respond to this shift from a dining room in Sydney to noisy tavern in Omira, the fictional nation where the game was set. Enki was a genasi bard; genasi are a race of humanoids related to genies. He was softly spoken at first, with a slight Irish lilt that was inconsistent but immediately accepted as a part of his character. Romeo, the frog druid, was voiced by Max mimicking the accents of the last character who spoke, but punctuating the sentences with sniffles and splutters. Max jutted their jaw out to mimic the jowls of a frog and often stroked just beneath their chin with their index and thumb to evoke the presence of a frog's vocal sac.

Fred, the human barbarian, was an imposing man, adorning his body with the skulls of animals he had slain. Jace spent the first couple of sessions speaking only in the narrative frame. He admitted that performing as Fred was difficult at first, because the point of the character was that he was designed to be as "generic" as possible, the counterpoint to a party of colorful characters. This was a play on Jace's status as the only straight- and cisgender-identifying member of the group. However, the role-play space eventually changed how Fred was performed and interpreted. Jace's voice for Fred was his own, a parody of his personality, as he leaned further into his Australian accent. He inserted anachronistic Australian slang into his dialogue. Often he would respond to the verbose and refined nonplayer characters (NPCs) played by Dungeon Mum with a laconic "yeah alright mate" or "you right?" The juxtaposition of a medieval setting recast Fred's generic larrikinism as unique and humorous. Cereza (named after the protagonist from *Bayonetta*) was my character, a human monk. I had based my characterization on Nigella Lawson. And as we spent more time with one another in character, hearing things like "you looked so much like your character then," when someone did an action that was interpreted through a "*D&D* way of thinking," became a common occurrence.

Dungeon Mum continued her generation of the role-play space by consistently giving the characters that we met different affectations. She altered her accent, shifted her tone, and maintained a consistent performance for return characters. The performance was not only vocal, as she would rise higher or lower in her chair to indicate stature and evoked imposing characters with a raised chin or enthusiastic characters with gesticulations. Touch played an important role too, with Dungeon Mum reaching across the table to hold players' hands or head when they greeted an NPC who was particularly close to them. Touch-based spells, which are abilities in the game transferred through the hands, were often acted out with one another—especially in pivotal story moments, such as a character saving someone from the brink of death with a healing touch. Occasionally players would place their hands on other players' arms or shoulders. In these moments, the touch occurred in both the third frame and the primary frame; in Dungeon Mum's lounge room as well as in the shared fantasy. This shared fantasy is differently imagined for each person, regardless of the images used to evoke the world.[26] This is why this world was grounded in tactile things, physical touch, the player's bodies. The common point of reference was the physical touch that occurred at the table. Through this, the imagined world became grafted over this visual for onlooking players and, through that touch, for those involved in the specific action. These characters were granted life by both the imagined action in the game and the physical, bodily performances that were never precontrived.

FORGING FAMILY

The space in which play occurred generated a particular kind of favorable role-play for the players, and in turn, this role-play perpetuated the space, in the fashion of a feedback loop. Role-play includes performative and narrative elements and imbues material surroundings with new virtual meanings. These new virtual meanings perpetuate a feeling of closeness because they generate a *"D&D* way of thinking" about the world that is experienced as a shared perspective between players.[27] Contrary to Sherry Turkle's predictions, this way of thinking in this context stimulated chaotic storytelling and humor as opposed to a computational worldview that valued rules over creativity.[28] I contend that the synthesizing of my participants' queer lifeworlds and their *D&D* lifeworlds caused them to view one another through familial categories. I call this process *forging family* because it was ongoing, continuously tested, and created a particular type of kinship that falls under the umbrella term of *fictive kinship*.

Players developed their own *"D&D* way of thinking" that was applied during and outside of the game, increasing the pleasure and power of both spaces. During my year of ethnography with my *D&D* family, I encountered many examples of a *D&D* way of thinking adding joy, inspiring action, and forging bonds in the so-called real world. From Cerys being the family's default for fielding difficult phone calls, to Max's skill with formal documentation, the same logic that was applied to problem-solving as a *D&D* party was applied to everyday experiences. Character aptitudes such as Enki's intelligence or Jace's survivalist instincts were grafted onto the identities of the players that embodied those characters. To illustrate further the rousing quality of a *D&D* way of thinking, I will tell a small story about Dungeon Mum and Cerys drinking in a park. In the darkness, a troop of three men had descended on two young women. Watching for signs of distress, Dungeon Mum and Cerys spotted the women subtly shuffling away from the intoxicated trio. They leaped to their feet, approached the group, and plonked themselves down between the women and the drunkards. Loudly, they declared their apologies for being late and role-played a story of yet more fictional friends who were due to arrive. Outnumbered and dissuaded, the men slunk away into the night, and Dungeon Mum and Cerys dropped the act and left the relieved women in peace. When asked about the incident, Cerys replied, "Well, I just thought to myself, what would Helkis do?"

I will illustrate one of the more formative moments that is constantly spoken about by participants as an event that forged the familial bonds they experience. The forging of family was an ongoing, everyday process that built on shared moments of relatability that occurred in the chat, at the *D&D* table, and out in the world. But, by focusing on one specific moment, I will make clear the kinds of narratives and sensory experiences that actualized feelings of family and thus became crucial to the lifeworlds of those I studied. After we had been playing *D&D* together for a few months, I was invited to a games night on the same night as our weekly *D&D* campaign. Nervously, I asked the *D&D* family if they wanted to skip the session that night and attend the games night. The *D&D* family responded enthusiastically, with Dungeon Mum expressing her excitement about meeting other queer gamers.

We all filed into the house where the games night was being held. The place was geographically and socioeconomically very far away from our homely, if not slightly moldy, share house. (At this point in the fieldwork,

I had moved in with Dungeon Mum, and the house was aptly named Dungeon.) There was small talk about our current campaign as more people began to arrive. Soon there was a group of gay men, El, Max, Cerys, Dungeon Mum, and me. The first game we played was called *Werewolf*. The game is a "social deduction" game because the majority of the gameplay occurs in the interactions between players. It involves deception and strategizing with others to uncover the people who have been tasked with betraying everyone else. The rules are less important for this anecdote because I want to focus on the clash of two very different kinds of groups who generated conflicting spaces.

The rules were explained to us by a particularly vocal member of the host's group named Anthony. Despite how the roles were allocated, the teams fell into established divides. The majority of the host's group spent much of the time talking and strategizing with each other, with Anthony leading most of these discussions. They spoke past Dungeon Mum, Cerys, or Max to ask questions from people across the table. They had decided between themselves that it was either Cerys or Dungeon Mum who received the role of the traitor, without addressing either of them. Cerys sent a message to the *D&D* chat on Facebook Messenger, "I haven't said anything in 5 minutes." This was out of character for Cerys, who was usually quite vocal. None of the men were explicitly preventing Cerys from talking, but the kind of social space they created made Cerys feel that her voice would go unheard. It appeared that the men had nothing on which to base their claims but refused to engage with others to test their hypothesis.

Anthony's group discussed reasons why Cerys or Dungeon Mum were werewolves without addressing either of them. This was interpreted by the *D&D* family as the classic trope of an all-male gaming group who valued game strategy and their own opinions over inclusion and the voices of those they saw as other.[29] They deployed paternalistic language to assert their space, referring to Dungeon Mum and Cerys with terms that sounded patronizing, like "dear" and "honey." They embodied the gaming cultural trope of "rules lawyers," who brought the "real and ordinary into the imaginary and fantastical."[30] In protest, Dungeon Mum adopted a high-pitched, Eastern European accent and slouched her shoulders to portray a village maid. She responded to their accusations with "but I am just a poor *willager*." She turned the *v* into a *w* to emphasize the parodic aspects of her character and to deploy humor as a strategy to assert her voice. She redirected the game into the narrative frame, which disrupted the perceived flow of the game for Anthony's group. The character was not simply created to perpetuate world-building, but the villager was mobilized as a disruptive tool, designed to challenge the status quo of the game.

Despite the mounting confusion of Anthony's group of accusers, she maintained this character, which channeled an NPC from our *D&D* campaign. Cerys accepted the offer from Dungeon Mum and assumed her own villager persona, which was more akin to a vengeful witch. Max and I followed suit as we shifted into the performative frame as well. Meanwhile, in the online *D&D* chat, a parallel game of *D&D* was being played alongside the game of *Werewolf* occurring at the table. The players were filling the chat with the reactions of their *D&D* characters to the real-world situations. Thanks to the collectively cultivated *D&D* way of thinking, we generated a role-play space to change the predicted script that valued strategic play over any other type of play. Soon the table was divided, not just between men and nonmen but between non-role-players and role-players. Soon enough it was revealed that Cerys's character was indeed the werewolf. Anthony's group took much enjoyment in the murder of Cerys's character, to which Cerys simply responded, "I just want everyone to know that my character is screaming right now." Which, to the *D&D* family, conjured images of Cerys's ferocious character Helkis, who could set people aflame with a verbal rebuke. Unfortunately for the boys, Cerys's death did not come swiftly enough for them to claim victory, as she had already murdered too many. This spelled defeat for all of us (except Cerys) in game terms, but sweet victory for the *D&D* family in role-play terms.

FORGED FAMILY

I'm glad we've found a supportive group of humans* that will love each other unconditionally and won't stand by and let dictators reign. 😊

*Frog persons, tieflings, dragon monks, genasi types, goliaths, elves, tabaxi, cyclops and gods.

This message was sent by Cerys to the chat immediately after we left the games night. "Let dictators reign" was a reference to the rules lawyers the gay gamers had become. The smirk emoji that followed was an example of "communicative irony" that drew attention to the hyperbolic use of "dictators" as both sarcastic and honest.[31] It was also a callback to recent events in our campaign involving our party challenging corrupt leadership in-game. Cerys lists the fantastical races that make up the *D&D* family with an asterisk after "human." This is yet another piece of communicative irony that positions all of us as both human and, virtually, our chosen fantasy race. This is less about identifying as other and more about solidifying familial ties through a *D&D* way of thinking, despite the differences between us.

The "trials" that forged family happened both in-game and out of the game. The incident with the gay gamers brought my *D&D* family up close with precisely the sorts of gaming that made them uncomfortable. This group of gay gamers embodied the hegemonic style of gaming many queer gamers associated with straight male gamers, even though this was not the gay gamers' intention. The types of prescriptive gaming, involving specific interpretations of the rules, a lack of role-play and an exclusive mentality to anyone considered an outsider, turned a queer safe space into a microcosm of the broader gaming landscape. This may appear like a simple disagreement, but the ramifications for the *D&D* family were massive. This experience, seen through a *D&D* way of thinking, became a formative narrative that, like a crucible, forged a sense of family.

The *D&D* family emerged as a result of influential gaming encounters, shared queer experiences, unstable housing situations, and common financial circumstances, as well as geographic and, in many cases, ideological separation from biological family. This is not to say that shared hardships alone forged a sense of family, but these conditions created the foundations for the kinds of fantasies that eventually forged a family. I choose to see that *D&D*, especially in the way my participants and I played it, was about generating the "collective affect" of "family get-togethers."[32] In my research, I combined the emphasis on *why* people played with ethnographic evidence of *how* they played, to give an account of what *D&D* did for my participants and what my participants did with *D&D* in an everyday context. What my participant observation revealed was that the *D&D* family used *D&D* to position themselves within their own life-worlds.[33] After a few sessions, I found that they had adopted a *D&D* way

14.2 Another drawing of the party by Dungeon Mum. The party members are depicted facing down a worthy opponent as a united (and stylish) front.

of thinking, and this became a specific mode of sociality, even when the game was not being played. The norms that were invented during play, and were unique to the world created by our Dungeon Mum, became frames through which everyday life was remade and reenchanted.[34]

Queer ethnography calls less for a focus on identity and more for a focus on the discursive spaces that make certain identities possible.[35] I united this focus with the study of *D&D*, as previous ethnographic engagements with queer players have focused on the unique capacity *D&D* has for in-game identity validation.[36] I propose that the concept of the *D&D* family and the idea of a positive *D&D* way of thinking demonstrate the particular relationships between *D&D* and queer players. The specific way of thinking, developed through *D&D* play, persisted into participants' everyday lives, concretizing fictive kinship ties that are forged in-game. I contend that the power of *D&D* for queer people, in addition to providing a framework for experimentation, is its unique ability to forge validating and familial relationships through creative and constructive trials. Moreover, the kinds of familial ties the game creates are based on identities that are thought of as simultaneously fantastical and very real. These notions, which straddle the virtual and the actual, have always been central to imagining queer utopias.[37] This chapter calls for a similar move away from praising all forms of queerness as equally liberating or safe to all queer people. I join a growing chorus of works that seek to point out that not all "homosexual" groups are "alternative," just as not all heterosexual groups are "dominant."[38] Indeed, I bring stories from the field that show how hegemony can quite often present itself and be perceived in the everyday, through the actions of other minority groups. *D&D* is a tool that allows for the cultivation of different collective ways of thinking that can create safe spaces in which players can resist dominant narratives. *D&D* is an effective crucible for the formation of collective resistance that can push out from the game itself, thanks to the kinship ties forged through emotive and affective play in fantastical safe spaces.

NOTES

1. T. L. Taylor, "The Assemblage of Play," *Games and Culture* 4, no. 4 (October 1, 2009): 331–339, https://doi.org/10.1177/1555412009343576.

2. Katherine Angel Cross, "The New Laboratory of Dreams: Role-Playing Games as Resistance," *Women's Studies Quarterly* 40, nos. 3–4 (2012): 82, https://doi.org/10.1353/wsq.2013.0026.

3. Jerome Bruner, "The Narrative Construction of Reality," *Critical Inquiry* 18, no. 1 (1991): 13.

4. Kerryn Drysdale, "Tactile Places: Doing Sensory Ethnography in Sydney's Drag King Scene," *Continuum* 30, no. 2 (March 3, 2016): 206–217, https://doi.org/10.1080/10304312.2016.1143190.

5. Marcel Danesi, "Emoji Semantics," in *The Semiotics of Emoji: The Rise of Visual Language in the Age of the Internet* (London: Bloomsbury, 2016), 53, https://www.bloomsbury.com/uk/semiotics-of-emoji-9781474282000/.

6. Danesi, "Emoji Semantics," 53.

7. Richard Page, "Leveling Up: Playerkilling as Ethical Self-Cultivation," *Games and Culture* 7, no. 3 (May 1, 2012): 238–257, https://doi.org/10.1177/1555412012440319.

8. Gary Alan Fine, "Frames and Games," chap. 6 in *Shared Fantasy: Role-Playing Games as Social Worlds*, paperback ed. (Chicago: University of Chicago Press, 1983), 186.

9. Margaret K. Nelson, "Introduction," in *Like Family: Narratives of Fictive Kinship* (Rutgers University Press, 2020), 1–16, https://www.degruyter.com/rutgers/view/title /588817.

10. Nelson, *Like Family*; Gary Alan Fine, "Players," chap. 2 in *Shared Fantasy: Role-Playing Games as Social Worlds*, paperback ed. (Chicago: University of Chicago Press, 1983), 39–72; Nicholas J. Mizer, "Introduction," in *Tabletop Role-Playing Games and the Experience of Imagined Worlds* (Palgrave Macmillan, 2019), 1–23.

11. Felix Rose Kawitzky, "Magic Circles: Tabletop Role-Playing Games as Queer Utopian Method," *Performance Research* 25, no. 8 (November 16, 2020): 129–136, https://doi.org/10.1080/13528165.2020.1930786; Toriana Shepherd, "Roll for Identity: A Study of Tabletop Roleplaying Games and Exploring Identity" (MA thesis, University of Wyoming, 2021), https://www.proquest.com/docview/2543475498 /abstract/606FD1B6069C47BEPQ/1; Scott Storm and Karis Jones, "Queering Critical Literacies: Disidentifications and Queer Futurity in an Afterschool Storytelling and Roleplaying Game," *English Teaching: Practice and Critique* 20, no. 4 (January 1, 2021): 534–548, https://doi.org/10.1108/ETPC-10-2020-0131.

12. Sherry Turkle, "Introduction (1984)," in *The Second Self: Computers and the Human Spirit* (Cambridge, MA: MIT Press, 2005), 18.

13. Antero Garcia, "Gaming Literacies: Spatiality, Materiality, and Analog Learning in a Digital Age," *Reading Research Quarterly* 55, no. 1 (2020): 9–27, https://doi.org/10 .1002/rrq.260.

14. Cross, "New Laboratory of Dreams"; Storm and Jones, "Queering Critical Literacies"; Shepherd, "Roll for Identity."

15. Cross, "New Laboratory of Dreams"; Kawitzky, "Magic Circles"; Jay Malouf-Grice, "Virtually Safe: Spaces of Fantasy and Family amongst Sydney's Queer Gaming Communities" (PhD thesis, 2021), 141–143, https://hdl.handle.net/2123/25123.

16. Malouf-Grice, "Virtually Safe," 148–150.

17. Leigh E. Fine, "The McElroy Brothers, New Media, and the Queering of White Nerd Masculinity," *Journal of Men's Studies* 27, no. 2 (June 1, 2019): 132, https://doi .org/10.1177/1060826518795701.

18. Alistair John and Brent McDonald, "How Elite Sport Helps to Foster and Maintain a Neoliberal Culture: The 'Branding' of Melbourne, Australia," *Urban Studies* 57, no. 6 (May 1, 2020): 1184–1200, https://doi.org/10.1177/0042098019830853.

19. Fine, "McElroy Brothers."

20. Taylor, "Assemblage of Play."

21. Adrienne Shaw, "Talking to Gaymers: Questioning Identity, Community and Media Representation," *Westminster Papers in Communication and Culture* 9, no. 1 (October 1, 2017): 67–89, https://doi.org/10.16997/wpcc.150.

22. Daniel Mackay, *The Fantasy Role-Playing Game: A New Performing Art* (McFarland, 2001); Fine, chap. 6, "Frames and Games."

23. Mackay, *Fantasy Role-Playing Game*, 102.

24. Mackay, 102.

25. Mackay, 102.

26. Fine, chap. 2, "Players."

27. Turkle, "Introduction (1984)," 18.

28. Sherry Turkle, "Growing Up with Computers: The Animation of the Machine," in *The Second Self: Computers and the Human Spirit* (Cambridge, MA: MIT Press, 2005), 31–152.

29. Genesis Downey, "The Here and There of a Femme Cave: An Autoethnographic Snapshot of a Contextualized Girl Gamer Space," *Cultural Studies ↔ Critical Methodologies* 12, no. 3 (June 1, 2012): 235–241, https://doi.org/10.1177/1532708612440259; Shaw, "Talking to Gaymers"; Adrienne Shaw, "Circles, Charmed and Magic: Queering Game Studies," *QED: A Journal in GLBTQ Worldmaking* 2, no. 2 (2015): 64–97, https://doi.org/10.14321/qed.2.2.0064; Robert Yang, "On 'FeministWhorePurna' and the Ludo-Material Politics of Gendered Damage Power-Ups in Open-World RPG Video Games," in *Queer Game Studies*, ed. Bonnie Ruberg and Adrienne Shaw (University of Minnesota Press, 2017), 97–108, http://www.jstor.org/stable/10.5749/j.ctt1mtz7kr.14.

30. Malouf-Grice, "Virtually Safe," 148.

31. Mitchell Green, "Irony as Expression (of a Sense of the Absurd)," *Baltic International Yearbook of Cognition, Logic and Communication* 12, no. 1 (2017), https://doi.org/10.4148/1944-3676.1116.

32. Ian Skoggard and Alisse Waterston, "Introduction: Toward an Anthropology of Affect and Evocative Ethnography," *Anthropology of Consciousness* 26, no. 2 (2015): 112, https://doi.org/10.1111/anoc.12041.

33. Terje Rasmussen, "Introduction: Personal Media," in *Personal Media and Everyday Life: A Networked Lifeworld*, ed. Terje Rasmussen (London: Palgrave Macmillan, 2014), 1–15, https://doi.org/10.1057/9781137446466_1.

34. Richard Jenkins, "Disenchantment, Enchantment and Re-Enchantment: Max Weber at the Millennium," *Max Weber Studies* 1, no. 1 (2000): 11–32.

35. Natalie Oswin, "Critical Geographies and the Uses of Sexuality: Deconstructing Queer Space," *Progress in Human Geography* 32, no. 1 (February 2008): 89–103, https://doi.org/10.1177/0309132507085213; April Scarlette Callis, "Bisexual, Pansexual, Queer: Non-Binary Identities and the Sexual Borderlands," *Sexualities* 17, nos. 1–2 (January 2014): 63–80, https://doi.org/10.1177/1363460713511094; Sofian Merabet, "Queer Habitus: Bodily Performance and Queer Ethnography in Lebanon," *Identities* 21, no. 5 (September 2014): 516–531, https://doi.org/10.1080/1070289X.2014.907168.

36. Kawitzky, "Magic Circles"; Storm and Jones, "Queering Critical Literacies."

37. Tom Boellstorff, "The Subject and Scope of This Inquiry," in *Coming of Age in Second Life: An Anthropologist Explores the Virtually Human* (Princeton University Press, 2008), 3–31, https://doi.org/10.2307/j.ctvc77h1s; Kawitzky, "Magic Circles."

38. Oswin, "Critical Geographies," 98.

A party of *D&D* characters in a classroom setting. C Liersch, *Classroom D&D*, 2023. Pen and ink on paper.

CRITICALLY PLAYING
DUNGEONS & DRAGONS

(*continued*)

Designer Vignettes III (continued)

You can't have *D&D* without crunch, and you can't have it without role-play. The two extremes think they can exist without each other, but they'd be playing a stripped down version of the game. . . . That's the beauty of *D&D*. The words on the page aren't the game. The game is the communication between the people at the table.

—**Hannah Carlan**
Game designer; coauthor of *Icewind Dale: Rime of the Frostmaiden*

When I play *D&D*, I get the same satisfaction I get when I have created something with a group of people. I produced a lot of theatre in college through student productions, and I worked in television for a long time. And to me, *D&D* is less a group of actors sitting around playing roles than it is a TV writers room, writing an episode.

—**James Introcaso**
Lead designer for MCDM; contributor to many official *D&D* books; designer of *Burn Bryte*; host of *Table Top Babble*

15

"RACE" AND RACE: LONGITUDINAL TRENDS IN *DUNGEONS & DRAGONS* CHARACTER CREATION

Amanda Cote and Emily Saidel

Any *Dungeons & Dragons* (*D&D*) player—or fan of high fantasy in general—is no doubt familiar with the common tropes surrounding different character "races," from gruff dwarven miners to haughty, magical elves.[1] These archetypes have been genre staples since J. R. R. Tolkien's creation of Middle-earth in the 1930s, and of *D&D* since its inception in the 1970s. They have also been essential to gameplay. Players start creating a character by choosing a "race" and a class, often coordinating the two to ensure that their character's innate "racial" characteristics, such as increased strength and constitution for half-orcs, advance the skills needed for their chosen class.

Critics have long pointed out, however, that using "racial" characteristics as a play mechanic risks essentializing the very idea of race itself. Because "race" determines everything from skill set and intellect to temperament and background, games like *D&D* position race as a static, biological fact, rather than as a sociocultural construction. Race scholars and players of color have also advocated for changes to *D&D*'s "race"-based system on the grounds that many in-game "races" risk reinforcing real-world stereotypes. For instance, critics point to how descriptions of orcs or drow elves (dark-skinned elves that are generally depicted as evil) often mirror language used to stereotype and dismiss people of color.[2]

Playing with ethnocultural stereotypes invites overly simplistic interpretations of real-world cultures and individuals.

While researchers such as Aaron Trammell and Antero Garcia,[3] as well as many journalists, have identified overall issues in *D&D*'s representations of race, an in-depth longitudinal assessment can reveal how representation has—and has not—changed over time. To this end, we conducted a qualitative analysis of *D&D*'s *Player's Handbooks* (*PHBs*) from the first edition onward, examining both imagery and language to determine how "racial" characteristics and racial stereotypes are embedded in game materials. The study also addresses when and in what format changes occur. Collectively, these analyses demonstrate how *D&D*'s structures interweave with real-world racial hierarchies, beliefs, and stereotypes, as well as how progress toward inclusion is occurring, albeit unevenly.

"RACE" AND ITS FOUNDATIONS

Race scholars have long pointed out fantasy media's issues with "race." Medievalist Paul Sturtevant even calls race "the original sin of the fantasy genre."[4] Looking back to the work of Tolkien, Sturtevant argues that Tolkien chose to "[conflate] race, culture, and ability." In assigning different "races" set characteristics—and separating them into a hierarchy based on these—Tolkien treated race as a deterministic factor, limiting how any individual character could act or behave. Owing to Tolkien's outsize influence on the genre of fantasy,[5] his uses of race, and many of his archetypes, have spread beyond literature into other media.

In games, "race" is foundational, setting character types apart based on abilities. For instance, while studying *World of Warcraft* (*WoW*), media scholar Melissa Monson argued that determining characters' traits based on their "race" "draws upon and reinforces the preconceived notions of a race-based society."[6] In *D&D*, although players can alter tabletop game rules if they wish, the game's written materials "model race as a fixed biological species with fundamental bodily differences. . . . This reproduces an essentialist understanding of race found in eugenics."[7] This is an outdated, inaccurate perspective, as modern genomic research concludes that perceived race does not consistently map onto biology.[8] Only

Advanced Dungeons & Dragons second edition (*AD&D* 2e, 1989)[9] explicitly tries to disentangle "race"/race, stating that "race" in the game "is not a race in the true sense of the word: caucasian, black, asian, etc. It is actually a fantasy species for your character."[10] Most *PHBs* do not acknowledge rhetorical issues in their use of "race," allowing deterministic racial understandings to permeate several editions and reinforce biased beliefs.

Fantasy "races" also have a history of drawing on real-world stereotypes to set different character types apart. The hierarchy of "races" in Tolkien's Middle-earth novels often problematically associates blackness with evil and whiteness with good.[11] Analysts have also suggested that Tolkien's dwarves, which the author explicitly connected to Judaism, potentially extend antisemitic stereotypes.[12] Scholars do not fully agree about how to interpret Tolkien's writings, especially as several of his letters strongly repudiate antisemitism.[13] Nevertheless, even if only some readers interpret stereotypes in harmful ways, the emotional impact of exposure to those stereotypes can be a significant barrier to inclusivity.

Games also incorporate real-world stereotypes both visually and mechanically. In *D&D*, Trammell found Edward Said's concept of Orientalism—"a way of reducing the complexity of eastern culture to a set of problematically racist and sexist stereotypes"[14]—to be a pervasive influence, pointing to examples from *Oriental Adventures* (1985) as well as recent editions.[15] Garcia finds similar tropes in modules such as *Al-Qadim* (1992).[16] Game critics Graeme Barber and James Mendez Hodes[17] argue that descriptions of half-elves and half-orcs often reproduce the racialized trope of the "tragic mulatto," the stereotype that mixed-race individuals must constantly feel split between worlds.[18] Similarly, the treatment of "races" like orcs as *inherently* violent calls back to savage, "martial race" stereotypes, long a justification for white settler colonialism. Just as Tolkien influenced *D&D*, *D&D* has influenced subsequent properties. Within *WoW*, for instance, humans and several of their allies are coded as white and European.[19] Enemy races that make up the Horde, on the other hand, are coded as a variety of ethnic "Others," for example, invoking Native American and Jamaican stereotypes.[20]

Relying on existing tropes can be a means for game designers to manage risk. Developers are under pressure to create easily understandable games, seeing these as more likely to sell. Therefore, racism—in the form of widely recognized stereotypes—"might be enabled because it is believed to be a hedge against market uncertainty."[21] Collapsing an entire group of people to a specific set of characteristics, however, minimizes our ability to recognize difference and to interact with people on individual, rather than essentialized, terms. Stereotypes also reinforce social hierarchies, bolstering beliefs that justify inequality and discrimination. Therefore the repeated use of "race," racial essentialism, and racial stereotypes in games can affect real-world beliefs and relationships.[22]

Players and critics are not the only ones to acknowledge the links between game terminology and real-world beliefs; D&D's publisher Wizards of the Coast (WotC), too, has acknowledged the overlap of race and "race" and the need to adjust the game to be inviting to all players. In 2020, D&D's development team promised to redo problematic historical texts, increase the use of sensitivity readers, and hire more diverse staff and writers.[23] Tasha's Cauldron of Everything (2020), a supplemental rule book published that same year, also works to divorce players' choice of "race" from innate characteristics.[24] In December 2022, WotC announced that the next generation of D&D would remove the word "race" entirely, replacing it with "species." In a press release, the company stated, "We understand 'race' is a problematic term that has had prejudiced links between real world people and the fantasy peoples of D&D worlds. The usage of the term across D&D and other popular IP has evolved over time. Now it's time for the next evolution."[25] WotC also stated that "species" was chosen as an alternative term "in close coordination with multiple outside cultural consultants."

Overall coverage of these changes has been positive.[26] Some critics, though, point out that the Tasha's changes merely encourage players to "homebrew" their own rules, rather than reimagining the game itself.[27] Moreover, as tabletop scholars Aaron Trammell and Steven Dashiell stated in an interview with PBS NewsHour, the shift from "race" to "species" may be "an earnest appeal to fans that WotC is taking the representation of race seriously in its games," but "the issue was never really 'race' but essentialism,"[28] Thus it remains important to assess where and how deeply "race" and race have changed in D&D over time, as well as the extent to which they have not. For instance, visual shifts may be more obvious—as when fifth edition (5e, 2014) depicted a Black woman as the default image of a human—but the impact of diversified visuals could be undermined if written components do not change accordingly.

METHODS

We collected every *Player's Handbook* (*PHB*) from the first edition to the fifth (*n* = 14). We focused on *PHBs* both to keep the project scope manageable and because *PHBs* are the base material one needs to play a game of *D&D*; most other materials are optional or read only by dungeon masters (DMs). Over fifty years, *PHBs* follow the same general order of information, beginning with character creation, thus providing consistency and a longitudinal perspective. Using the qualitative analysis software package NVivo, we categorized the *PHBs* through a combination of open and axial coding,[29] tagging individual lines and images for their meaning, then sorting the resulting codes into overall themes and conclusions.

To provide a comprehensive perspective, we conducted both textual and visual analyses. Our textual analysis focused on the *PHBs*' character creation sections; although other sections of the *PHBs* occasionally reference "race" (for example, "Elven boots" that allow players to move silently), "racial" descriptions are mostly employed to facilitate character creation. This section is thus most likely to impact how players understand and implement different "racial"/racial characteristics. In analyzing imagery, we assessed how and how often different characters were represented, as well as how these images draw on real-world conceptions of race and appearance. We coded every handbook image (*n* = 582) that contained a character for their "race," perceived race, and, if possible, their in-game class. Overall, we found that *D&D*'s treatment of "race" and race could best be assessed through three lenses: mechanics, written descriptions, and visuals.

MECHANICS

A game of *D&D* requires at least two people: a DM, who controls the fantasy scenario, and a player, who creates a character and makes decisions in the DM's world. Although "house rules" can vary, both DMs and players operate according to a set of provided mechanics. *D&D* explains this relationship as "your character is a combination of the fantastic hero in your mind's eye and the different game rules that describe what he or she can do."[30] Modeling from the work of scholars such as Gerald Voorhees and Helen Young, who illuminate how games' ludic elements help structure their ideological perspectives,[31] this section explores the tensions between imaginative play, codification of "race," and game mechanics.

THE INTERWEAVING OF "RACE" AND CLASS

Character creation in *D&D* begins with a player's choice of "race" and class, and many mechanics in the game link these components to build "an essentialist claim about the possibilities life affords an individual."[32] For instance, original *D&D* (*OD&D*, 1974) provides three choices for class—Fighting-Men, Magic-Users, and Clerics—and four playable races: humans, elves, dwarves, and halflings (fig. 15.1). However, races and classes cannot be combined haphazardly. Humans, dwarves, and halflings could be Fighting-Men, Magic-Users "includes only men and elves," and Clerics "are limited to men only."[33] The choice of race limits the choice of the class, and vice versa—except for human characters.

Further detriments and benefits are assigned to the intersection of race and class. Elves can only progress to fourth-level Fighting-Men or eighth-level Magic-Users, whereas dwarves can only rise as high as sixth-level Fighting-Men but have increased magic resistance. The *PHB* notes that "there is no reason that players cannot be allowed to play as virtually anything, provided they begin relatively weak and work up to the top."[34] This apparent flexibility is undermined, though, because the "virtually anything" the *PHB* imagines is a dragon, rather than a dwarf who can do magic. Before a campaign truly begins, "race" and class are mutually constitutive and mutually restricting; abilities and opportunities are racially essentialized.

The imbrication of "race" and class continued in *D&D* editions published through the early 2000s, even as character options grew. Third edition (3e, 2000) was the first edition that allowed players to choose any "race"/class combination, with eleven classes to choose from and seven playable "races."[35] Despite these expansive possibilities "race" and class remain deeply interwoven in restrictive ways. The *PHB* repeatedly reminds

Table 15.1 D&D's playable races, by analyzed PHB.

	Dungeons & Dragons 1974 (1e)	Advanced Dungeons & Dragons 1978 (AD&D)	Dungeons & Dragons Basic Set 1978 (Basic)	Dungeons & Dragons Basic/Expert Set: Basic 1981 (B/X Basic)	Dungeons & Dragons Basic/Expert Set: Expert 1981 (B/X Expert)	Advanced Dungeons & Dragons 2nd Edition 1989 (AD&D2)	Classic Dungeons & Dragons 1994 (Classic)	Dungeons & Dragons 3rd Edition 2000 (3e)	Dungeons & Dragons 3.5 Edition 2003 (3.5e)	Dungeons & Dragons 4th Edition: Arcane, Divine & Martial Heroes 2008 (4e1)	Dungeons & Dragons 4th Edition: Primal, Arcane & Divine Heroes 2009 (4e2)	Dungeons & Dragons 4th Edition: Psionic, Divine & Primal Heroes 2010 (4e3)	Dungeons & Dragons 5th Edition 2014 (5e)	Dungeons & Dragons 5th Edition: Basic Rules 2018 (5e Basic)
Human	x	x	x	x	x	x	x	x	x	x			x	x
Dwarves	x	x	x	x	x	x	x	x	x	x			x	x
Elves	x	x	x	x	x	x	x	x	x	x			x	x
Halflings	x	x	x	x	x	x	x	x	x	x			x	x
Gnomes	x	x				x		x	x		x		x	
Half-elves	x	x				x		x	x	x			x	
Half-orcs	x	x						x	x		x		x	
Dragonborn										x			x	
Eladrin										x				
Tiefling										x			x	
Deva											x			
Goliath											x			
Shifter											x			
Githzerai												x		
Minotaur												x		
Shardmind												x		
Wilden												x		

players: "Some races are better suited to some classes."[36] Human, half-orc, and dwarf barbarians, for instance, are common, but "barbarians of other races are very rare." "Bards are commonly human, elven, or half-elven," but "there is no bardic traditions among dwarves, gnomes, or halflings."[37] Mechanically, players also benefited from choosing a "favored" "race"/ class combination, such as a halfling rogue, to avoid facing penalties for things like multiclassing.[38]

Thus it was not until fourth edition (4e, 2008–2010) that *PHBs* truly started disentangling race and class. Fourth edition advises that "you should pick the race and class combination that interests you the most,"[39] focusing on the role a character fulfills in a specific party. While there are still some encouragements to choose "race" and class strategically, especially when creating a hybrid character,[40] these take the form of advice more than mechanical restrictions. Both 4e and 5e also distinguish "race" from class within the ordering of character creation. Fifth edition clarifies that "the race you choose contributes to your character's identity in an important way, by establishing a general appearance and the natural talents gained from culture and ancestry," while class "broadly describes a character's vocation, what special talents he or she possesses, and the tactics he or she is most likely to employ."[41] Whereas these choices were previously simultaneous, these later editions direct a selection of "race" before a selection of class, potentially encouraging players to view them as more distinct entities. This design change invites more imaginative play and creative representation. It also reduces the emphasis on humans as the only characters with access to all class options.

NUMERICAL "RACIAL" ABILITIES

In addition to linking "race" and class, mechanics also mark "race" as deterministic via numerical racial abilities and skills. Within *D&D*, all characters share a set of six abilities: strength, intelligence, wisdom, constitution, dexterity, and charisma. These affect gameplay by providing bonuses or penalties to players' rolls; a character high in charisma is more likely to succeed on persuasion rolls, while a character low in strength might fail an athletics check. Players have some control over how they assign their character's ability points, but "race" influences the final result.

In *AD&D* (1978),[42] racial advantages and disadvantages are codified by tables that specify maximums and minimums.[43] Halflings, for instance, not only have a maximum strength of 14 (female) or 17 (male) but also have a standard −1 penalty to strength (although +1 to dexterity.) Third edition drops maximums/minimums and gendered differences but continues "racially" specific modifiers: gnomes receive +2 to constitution and −2 to strength, whereas halflings receive +2 to dexterity and −2 to strength.[44] Mechanics also confer "racial" bonuses to skills such as listen or search, turning inherent "racial" characteristics into professional advantages. While these codifications of physical abilities may seem straightforward—halflings are, one might say, half the height and size of larger "races"—this mechanic also applies to mental acumen. In *AD&D*, both "race" and class choices define minimums and maximums of wisdom, intelligence, and charisma. Half-orcs have prescribed maximums below the minimums needed to play magic-users, paladins, or monks, thus excluding half-orcs from those classes. Humans, with the flexibility to play any class, face none of these mechanical restrictions.

Gary Gygax explains the rationale behind these mechanics: "Classes have restrictions in order to give a varied and unique approach to each class when they play, as well as to provide play balance. Races are given advantages or limits mainly because the whole character of the game would be drastically altered if it were otherwise."[45] Gygax's rationale asserts the codification of different "racial" abilities as *intrinsic* to the character of the game and the world of *D&D*—without articulating how or what that character is. This narrative of "meaningful choice," however, "overlooks how these rules reinforce outmoded notions of race."[46] Further, later editions expose how mechanics of restriction are *not* essential to gameplay, by eliminating level caps (3e, 2000)[47] and then "racial disadvantages" (4e, 2008).[48] By 5e, although "race" still "grants particular traits, such as special senses, [or] proficiency with certain weapons or tools," these come to be phrased as benefits, "racial" skills "dovetail" with classes rather than dictate them, and "playing against type" is acknowledged as a fun option.[49]

The role that racial essentializing plays in *D&D* has had a mixed evolution over fifty years. Early editions firmly restricted all nonhuman "races," creating a system that encouraged players toward human characters. Later editions decreased these penalties, allowing players more freedom of choice, and also shifted "racial" characteristics from a mixed bag of pros and cons to only advantages. This transition is a move away from racialized blame but even beneficial racial traits (with specific "races" being explicitly better at specific skills) can invoke restrictive "model minority" stereotypes. Further, the continued use of "racial" characteristics can still reinforce ideologies of racial essentialization.

THE ROLE OF THE DM

In recognition of these ongoing constraints, WotC introduced some of the aforementioned changes.[50] *Tasha's Cauldron of Everything*[51] allows players to customize their character's origins, including reassigning their "racial" bonuses to different abilities if they want to play against archetypes. Many players appreciate the changes in *Tasha's* and the increased character design freedom they offer;[52] others, however, have criticized the expansion as "a very basic, uncreative, and status quo supporting rough guide to homebrewing your player race a little bit."[53]

This mention of homebrewing leads into the final mechanical change we noted in our analysis: the growing attention that *PHBs* pay to the DM's role in customizing game rules. While many editions mention the players' and DM's ability to collectively negotiate new rules, as when the *D&D Basic Set* (1977) states, "At the Dungeon Master's discretion a character can be anything his or her player wants him to be,"[54] most early *PHBs* prioritized the rules as written.[55] Over time, manuals normalized flexibility, positioning game mechanics more as guidelines.[56] The third, fourth, and fifth editions repeatedly remind players to "talk with your DM" to negotiate new character backgrounds or abilities. Lead designer Mike Mearls featured this ability in 5e, writing: "To play *D&D*, and to play it well, you don't need to read all the rules, memorize every detail of the game, or master the fine art of rolling funny looking dice. . . . Read the rules of the game and the story of its worlds, but always remember that you are the one who brings them to life."[57] The developers thus attempt to overcome mechanical design limitations by highlighting *D&D's* collaborative aspects.[58]

WRITTEN DESCRIPTIONS

In analyzing the written descriptions of "races," we found longitudinal shifts in terminology, the "subraces" available to players, and the temperament and appearance descriptions of different "races." These themes extend both the improvements and limitations found in mechanics, such as when the increased diversity of choices and appearances offered to players remains somewhat hindered by the baggage of high-fantasy archetypes.

"RACE" AND RACE TERMINOLOGY

Early *D&D* editions occasionally lapse into terminology associated with scientific or biological racism, the pseudoscientific practices and theories that posited that different groups of humans had unique origins and therefore could be better understood as different species.[59] These theories, common from the late seventeenth century to the early twentieth, were used by white, Western physical anthropologists and eugenicists to differentiate racial types based on anatomical characteristics such as skull and jaw shape, skin color, and hair type. Their supposedly "objective" taxonomies promoted social hierarchies not only among races but also among nationalities and socioeconomic classes. Original *D&D* and *AD&D* both reinforce this hierarchical view of "race" in which "in general human is superior to the others."[60] *AD&D* also echoes these disavowed theories through the use of the term "racial stock" to describe different groups of characters. The prevalence of racial science likely affected the development of high fantasy,[61] and considering *D&D*'s early inspirations— including *The Lord of the Rings*, Robert E. Howard's Conan books, or Edgar Rice Burroughs's Barsoom series—it is unsurprising that this discriminatory language made it into early versions of the game.

The language of "racial stock" drops out of *PHB*s after *AD&D* (although it does appear in other texts, such as campaign manuals),[62] but the accompanying framework of a "race" hierarchy remains embedded. *D&D Basic*, the *Basic/Expert Set* (1981), *AD&D* 2e, and *Classic D&D* (1994) all refer to nonhuman playable races as "demi-human." This language of partialness, and its focus on humans as the standard against which others are measured, combines with the aforementioned mechanical limitations placed on "demi-human" races to reemphasize humans' role as dominant.

With 3e, the first edition published by new *D&D* owners WotC in 2000, there is less of a hierarchy in racial terminology. The term "demi-humans" is removed, and there are fewer direct comparisons between humans and other "races." Remaining comparisons focus more on how humans tend to be "somewhat more numerous than other races," rather than inherently better. This echoes the mechanical changes that helped even the playing field between human and nonhuman characters in later editions (although humans remain by far the most commonly chosen characters, likely due to their continued mechanical flexibility).[63]

SUBRACES AND ETHNICITIES

One lingering area in which humans are prioritized is in the use of "subraces." Early editions make only general races available: humans, elves, dwarves, and so on. Later editions, in their quest for variety, describe certain "races" as having "subraces." Elves, for instance, are often divided among agile and nature-oriented wood elves, high elves with the strongest affinity for magic, and dark or drow elves who dwell in subterranean cities and, unlike their kin, have a tendency toward evil.[64] Subraces receive different skills and bonuses, reinforcing "race"-based game mechanics. In 5e, for instance, lightfoot halflings receive charisma and stealth bonuses, while stout halflings receive a benefit in constitution and saving throws.

By contrast, human types are referred to as "varieties" or ethnicities, not subraces, and they differ only in appearance, not ability. This treats *D&D* humans as comparable to real-world humans, recognizing their potential for intraspecies diversity, while other "races" are taxonomically classified similarly to animals. Drawn from the Forgotten Realms novels and campaign settings,[65] human ethnicities first appeared in the 5e *PHB*. Without speaking to the game's designers, we cannot definitively state why this material was included but there are some obvious possibilities. First, the world of *D&D* extends well beyond the *PHBs*, or even the tabletop game, through novel series, video games, and movies. Fifth edition's inclusion of the Forgotten Realms' nine human varieties strengthens branding between the game and other media. Listing the range of human ethnicities found in the world of *D&D* may also have been meant to encourage players to create more diverse characters, a design goal WotC highlighted for 5e.[66]

The addition of human ethnicities stands out, however, due to their explicit connections to real-world referents. The most jarring of these comes in the portrayal of the Shou ethnic group. With suggested names like Chen, Huang, and Mei, the Shou are loosely based on Chinese culture, making the description of their "yellowish-bronze" skin problematic. Such terminology calls back to racist depictions of Asians as a "yellow peril," as well as to the use of "yellowface" caricatures.[67] These historical stereotypes could result in players engaging in what Lisa Nakamura calls "identity tourism," "which allows a player to appropriate an Asian racial identity without any of the risk associated with being a racial minority in real life."[68] Other human ethnicities, as described in the *PHB*, often draw from real-world influences as well, but with less evident reference to historical or racist stereotypes. Therefore we point out the use of ethnicities in *D&D* not to argue that such use is inherently problematic, but rather to encourage designers to be reflective when drawing on real-world inspirations.

CHARACTERIZING APPEARANCES

This caution is also applicable to how different "races" are physically described in the *PHB*s. Although early editions did not include many details regarding characters' appearances, later editions clarified how different "races" are expected to look. The range of skin, hair, and eye options often differed by "race." In 3e, for instance, humans are described as "more physically diverse than other common races, with skin shades that run from nearly black to very pale, hair from black to blond (curly, kinky, or straight)."[69] In contrast to this array of options, "dwarves' skin is typically deep tan or light brown, and their eyes are dark,"[70] elves "tend to be paleskinned and dark-haired, with deep green eyes,"[71] halflings' "skin is ruddy, their hair black and straight. They have brown or black eyes,"[72] and gnomes' "skin ranges from dark tan to woody brown, their hair is fair, and their eyes can be any shade of blue."[73] While human appearance has inherent variety, the physical characteristics of other "races" tend to be limited to a small spectrum of colors.

This balance changes in 4e, which makes a point of noting that most humanoid characters can have "the same variety of skin, eye, and hair colors as humans" and more—dwarves could be gray or sandstone red, elves may have green or gold hair, and tieflings' "skin color . . . extends to reds, from a ruddy tan to a brick red. Their hair . . . is as likely to be dark blue, red, or purple as more common human colors."[74] While earlier *D&D*'s "demi-human" terminology positioned nonhuman characters as partial or measured them against a human standard, the 4e appearance descriptions position these characters as surpassing the range of options available to humans. This again works to counter the "racial" hierarchy of early editions, allowing players to choose nonhuman characters while still embodying their real-world appearances if they desire. As players of color often struggle to find their skin, hair, or face characteristics represented in games,[75] the increased range of described appearances is a significant step toward inclusion.

Fifth edition maintains some of these changes; for instance, elves and tieflings continue to "cover the full range of human coloration"[76] plus additional options, while humans still range "from nearly black to very pale, and hair colors from black to blond (curly, kinky, or straight)."[77] Dwarves, gnomes, and halflings, conversely, return to being described as primarily brown, tan, or pale. Overall, our textual analysis reveals some tension between progress and regression in terms of character appearances.

OLD AND NEW "RACES"

The previous sections describe several ways in which the use of "race"/race has shifted over time; *D&D*'s reliance on traditional high-fantasy archetypes, however, has remained consistent throughout the years. Elves, for instance, are repeatedly portrayed as "hauntingly beautiful," magical forest dwellers with a special connection to nature and propensity for archery.[78] WotC likely benefits from this consistency; recognizable character tropes appeal to existing high-fantasy fans and provide easy entry points into *D&D*'s mythos. Yet, as described earlier, some long-standing fantasy archetypes come with racialized baggage, meaning that the industrial logic of consistency can have unintended ideological repercussions.

Whereas the description of elves does not immediately activate stereotypes, that neutrality is not true for all of *D&D*'s core races. Dwarves remain consistent as short, stocky mountain dwellers whose interests lie in fighting, mining, clan, and—most significantly—gold. Eleven of fourteen *PHBs* describe dwarves as being focused on gold or money; this is often seen as a strength, inherent in their status as "miners of great skill,"[79] but sometimes "festers into avarice."[80] These aspects reflect previous critiques of *The Lord of the Rings*, where "dwarves, with their large noses, greedy behavior, and short stature, can be equated to many racist Jewish stereotypes."[81] *D&D's* repeated reliance on this source material brings with it these implicit racialized subtexts.

This is not to argue that written "race" descriptions show no change over time. While early halflings were indebted to Tolkien's hobbits, described as small, stout, and living in pastoral shires, later halflings transition into wanderers, "a nomadic folk who roam waterways and marshlands."[82] Fifth edition splits the difference, stating "some halflings live out their days in remote agricultural communities, others form nomadic bands that travel constantly, lured by the open road and the wide horizon."[83] This shift represents the greatest change halflings undergo over time, and, while their location changes, their overall characterization as small, good-natured, or rogue-like does not.[84] That this change was noteworthy in comparison to other "races" highlights the embeddedness of standard "racial" tropes—even over the course of fifty years.

The only *PHBs* that offer real experimentation are those of 4e, which introduced new "races" such as dragonborn, shardminds, tieflings, and wilden that deviate from *D&D's* standard offerings. Because these "races" are not long-standing fantasy archetypes, they offer an opportunity to divorce *D&D* from real-world conceptions of race and stereotypes.[85] A 4e developer Andy Collins explicitly made this connection in an interview with *The Escapist*, stating that the team had introduced new "races" because "we wanted the *Player's Handbook* to represent a broad cross-section of races, not only from an in-game cultural standpoint but also from players psychographics."[86] But, by 5e, many of the new "races" disappeared, leaving only dragonborn and tieflings. While players can continue to play the previously introduced "races" using older rule books or supplementary materials, transitioning older "races" to newer editions in a balanced way can take some skill. It also requires a flexible DM. Fifth edition's reaffirmation of traditional high-fantasy archetypes steps back from the increased diversity offered by 4e, foreclosing more imaginative "racial" and play possibilities.[87]

IMAGES AND VISUALS

Perhaps the most dramatic changes in the *PHBs* over time are visual, due to the game's shifting artistic influences, attention to visual diversity, and instructions to artists. As a tabletop game, rather than a video game, *D&D* relies on players and DMs to describe scenes or characters in detail. *PHBs*, however, are often new players' first introductions to the world, lore, and peoples of *D&D*, and their illustrations serve a foundational role in how players envision, craft, and describe their characters. Therefore diversifying visuals can be a starting point for making *D&D* more inclusive.

While almost all versions of *D&D* contain full-color cover art, early interior art consisted primarily of simple black-and-white line drawings. Artists were primarily told how much space they had, where their illustration would be located on the page, and what information was on that page. They then tried to draw something that would fit both space and topic.[88] Illustrators drew on a long history of fantasy art but were also inspired by contemporary artists such as Frank Frazetta, who famously illustrated the Conan and Barsoom series starting in the 1960s. Not only did these two series influence the creation of *D&D*, but they also influenced the game's visuals (fig. 15.2).

Most early drawings display humans as white coded, as do the rare illustrations of dwarves, elves, and halflings. Wizards tend to be older men with beards; fighters have Conan-style muscles and loincloths, and armored knights ride horses and carry swords or lances. Female characters, when they appear, are thin yet buxom, often with a great deal of

15.2 Examples of pulp-inspired illustrations from *OD&D* (1974).

bare skin. In these ways, *D&D* illustrations exemplify the visual tropes of classic pulp fiction. As in video games like *WoW*, these illustrations also construct a world that foregrounds European whiteness. Generally, only monsters are left to be read as nonwhite; the few illustrations that depict people of color often draw on racist stereotypes. In the *D&D Expert Set* (1981), a caricature of an Asian apothecary mixes potions by candlelight. In *Classic D&D*, a potentially Jewish-coded man picks the lock of a chest and chortles over his resulting treasure, playing into antisemitic representations (a characterization apparently not reserved for dwarves alone).[89]

In 3e, we see a range of visual changes. Not only does this edition depict humans and elves with a broader range of skin tones and facial features,[90] but it also includes illustrations of many different "races" rather than prioritizing humans.[91] These additional drawings, however, sometimes essentialize differences between characters or rely on racialized visual tropes. For example, in a move reminiscent of phrenology/craniology and "racial stock," 3e contains sketches that distinguish dwarves, humans, half-elves, and elves based on the shape of their skulls (figs. 15.3, 15.4). As with the addition of human ethnicities to 5e, this shows how otherwise well-meaning changes can be undermined without sufficient attention to context and history.

These concerning images were removed in 4e and 5e, which instead continued to diversify illustrations. In addition to introducing the first Black halfling in a *PHB*, the 4e handbooks show Black and Asian humans, darker-skinned dwarves and gnomes, and even a greater variety of hairstyles, such as braids and locs (fig. 15.5). Subraces such as drow also appear more in these later editions, helping to reclaim them from their monstrous background. This choice to expand representations over time appears to be deliberate on the part of WotC. According to freelance *D&D* illustrator Brynn Metheney, "People of all genders, races, everything have always been playing Dungeons & Dragons. It's who we start to feature more. When we got the descriptions, they [WotC] were very adamant. They were like, 'Try not to make it, like a white blond guy. Like, please. We love 'em, but there's like 500 million of 'em.'"[92] Matt Stawicki, an artist who has freelanced on *D&D* since 1999, echoed Metheney's perspective.

There are, of course, ongoing tensions in *D&D*'s visual representations. While many players enjoy seeing real-world influences slip into in-game

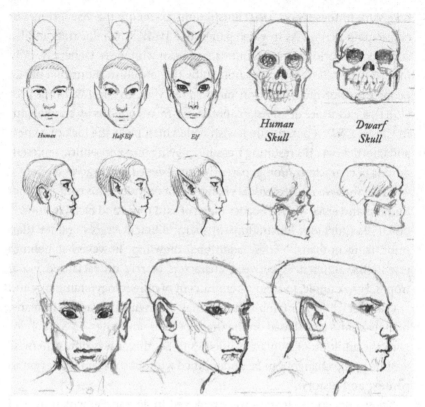

Human   Half-Elf   Elf   Human Skull   Dwarf Skull

15.3 Examples of "race" drawings in the 3e *Player's Handbook* (2000), 14, 15, 19.

illustrations, others find continuing "race"/race crossovers problematic. For instance, Trammell argues that some 5e visuals remain Orientalist, and a prominent image of a female dwarf sporting Native American–inspired face paint mirrors Sturtevant's critiques of "racist depictions of Indigenous peoples" in the barbarian class (figure 15.6).[93] Under the weight of other game components like mechanics and terminology, diversifying visuals alone may not be enough to overcome the game's structural racial assumptions.[94]

CONCLUSIONS

Our longitudinal analysis of how *D&D* represents "race"/race visually and textually reveals that the game has undergone several changes over time,

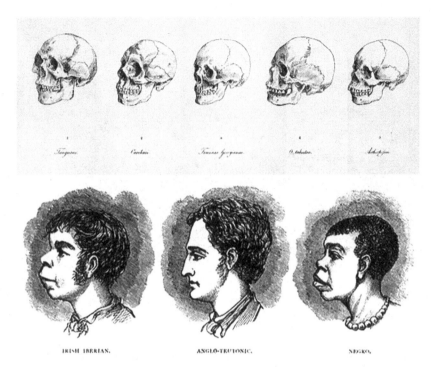

15.4   Examples of racialized craniology. Johann Friedrich Blumenbach, *De Generis Humani Varietate Nativa* (Gottingae: Vandenhoek et Ruprecht, 1795); Henry Strickland Constable, *Ireland from One or Two Neglected Points of View* (Liberty Review Publishing Company, 1899).

15.5   Changing human imagery in *AD&D* (1978), 3e (2000), 4e (2008), and 5e (2014).

15.6 A Native American–inspired dwarf barbarian in the 5e *Player's Handbook* (2014), 48.

many of which contribute to inclusivity. These include an expansion of available "race" and class options, as well as greater encouragement for players to take on nonhuman roles; an increased emphasis on DMs' ability to modify rules and mechanics; updated terminology for "race"; and increased attention to diversity of appearance, both in written and in visual depictions. Collectively, these changes provide some support for the developers' contention that they are working to welcome more types of players, and upcoming changes to *One D&D* may continue this progress.

Some ongoing challenges remain. First, as Metheney has pointed out, "Fantasy in general suffers from being very European. And there are so many more amazing cultures and stories and worlds out there that I think are starting to kind of penetrate into fantasy realms."[95] This process is not always smooth, as when intentionally non-European expansions veer into Orientalism, anti-Blackness, or other racialized tropes.

Second, while WotC has tried to diversify playable characters—adding new races, altering mechanics and descriptions, and so on—it has also stepped back from some of the more dramatic changes introduced in 4e, such as new "races" and the broadest possible appearance descriptions. Further, the sheer consistency of "racial" tropes, many of which originally emerged from racialized stereotypes, belies the appearance of change. Given how deeply embedded these archetypes are in the *D&D* mythos, as well as within high fantasy in general, these factors may be too interwoven into the game for players to expect full change or for the game to remain recognizable as *D&D*. It is also unlikely, as critics point out, that simply renaming "race" to "species" will be sufficient to change these tropes.[96]

Finally, many of the game's changes focus on encouraging players to take ownership of diversity and inclusion, rather than altering the game structures that complicate this task. As disability advocate Elsa Henry noted in critiquing role-playing games' fraught relationship with disability, "Inclusion means more than assuming that one is included, it means being named."[97] Several *D&D* aspects still off-load responsibility for inclusion from the developers to the individual players, forcing players to invite themselves in rather than being explicitly welcomed.

This is not to say that players cannot build more inclusive gaming spaces. Invested players and DMs can work together to creatively apply new ideas and call out problematic tropes around race, as well as gender, ableism, and more. Players should learn more about real-world stereotypes and how they permeate fantasy's background to avoid replicating these viewpoints in their own play. (See works from Barber and Sturtevant for some starting points.)[98] The work of individuals like James Mendez Hodes, a game designer and cultural consultant, can be useful in this process. Mendez Hodes's work on orcs and cultural appropriation provides actionable suggestions for players to alter their gameplay away from stereotypes.[99] Finally, we want to highlight that we are not demonizing *D&D* or its players; instead, we are calling for both designers and players to recognize how fantasy worlds emerge from real-world reference points. Through increased attention to those connections, it is possible to construct better, more inclusive spaces of play.

It is important to recognize that rule books alone represent only part of the story; textual analysis allows us to understand what the game itself says, but it cannot give us insight into the motivations behind design changes. Playing a game is also interactive and can generate communal or emergent meanings.[100] As Esther MacCallum-Stewart argues in chapter 9 of this collection, *D&D* play has also become increasingly inventive over time, with players often using "the rule books as a guideline rather than a definitive text." Further, individuals bring their own experiences and backgrounds to engaging with popular media and can therefore interpret the same text in different ways.[101] At the same time, a game's meaning is generated within a shared system of expectations—namely, the mechanics and rules of the game, as well as genre and social gameplay conventions.[102] While *D&D* can help players develop "alternative social worlds," these worlds are still "governed by a complicated set of rules and constraints."[103] The game's structures can make some meanings, actions, and outcomes more accessible than others. Understanding what those structures encourage thus remains a priority, especially as *D&D* exerts an outsize influence on the overall world of fantasy media (see Dimitra Nikolaidou, chap. 11, this collection).

Thus we conclude by celebrating the steps *D&D* has taken over its fifty-year history, especially in the area of illustrations, but we also encourage developers to continue reimagining the expansive fantasy world the game offers.[104] As Trammell points out, "The TRPG community has historically been a site of struggle and ignorance over representation and discrimination."[105] Understanding how *D&D*, as a cornerstone text in that field, has represented "race" and race over time highlights what work still needs to be done to overcome historical exclusions and inequalities. This multifaceted content analysis, which draws together descriptions, language, and imagery, takes one step further toward achieving that goal.

NOTES

1. Within games, "race" is often used to mean species, rather than culture, ethnicity, or social category. Because we discuss both these uses simultaneously, we use "race" (in quotes) to denote race-as-species, while race (without quotes) denotes race-as-ethnicity.

2. Cecilia D'Anastasio, "D&D Must Grapple with the Racism in Fantasy," *Wired*, January 24, 2021, https://www.wired.com/story/dandd-must-grapple-with-the-racism-in-fantasy/; Cass Marshall, "Wizards of the Coast Is Addressing Racist Stereotypes in *Dungeons & Dragons*," Polygon, June 23, 2020, https://www.polygon.com/2020/6/23/21300653/dungeons-dragons-racial-stereotypes-wizards-of-the-coast-drow-orcs-curse-of-strahd; Melissa J. Monson, "Race-Based Fantasy Realm: Essentialism in the *World of Warcraft*," *Games and Culture* 7, no. 1 (2012): 48–71, https://doi.org/10.1177/1555412012440308; Nathaniel Poor, "Digital Elves as a Racial Other in Video Games: Acknowledgment and Avoidance," *Games and Culture* 7, no. 5 (2012): 375–396, https://doi.org/10.1177/1555412012454224; Paul B. Sturtevant, "Race: The Original Sin of the Fantasy Genre," *Public Medievalist*, December 5, 2017, https://www.publicmedievalist.com/race-fantasy-genre/.

3. Aaron Trammell, "Representation and Discrimination in Role-Playing Games," in *Role-Playing Game Studies: Transmedia Foundations*, ed. José P. Zagal and Sebastian

Deterding (New York: Routledge, 2018), 440–447; Antero Garcia, "Privilege, Power, and Dungeons & Dragons: How Systems Shape Racial and Gender Identities in Tabletop Role-Playing Games," *Mind, Culture, and Activity* 24, no. 3 (2017): 232–246, https://doi.org/10.1080/10749039.2017.1293691.

4. Sturtevant, "Race."

5. Brian Attebery, *The Strategies of Fantasy* (Bloomington: Indiana University Press, 1992).

6. Monson, "Race-Based Fantasy Realm," 54.

7. Trammell, "Representation and Discrimination," 444; Garcia, "Privilege, Power, and *D&D*."

8. Vivian Chou, "How Science and Genetics Are Reshaping the Race Debate of the 21st Century," *Science in the News: Harvard Medical School*, April 17, 2017, https://sitn .hms.harvard.edu/flash/2017/science-genetics-reshaping-race-debate-21st-century/; Noah A. Rosenberg et al., "Genetic Structure of Human Populations," *Science* 298, no. 5602 (2002): 2381–2385.

9. David "Zeb" Cook et al., *Player's Handbook* (*AD&D* 2e) (Lake Geneva, WI: TSR, 1989), 20.

10. Here and throughout the chapter, we replicate the capitalization used in the original *PHBs*.

11. Dimitra Fimi, "Revisiting Race in Tolkien's Legendarium: Constructing Cultures and Ideologies in an Imaginary World," lecture at *Politics of Contemporary Fantasy* conference, Wurzburg, Germany, 2012, released online 2018, http://dimitrafimi.com/2018 /12/02/revisiting-race-in-tolkiens-legendarium-constructing-cultures-and-ideologies -in-an-imaginary-world/; Anderson Rearick, "Why Is the Only Good Orc a Dead Orc? The Dark Face of Racism Examined in Tolkien's World," *MFS Modern Fiction Studies* 50, no. 4 (2004): 861–874, https://doi.org/10.1353/mfs.2005.0008; Helen Young, "Racial Logics, Franchising, and Video Game Genres: The Lord of the Rings," *Games and Culture* 11, no. 4 (2015): 343–364, https://doi.org/10.1177/1555412014568448.

12. Rebecca Brackmann, "'Dwarves Are Not Heroes': Antisemitism and the Dwarves in J. R. R. Tolkien's Writing," *Mythlore* 28, no. 3 (2010): 85–106, https://dc.swosu.edu /mythlore/vol28/iss3/7.

13. Rearick, "Racism Examined in Tolkien."

14. Aaron Trammell, "How *Dungeons & Dragons* Appropriated the Orient," *Analog Game Studies* 3, no. 1 (2016), http://analoggamestudies.org/2016/01/how-dungeons -dragons-appropriated-the-orient/; see also Edward Said, *Orientalism* (London: Vintage Books, 1978).

15. In *Oriental Adventures*, Gary Gygax states, "When the *Dungeons & Dragons* game system was envisioned and created, it relied very heavily upon the former work [the tabletop game *Chainmail*], medieval European history, and mythos and myth most commonly available to its authors." Gary Gygax, David "Zeb" Cook, and François Marcela-Froideval, *Oriental Adventures* (TSR, 1985), 3. Gygax positions the *D&D* universe as Western, European, and white. *Oriental Adventures* also leaned heavily into both mechanical and narrative Orientalism, exoticizing the new setting.

16. Garcia, "Privilege, Power, and *D&D*"; see also Jeff Grub, *Al-Qadim: Arabian Adventures* (*AD&D* 2e) (TSR, 1992).

17. Graeme Barber, "Mired in the Past," *POCGamer*, January 1, 2014, https://pocgamer.com/2014/01/01/mired-in-the-past/; Graeme Barber, "Decolonization and Integration in D&D," *POCGamer*, February 8, 2019, https://pocgamer.com/2019/08/02/decolonization-and-integration-in-dd/#more-1080; James Mendez Hodes, "Orcs, Britons, and the Martial Race Myth, Part I: A Species Built for Racial Terror," jamesmendezhodes.com (blog), January 14, 2019, https://jamesmendezhodes.com/blog/2019/1/13/orcs-britons-and-the-martial-race-myth-part-i-a-species-built-for-racial-terror; James Mendez Hodes, "Orcs, Britons, and the Martial Race Myth, Part II: They're Not Human," jamesmendezhodes.com (blog), June 30, 2019, https://jamesmendezhodes.com/blog/2019/6/30/orcs-britons-and-the-martial-race-myth-part-ii-theyre-not-human.

18. Although we do not have space to address this fully, our research supports their argument; for instance, 5e (2014) states, "Half-elves and half-orcs live and work alongside humans, without fully belonging to the races of either of their parents" (17).

19. Tanner Higgin, "Blackless Fantasy: The Disappearance of Race in Massively Multiplayer Online Role-Playing Games," *Games and Culture* 4, no. 1 (2009), https://doi.org/10.1177/1555412008325477; Jessica Langer, "The Familiar and the Foreign: Playing (Post)Colonialism in World of Warcraft," in *Digital Culture, Play, and Identity: A World of Warcraft Reader*, ed. Hilde G. Corneliussen and Jill Walker Rettberg (Cambridge, MA: MIT Press, 2008), 87–108; Monson, "Race-Based Fantasy Realm"; Poor, "Digital Elves."

20. See Dimitra Nikolaidou (chap. 11, this volume) for further examples of *D&D*'s influence on broader fantasy media.

21. Sam Srauy, "Professional Norms and Race in the North American Video Game Industry," *Games and Culture* 14, no. 5 (2019): 478, https://doi.org/10.1177/1555412017708936.

22. See Daniel Heath Justice (chap. 16, this volume) and Aaron Trammell and Antero Garcia (chap. 17, this volume) for details on how *D&D*'s racial stereotypes affect real players.

23. Wizards of the Coast, "Diversity and Dungeons & Dragons," June 17, 2020, https://dnd.wizards.com/articles/features/diversity-and-dnd.

24. Jeremy Crawford, *Tasha's Cauldron of Everything* (Renton, WA: Wizards of the Coast, 2020).

25. D&D Beyond Staff, "Moving On from 'Race' in One D&D," D&D Beyond, December 1, 2022, https://www.dndbeyond.com/posts/1393-moving-on-from-race-in-one-d-d.

26. Vanessa Armstrong, "Dungeons & Dragons Pledges to Add 'New Voices' to Diversify Its Storytelling," *Syfy Wire*, June 19, 2020, https://www.syfy.com/syfywire/dungeons-dragons-new-voices-to-diversify; Charlie Hall, "How Dungeons & Dragons' Next Book Deals with Race, plus Exclusive New Pages and Art," Polygon, November 2, 2020, https://www.polygon.com/2020/11/2/21538090/dungeons-dragons-tashas

-cauldron-of-everything-race-monk-art; Corey Plante, "'Tasha's Cauldron of Everything' Is the Most Important New *D&D* Book of 2020," *Inverse*, August 24, 2020, https://www.inverse.com/gaming/tashas-cauldron-of-everything-release-date -subclasses-lineage-rules; Luke Plunkett, "Dungeons & Dragons Removing 'Race,' Wants to Use 'Species,'" *Kotaku*, December 1, 2022 https://kotaku.com/dungeons -dragons-d-d-race-species-racism-change-1849844249; Samantha Puc, "Why It Matters That D&D Is Replacing the Term 'Race,'" *The Mary Sue*, December 1, 2022 https://www.themarysue.com/why-it-matters-that-dnd-is-replacing-the-term-race/.

27. Graeme Barber, "Tasha's Cauldron of No Change," *POCGamer*, November 20, 2020, https://pocgamer.com/2020/11/20/tashas-cauldron-of-no-change/; D'Anastasio, "D&D Must Grapple."

28. Christopher Thomas, "How a New Generation of Gamers Is Pushing for Inclusivity beyond the Table," *PBS NewsHour*, January 2, 2023 https://www.pbs.org/news hour/arts/how-a-new-generation-of-gamers-is-pushing-for-inclusivity-beyond-the -table.

29. Thomas R. Lindlof and Bryan C. Taylor, *Qualitative Communication Research Methods*, 2nd ed. (Thousand Oaks, CA: Sage, 2002).

30. Rob Heinsoo, Andy Collins, James Wyatt, et al., *Player's Handbook: Arcane, Divine, and Martial Heroes* (*D&D* 4e) (Renton, WA: Wizards of the Coast, 2008), 12.

31. Gerald Voorhees, "The Character of Difference: Procedurality, Rhetoric, and Roleplaying Games," *Game Studies* 9, no. 2 (2009), http://gamestudies.org/0902/articles /Voorhees; Young, "Racial Logics."

32. Voorhees, "Character of Difference."

33. Gary Gygax and Dave Arneson, *Dungeons & Dragons Volume 1: Men & Magic* (Lake Geneva, WI: Tactical Studies Rules, 1974), 6.

34. Gygax and Arneson, *Men & Magic*, 8.

35. Monte Cook, Jonathan Tweet, Skip Williams, et al., *Player's Handbook* (*D&D* 3e) (Renton, WA: Wizards of the Coast, 2000).

36. Cook et al., *Player's Handbook* (3e), 4.

37. Cook et al., 24–26.

38. Cook et al., 11.

39. Heinsoo et al., *Player's Handbook* (4e), 14.

40. Heinsoo et al., 136.

41. Wizards of the Coast, *Player's Handbook* (*D&D* 5e) (Renton, WA: Wizards of the Coast, 2014), 11.

42. Gary Gygax, *Advanced Dungeons & Dragons Players Handbook* (Lake Geneva: WI, TSR/Random House, 1978), 6.

43. These limitations are affected by gender as well as "race"; see Aaron Trammell, "Misogyny and the Female Body in *Dungeons & Dragons*," *Analog Game Studies* 1, no. 3 (2014), http://analoggamestudies.org/2014/10/constructing-the-female-body -in-role-playing-games/.

44. Cook et al., *Player's Handbook* (3e).

45. Gygax and Arneson, *Men & Magic*, 6.

46. Trammell, "Representation and Discrimination," 444.

47. Cook et al., *Player's Handbook* (3e).

48. Heinsoo et al., *Player's Handbook* (4e).

49. WotC, *Player's Handbook* (5e), 8.

50. WotC, "Diversity and *D&D*."

51. Crawford, *Tasha's*.

52. For example, Plante, "Most Important New *D&D* Book."

53. Barber, "Tasha's Cauldron of No Change."

54. Gary Gygax and Dave Arneson, *Dungeons & Dragons Basic Set*, 1st ed., ed. John Eric Holmes (Lake Geneva, WI: TSR Hobbies, 1977), 7.

55. See also Garcia, "Privilege, Power, and *D&D*."

56. See Esther MacCallum-Stewart (chap. 9, this volume) for more discussion of *D&D*'s move toward imaginative play.

57. Mike Mearls, "Preface," in *Player's Handbook* (5e), by Wizards of the Coast (Wizards of the Coast, 2014), 4.

58. It is worth noting, however, that players cannot use homebrewed content in official contexts like the *D&D* Adventurers League.

59. Johann Friedrich Blumenbach, "De Generis Humani Varietate Nativa" (On the Natural Varieties of Mankind), 1775, reproduced in *The Anthropological Treatises of Johann Friedrich Blumenbach and the Inaugural Dissertation of John Hunter*, ed. and trans. Thomas Bendyshe (London: Longman, Green, Longman, Roberts, and Green, 1865), 65–144; Henry Strickland Constable, *Ireland from One or Two Neglected Points of View* (London: Liberty Review Publishing Company, 1899).

60. Cook et al., *Player's Handbook* (*AD&D* 2e), 3.

61. Fimi, "Revisiting Race in Tolkien"; Dimitra Fimi, *Tolkien, Race and Cultural History: From Fairies to Hobbits* (Palgrave Macmillan, 2018).

62. For example, Eric L. Boyd, James Jacobs, and Matt Forbeck, *Dungeons & Dragons Campaign Accessory: Races of Faerûn* (Wizards of the Coast, March 2003).

63. Gus Wezerek, "Is Your *D&D* Character Rare?" *FiveThirtyEight*, October 12, 2017, https://fivethirtyeight.com/features/is-your-dd-character-rare/.

64. This aligns with common representations of elves across fantasy media (Poor, "Digital Elves").

65. Garcia, "Privilege, Power, and *D&D*."

66. WotC, "Diversity and *D&D*."

67. Robert G. Lee, *Orientals: Asian Americans in Popular Culture* (Philadelphia: Temple University Press, 1999); Gary Y. Okohiro, *Margins and Mainstreams: Asians in American History and Culture*, 2nd ed. (Seattle: University of Washington Press, 2014).

68. Lisa Nakamura, "Race in/for Cyberspace: Identity Tourism and Racial Passing on the Internet," in *Reading Digital Culture*, ed. David Sharp (New York: Wiley Blackwell, 2001), 229.

69. Cook et al., *Player's Handbook* (3e), 12.

70. Cook et al., 14.

71. Cook et al., 15.

72. Cook et al., 20.

73. Cook et al., 16.

74. Heinsoo et al., *Player's Handbook* (4e), 49.

75. Ash Parrish, "I Spent Three Hours in *Baldur's Gate 3*'s Character Creator and It's Pretty Good," *Kotaku*, October 9, 2020, https://kotaku.com/i-spent-three-hours-in -baldur-s-gate-3-s-character-crea-1845328223.

76. WotC, *Player's Handbook* (5e), 42.

77. WotC, *Player's Handbook* (5e), 29.

78. Elves were also, before 5e, predominantly represented as white, with the dark-skinned drow portrayed as enemies rather than playable options.

79. Cook et al., *Player's Handbook* (2e), 15.

80. WotC, *Player's Handbook* (5e), 19.

81. Higgin, "Blackless Fantasy," 11.

82. Heinsoo et al., *Player's Handbook* (4e), 44.

83. WotC, *Player's Handbook* (5e), 29.

84. The newer, nomadic characterization of halflings does activate some real-world stereotypes about the itinerant Romani people. Thus developers must be cautious in *how* they change characterizations, to avoid contributing to new prejudices.

85. Not all new "races" accomplish this split; the deva, for instance, can be read as Orientalist through the use of Hindu or Buddhist terminology, beliefs in reincarnation, and vaguely Asian or Middle East–inspired dress.

86. Andy Collins, quoted in Greg Tito, "The Truth about 4th Edition: Part One of Our Exclusive Interview with Wizards of the Coast," *Escapist*, March 3, 2010, https:// www.escapistmagazine.com/the-truth-about-4th-edition-part-one-of-our-exclusive -interview-with-wizards-of-the-coast/.

87. While some critics felt that 4e took away "the flavor of these races" by unlinking "race" and mechanics (John Baichtal, "GeekDad Review: D&D 4th Edition [part 1 of 3]," *Wired*, July 19, 2008, https://www-wired-com.proxy.lib.umich.edu/2008 /07/geekdad-revie-1-6/), many players struggled with 4e's overall changes, arguing that it was too battle oriented, rather than role-playing based. Therefore it's difficult to disentangle specific critiques of 4e's approach to "race" from more general feedback.

88. Kelley Slagle and Brian Stillman, dirs., *Eye of the Beholder: The Art of Dungeons & Dragons* (Cavegirl Productions and X-Ray Films, 2019), film, 90 min.

89. Gary Gygax and Dave Arneson, *Dungeons & Dragons Expert Set*, (Lake Geneva, WI: TSR Hobbies, 1981), x21; Gary Gygax and Doug Stewart, *Classic Dungeons and Dragons* (Lake Geneva, WI: TSR, 1994), 18, 102.

90. Third edition included more color illustrations than several earlier editions. However, the diversity of its depictions cannot solely be attributed to this technological change; *AD&D* 2e (1989) was also printed in color and did not display the same variety of characters.

91. For a more quantitative assessment of *PHB* imagery, see TiMar Long, "Character Creation Diversity in Gaming Art," *International Journal of Role-Playing* 7 (2016): 23–29.

92. Brynn Metheney, in Slagle and Stillman, *Eye of the Beholder*.

93. Trammell, "How *D&D* Appropriated the Orient"; Paul B. Sturtevant, "Improving Dungeons and Dragons: Racism and the 'Barbarian,'" *Public Medievalist*, March 18, 2021, https://www.publicmedievalist.com/dungeons-dragons-racism-barbarian/.

94. Long, "Character Creation Diversity."

95. Metheney, in Slagle and Stillman, *Eye of the Beholder*.

96. Thomas, "How a New Generation of Gamers."

97. Elsa S. Henry, "Reimagining Disability in Role-Playing Games," *Analog Game Studies* 2, no. 2 (2015), http://analoggamestudies.org/2015/02/reimagining-disability-in-role-playing-games/.

98. Barber, "Decolonization and Integration"; Sturtevant, "Race: The Original Sin"; Sturtevant, "Improving *D&D*."

99. Mendez Hodes, "Orcs, Britons: Part II"; James Mendez Hodes, "How to Change Your Conversations about Cultural Appropriation," jamesmendezhodes.com (blog), January 2, 2020, https://jamesmendezhodes.com/blog/2020/1/2/how-to-change-your-conversations-about-cultural-appropriation.

100. Joseph Packer, "What Makes an Orc? Racial Cosmos and Emergent Narrative in *World of Warcraft*," *Games and Culture* 9, no. 2 (2014): 83–101, https://doi.org/10.1177/1555412013512420.

101. Stuart Hall, "Encoding and Decoding in the Television Discourse," in *Essential Essays*, vol. 1 (Durham, NC: Duke University Press, 2019), 257–276.

102. Voorhees, "Character of Difference"; Garcia, "Privilege, Power, and *D&D*"; Gary Alan Fine, *Shared Fantasy: Role-Playing Games as Social Worlds* (Chicago: University of Chicago Press, 1983).

103. Fine, *Shared Fantasy*, 182, 186.

104. See, for instance, the new cultures introduced in *Journeys through the Radiant Citadel* (Ajit A. George and F. Wesley Schneider, *Journeys through the Radiant Citadel* (Seattle, WA: Wizards of the Coast, 2022), which released as we were completing this chapter.

105. Trammell, "Representation and Discrimination," 442.

16

HACK THE ORCS, LOOT THE TOMB, AND TAKE THE LAND: REFLECTIONS ON SETTLER COLONIALISM, INDIGENEITY, AND OTHERWISE POSSIBILITIES OF *DUNGEONS & DRAGONS*

Daniel Heath Justice
(citizen, Cherokee Nation)

In the United States, the Indian is the original enemy combatant who cannot be grieved.

—Jodi Byrd (Chickasaw Nation), *The Transit of Empire* (2011)[1]

I grew up in a world of ruins, both literal and imagined. My mom's hometown was Victor, Colorado, once a thriving Gold Rush city of over ten thousand reduced to around three hundred when I was a child. Everywhere around me were the picturesque remnants of nineteenth-century mining headframes, ore processing mills, fraternal-order temples, mercantile shops, and churches of crumbling brick, rough-hewn stone, and rusting iron, the askew residue of stolid industrial pragmatism and flamboyant *nouveau riche* fantasy. There were countless half-hidden old shacks, long-abandoned mines, and bleached tailings piles to be discovered throughout the arid pine- and aspen-covered mountains, a landscape seemingly forgotten and untouched by the modern world, discovered only by those willing to explore beyond the bounds of the past-haunted town we called home.

And then there were the "Indian relics" that occasionally surfaced, the arrowheads and spearpoints and the story of an unearthed Native burial site on the southern slopes of the mountain where my hometown sprawled, most of its buildings empty of all but dusty detritus and memory.[2] In the account that my mom learned in her short stint as a tour bus driver for a local mine, early white "pioneers" in the area discovered a Native woman's remains interred in a sealed grave, either somewhere on the slopes of the mountain or in a nearby gully. In that account, the body was looted and put on display in one of the nearby mining camps, but what happened afterward isn't known. I don't know if there's any truth to the story, or if it was invented to explain the mountain's racist toponym, but there's a long and ugly settler history of grave robbing and exhibiting Native bodies—living and dead alike—so the story certainly has the ring of truth.[3] Either way, the unmistakable message growing up in that place was that the Native presence in the region was fully in the past, and whatever ruins and fragments remained were little more than mildly interesting historical curiosities undeserving of dignity or care.

Those were the literal and storied ruins, but the familial ones, too, loomed large in our consciousness. "Heinz 57" is how my mom referred to her background, a motley assortment of British and western European settlers, including Ashkenazi Jews. (Like so many white Americans, they also claimed Native heritage through a convoluted and implausible story that seems to have been a way of laying claim to Chickasaw land during the allotment period of the late nineteenth and early twentieth centuries.)[4] We didn't know much about the Fay, Small, or Schryver families, as emigration, economic peril, sexual abuse, and class shame had severed many of the pathways through which meaningful stories might have been shared across the generations of my maternal kin.

Through my father's maternal line, I am a citizen of the Cherokee Nation in what is today northeast Oklahoma, but while our kinship, political, and heritage links to the Nation are deep and significant, Grandma Pearl died of tuberculosis when Dad was a teenager, and between his own profound grief and his father's hostile relationship to Pearl's family, Dad was largely distant from his Cherokee kin (although his long-estranged sister Alverta maintained strong ties to our Spears relatives throughout her life). He was phenotypically Native, with dark skin and black hair buzzed to an invariable flattop; he was rarely seen without a well-weathered hat and had a seemingly endless supply of flannel shirts. But he wasn't culturally connected, and what he knew of our family heritage was fractured at best until I was old enough to help him start putting those pieces together.

Though I had siblings from Dad's first marriage, in many ways when growing up it was just Mom, Dad, and me. We lived in something of a closed bubble among Gold Rush ruins, in lands that had been violently seized from the Utes, Cheyennes, and Arapahos in the nineteenth century, a place haunted with stories of gold-hungry white miners and dead Indians, entangled in, but largely unfamiliar with, the complicated legacies of our mixed family lines. I would be in my late teens before we would reconnect with Dad's sister and start to reweave those ties and gingerly attend to those histories, to begin to understand our place in our families and in relation to the very much living Nation.

On both sides of my family there was a sense that we were connected to a once-great past, that we were the unstoried remnants—sometimes bedraggled, sometimes just stubbornly enduring—of greater people with a firmer sense of their place in history and in the world. In the absence of any stories that might have helped me make sense of who we were in relation to our tangled histories, or active engagement with the living people and traditions I'd come to think of entirely in the past tense, I looked elsewhere for a sense of belonging. And where better for a dreamy, mixed Cherokee bookworm than a storytelling game set among the treasure-strewn ruins of a world inhabited by the scrappy but watered-down descendants of nobler peoples and their now-fallen greatness?

The great story of Faerûn is, in many ways, that of the rise of humankind and the fading of the ancient empires of those who came before. Over thousands of years, humans have brought an end to the old ways. Elven cities lie in ruins, abandoned to human encroachment. Hills and dells once the homes and hunting grounds of goblins and giants are now dotted with human fields and pastures.

Human pride and folly have brought untold disaster down on Faerûn more than once, and the ever-growing lands of humans encroach on the territories of older races both benign and fierce. . . . Can the old races survive the dominance of humankind?
—Ed Greenwood et al., *Forgotten Realms Campaign Setting* (2001)

My first clear memory of *Dungeons & Dragons* (*D&D*) is of two beat-up boxes. The first was the 1981 *Basic Set*, referred to by old-school *D&D* nerds as the "Magenta" edition for the purple tones of the subterranean lair featured in Erol Otus's cartoonish cover art of a sorceress and spear-wielding fighter fending off a green dragon. The other was the iconic 1983 "Red Box" featuring artwork by Larry Elmore, with a fierce red dragon bearing down on a courageous, horn-helmed warrior whose sword is captured in midswing at the moment of attack.

I'm not sure how these boxes came into my possession, but I was about ten or twelve, so likely 1985 or a bit later, likely a summer flea market purchase with my dad. I was too young to really understand the game, especially without other close friends to play with, but its storytelling possibilities fascinated me. I was delighted to discover that one of my favorite Saturday morning cartoons was connected to these books and had more than a superficial relationship to J. R. R. Tolkien's sprawling legendarium, which I'd only just started to explore through *The Hobbit* novel and the animated films of Rankin/Bass and Ralph Bakshi. Soon after I found other *D&D* paraphernalia, including Endless Quest books, action figures, pewter miniatures, and gaming supplements from TSR and other companies.

I was hooked. *D&D* had everything I liked: storytelling, fantasy, adventure, inhabiting other worlds and characters. And the foundational template for all these works was one with which I was already intimately familiar, even as a child: savagism versus civilization. The stories of fallen empires and rising powers, decline and progress, primitive tribespeople and cultured settlers, made a kind of twisted sense to me, even though, deep down, I feared that I already knew where my family and I sat in that binary, and it wasn't where I wanted to be.

Even so, when I started to create my characters, it wasn't the brash (white) warriors who appealed to me, or the dignified (white) princelings seeking to regain their thrones, or the noble (white) paladins charging down the dragons to rescue the swooning (white) maidens in distress. These weren't characters who reflected where we lived or where we came from. I struggled with shame about my little mountain town, far from what I envisioned as the center of culture, art, and intellectual achievement, but I loved the place, too; and so, to manage the cognitive dissonance, I began imagining myself in worlds of magic and mystery where difference was valued, not despised, where the game's explicit insistence on the dungeon master's (DM's) ultimate authority as storyteller made it possible to ignore the parts that wounded and enhance those that empowered, no matter what the canonical rule books might otherwise state. The DM was the ultimate creator of worlds through story, and that was something I understood at a visceral level.

These sideways and otherwise fantasy worlds I cobbled together from scraps of game supplements, novels, comic books, cartoons, and my own imagination were the ones I wanted to be in, not the one of my everyday existence. For all that my home life was deeply loving and supportive, I internalized other corrosive ideas from my peers, from our neighbors, from popular culture, and even from the ruptures and absences in our own family. I came to see myself and my family through more judgmental eyes: the faggy, back-country weirdo with the run-down house and the loving but rough-hewn, brown-skinned dad and mountain-bred mom.

But rather than imagine myself among the privileged, I doubled down on the outsiders. My imagination wasn't so detached from reality that I easily envisioned being one of the cool, the privileged, the easy elite. Misfits were the only characters with whom I really related, but misfits with power and purpose, motley fey folk and half-elves and wise women and witches of inborn talent and trained skill, for whom courage and intelligence were more than a match for plain physical prowess. Though displaced and erased in most fantasy settings, they at least had a certainty and clarity that my own world seemed to lack.

It was the *Basic Set*'s "demi-humans" who appealed the most, in spite of being manifestly less powerful and having fewer ability options than humans: the elves, dwarves, and halflings whose character class was the same as their race. They were outsiders, associated with the land and the wild places of the world; even if they were inferior in skills compared to the human characters in the game, they felt far more recognizable to me than their more powerful human counterparts. For all that they drew on stereotypes, some of those stereotypes were ostensibly positive, the noble savage infinitely more appealing than its ignoble counterpart. These were the figures that spoke to me and my growing interest in fantasy role-playing. And that continued even as I moved to *Advanced Dungeons & Dragons*, where more scope existed for character advancement, if not much change in the foundational ethos of the game. (In chapter 17 of this collection, Aaron Trammell and Antero Garcia share their own reflections on these retrograde racial taxonomies and game mechanics as young mixed-race players. How many of us similarly found both empowerment and ensnarement alike in our first racialized engagements with *D&D*?)

It's fair to say that I didn't feel entirely human myself; among the vast majority of people who lived in Victor in the 1980s and '90s, as in so many places throughout the United States then and now, full human status was determined by proximity to unsullied whiteness and Euro-Western culture. Whiteness determined both dignity in life and grievability in death, and even though my own features were lighter than my dad's, and my own proximity to the myriad privileges of whiteness infinitely more secure, there was always a shadow of uncertainty, one compounded by the instabilities of heritage, class, income, education, and the growing awareness—my own and others'—of my nascent queerness. Social acceptability seemed tenuous at best, as the harder I tried to embody what my world deemed "normal"—white, straight, culturally sophisticated, well-spoken, and so on—the more that goal receded into an inevitably unachievable distance. Everything seemed to betray me: my parentage, my hometown, my education, my desires, my features, even the pitch of my voice. So if my humanity could only ever be a constant and embarrassing failure, my fantasy demi-humanity could at least be successfully realized. As a half-elf druid or a halfling ranger, I could be a celebrated hero, an honored compatriot, a desired lover; as myself, I could only ever stumble awkwardly toward belonging. Better to imagine the integrity of being an outsider in totality and not just in pieces and parts that were destined to betray me in spite of my best efforts to fit in.

Of course, humans and demi-humans weren't the only beings in *D&D*: these worlds were full of monsters, too, the "savage peoples—goblins, orcs, ogres, and all their kin . . . [who] regularly burst forth from their strongholds to pillage and slaughter villages and towns unfortunate enough to be in their path."[5] From tribal goblinoids to dragons, beholders and bullywugs, even the degenerate civilizations of the fallen-from-grace dark elves, monsters were obstacles—not just to the adventurers, but to civilization itself. Thus their subjugation was not only an act of self-preservation but the highest possible good to defend civil society, history, family, and social order.

And this is where the savagism-versus-civilization binary really came in, for the function of monsters was—like that of all savages in this ideological structure—to die, and thereby give certainty of purpose to the civilized. One side in this binary is culturally complex, sophisticated, literate, and ambitious, and the other is brutish, superstitious, and little better than mindless beasts. Civilization depends on its opposite; without savagery for negative comparison, there is no civilization. Even when the savages are given complex emotions and cultures, they rarely escape the binary—noble savages from once-great cultures die just as readily as ignoble savages, but there is a sense of resigned if nostalgic sadness for the inevitable fall and fading of the former, while the latter are mown down like so much crabgrass. The Ignoble Savage is a menace, but the Noble Savage is a warning: it heralds what can happen when a civilization becomes complacent, soft, or degenerate. Together they are an object lesson for the rising powers: stay virile, stay robust, stay vigilant; otherwise, you degrade or you fade.

And the association of both the demi-humans and the monsters with Indigenous and colonized peoples was hardly coincidental. Indeed, it was baked into the earliest iterations of the game, as Eugene Marshall notes: "It's hard to ignore the fact that, when he first created miniatures for the fantasy races, Gary Gygax chose Turk minis to depict orcs and repainted Native American figures for trolls and ogres."[6] Indigenous peoples were rendered monstrous and therefore killable, neither one worthy of mourning or compassion; the savage dies so that the civilized may flourish, no matter how bloody the cost.

But I didn't relate to the righteous killers. I can't remember even once playing a human character in *D&D*—all my characters were fully demi-humans or half-elves, and most were women or genderqueer. Only later did I realize that was because I related not to the masculinist human champions but to the goblins they killed without mercy, to the elves and dwarves they sent fading into history, to the seemingly weak halflings slipping through the shadows of lands they'd always called home. My imagination lay with those who inhabited the ruins, those who remained, furtive but defiant, the peoples far less cruel than the ones who persecuted them and called them monsters.

The Indian who was important to Americans setting out to make their new society was not the person but the type, not the tribesman but the savage, not the individual but the symbol. The American conscience was troubled about the death of the individual. But it could make sense of his death only when it understood it as the death of the symbol.

—Roy Harvey Pearce, *Savagism and Civilization* (1953)

In spite of the superficial polytheism and diverse deities influencing the various world orders, there's also a kind of Christian triumphalism at play in *D&D*, with clerics and paladins in righteous crusade against the forces of darkness, with darkness versus light mapped readily onto the savage-versus-civilized underpinnings.[7] (This might have reassured the Christian fundamentalists during my youth who insisted that the game was inherently satanic.) As befit its wargaming origins, *D&D* depended on such dualistic conflicts at all levels, in all interactions. The bold and righteous fight to survive and bring civilization to the wilderness, but the unrighteous—the savages, the heretics, the cultists—exist only to be killed. Indeed, beyond the cultural crusade of civilization, killing savages—religious as well as racial and cultural—has been, for most of *D&D*'s history, the main way for characters to advance in level, power, and skill. In the game, they are heroes and champions; in life, they would be sociopathic war criminals at best. But in colonial frameworks, Turks readily become orcs, Native Americans readily stand in for trolls, and if you accept the binary, there's only one direction that story goes.

As I grew older and began to connect the dots between my family's entangled histories and my love of fantasy, it became increasingly clear that, in the dualistic Christo-colonial cosmologies of *D&D*, my world and so much of my family could only ever be on the savage side of that system. The plundering of lost tombs lost its excitement when I began to learn how many treasure hunters had robbed Indigenous graves and burial sites, how many looters had destroyed important cultural sites, how many companies and individuals had wrested vital ceremonial places and objects away from our nations, how the lives and livelihoods of working-class people were so easily taken away by those with power and impunity. The destruction in the 1930s of the Craig Mound in Oklahoma—part of the Spiro Mounds site on the Choctaw Nation reservation—put all treasure-hunting adventure stories in a very new and unpleasant light, while an ugly repatriation controversy during my graduate school years also opened my eyes to the myriad harms such thefts enacted on living communities, even long after the initial robbery.[8] A lifetime of watching multinational mining companies use up the land and the people and then abandon both when profits went down made it clear that the hierarchies of that binary had their class dimensions too.

No longer satisfied with pseudomedieval, pseudo-European worlds of prophesied monarchs returning to thrones they claimed by right of blood, I was far more interested in stories that spoke to lands, cultures, and contexts closer to home. And soon the Tolkienesque template of *D&D* began to chafe, as did the varied inheritors of Tolkien's literary imaginings. (The other great influence on *D&D*'s world-building, Robert E. Howard, especially his *Conan* works, held no appeal for me whatsoever, as there was no beauty, no grace, no romance—just blood, brutality, butchery, and overt racism.) As much as I loved Middle-earth, it was still a world where lordship was borne in the blood, where inheriting country gentry were served faithfully by loving and dutiful servants, of the uncertain triumph of "Western civilization" over the dark and fallen peoples who stood against it. And while Tolkien's orcs and their filmic, gaming, and media iterations have been shaped by and expanded on savagist anti-Black and anti-Asian stereotypes, they're also informed by stereotypical ideas about Indigenous primitivism (as are his Drúedain, the reclusive Woses who aid the Rohirrim on their way to the Battle of the Pelennor Fields).

I still loved *D&D*, but everywhere I turned, the savage versus civilized binary flourished. The designers of every edition grappled with it in different ways, sometimes challenging it, sometimes burying it, but as Amanda Cote and Emily Saidel have demonstrated (see chap. 15 in this collection), the basic template has remained troublesome, making it extremely hard to shift these deeply rooted and widely held cultural biases. *The Atruaghin Clans* of Mystara recycled almost every problematic Hollywood and pulp western stereotype about Native peoples, in both the noble and ignoble savage modes; *Dragonlance* had its noble savage (but blond!) Plainsmen right out of *Dances with Wolves*, along with the execrable gully dwarves, a people depicted as so primitive, degenerate, filthy, and simpleminded that their more civilized dwarven kin actively sought their extermination; *Forgotten Realms* was explicitly based on the civilized-versus-savage binary and leaned in hard on racial essentialism in its sadistic black-skinned drow led by vicious matriarchs and their terrible spider goddess, firmly melding anti-Blackness with misogyny, a once-civilized people gone feral under the debased rule of women. *Ravenloft* had its pseudo-Roma Vistani, complete with the worst "gypsy" stereo-types of criminality and charlatanism. And where to begin with the tribal cannibals that were the *Dark Sun* halflings? With savagism versus civiliza-tion as the structuring logic, changes could only ever be superficial, and those supplements that extended too far outside the logic didn't tend to do well. (For all that I objected to *The Atruaghin Clans*, I still think that the 1990 Mystara gazetteer *The Shadow Elves*, by Carl Sargent and Gary Thomas, offered a fascinating spin on the "dark elf" trope that was far more complex, more imaginative, and less burdened by racist stereotypes than the drow have ever been.)

Other fantasy game systems and imagined RPG worlds weren't much better. *Warhammer, GURPS, HârnMaster, Palladium, Shadow World*—few systems seemed able to imagine beyond the underlying dualistic and extractivist logic that so deeply informed *D&D*, even when seemingly inclined to do so. So I started looking elsewhere. The first few story lines of Wendy and Richard Pini's *Elfquest* series of fantasy comic books shook me, for here was a world that, while not without its essentialist limita-tions, nevertheless showed cultures not simply in conflict but in quite complicated *relationship*. Some of the elves were brown-skinned desert dwellers; others were light-skinned forest folk with deep other-than-human kin bonds; all were complex, and all had sophisticated cultures and social systems. Sex and desire were natural parts of the characters' lives; there were triads, queer relationships, and even a lovingly rendered group love-in in one issue.

Octavia Butler's *Wild Seed* and other Patternist volumes in the "Seed to Harvest" series were all about people of color finding a space of their own in a world that too often subjected them and their desires to bodily indignities; Butler was the first fantasist of color whose work I ever read, and she had a profound impact on my own desire to write Indigenous fantasy novels of my own, stories that took Indigenous cosmologies and relations and power dynamics seriously, and where identity was rooted in land, language, and kinship that included other-than-human beings and subjectivities. Dignity, love, passion, courage, complexity—these were the motivating forces of these otherwise worlds, and they opened up vistas I'd longed for but couldn't quite see in my solitary imaginings in the mountains.

In these new fantastical places, the "civilization" and "savagery" binary didn't dominate or even operate; the main characters were driven by purpose and principle, not by unearned power, and struggled with the very real effects of colonization, enslavement, bigotry, and fear, not simply reacted passively or without reflection against an externalized threat. It's no surprise to me now that most of these writers were feminists who were, to varying degrees, politically and intellectually sensitized to the struggles of oppressed peoples, with the linguist Suzette Haden Elgin and the visionary Ursula K. Le Guin joining Butler among my literary favorites. And there have been so many justice-oriented feminist and queer and BIPOC (Black, Indigenous, and People of Color) writers and artists since, each imagining other worlds beyond the extractive limitations of settler colonialism and its impossibly narrow dualisms.

But I didn't let go of *D&D*, not completely; I remain a player and a DM, in homebrew worlds where the savagism versus civilization binary is actively contested, where diverse genders and queerness are normalized but rape and sexual objectification aren't, where restoration of lands, languages, and kinship are far more important than achieving wealth or glory. In these imagined worlds, grave robbers are villains, not heroes; today's peoples aren't the pathetic remnants of once-great cultures but complicated and enduring people doing their best to thrive even in difficult circumstances. My fantasy series *The Way of Thorn and Thunder* directly explores issues around Indigenous dispossession and restoration in a secondary-world fantasy setting that started as one of my homebrew worlds, and three of the main characters were my own player characters (PCs): Tarsa and Tobhi were my first PCs (though fortunately very different in the novels than when I first conceived of them), and Denarra was my unashamedly queer alter ego from a multiyear gaming group during my undergraduate years. These characters embodied and expressed parts of me I didn't understand at the time. We've been on a lifelong adventure together.

Though decidedly not the only influence or source of inspiration in my life, and though not without its myriad problems, *D&D* was one way

I found a partial if imperfect language for naming my world, its limits, and its possibilities in all its contradictions, complexities, and diversity. The game's own limitations—and the alternate visions of BIPOC, queer, and allied fantasists—helped me see myself and my family as not simply broken and ruined but meaningful and complicated in our own ways, and to understand the very real kinship and cultural fractures in our histories not as an inevitable consequence of our essential natures but as the results of historical forces, violent structures and institutions, and individuals who made choices—some of which we were actively complicit in, some of which we resisted, some of which we embraced, and some of which were forced on us.

The world of tabletop role-playing is very different now from when I was coming of age in the game: no more accepting the most overbroad stereotypes simply because they at least had a slim hint of Indigenous resonance, the thin leavings on bones tossed from an imaginative banquet others could enjoy with more gusto. I'm delighted that there are Indigenous gamers and game designers working hard to present otherwise possibilities in their own gaming worlds and systems (with *Coyote and Crow* being an important step forward), alongside Black game designers and visionaries from other communities, cultures, and contexts. BIPOC, queer, and otherwise marginalized players haven't entirely given up on *D&D* itself, either; a lot of us still work to make it our own, with our own stories and our own cosmologies, and have brought this to a broader public, as the NDND All-Native *D&D* gamers have done on their YouTube adventures and as seen on the Indigitek Blak All-Stars game on Twitch. While not entirely escaping some of the problematic underlying structures of *D&D*, the Arcanist Press *Ancestry and Culture* fifth edition gaming supplements are helpful reimaginings of identity outside the static essentialisms of race.

Even Wizards of the Coast (WotC) is responding in official *D&D* content—part of a larger company-wide move to address sexism, homophobia, and racism in published content—although not entirely successfully, with the controversy around Graeme Barber's experience with content he wrote for *Candlekeep Mysteries* (2021) a case in point. Barber's original material intentionally complicated the frog-like Grippli people, taking them from past representations as a simplistic and "primitive" bipedal frog folk to a more nuanced and complex society. According to Barber, the WotC editorial team revised his material toward more retrograde, primitivist directions before the book was released, which he discovered only after its publication.[9] A disappointing retrenchment into savagist stereotypes, but new designers and new projects in development give me hope that these reversals will be the exception rather than the rule.

Indigenous fantasists and wonder-workers are flourishing globally, especially in the last decade, finding appreciative audiences within and beyond our nations: Daniel H. Wilson, Andrea Rogers, Richard Van Camp, Chelsea Vowel, Darcie Little Badger, Stephen Graham Jones, Sara General, Gina Cole, Tihema Baker, Ambelin Kwaymullina—just a few of the visionaries creating Indigenous worlds beyond the colonial now. Indigenous gamers are using social media to find one another, and we're playing and learning with and celebrating one another all over the world. Our writers and artists and gamers and DMs are creating richly imagined and complex Indigenous futures where Indigenous lives, lands, and relations continue to be strong, unbroken, and undeterred, collectively enriching our imaginative horizons in ways that were far outside my lonely, limited scope when I was a disconnected mixed Cherokee kid in that little Colorado mountain town flipping through my *Basic Set.*

The solitary worlds I made up in my head were one way I could imagine my way around the ruinous settler presumptions of mainstream society, presumptions I had internalized in so many ways but still struggled against. If I'm honest, I still grapple with them even now. I can't know how much more my imagination might have expanded, and my journey into accepting so many parts of myself been so much easier, had I been part of an online community like NDND, read wondrous fantasy novels by Indigenous writers, or even had just one other Indigenous gamer to play with in my hometown. The internet has made these connections possible in ways that were unimaginable when I was an awkward and lonely kid in a world that just didn't seem to have a place for people like me and my family except among the ruinous reminders of a distant past.

For all its problems, I'm still glad I've had *D&D* in my life. I'm glad that so many people from so many backgrounds and identities have found something worthy and affirming in this strange, empowering, problematic, and complicated game. I'm also glad that people are challenging the game, pushing back against its calcified traditions, refusing its baked-in bigotries. I'm certainly not one of those longtime gamers who bemoans the growing popularity and social justice concerns that now inform so much of the game and the way it's played—I wholeheartedly celebrate these changes. My own experience would have been far less vexed, the struggle and uncertainty far less onerous, had these been part of our conversations back then.

But even more than all that, I'm immensely grateful that *D&D* has inspired, in both its best and its worst, new ways of imagining vibrant Indigenous futures far beyond the haunted ruins of the settler colonial imaginary. Had he known about them back then, I think that queer Cherokee kid rolling his d20 and dreaming of wondrous vistas within and beyond his little mountain town might have taken great comfort in these otherwise possibilities, too.

NOTES

1. Jodi Byrd, *The Transit of Empire: Indigenous Critiques of Colonialism* (Minneapolis: University of Minnesota Press, 2011), xviii.

2. For over a century, the mountain and a nearby ravine shared the name of a degrading and abusive term used against Indigenous women. In 2022 the US Department of the Interior removed these violent place names, replacing them with the far more evocative Evening Star Mountain and Maize Gulch. See US Department of the Interior, "Interior Department Completes Removal of 'Sq___' from Federal Use," September 8, 2022, https://www.doi.gov/pressreleases/interior-department-completes -removal-sq-federal-use.

3. The terrible story of Julia Pastrana, an Indigenous woman from Mexico who was exhibited as a sideshow "freak" by her white husband in the mid-1800s and who was, along with their infant son, stuffed and displayed after dying from complications of childbirth, is one of the most ghoulish cases, but by no means anomalous. See Warren Cariou, "The Exhibited Body: The Nineteenth-Century Human Zoo," *Victorian Review* 42, no. 1 (Spring 2016): 25–29; Linda Frost, *Never One Nation: Freaks, Savages, and Whiteness in U.S. Popular Culture* (Minneapolis: University of Minnesota Press, 2005); Pascal Blanchard et al., eds., *Human Zoos: Science and Spectacle in the Age of Colonial Empires* (Liverpool: Liverpool University Press, 2008).

4. See Daniel Heath Justice, "Narrated Nationhood and Imagined Belonging: Fanciful Family Stories and Kinship Legacies of Allotment," in *Allotment Stories: Indigenous Land Relations under Settler Siege*, ed. Daniel Heath Justice and Jean M. O'Brien (Minneapolis: University of Minnesota Press, 2022).

5. Ed Greenwood, Sean K. Reynolds, Skip Williams, and Rob Heinsoo, *Forgotten Realms Campaign Setting* (Renton, WA: Wizards of the Coast, 2001), 6.

6. Eugene Marshall, *Ancestry and Culture: An Alternative to Race in 5E* (Arcanist Press, 2020), 5.

7. Roy Harvey Pearce, *Savagism and Civilization: A Study of the Indian and the American Mind* (Baltimore, MD: John Hopkins University Press, 1953), 73.

8. See David La Vere, *Looting Spiro Mounds: An American King Tut's Tomb* (Norman: University of Oklahoma Press, 2007); Ellie Churchill, "Bones Unearthed and Respect Burned," *Nebraska U: A Collaborative History*, n.d., accessed February 25, 2022, https://unlhistory.unl.edu/exhibits/show/bones-unearthed/unearthed-respect.

9. Chase Carter, "An Author Is Questioning Wizards of the Coast's 'Problematic' Changes to His Adventure in the Newest *D&D* 5E Sourcebook," *Dicebreaker*, March 24, 2021, accessed February 25, 2022, https://www.dicebreaker.com/games/dungeons -and-dragons-5e/news/dungeons-dragons-candlekeep-mysteries-freelance-alterations.

17

SEEKING THE UNIMAGINABLE: RULES, RACE, AND ADOLESCENT DESIRE IN *DUNGEONS & DRAGONS*

Aaron Trammell and Antero Garcia

Dungeons & Dragons (D&D) has long been a game about playing within the limits of imagination. These limits, unfortunately, prefigure a knowledge of race that is pregnant with harmful stereotypes and tropes. For us, two critical game scholars who both grew up mixed-race, the unimaginable aspects of *D&D* are just as important as the imaginable. By recollecting our earliest moments with the game, we consider what it meant to locate belonging in fantasy worlds where encountering other mixed geeky kids was unimaginable. These autobiographical sketches aim to illuminate the power that *D&D* had to help us make sense of our own identities, our shared placelessness in the white suburban worlds we inhabited, and, perhaps most of all, how being mixed was unimaginable in fantasy and otherwise.[1]

AARON

I remember reading the *Dungeons & Dragons Rules Cyclopedia* when I was ten years old in elementary school.[2] While the other kids were busy practicing arithmetic and learning basic social studies, I sat with the book under my desk, learning about how nimble a thief had to be to disarm a trap and how strong a warrior had to be to bend prison bars. I pored over full-color maps that seemed just as real as the Mercator map that hung on the wall beside the teacher. I weighed the differences between scale mail and plate mail, halberds and pikes, in my head as I considered which tools would be most effective for slaying a hydra.

In rapt curiosity, as I sat reading about the different "classes" of characters in this vivid new world, I learned that even in this fantasy world, whiteness was as powerful as it was invisible. My ten-year-old mind believed and internalized what my adult self shudders to read today: "Demihumans [elves, dwarves, and halflings] are more limited in their options than humans are, so the entire race can be represented by a single character class."[3] Here it was, hidden in plain sight: the language and logic of white supremacy—that some "races" are less than human, they can be reduced to a singular and monolithic "species," and these races simply have fewer career "options." The designers even built in a glass ceiling and determined that no dwarf could rise above level twelve, no elf above ten, and no halfling above eight. Of course, this all made sense to me at the time; I had read *The Hobbit*. Thus the *Rules Cyclopedia* simply seemed like an encyclopedia, an authoritative text that confirmed what I already knew: that even in the deepest realms of fantasy, humans were central, powerful, and even invisible, marked more by their occupation (fighter, thief, cleric, wizard) than their race.

The invisibility of whiteness works by positing a formula wherein to have race is to be nonwhite, and to be white is to control the conversation around who is visible and who is not. To this point, I was surrounded by white friends and students in a middle-class New Jersey suburb, where whiteness was an assumed and invisible norm. Here I rarely saw Blackness reflected back at me through the experiences of my peers. I assumed that we were unified in our shared humanness, even though I know now that my friends saw my Blackness far more clearly. So while the teacher explained America's immigration policy through the metaphor of the melting pot, I absorbed a twisted hidden curriculum from the *Rules Cyclopedia* that encouraged me to internalize the opportunities granted to an invisible, idealized, and imaginary white hero.

The illustrations in the *Rules Cyclopedia* even revealed this hero could be Black, as long as they saw themselves as human in a system that classified others as a different species entirely. In other words, by depicting Black humans in the illustrations of the *Rules Cyclopedia*, the manual itself offered an assimilationist perspective that promised a multicultural inclusivity within a belief system that evinced the most toxic fiction of white supremacy—that some races are fundamentally inferior to an invisible white standard of humanity. The multicultural illustrations of characters from different ethnic backgrounds in the *Rules Cyclopedia* were clearly more diverse than those in early core sets, which featured only white men in their illustrations; yet the rules were still just small iterations on the systems that had already been published. Thus inclusivity in this context was inclusion in a game system that reinforces the racist cultural norms of white supremacy and white privilege. But for me, the Black characters illustrated in the *Rules Cyclopedia* didn't resonate; they were exotic, prominently featuring a more traditional African garb, and identifying with these illustrations meant disidentifying with the culture and icons of my white suburban friends in New Jersey.

Tragically, in this context, humanity is the ideology of white supremacy. The rules of *D&D*, in other words, show how the game's multicultural facade is a gateway to white supremacist ideology. By producing an acute sense of hierarchical difference between the different races of the game and the invisible white standard of humanity against which these fantasy races are judged, the game captures players in the logic of racism. I have written elsewhere about how fans of the game have used statistical tables to infer how attractive the different races of the game might find one another (from the fair-skinned elf who is universally attractive to the dark-skinned half-orc who is undesirable),[4] and how the game's original designers went to great lengths to offer an Orientalist vision for adventures in both Middle Eastern and East Asian settings.[5] For most of the 1970s, 1980s, and even 1990s, the players and designers of *D&D* were engaged in a white supremacist feedback loop that takes for granted and centers the human experience as universal, powerful, attractive, and good, while simultaneously producing an inferior racialized other against which one's humanity can be judged.

This was all over the mop of curly hair on top of my head. I just knew that I held in my hands an encyclopedia that literally offered a mathematical logic, via charts, dice, and tables, through which I could understand the reasons why Gandalf was so much more powerful than Bilbo and the Dwarves in *The Hobbit*. It showed me the statistical differences between characters of different races, differences that would be mimicked in my favorite video games like *Rogue, Final Fantasy, Ultima,* and more. And, most important of all, it helped me fit in with my small but tight circle of friends, who saw in it also a set of rules that reinforced the norms of our white suburban worldview. Certainly white supremacy and racism all predate *D&D,* but an open question remains: how deeply ingrained are the tropes of *D&D* in the hearts and minds of gamers and designers? And even today, as the franchise releases core rule sets such as the progressive *Tasha's Cauldron of Everything,* which (optionally) untethers race from statistics (and thus biology), has the damage been done, and has the invisible white model of humanity that was invented by *D&D* become so popular that it has colonized the hearts and minds of designers in games across all genres?

ANTERO

I fell in love with rules and possibilities. Character statistics offered a rigid proof of humanity—personhood—unlike my own. I lingered in the realm that began at the margins of the *D&D* rule books I grew up with. These rules acted as a guide toward imagining a world unlike my own and offering strict heuristics for making it viable through dice rolls and precise recordkeeping. What was permissible hung in the balance of probability scores and eraser-scuffed record sheets.

I was a bookish ten-year-old when a copy of the *Advanced Dungeons & Dragons* second edition (*AD&D* 2e) *Player's Handbook* was left in my mother's classroom and never claimed. I inherited the title, and it didn't leave my side for months. I pored over its pages, consumed with the potential of who I *could* be based on an amalgamation of numbers and agency.

I would return, later on, to the same *Rules Cyclopedia* that Aaron describes. The seeming totality of its rules was even more alluring to me. But, in the beginning, it was my pockmarked copy of the *Player's Handbook*—complete with its furious white man charging on the cover—that beckoned me to an elsewhere. Like Aaron, I have spent a substantial part of my life studying and playing *D&D.* I am struck by how the rules printed on the page both approximate a world familiar enough for open exploration and yet paradoxically enclose that fantastical world. The borders of race, of gender, of culture, are bound by the authorial visions of the storied geeks from the American Midwest who collaboratively developed

the first role-playing game. The game is "charismatic," problematically creating enmity between different races within the game. It is also charismatic
in the same way that the technology scholar Morgan Ames describes the
allure of cognitive technologies as moving beyond the fully realized limitations with which they are imbued.[6]

These books also contain important limits to the imagination that
need to be addressed. Magical spells and enchantments have to look like
culturally acceptable, perhaps *familiar*, forms of magic. Flying, fireballs,
bags with endless space for collection—these lie at the heart of the game's
storytelling because these were references familiar to the genre-reading
players of *D&D*. The "magic" of *D&D*, both figuratively and literally, was
of a familiar and Eurocentric variety. When games are performed in the
theater of the mind, the unimaginable is also the unplayable; biases of
familiarity and cultural representation dictate fictitious reality. A non-
exotic Black character in a fantasy setting like the *Rules Cyclopedia*, for
instance, was unimaginable in 1991, when the manual was produced. In
this way, the game's tables, percentages, and progression charts—these
carefully designed and numerically driven guidelines for play—ascribe a
level of empirical believability to the fantastic.

It is important to recognize that these systems do not simply limit
where and how representations of race and gender show up in gaming
systems;[7] they also reinforce values of colonialism and capitalism. These
are baked into the mechanics and function of progression and exploration in these games. The very nature of conflict—with few exceptions—
hinges on players' tacit willingness to pillage, to lead with violence, to
develop approaches for accumulating wealth. Systems of accumulation,
of hoarding, of intentional capitalism, invisibly course through the
veins of the *D&D* system. Everything is ascribed a value in the *Player's
Handbook*, not because the ontological truth of "real" life requires it, but
because it is the truth that most players and designers naturally intuit. As
an adolescent reader, I wasn't reading critically; I was consuming this text
and understanding the given truths of the world around me: meritocracy,
prescribed values of normalcy and excellence, and predetermined limits
of my capabilities were all ideological viewpoints from the rules of a game
that implicitly shaped me as a reader and my worldview in my suburban
upbringing.

All of this is to say that racial ambiguity and the lack of representation thereof are justified by this system. Real-world analogues to race are not found in the tables and character descriptions, because they are invisible and inscrutable to the game's logic. Further, because a central tenet in role-playing circles is that anything not found within the system can be imagined and designed by players and the jurisprudence of a dungeon master, the open-ended nature of role-playing games allows us to hand wave away the concerns of the killjoys at the table. Because a group of players *could* use the gaming system to imagine and play a game based on non-European tropes and nonwhite character backgrounds, *D&D* begat a form of play that seemingly dismantles arguments of essentialism.

Except it doesn't.

I think that what the ten- and thirteen- and thirty-year-old versions of me (all years ago!) were looking for in *D&D* were mirrors that could offer a nondistorted version of my identities.

And I found none.

I wanted the me that was half-white, half mexi-pino, and fully-confused to find some kind of landing space in a world that was filled with talking monsters, attainable treasures, and incredible power. In some ways, it doesn't matter for most readers if a Black character or a racially ambiguous individual—my history is a litany of the legacies of US imperialism—is reflected in the pages of *D&D*'s rules. Aaron and I weren't even marginalized in these rules systems, because we lived beyond the boundaries of the imaginable and thus were not ludically figured into existence.

CONCLUSION

The unimaginable is not the impossible. As we reflect back on what *D&D* meant to us in the formative years of our youth, it is striking how the limits to our imaginations were shaped by the white suburban spaces that we inhabited. Within this imaginary, where "Black" toggles between "urban" and African, and the Latinx diaspora is reduced to Mexico and Puerto Rico, we were attracted to *D&D* because it offered a potential path forward to exceeding these stereotypical limits and finding ourselves in a game where we could play as anyone and do anything. Sadly, despite this promise, we never left the sandbox of the white suburban imagination when playing.

These are the hard truths that the world deals mixed kids. In a world where identities are essential, binary, and stable, we have to learn to swim with uncertainty and seek the unimaginable. Antero's pockmarked *Player's Handbook* and Aaron's trusty *Rules Cyclopedia* were atlases that taught us how to navigate these waters, even if at the voyage's end we found that we knew no more than we did when we began. This is how culture and imagination conspired to imprison us—two goofy mixed kids who just sought to make friends and find a sense of belonging—in identities that fit like a dead man's suit. How were we to know that the frontiers of imagination that *D&D* advertised would take us only as far as the back room of the hobby shop downtown?

Yet this story has a silver lining, despite our nihilistic meanderings. The unimaginable is aspirational; it is a space of potential that we both learned to swim in, despite the phony maps and stumbling blocks along the way. Even though no part of the *D&D* franchise could guide us there in 1992, we were nonetheless inspired to read, explore, and try to find our own way. Perhaps this is why, even though we shared the painful experience of encountering whitewashed reflections of ourselves in the game's manuals, we are both still fans of it to this day. We know that our stories are not unique either, and many others like us also learned, by playing *D&D*, how to swim in the choppy waters of the white suburban imagination before breaking through, breaking out, and seeking the unimaginable.

NOTES

1. Of course, the rules of *D&D* did imagine ways for players to play a mixed character—they offered rules for playing half-elven characters—yet these rules missed the bull's-eye in any number of ways. Perhaps it was because half-elven characters like Tanis from the Dragonlance series perceived their mixed heritage as a burden. Or it could have been that half-elven characters were seemingly a mix of white and whiter. It could even have been that the half-elven build package was simply less interesting than what was provided to all other races. Whatever the reason, half-elven never stuck; it essentializes the mixed experience to a category all of its own, and so forgive us as we gloss over it in the meanderings to come.

2. Aaron Allston, Jon Pickens, and Steven Schend, *Dungeons & Dragons Rules Cyclopedia* (TSR, 1991).

3. Allston, Pickens, and Schend, *Rules Cyclopedia*, 7.

4. Aaron Trammell, "Misogyny and the Female Body in *Dungeons & Dragons*," *Analog Game Studies* 1, no. 3 (2014), https://analoggamestudies.org/2014/10/constructing -the-female-body-in-role-playing-games/.

5. Aaron Trammell, "How *Dungeons & Dragons* Appropriated the Orient," *Analog Game Studies* 3, no. 1 (2016), https://analoggamestudies.org/2016/01/how-dungeons -dragons-appropriated-the-orient/.

6. Morgan G. Ames, *The Charisma Machine: The Life, Death, and Legacy of One Laptop per Child* (Cambridge, MA: MIT Press, 2019).

7. Antero Garcia, "'I Piss a Lot of People Off When I Play Dwarves like Dwarves': Race, Gender, and Critical Systems in Tabletop Role-Playing Games," *Teachers College Record* 123, no. 13 (2021): 1–26, https://doi.org/10.1177/016146812112301302.

18

DEFAMILIARIZING *DUNGEONS & DRAGONS*: PLAYING OUT WESTERN FANTASY IN SINGAPORE

Kellynn Wee

INTRODUCTION: WINGS OR WHISKERS?

"I mean, it depends on where the dragon is from," said Jacob. "Is it a Chinese dragon, or is it an *angmoh* dragon? Does it have wings or, like, whiskers?"[1] An amused pause settles over the table at a game studio in Singapore as we contemplate the provenance of the titular dragon in *Dungeons & Dragons (D&D)*. We are having a pregame dinner in a specialized play studio where members pay a fee every month for access to weekly *D&D* games tailored to each group's specific personality profiles. While we play *D&D* without irony—the iconic dragon queen Tiamat makes an appearance later in the game, wings and all, per the book—for a brief moment the whiskered, winding, snakelike body of the Chinese dragon, emblazoned on wedding decorations, Chinese New Year red packets, and astrological prediction boards outside shopping malls, flashes through our minds. In English-speaking, highly globalized Singapore, Western fantasy originating from British and American literary traditions has dug its roots in deep: *Game of Thrones*, *Harry Potter*, and *The Lord of the Rings* have as avid a following here as anywhere else in the world. But Southeast Asia has its own monsters, its own ghosts, and its own reckoning with the way imagined worlds are shared and shaped, and in Singapore, our fantastical worlds carry the imprint of our realities.

D&D's enduring legacy derives from an imagined medieval white Europe.[2] Asians and other nonwhite cultures have been depicted in questionable ways in *D&D* texts and paratexts,[3] and critical examinations of the way that Asian gamers are treated at the table and beyond have been growing. Change, however, is in the air: the recent publication of *Journeys through the Radiant Citadel* by Wizards of the Coast featured Black and brown writers,[4] and *D&D's* growing sensitivity toward responsibly depicting worlds beyond the game's Anglo-American origins has not gone unnoticed. Yet—even when one is careful about an essentialist approach to cultural and national identity—these attempts at making room for nonwhite players and creators still often feature the diasporic Asian experience, which differs from the experience of the Southeast Asian player. As *D&D's* player base balloons, studies that decenter the American experience of *D&D* are necessary, particularly when scholarly literature has also remained attentive mainly to Anglophone contexts in the West.

This chapter looks at how *D&D* is being played, and being played with, in the island nation of Singapore, a highly urbanized metropolis that is home to six million individuals, by offering a description of Singapore's tabletop role-playing scene. Singapore, briefly: situated in Southeast Asia; a former British colony; wealthy, globalized, and highly connected; home to the largest Chinese majority population in the world outside of China, mixed with diverse Indian, Malay, and other indigenous Southeast Asian racial identities. In Singapore, the experience and making of a white Euro-American world is experienced through a prism of class, gender, and race in a context that strays far from the young American men who played *D&D* in a police clubhouse in the 1970s.[5]

The relationship of Southeast Asians to the legacy of empire shimmers throughout game experiences in ways that are dissimilar from the perspectives and experiences of the Asian diaspora worldwide. Role-playing games (RPGs), as fleeting and unwitnessed forms of creative authorship, can serve as indexes of social and cultural transformations as everyday sites of emergent narrative making. RPG's transient and unrecorded nature also allows subaltern commentaries to take place beyond the public archive. Using ethnography to extend analyses of race beyond the text of the game book, as this research does, permits us to observe and record the quickly evaporating realities of playing the text as a game. It also allows us to understand the disjunctures, fractures, and dissonances that characterize Singaporeans' relationship with *D&D* and other tabletop role-playing games (TTRPGs). Additionally, an emphasis on the material realities of the game coheres with the spatial realities and leisure expectations characteristic of Singapore, emphasizing that *where* we play is also critical to *how* we play—and also that the game we strive to play rearranges the material constitutions of the conventional "tabletop" in TTRPGs.

THE CENTERING OF WHITENESS IN WESTERN FANTASY AND *D&D* SCHOLARSHIP

The genre of fantasy has a habit of whiteness.[6] Because the genre of fantasy incorporates impossible elements such as dragons and magic, it offers rhetorical distance from reality. Helen Young shows how imperialist nostalgia anchored the development of fantasy as a genre of popular fiction by white men in the United States and the United Kingdom in the early twentieth century, creating genre habits that are difficult to break even today. The violence of empire is revealed in the way that the player characters of the world are pitted against the savage, antagonistic, and brutish 'Other', who are often stand-ins for Indigenous and colonized peoples within the game (see Daniel Heath Justice, chap. 16 of this collection). Emma Vossen makes the direct link between fantasy epics such as *The Lord of the Rings* and *D&D* clear:[7] neo-medieval fantasy worlds of whiteness are entirely imaginary, yet historical accuracy is bizarrely invoked when calls for greater diversity are made, such as in angered responses to race-blind casting in TV remakes of Robert Jordan's *The Wheel of Time* (2021) and *The Lord of the Rings: The Rings of Power* (2022).[8]

The East as represented in *D&D* is an exotic place—a facsimile of East Asia and the Middle East, a wild, lush land populated by warlords where obscure rules elaborately govern social custom.[9] Aaron Trammell points out the Orientalism inherent in such a depiction and further argues that this Orientalism extends beyond representation: it is also enacted as a procedural practice by the rules introduced in supplements such as *Oriental Adventures*, which dictate characters' comeliness, weapon proficiencies, and moral alignments in specific ways. In *D&D*, race is not merely a matter of representation but also an essentializing logic: before the rule change in 2020 where race was disentangled from characters' ability score bonuses,[10] race was initially tied to specific characteristics that affected characters' ability to fight and interact within the game world.

Nonetheless, as alluded to in the introduction, a growing awareness of these issues has led to changes in the texts and paratexts published by Wizards of the Coast.[11] Over time, texts produced in each successive edition of *D&D* are more likely to depict women as well as nonwhite humanoid heroes.[12] *D&D*'s approach to race, as portrayed both visually and in the game's rules, has also been increasingly, if unevenly, progressive (see Amanda Cote and Emily Saidel, chap. 15 of this collection). A wave of newer research is further attuned to how *D&D* can be used to explore and center marginalized identities, specifically queer identities.[13] Yet studies have still tended to focus on a close analysis of the *texts* of the game as a barometer of *D&D*'s inclusiveness. Research that connects playing *D&D* to a wider cultural context—what its practices look like outside white Euro-American spaces, and how and why people's *D&D* practices ripple outward into the society in which they dwell (and vice versa)—is less common. Aaron Trammell and Antero Garcia's chapter in this collection (chap. 17) offers a welcome addition to this research by extending the lived experience of race beyond *D&D*: by reflecting on their mixed-race identities, the authors show how their white suburban childhoods immured them in inescapable hierarchies of race even as they tested new, playful identities through *D&D*.

American sites, actors, and networks produce specific cultures of play and should not be taken for granted as a neutral backdrop against which to conduct research on role-playing games. Beyond an interest in Nordic LARPs, studies of how RPGs have been globalized beyond the United States are fairly scant. Nicholas Mizer's focus on Spain shows how, in contrast to the informal gaming groups that grow loosely out of friendships in the United States, Spanish gaming centered around formally organized, state-registered clubs.[14] By publishing game magazines, registering themselves with local governments, and encouraging players to participate in festivals and youth fairs, clubs were instrumental in shaping public play cultures in Spain.

An additive approach to studies of *D&D*, where researchers collect "new" contexts of play beyond Europe and America, is also unsatisfying.

As Björn-Ole Kamm points out in his work on RPGs in Japan, to say that there is such a thing as a "Japanese RPG" is to essentialize a dynamic and emergent assemblage of practices into an artificially stable entity circumscribed within nation-state borders.[15] This way of thinking about RPGs as nationally bound, Kamm notes, does not reflect the transcultural entanglements of RPGs in Japan. Instead of presupposing that there is such a thing as a Japanese RPG, Kamm focuses on "modes of ordering, which have produced some more or less stable forms of practice, spaces to talk about them, and related subject positions from which to speak."[16]

SITUATING SINGAPORE

A thriving trading entrepôt colonized by the British in 1819, Singapore is a young nation, having only gained independence as a nation-state in 1945 at the end of World War II. It is considered a high-income economy and depicted as a marvel of economic development: wealthy, safe, and clean.[17] Its populace of 5.7 million individuals[18] consists of a diverse mixture of ethnic and religious backgrounds, the vast majority of whom are descendants of migrant settlers who came to Singapore when it was a British colony.[19] Liberal immigration policies attract temporary economic migrants to its shores to work in sectors ranging from construction to finance, but generally preclude permanent settlement.[20] Play is not an activity that is valued in Singapore, largely because of the persistence of a survivalist ideology:[21] even its playgrounds were created as part of a nation-building project that sought to zone, bind, and tame shared spaces.[22] Singapore's autocratic government has little patience for experimentation,[23] scripting its inhabitants' life trajectories through heavy-handed state policies that tie marriage, military conscription, home ownership, aging, and health care to idealized heteropatriarchal social and cultural formations. Within this context, Tan Shao Han, a game designer, writer, and educator, draws from Victor Turner to propose that role-players in Singapore create a "liminoid" space where they are able to test out different subject formations and situations for themselves outside the ossifying structures of an authoritarian state.[24]

Racial categories in Singapore are naturalized through an official policy of multiracialism.[25] Many of Singapore's social distribution mechanisms, such as the allocation of public housing, the distribution of public holidays, and the makeup of political parties, are premised on race, a category printed on Singaporeans' state-issued identity cards and all official documents. This is known as the CMIO model—Chinese, Malay, Indian, and Other. While this formulation is ostensibly aimed at acknowledging and encouraging racial diversity in Singapore, it also fixes, formalizes, and essentializes racial categories. Non-Chinese races face discrimination and prejudice, most notably in the workplace[26] and in the rental market,[27] and experience microaggressions that relate to skin color and other phenotypical categorizations.[28] As mentioned, waves of new migrants, particularly from India and China, invoke nationalistic contestations of what it means to be Singaporean as well as a new set of complications around discrimination and inclusion.[29] Questions of racial categorization and symbolic diversity are therefore not new to Singaporeans, who are accustomed to the symbolic representation and repeated encoding of race in state pageantry, media portrayals, and other nation-building tools.[30]

This chapter now moves on to offer a broad sketch of the *D&D* scene in Singapore, based on twenty months of ethnographic research and thirty-eight interviews that make up my PhD fieldwork, before reflecting on how Singaporean players remake the fantastical worlds of *D&D*.

FROM BOYS' SCHOOLS TO PLAY STUDIOS

Tabletop role-playing games (TTRPGs) were initially the province of a fairly niche subcultural community in Singapore but have grown more mainstream since 2014, after the introduction of *D&D* fifth edition (5e), as well as the stratospheric popularity of actual-play shows.[31] As of 2021–2022, many of the newer players I have encountered in the play communities here mention the widely acclaimed actual-play show *Critical Role*—where *D&D* is played "live" by a cast of well-known voice actors—as the reason why they grew interested in *D&D* and TTRPGs in general (see also Esther MacCallum-Stewart, chap. 9, this collection). The surge in popularity of *D&D* in broader popular consciousness is marked by a flourishing local market in imported game books, dice, miniatures, and other supplements to facilitate role-playing, but more visibly by the opening of several new game studios dedicated to running TTRPGs in the 2020s.

In the late 1970s and 1980s, the RPG-playing base drew from a more narrow subset of English-educated Singaporean players—mainly (but certainly not exclusively) young male students from Anglo schools established in the colonial era,[32] who had the literacy, access to privacy, money, cultural capital, and leisure time to invest in the time and materials needed for a role-playing game like *D&D*. As researcher Aaron Neo put it, to play *D&D*, you needed to have "affluence, free time, and linguistic capability."[33] Most importantly, many of the game's earliest players were comfortable using English, a prerequisite for parsing the text-heavy game. Facility in English was not a given in those days; while English was used for public administration and commerce as a holdover from Singapore's past as a British colony, it only became the primary language for education at all levels in 1974. Fluency in English therefore mapped itself along class lines more so than racial categories,[34] which in turn also inflected the composition of *D&D*'s earliest players.

The usual public sites for games in Singapore from the 1980s to the 2000s were comic book and hobbyist specialty shops that served also as hangouts for gamers. Shops like Comics Mart, for example, located by a belt of elite boys' schools in Bukit Timah and the Botanic Gardens, hosted groups of *Magic: The Gathering* players, *Warhammer* aficionados, and *D&D* players who gathered and gamed in rowdy groups until the shop closed in 2010. Other shops such as Gamersaurus Rex (opened in 2012), Grey Ogre Games (2013), and Sunny Pair O'Dice (2017) soon arose to fill the gap. These sites were a mix of retail and community spaces. As one of my respondents recalls, although Grey Ogre Games was particularly known to be a watering hole for *Magic: The Gathering* players, it also soon began to attract groups of *D&D* players, playing mostly Adventurers League (AL) modules, circa 2017.[35] The nature of AL modules does not generally lend itself to long-term storytelling due to the carousel-style tables of players.

As the *D&D* scene grew, players also began to pay a small fee for every game they played to help cover the store's operational costs, usually ranging between SGD$4 and $10, though the intent of the games is mainly still to attract footfall to the shop's retail space rather than to generate profit.

An important parallel strand to this history was how, in the '90s, the internet became a vehicle for a wider range of players to participate in *D&D* games. One player, Cheryl, talks about how the act of joining a locally run IRC channel was like entering a gateway that connected her to *Vampire: The Masquerade* and *D&D* players during a period where female players were scant: before that, she had no idea that such a community existed in Singapore.

In the 2020s, a new wave of specialized studios such as Tinker Tales, TableMinis, and Guild Hall, rose to popularity in the play scene just before the COVID-19 pandemic struck, and fully hit their stride when local restrictions around face-to-face play lifted in late 2021 and early 2022. Unlike previous shops, which were primarily *retail* spaces that occasionally hosted community games, these studios market themselves as offering the *D&D experience* as the primary part of their operations. They differentiate themselves in two ways: first, with the material constitution of their studios, which offer state-of-the-art lighting, sound, and furniture to facilitate play, as well as an enormous range of miniatures, battle terrain, and game books for players to use as part of the game experience; and second, with the gameplay style, which promises a focus on the narrative experience over all else, as delivered by professional GMs. The demographics of Singapore's play community have also broadened far beyond its initial constitution and incorporate a greater diversity of gamers as *D&D* broaches mainstream popular culture.

The cost of a game has also risen sharply alongside the promised elevation of the *D&D* experience: a player can now expect to pay an average of SGD$25–$35 per person for a game lasting three to four hours, and up to $50–$70 for games that require extensive preparation. Gamers who frequent these play studios are also far more likely to sign up for long-term shop-wide sandbox campaigns or multiple sessions that follow a published adventure. Instead of the drop-in, drop-out style of AL, gamers want to play characters who undergo a cohesive narrative arc across time. Many players desire studio atmospheres that mimic actual-play production values hoping that this will give them the *D&D* experience they seek.

THE QUESTION OF GENRE: SPICEPUNK, WUXIA, AND MORE

Beyond the material constitutions of play spaces and the social compositions of the play community, how do *D&D* games in Singapore deal with Western fantasy? Racial histories are interconnected, but not identical, and race as reflected in the mirror of Western fantasy does not map neatly onto Singapore or to other parts of Southeast Asia. Even within Southeast Asia, Singapore itself occupies an uneasy position in relation to its geographical neighbors. As a Chinese majority country, Singapore's policies and everyday politics, as mentioned earlier, racialize and disenfranchise poorer brown bodies, whether its own citizens or the million migrant laborers from India, Indonesia, Bangladesh, and the Philippines who work in the construction or domestic work sector.

With this in mind, answering the question of how *D&D* is localized or transformed through an Asian context is difficult. To work through the questions in turn, one first asks: What constitutes Singaporean fantasy? What is considered canonical and influential in the way that we think about Singaporean imaginings of the nonmimetic, a world of otherwise? How, and should we, excerpt Anglophone Singapore from its position within the Southeast Asian region, keeping in mind the constructed nature of the nation-state—and even the region—as a project of imagined community? The speculative fiction author Ng Yi-Sheng, in an essay where he coins the term "spicepunk," asks the same questions, pointing out the erasure of seafaring Southeast Asia from the world stage in favor of fantastical imaginations of Chinese bureaucratic empires.[36] Part of the difficulty in establishing Southeast Asian fantasy as a genre is also the marginalization of non-English languages and the loss of local accounts of history and social life from Southeast Asia as a consequence of colonial violence. The writers of *The Islands of Sina Una*, a critically acclaimed *D&D* 5e supplement that offers races, subclasses, and settings based on precolonial Philippines, reflect on how historical accounts of the Philippines are "filtered through the colonial machinery and non-Filipino perspectives, which renders the 'truth' they present as relative to the authors' own biases."[37] In short, Southeast Asian fantasy is read and circulated by a niche group of readers, and knowledge of Southeast Asian fantasy is not detailed among the gamers whom I have met. Even in formal education, students earn qualifications such as the UK-administered GCSE O- and A-levels, which are more likely to center on British and American literature or Asian realist fiction. So if a *D&D* player in Singapore wants to play or create an Asian *D&D* game, where do they look?

The answer, for some Singaporean Chinese players, is *wuxia* or *xianxia*. Attending to the debates around the definition and history of this Chinese fantasy genre is beyond this chapter, but to draw simply from Dang Li's work,[38] wuxia is a Chinese literary genre that features a noble warrior (the eponymous *xia*) who cultivates their martial arts skills (*wu*) through a process of arduous self-making, usually set in a quasi-historical ancient China. Xianxia, on the other hand, is a more contemporary interpretation of wuxia; *xian* implies a transcendent hero or an immortal, not merely a warrior,[39] and in general the genre incorporates a high-fantasy approach to magic, gods, demons, and the supernatural. Both genres are heavily influenced by Chinese mythology as well as Taoist and Buddhist principles.

Wuxia or xianxia works well for two reasons. First, the premise of wuxia is that of a striving warrior set apart by their quest to cultivate themselves diligently enough to attain supernatural power. This premise aligns with the *D&D*-style notion of "leveling up" as each character gains experience. Zhange Ni makes a direct connection between the development of the xianxia genre and video games, calling characters who seek cultivation "video game avatars who must accumulate qi-energy, quantifiable like points or coins, to level up."[40] Mechanically and narratively, to port a character from *D&D*'s established settings into a xianxia or wuxia world is fairly straightforward. Secondly, turning to wuxia aligns the playing of *D&D* with an experience of nostalgia. Nostalgia is a key part of playing *D&D*, especially for older adult players: Nicholas Mizer argues that it forms a fundamental part of the Old School Renaissance revival in *D&D* play in America,[41] and Anh Quang Phan connects Vietnamese gamers' cultural receptivity to wuxia games with nostalgia, rooted in Sino-Vietnamese relations.[42] Singapore's experience with Chinese fantasy is much more extensive than with Southeast Asian fantasy, stemming broadly from popular media productions such as serialized Chinese TV dramas. These include Hong Kong–produced wuxia dramas in the 1980s such as *Legend of the Condor Heroes* and Chinese mythology dramas such as the *Legends of the Eight Immortals*, which was broadcast widely between 1998 and 2000. Wuxia, and more recently xianxia, is a far more established genre than spicepunk, with a gamut of movies, comics (known as *manhua*), and TV shows to draw inspiration from.

One of the ways that xianxia is played in Singapore is through an actual-play show on Twitch known as *Xianxia D&D*. Cheekily self-described as "a bunch of nerdy-ass middle-aged Singaporean TTRPG players," the group comprises a party of friends and their DM, KC. For KC and his gaming group, many of whom he has played with since childhood, the desire to play in a wuxia game connects to how specifically located his childhood was in a particular time and space. Growing up with primarily Mandarin Chinese–speaking parents, KC and his brother spoke Mandarin at home, watched TVB wuxia dramas beamed in from Hong Kong, and listened to Teresa Teng on the radio; at school, however, KC read Tolkien, joined the Science Fiction Association, and played *Marvel Super Heroes*. For him and his brother, the desire to play in a wuxia game was a consequence of straddling two linguistic worlds at a moment when the Singaporean state had just formalized English as the main language of formal education. KC says that the wuxia game was a:

pipe dream for many, many years. Even back in the days of when we were first gaming, we were all looking for this wuxia game. We were all trying to do this TVB thing, which I discovered is a very Singaporean impulse. You have these guys who can speak English really well, and they're the same guys who go and watch *Legend of the Condor Heroes* and stuff like that. All of us have been trying to find this Holy Grail [of a wuxia game experience specific to Singaporean players].

While nostalgia is a part of this impetus, KC's deeper motivation is to return to the intent of the wuxia genre as one of antiauthoritarianism, where its martial heroes seek and enact justice in ways the government is incapable of executing. With his stream, KC's world challenges sleek contemporary Chinese productions of xianxia as epic romances and calls into question Han Chinese chauvinism in the way that Chinese history is presented. He incorporates, for example, the instrumental role of Arab mercenaries in China in repelling an invasion from the Liao, an event he says has otherwise been consigned to "a footnote of history." As KC says: "China was a sea of empires during that time. Where was that myth-making in that process? It's all gone. It's all kind of tarred over, the same way that my beloved wuxia has been tarred over."

The confluence of KC's childhood, his cultural experiences, and his position as an "overseas Chinese" outside of China, imbricated with his position as a member of the majority race in Singapore instead of a minority one, were all formative in the way that he created his *D&D* wuxia homebrew. KC's decision to stream his game is deliberate, motivated by a desire to publicly archive a snapshot of wuxia's genre underpinnings as countercultural commentary rather than romanticized Sinicism.

Beyond streamed games, private games also incorporate popular Chinese mythology into their shared worlds and serve different purposes. Kenneth, a Singaporean Chinese man in his thirties, runs a homebrew *D&D* game where his players occupy roles from all odds and ends of Chinese folk mythology. For Kenneth, like KC, anything that has ever surfaced in TV dramas, sat on altars, or been celebrated as part of a Chinese public holiday in Singapore is fair game, and he mixes and matches settings and story lines with playful irreverence, depending on casual Google searches to patch holes in his knowledge, but not overly concerned with being truthful to Chinese lore. For this group, Kenneth says, it is an endeavor of nostalgia: simply put, it is *fun* to put the Jade Rabbit (a key figure in Chinese folklore), Cai Shen Ye (the God of Fortune), and Yang Gui Fei (a historical figure and an infamous imperial consort) in the Heavenly Realm together and see what happens next. Kenneth's players attempt to speak Mandarin Chinese when in character, which is an often fraught, funny, but earnest endeavor that inspires reflection about the dominance of English in their lives. That Kenneth's games are played privately (unlike KC's Twitch stream) is important, as it creates a space for players to try and fail when dealing with their capacity to speak Mandarin Chinese.

While Chinese Singaporeans may look to Chinese genres and popular culture productions for inspiration, other players in Singapore are interested in exploring Singaporean identities that are less focused on China and Chineseness as a cultural referent. A local studio called Tinker Tales offers players a chance to inhabit a homebrewed *D&D* setting called the Huro Federasi that is based on a mixture of Southeast Asian, Malay, and Celtic myths. Game-master Suffiyan draws from Malay ghost stories told by his mother, grandmother, and aunts to create the dreamlike settings that players find themselves in. Immersed in the sounds of Indonesian gamelan that float through the studio during one of Suffiyan's games, players tempt fate by eating Balinese-style offerings to gods and travel through archipelagic seas under the light of the full moon. In this world, the ghosts that Suffiyan conjures feel piercingly real, inviting players to glance nervously over their shoulders: the supernatural is palpable in the moods, referents, and music he uses, because they are the ghost stories that Singaporean children grew up with. Another studio, TableMinis, runs a live game called Makcik and Magicks. Their DMs play in a game that is performed to a live audience every week at the studio, and the game approaches its modern-day Singaporean setting with a greater emphasis on its more realist locatedness in Southeast Asia as opposed to turning towards wuxia or xianxia as a fantastical genre. Its cast incorporates characters from a range of class backgrounds—including a handphone seller, an influencer, and a mover—as well as from different ages and races. One of its most moving characters, Makcik Jenab ("Makcik" is an affectionate term for an older Malay woman in Singapore and other parts of Southeast Asia), is a 57-year-old Malay woman who sells a popular local dish called nasi padang; her storyline incorporates an exploration of her sexuality and religion that has, at times, brought audience members to tears. The characters also speak in Singlish—a localized version of English that mixes in loanwords and syntax from other languages used in Singapore. Prior to this, the appearance of Singlish at the *D&D* table in my experience had always felt clunky, even comedic, but the players choose to use it here with artful seriousness to reflect their characters' histories and social positionings. The popularity of Makcik and Magicks led to a live play to a receptive audience beyond the studio from which it originated at the Singapore Repertory Theatre. By transposing *D&D* into a contemporary Singaporean setting and refusing to allow it to falter into parody or satire, Makcik and Magicks explores the complexity and contradictions of Singaporean identities.

If one looks beyond *D&D*, other types of role-playing games have been more popular sites for exploring questions of race and identity in Singapore. Games that are either historical or realist in their approaches reveal that these tensions very much exist in a different, more intimate context. For example, at Tinker Tales, I played a *Call of Cthulhu* game where the Singaporean Chinese players role-played white explorers with a heavy dose of irony, deliberately exaggerating imperialist and racist behavior. Tinker Tales also runs a *Vampire: The Masquerade* game set in 1920s Singapore, where different factions jockey for power: the vampires' court of elites is filled with white men, and the Asian characters must find a way to establish themselves amid shifting racial and class tensions. This also incorporates racial tensions between new migrant settlers and Indigenous Malays, with the gameplay revealing uneasy alliances formed during these uncertain times. Ultimately, in Singapore, the fantastical worlds created through *D&D* gameplay extend far beyond the covers of a *D&D* book and into the specific trajectories of life lived by people beyond an American center.

CONCLUSION

In Singapore, the *D&D* community was dominated by English-speaking boys from elite Anglophone schools in the early '80s and '90s but has since widened to incorporate a broader range of players for several reasons: the popularization of English as Singaporeans' native language; Singaporeans' growing affluence and appetite for leisure activities; the globalization of our media consumption habits; the geekification of pop culture more broadly; and the influence of actual-play podcasts and shows in the late 2010s. This has led to the development of TTRPG play studios in the 2020s aimed at engineering a specific narrative experience. Players in Singapore are also interested in exploring fantastical worlds set in Asia in their *D&D* games but face a number of challenges while doing so: a lack of knowledge about Southeast Asian fantasy; the way that *D&D* deals with race as white/Other, which does not reflect Singaporeans' own experiences of race; and the game mechanics themselves, which create characters that interact with the world with force and violence.

An overview of Singapore's *D&D* play communities and playful worlds unravels multiple threads that stretch into an enticing darkness, allowing us to reframe our questions more broadly—to be deliberate about grounding players in time and place when we try to understand what *D&D* is and what it does. Through the development of studios that attempt to elevate storytelling by immersing players in conditions similar to actual-play podcasts, what sort of experiences are gamers seeking, and why? How do geopolitical relationships between Singapore and China play out in a *D&D* xianxia stream, and what does that tell us about how everyday citizens participate in broader social discourses, and to what end? What sort of characters do localized game worlds feature, what are the stories told by and about these characters, and what are the techniques used to tell these stories? Where does whiteness sit in the stories that are told? In the context of a nation-state that has been founded on urgent survivalism, what sort of stories are people telling together for fun, what other lives do they seek in collective imagination, and what are they doing when they conjure these emergent worlds to life?

TTRPGs, often overlooked in "serious" scholarship, can help us understand how players—who might not necessarily define themselves as creative producers with the intention of performing to an audience or publicly archiving their work—have authorial power to experiment with broader cultural narratives within the private space of the table, revealing complicated everyday attitudes toward broader structural issues. Emerging strands of research that center an ethnographic approach to *D&D* beyond an analysis of *D&D* as media will help us to realize the cultural import of these games better and more fully. Understanding how *D&D* affects players' experiences of race can and should go beyond analyzing textual and visual material, particularly since the text itself can so often be ignored, used selectively, or even discarded. Paying attention to the sites where games are played, and how these spaces inscribe themselves on the unfolding narratives of the game—and vice versa—also helps us to understand what narrative experiences we are seeking, and why.

Looking at what emerges in the negative space beyond the market saturation of *D&D* is also important. In Southeast Asia, the independent RPG scene is vibrant; creators refuse to bear the imperialist mechanics of *D&D* and the burdens of its genre habits and instead have chosen to write and play a rich tapestry of independent games. Across RPGSEA, an online community of Southeast Asian independent game creators, was recently recognized in the 2022 ENNIE Awards for best online content and features games such as *Gubat Banwa*, a postclassical fantasy martial arts TTRPG; *A Thousand Thousand Islands*, a Southeast Asian–themed fantasy visual world-building project; and *Mangayaw*, a game set in the Philippine archipelago and inspired by Philippine legend, folklore, culture, and history. Despite this, issues with funding and access as well as the long shadow of *D&D*'s popularity limit the reach of these games. Perhaps the question is not whether dragons have wings or whiskers, but whether the games we play should necessitate our needing to ask this question at all.

NOTES

1. *Angmoh* is a term used to refer to a Caucasian person. It is seen as a casual descriptor but is not necessarily intended to be pejorative, depending on the context. The term is also used as a shorthand for places, things, or people who appear Westernized, for example, "She went overseas to study, then she came back and became very *angmoh*."

2. Emma Vossen, "There and Back Again: Tolkien, Gamers, and the Remediation of Exclusion through Fantasy Media," *Feminist Media Histories* 6, no. 1 (2020): 37–65, https://doi.org/10.1525/fmh.2020.6.1.37.

3. Aaron Trammell, "How *Dungeons & Dragons* Appropriated the Orient," *Analog Game Studies* 3, no. 1 (2016), https://analoggamestudies.org/2016/01/how-dungeons -dragons-appropriated-the-orient/.

4. Samantha Nelson, "*Journeys through the Radiant Citadel* Is *D&D*'s Answer to *Star Trek*," Polygon, July 19, 2022, https://www.polygon.com/23269854/dnd-journeys -through-the-radiant-citadel-review.

5. Gary Alan Fine, *Shared Fantasy: Role-Playing Games as Social Worlds* (Chicago: University of Chicago Press, 2002).

6. Helen Young, *Race and Popular Fantasy Literature: Habits of Whiteness* (Routledge, 2015).

7. Vossen, "There and Back Again."

8. James Poniewozik, "Guess Who's Coming to Mordor," *New York Times*, September 29, 2022, https://www.nytimes.com/2022/09/29/arts/television/the-rings-of-power-ca st-diversity.html.

9. Trammell, "How *D&D* Appropriated the Orient."

10. Charlie Hall, "How *Dungeons & Dragons*' Next Book Deals with Race, plus Exclusive New Pages and Art," Polygon, November 2, 2020, https://www.polygon.com /2020/11/2/21538090/dungeons-dragons-tashas-cauldron-of-everything-race-monk -art.

11. Sarah Stang and Aaron Trammell, "The Ludic Bestiary: Misogynistic Tropes of Female Monstrosity in *Dungeons & Dragons*," *Games and Culture* 15, no. 6 (2020): 730–747, https://doi.org/10.1177/1555412019850059.

12. Antero Garcia, "Privilege, Power, and *Dungeons & Dragons*: How Systems Shape Racial and Gender Identities in Tabletop Role-Playing Games," *Mind, Culture, and Activity* 24, no. 3 (July 3, 2017): 232–246, https://doi.org/10.1080/10749039.2017 .1293691.

13. Philip J. Clements, "Dungeons & Discourse: Intersectional Identities in *Dungeons & Dragons*" (PhD diss., Bowling Green State University, 2019), http://www .proquest.com/docview/2354147787/abstract/AFE1500812684A3DPQ/1; Nathaniel L. Rogers, "'A World Where They Belonged': Queer Women's Use of a *Dungeons & Dragons* Game to Experiment with, Express, and Explore Identity" (MA thesis, San Diego State University, 2020), http://www.proquest.com/docview/2490736949/abst ract/4A8876F4E46F4086PQ/1; Harold Bosstick, "'To Become Who You Wish to Be':

Actual-Play Tabletop Roleplaying Game Podcasts as Oral Storytelling Outlets for Queer Community, Representation, and Identity" (MA thesis, Indiana State University, 2021); Felix Rose Kawitzky, "Magic Circles," *Performance Research* 25, no. 8 (November 16, 2020): 129–136, https://doi.org/10.1080/13528165.2020.1930786.

14. Nicholas Mizer, "No One Role-Plays the Spanish Inquisition! The Early History of Role-Playing Games in Spain," in *Wyrd Con Companion Book 2013*, ed. Sarah Lynne Bowman and Aaron Vanek (Wyrd Con, 2013), 77–85.

15. Björn-Ole Kamm, *Role-Playing Games of Japan: Transcultural Dynamics and Orderings* (Cham: Springer International Publishing, 2020), https://doi.org/10.1007/978-3-030-50953-8.

16. Kamm, *Role-Playing Games of Japan*, 22.

17. World Bank, "The World Bank in Singapore," April 9, 2019, https://www.worldbank.org/en/country/singapore/overview.

18. Department of Statistics Singapore, "Singapore Population," Singapore Statistics, June 30, 2020, http://www.singstat.gov.sg/modules/infographics/population.

19. Beng Huat Chua, "Multiculturalism in Singapore: An Instrument of Social Control," *Race and Class* 44, no. 3 (2003): 58–77, https://doi.org/10.1177/0306396803044003025.

20. Brenda S. A. Yeoh, "Cosmopolitanism and Its Exclusions in Singapore," *Urban Studies* 41, no. 12 (2004): 2431–2445, https://doi.org/10.1080/00420980412331297618.

21. Geraldine Heng and Janadas Devan, "State Fatherhood: The Politics of Nationalism, Sexuality, and Race in Singapore," in *Bewitching Women, Pious Men: Gender and Body Politics in Southeast Asia*, ed. Aihwa Ong and Michael G. Peletz (Berkeley: University of California Press, 1995), 195–215.

22. Raffaella Sini, "The Social, Cultural, and Political Value of Play: Singapore's Postcolonial Playground System," *Journal of Urban History* 48, no. 3 (2022): 578–607, https://doi.org/10.1177/0096144220951149.

23. Shao Han Tan, "Tabletop Role-Playing Games in Singapore: Case Studies for Education and Empowerment" (MA thesis, National University of Singapore, 2011).

24. Tan, "TTRPGs in Singapore."

25. Chua, "Multiculturalism in Singapore."

26. Peter K. H. Chew, Jessica L. Young, and Gerald P. K. Tan, "Racism and the Pinkerton Syndrome in Singapore: Effects of Race on Hiring Decisions," *Journal of Pacific Rim Psychology* 13 (2019): e16, https://doi.org/10.1017/prp.2019.9.

27. Ilynn Mei Xian Chew, Pei Ying Goh, and Wan Zhyi Ng, "Racial Discrimination against Prospective Tenants: Evidence from the Room Rental Market in Singapore," Nanyang Technological University Singapore, 2020, https://dr.ntu.edu.sg/handle/10356/138771.

28. Farah Bawany, "Multiethnicity in Multicultural Singapore: Critical Autoethnography to Understand Racism in Singapore," *Inter-Asia Cultural Studies* 22, no. 1 (January 2, 2021): 118–126, https://doi.org/10.1080/14649373.2021.1886469;

Selvaraj Velayutham, "Everyday Racism in Singapore," in *Everyday Multiculturalism*, ed. Amanda Wise and Selvaraj Velayutham (London: Palgrave Macmillan, 2009), 255–273, https://doi.org/10.1057/9780230244474_14.

29. Sylvia Ang, *Contesting Chineseness: Nationality, Class, Gender and New Chinese Migrants* (Amsterdam: Amsterdam University Press, 2022).

30. Chua, "Multiculturalism in Singapore."

31. Shelly Jones, ed., *Watch Us Roll: Essays on Actual Play and Performance in Tabletop Role-Playing Games* (Jefferson, NC: McFarland, 2021).

32. These schools included St. Joseph's Institution (founded in 1852 by the Catholic Church), Raffles Institution (founded in 1823 by British statesman Stamford Raffles), Victoria School (founded in 1876 as part of the Straits Settlement Government's efforts to improve education among Malay boys of varying social classes), and the Anglo-Chinese School (founded in 1886 by Methodist Reverend William Fitzjames Oldham).

33. Aaron Neo, "Role-Playing Games in Singapore" (BA thesis, National University of Singapore, 2001), 19.

34. Chua, "Multiculturalism in Singapore."

35. A large number of public games are played "Adventurers League" style, where players can "port" their characters in and out of different story lines to level them up and gain magical weapons and items. The Adventurers League system works well for players who cannot commit to the long-term demands of an episodic campaign, or who have more of an interest in crafting characters who are exceptionally powerful in combat rather than in extensive narrative construction. One of my respondents described this as "RPGs for people who actually want to play computer games."

36. Yi-Sheng Ng, "A Spicepunk Manifesto: Towards a Critical Movement of Southeast Asian Heritage-Based SFF," *Strange Horizons*, August 29, 2022, http://strangehorizons.com/non-fiction/a-spicepunk-manifesto-towards-a-critical-movement-of-southeast-asian-heritage-based-sff/.

37. Dang Li, *The Islands of Sina Una* (Ontario: Hit Point Press, 2020), 323.

38. "The Transcultural Flow and Consumption of Online Wuxia Literature through Fan-Based Translation," *Interventions* 23, no. 7 (October 3, 2021): 1041–1065, https://doi.org/10.1080/1369801X.2020.1854815.

39. Yujuan Jing, "Reconstructing Ancient Chinese Cultural Memory in the Context of Xianxia TV Drama" (MA thesis, Uppsala University, 2021), http://urn.kb.se/resolve?urn=urn:nbn:se:uu:diva-446181.

40. Zhange Ni, "Xiuzhen (Immortality Cultivation) Fantasy: Science, Religion, and the Novels of Magic/Superstition in Contemporary China," *Religions* 11, no. 1 (2020): 11, https://doi.org/10.3390/rel11010025.

41. Nicholas J. Mizer, *Tabletop Role-Playing Games and the Experience of Imagined Worlds* (Cham: Palgrave Macmillan, 2019), https://doi.org/10.1007/978-3-030-29127-3.

42. Anh Quang Phan, "From Print Texts to Online Gaming: The Cross-Cultural History of Wuxia Fictions in Vietnam," *Sage Open* 11, no. 2 (2021), https://doi.org/10.1177/21582440211021392.

19

SOFT COMMUNITIES AND VICARIOUS DEVIANCE IN *DUNGEONS & DRAGONS*

Victor Raymond and Gary Alan Fine

In Rona Jaffe's 1981 novel *Mazes and Monsters*, Robbie Wheeling is described as a young man who has lost his sense of self, assuming instead the identity of his "Mazes and Monsters" character, Pardieu the Holy Man.[1] The conclusion of the novel finds Robbie embedded in the game, lost to friends and fellow players.[2] Inspired by the disappearance of James Dallas Egbert III in 1979, *Mazes and Monsters* suggested a dangerous side to the emerging hobby of role-playing games.[3]

At the time of Jaffe's novel, *Dungeons & Dragons* (*D&D*) had already inserted itself into the public imagination. Created by Gary Gygax and Dave Arneson in 1974, the game, developed out of the wargaming community, appealed to players who wanted their gaming to be more imaginative.[4] With businesses such as TSR Hobbies (the publisher of *D&D*) selling rule books and other objects that contributed to the game, *D&D* became what is termed a "manufactured subculture"—one that some people outside the hobby might consider a social problem in an age when threats to and from children and teenagers were salient.[5] By implication, games such as *D&D* could be seen as culturally deviant, and at worst leading to psychiatric disorders. A year after the publication of *Mazes and Monsters*, Patricia Pulling asserted that playing *D&D* had contributed to the suicide of her son, and formed an organization, Bothered About Dungeons and Dragons (BADD), that continued to raise the issue until Pulling died in 1997. She alleged a link between the game and Satanism, a claim hotly disputed by TSR Hobbies and other gaming companies.[6] Although the controversy over the effects of playing *D&D* did not dissipate immediately, the number of provable suicides and direct ties to Satanism linked to the game were few. Perhaps instead *D&D* players benefited from a caring community of fellow players.[7]

Since the 1980s, *D&D* and the role-playing game hobby have become immensely more popular and increasingly mainstream, but a persistent perception exists that gamers are somehow "different." (Some suggest that this has changed, perhaps due to the commercial success of *D&D*.) Labels such as "nerd" and "geek" are often applied to participants, both by gamers themselves and by people outside the hobby.[8] Rather than using a psychological or religious frame to understand this divide, we suggest that role-playing as a social activity is better understood as a form of bounded and socially accepted behavior that permits the imaginative presentation of deviance,[9] revealed through the willingness to imagine oneself engaging in fantasy worlds where conventional norms do not apply. These explorations constitute *vicarious deviance*. These nonnormative actions are permitted precisely because of their lack of social repercussions in daily life: characters are distinct from players, and players are protected because of the embrace of a soft community. The walls separating gaming from the "real world" are strong and shielding.

Drawing on the in-group literature from the early years of *D&D*, we argue that the playful performance of deviance within the gaming community became an integral part of gameplay, found among the intersecting levels of persons, players, and characters, but, as we subsequently describe, also a source of concern for those who wished to promote and expand the hobby.[10] Worth noting is the historical frame of our discussion; the role-playing game hobby developed very quickly from its origins in the early 1970s to the mid-1980s, which is our focus in this chapter. The hobby has continued to grow, develop, and diversify since then, with new play styles and preferences emerging in the past thirty years. These changes have affected how gamers interact with one another, but that is outside the scope of this chapter.

ROLE-PLAY GAMING AS A SOFT COMMUNITY

Role-playing involves sustained interaction among small groups sharing an imaginative social world as a form of leisure. While participants often knew each other, this was not inevitably the case. Conventions, college clubs, and game store events provided opportunities for strangers to join together; sometimes the group would continue, but on other occasions the gathering would be temporary. Some players may have revealed social deficits that made them problematic participants in other domains, but if they demonstrated a level of competence and enthusiasm at the game table, they were likely to be accepted despite their idiosyncratic behavior. This included talking too loud or too often, not sharing food, or being notably unhygienic. This openness defines a soft community, as is true for the long-standing communities of competitive chess,[11] where individual members are acknowledged as sometimes behaving in ways that would be considered deviant in the larger world but are acceptable within the chess community. The gaming ideal was to establish a group of like-minded participants who played in ways that increased the hedonic experience for all and embraced the recognized gaming goals. Central was the acceptance of a dungeon master (DM)—often an older, more experienced player—who constructed adventures for the players' characters. The adventures must challenge the players' skill, be enjoyable, and lead to self-enhancing outcomes.

As noted, role-play gaming grew out of the older wargaming hobby but quickly became distinctive.[12] These groups formed in a variety of locations, and the contexts for these gaming groups have expanded still further in the half century since the publication of the original *D&D* rules in 1974. The transformation of "wargaming," with its focus on historical military simulation, into "role-playing," with primacy given to fantasy, science fiction, and more fictive settings, was profound. In particular, the differences between wargame clubs and science fiction fan clubs resulted in considerable variability in how those communities understood *D&D* and role-playing in general, emphasizing either the battles or the technology of the period.[13] What was once a small and esoteric hobby, numbering no more than a few thousand American young people and adults, has grown to be a widespread and influential part of popular culture, with millions of players meeting in a vast array of global scenes, including game stores, bars, schoolrooms, home basements, and now increasingly online.

The wide availability of game materials, as well as a rapidly growing body of texts, including magazines, books, and online resources, provides for shared understandings of how the games are to be played and how play is to be understood. Within this community, what constitutes appropriate behavior may be at variance with the larger society and may differ from group to group but always is affected by rules, both written and developed locally.[14] This in itself does not explain the possibility of psychological harm raised by *Mazes and Monsters* and by subsequent concern about Satanism or occult involvement, or the lessened prominence of these concerns over time. It is certainly true that many social activities are seen as deviant when first introduced, but early critics of *D&D* pointed to the game materials themselves as problematic. The suggestion that playing *D&D* is dangerous—that is, contrary to well-established norms—has remained a persistent and recurrent theme, despite the game's growing acceptance in the larger society.

To examine the role of deviance and community as discussed in early role-play gaming, we rely on data from 1975 to 1982 from two primary sources: the *Strategic Review* and *The Dragon*, both published by TSR Hobbies. Drawing on Erving Goffman's frame analysis approach,[15] we examine the communal labeling of deviant behavior in the context of playing *D&D* and other role-playing games.[16] For sociologists such as Howard Becker, deviance is not a set of objective behaviors but rather a construction by authorities that is applied unequally to acts committed by those judged unworthy. The labeling of deviance is further complicated because, in fantasy gaming, several frames of meaning operate simultaneously: the meaning framework of the natural person, the playing persona, and the played character.

Data from articles, letter columns, advice columns, and editorials demonstrate that, contrary to public belief, gamers were aware that behavior defined as deviant was encountered in the context of gameplay, and decisions were necessary as to whether these actions were acceptable and appropriate in this social context. Whether objective or not, gamers recognized that some behaviors were problematic and even sanctionable, and this became especially notable when knowledge of fantasy gaming expanded from the in-group to a wider public.

AWARENESS OF DEVIANCE AS PUBLIC REPUTATION

In 1979 Timothy Kask, the editor of *The Dragon*, wrote about the perception of gaming by outsiders to the hobby, using an unnamed friend's viewpoint:

He was of the opinion, as an "outsider," that some of us might just be a little freaky, and his appraisal is not uncommon. Our hobby suffers from some bad impressions and bad press. To many people, the appellation "wargamer" conjures up visions of a budding group of warmongers, intent on world destruction, or some sort of blood and violence freak that gets his jollies on carnage and mayhem. Mention fantasy, and many think that we are a bunch of hopeless Walter-Mitty-types, disassociated from the real world.[17]

Theron Kuntz agreed, writing in *The Dragon* the next year that wargaming (and, by association, role-playing) should be seen in the same light as other, better-known games: "There is no difference between a wargame and a Monopoly game when it comes down to the actual competition between opponents."[18] Kuntz's defensiveness was, in part, a response to the media attention to the case of James Dallas Egbert III that had been mounting since the young man's disappearance. Indeed, Timothy Kask had directly addressed this issue earlier in *The Dragon*, noting that "it may become incumbent now upon all of us to actively seek to correct the misconceptions now formed or forming whenever and wherever possible."[19]

But there was also an awareness that considerable variety existed among wargamers at the time. In the letters column of *The Dragon*, Garry F. Spiegle noted both positive and negative examples of social interaction, emphasizing the need to avoid rigid and inflexible attitudes toward gameplay, as such attitudes would discourage beginning players.[20] Pointing to problematic social behavior suggests the effect of public awareness and the need to control deviance when participants interact as part of a group in creating shared understandings of the moral context of the fictive or fantasy milieu of the game through their frames of understanding.[21]

CONFLATION OF SELVES AND CHARACTERS

To an external observer, unaware of the frame switching that occurs in the game, it is easy to conflate the seemingly deviant actions of fantasy characters with the personal intentions of the players, creating a frightening image that suggests that gamers were engaging in unacceptable behaviors with serious consequences if they were enacted in the larger world. Aside from *Mazes and Monsters*, perhaps the most widely distributed example of this claim of immorality at the time was the infamous Chick tract *Dark Dungeons*, which linked *D&D*, witchcraft, suicide, Satanism, and mind control.[22] Despite being satirized and derided, becoming something of a pop-culture classic, when initially published, the tract reflected the concerns of some people unfamiliar with the gaming subculture.[23]

From the outside, the different—and distinct—frames of role-playing experience were distorted into an alarming picture of adolescents casting off their identities and inhibitions to act in ways that appeared worrisome to parents, teachers, and authorities. It *was* possible to establish a direct connection to *some* allegations of deviance and Satanism (as understood by some on the outside), and perhaps to mental illness, as *D&D* supplements incorporated druids, witches, and demons into gaming culture.[24] Further, articles in *The Dragon* directly suggested Christian-inspired demonology as a theme for inclusion in gameplay.[25] As for mental illness, it was treated as a character's condition, moderated by game rules that, in turn, demanded role-playing.[26] Even before these gameplay articles were published, Harry O. Fischer's story "The Finzer Family—A Tale of Modern Magic,"[27] serialized in *The Dragon* in 1977, posited that magic was alive in modern America. This was *fiction*, but if one took it seriously, *Dark Dungeons'* dire allegations might seem *much* less outlandish. However, from within the frame of gameplay, *all* these identities and actions are forms of imaginative play. Indeed, one of Fine's informants was a devout student at a conservative Christian college. Early on, a few leading gamers, including Gygax, recognized that these disturbing images might be taken seriously by people outside the gaming world.

Realizing that a defense was needed, the Methodist minister Rev. Arthur Collins wrote a response in *The Dragon*. Collins contrasts gaming with his theological profession, noting that since he has explained his hobby (role-playing games) to his congregation, they have "come to accept him as 'normal.' "[28] He explains that he games with other "ministers and theo-logs" who eschew playing clerics and instead prefer playing other classes of characters, finding fulfillment in the activity. Collins attributes public misapprehensions to stereotyping: "Clergypersons are seen as inhibitors of fun rather than sharers of fun." In the context of the soft community of gamers, shared fun is the goal.

Collins emphasizes the place of fantasy in Christian theology, draw-ing on J. R. R. Tolkien's essay "On Fairy-Stories" and explaining that "for me (and for many others) fantasy is an important and natural human activity: It is a function of the human soul which brings me fully alive."[29] Turning to the use of fantasy in role-playing, Collins suggests that it offers three distinct benefits and one potential shortcoming. The first is the opportunity to be somebody else:

Role-playing is a liberating exercise. It frees you from the pretense of trying so hard to be what you want others to think you are. Instead, by assuming a role, you can be whatever you want to be, and in the process you grow in your under-standing of human behavior (your own, not the least). One of the geniuses of *D&D* and *AD&D* is the identification of a player with a continuing, developing character.[30]

Beyond the opportunity to take on the role of another, Collins argues that the second benefit of role-playing is that it allows one to learn how to understand others, suggesting that the interactions that occur during role-playing are an ongoing exchange between players who validate each other's role performance. If this is not accomplished, or if something negates that performance, the player may be perceived by other players as having acted in an antisocial way.

For Collins, the third benefit is that "role-playing gives us a sanity break. People ask me why I play Dungeons & Dragons. One reason is for my emotional health."[31] Collins argues, perhaps overly optimistically, that imaginative play in the context of a role-playing game might help avoid deviance in real life. The downside, he cautions, is that each of these benefits can be turned to negative ends: one can become obsessed with being someone else; gameplay can be enacted so that it disrupts the enjoyment of others, and fictive elements of gameplay such as demonol-ogy and magic can be pursued in real life. He ends his essay by saying that these concerns were not applicable to his experience: "On the whole, I think these fears are ungrounded. It is possible to misuse fantasy, role-playing, and any other hobby, but the great majority of people who dabble in them are healthy persons." To expand Collins's conclusion, we turn to the conception of role-playing as described by gamers themselves as a *vicarious* experience.

VICARIOUS EXPERIENCE

The description of role-players as taking on a different persona and acting in ways that might be inappropriate in "real life" is validated by the depiction of the gaming ideal. Thomas Filmore provides a representative example:

The dreamer's art, the ability to cut loose from the restraints of reality and touch new shores and lives, is the essence and lure of D+D. . . . Role playing is a side of D+D which gives it much of its flavor. As a player defines his character's desires, his hopes and fears, weaknesses and vices, his commitment to him becomes deeper and this investment leads the player to more dangerous but satisfying exploits.[32]

Role-playing as an enjoyable activity encourages playing the role of another, a novel identity, rather than acting as oneself. The situations occurring in the context of the game may involve acting in violent ways to vanquish dangerous foes. In game terms, success can be defined as defeating danger and acquiring more experience and ability as a fictive self. Successful play depends on interacting with other players in ways that contribute to that conclusion. This is achieved through interaction among the players:

Just as people open a conversation with "In *The Return of the King* where . . ." or "You know that part in *Star Wars* when . . ." one can overhear a couple players say, "Remember last month when we played in John's campaign . . ." and "You know, once I played in this game where . . ." Sure, you'll hear a lot of first-person accounts, "I did this," and "I did that," but that is only a convenient shorthand for "Eldric the Bold did this or that." It's *telling the story* that is important.[33]

Validation of the vicarious experience comes from mutual understanding as players frame their game activity. Fantasy role-playing involves imagining violent acts, but more broadly, *D&D* envisions having characters act in a wide variety of ways that might never be available in the mundane world. Actions seen as transgressive or deviant in everyday life are entirely appropriate in the realm of fantasy role-playing, framed as legitimate for the enacted characters. This should not be conflated with the concept of "transgressive play," which involves gameplay that might be considered as a form of norm violation *within* the context of computer games and their implied settings, which is distinct from norm violations among the soft community of gamers. (Here we distinguish among computer gameplay, such as *Oblivion* or *Skyrim*, which is a solitary experience only later shared with others; collective online games such as *World of Warcraft*; and tabletop role-playing games, such as *D&D*.)

A typical episode of *D&D* gameplay involves imagining battling and defeating dangerous foes, acquiring treasure from those foes, and sharing the benefits that then accrue to the players' characters. However, within the fictive realm of the fantasy setting, many more imagined social activities are possible outside the demands of the adventure narrative. What are characters to do with their acquired wealth? Are there altruistic acts in which characters engage? In the case of the first question, players may use characters' wealth in mundane ways: donating to charity, investing in business, or using money for training or research.[34] But that wealth might also be used in ways that would be perceived as deviant in the larger society: engaging in orgies, practicing socially unacceptable religions, or making donations to groups seen as disreputable in the setting of the game. The sociological point is that deviance is not an objective set of actions but should be understood only in context.

FRAMES OF SOCIAL MEANING AND DEVIANCE

To understand deviance in the soft community of role-playing games, we separate domains of social interaction. In this, role-playing games have three frames of meaning:[35]

1. The social frame of a *person*; their commonsense understanding of the world
2. The group frame of a *player*; their appreciation of the rules and conventions of the game
3. The fantasy frame of a *character*; how a player's character is conceived within the fictive setting of the game

Each of these frames affects how role-players interpret their interactions within a local community. Drawing on Becker's model of deviance as a form of labeling,[36] being considered deviant results from how others react to the person and judge their behavior. However, this is not based on a society-wide understanding of behavior; rather, meaning derives from inside the community itself. The reactions of the referee (game master or dungeon master), the other players, and occasional outside observers define which behaviors or roles are rejected. For players, this layered framing of gameplay provides the context for social interaction. To form and maintain a soft community, a communal understanding of what is expected of *persons* interested in role-playing games must develop. This understanding produces a lattice of social expectations that form a social contract that frames gameplay. In other words, players are expected to act consistently within the contours of their character: a player with a paladin character should be heroic in their gameplay; acting otherwise might be rejected as "inauthentic" by other players.

The rules of *D&D* provide the framework for evaluating actions taken by *players*. Since this is the most visible and tangible basis for mutual agreement available, the rules as seemingly objective structures have the most immediate effect on how players perform their characters and interact as a game-playing group.

Finally, the fictional environment of the fantasy setting of gameplay, the simulacrum of society, is presented as the context of the adventures undertaken by the players' *characters*. For purposes of gameplay, this fictional environment is the frame whereby the players' characters interact. When players portray other characters' actions as deviant in a fictive context, there may be imaginative consequences. For example, when a thief is apprehended by the (in-game) city watch, social sanctions may be directed at the character, which can lead to dissatisfaction by the player.

It is also the case that players (and the referee) simultaneously take into account each other's actions and react in ways ranging from strong approval to extreme rejection. But since this takes place in light of a need for group cohesion, the goal or objective is often to maintain group stability, keeping the group functioning. This interaction contributes to the socialization of players to the social world of the game on several levels:

within the context of the character and game setting, within the context of being a player in a soft community of gamers, and within the context of being a moral person in a larger society. While the in-game presentation of social situations is ostensibly targeted at the characters, players also react to the fantasy situation and modify their behaviors toward one another around the table as a result.

One might argue that the diversity of gameplay preferences that have emerged since the 1980s has blurred group definitions of deviance and lessened the influence of gaming groups as "soft communities." This view should be balanced against the emergence of a variety of popular and social media, particularly shows such as *Critical Role* and *Stranger Things*, which reinforce normative expectations of what is considered appropriate gameplay. Also worth noting is that definitions of what is considered deviant behavior are rooted in a larger social context, suggesting that more research is needed to understand these factors influencing gameplay.

VICARIOUS DEVIANCE IN THE SOCIAL WORLD OF GAMERS

Having presented the role of vicarious deviance within soft communities, we turn to how the perception of this deviance has been described, drawing on essays in the early volumes of the *Strategic Review* and *The Dragon*. Vicarious deviance occurs, but, as significantly, it is also discussed. These texts reflect how the early participants understood the problem. While many magazines and fanzines were published during the period, these two were the most organizationally authoritative.

With our focus on the levels of framing in *D&D*, tied to the person (in the natural world), the player (in the gaming community), and the character (in the fantasy domain), we briefly address three core ways in which vicarious deviances are contained. Specifically, we describe the implicit social contract through which adolescent behavior is made acceptable in the gaming context. The character's alignment constitutes a means through which a player's imagined deviance can be expressed. Each level of the framing of meaning is embedded in the soft community of players, in which a strong desire exists to keep the group together, satisfied over weeks and months, and continuing unless a sharp reason to disband arises.

THE SOCIAL CONTRACT OF "GAMING PERSONS"

As discussed, players recognized from the earliest days of *D&D* that a divide existed between "good" and "bad"—proper and improper—behavior by fantasy gamers. The former includes a serious interest in the games hobby, courtesy, mutual support, and tolerance of differences of opinion.[37] However, the rapid growth in the popularity of *D&D* meant that not all new players embraced or displayed these expectations.

These difficulties were detailed in a letter by Michael Sutton, printed in *The Dragon* in 1979. He described a *D&D* tournament allegedly sponsored by TSR Hobbies in which times for sessions varied, rules were applied inconsistently, and the organizers and referees acted in an abusive manner. Sutton appealed to the community of gamers to uphold the norms of the hobby and to sanction tournament organizers who were acting inappropriately. Within a few years, an extensive array of social norms and expectations among players and DMs had spread widely. For instance, Fred Zimmerman provided a set of questions for players to consider when selecting a DM, distinguishing a "superior DM" from a less acceptable one. Zimmerman asked, "Does the DM ensure that each player can and does act independently during resolution of encounters? It is essential that each member of the party feels that he has had a hand in the action."[38] The article's publication in *Dragon* suggests that it struck a chord with the editor. However, it is not only DMs who needed to be controlled. Thomas Griffith turned the tables and suggested that DMs should shape the behaviors of "problem players."[39]

THE FRAMINGS OF TEEN SPIRIT

Creating a moral gaming group is particularly challenging when incorporating teens, their follies, and their fantasies. Adolescents must determine what it means to be a responsible person and group member. For adolescents, the fictive setting of gameplay provides opportunities for wish fulfillment as well as for acting out and exploring the social boundaries of the imagined setting. As role-playing games developed as a hobby, these opportunities were experienced not only by White middle-class adolescent boys but also eventually by young women, people of color, and individuals from other demographic groups. The idea of role-playing a character as a robust hero in a larger setting of risk and reward provided a sense of agency to new players. The rules of the game provide guidance about expected gameplay but also imply what is acceptable (and what is not) in the context of the game. Centrally, players are expected to cooperate with one another, to overcome the risks and challenges presented in the game; those who do not are often marginalized, either temporarily or permanently This speaks to the adolescent's position both as a player and as the animator of a character, but it simultaneously suggests that players must behave as responsible citizens, treating others with respect and showing awareness of the rights of their fellow gamers. In our experience as researchers, these expectations were sometimes violated, and the responses of older players provided moral guidance to, or pungent teasing of, those younger players. The frame of gameplay mediated and justified this socialization process, affirming the "soft community" in which they participated.

Fantasy role-play gaming developed from wargaming, a hobby in which young adults dominated. This proved true in the early years of *D&D* as well. However, within a few years, teens and then preadolescents discovered the game, and the demographic changed.[40] Older players often resented the younger, less knowledgeable, less mature, and less "serious" players who desired to participate. The toleration of these newcomers varied according to local cultures and in light of whether they accepted the norms that group life demanded. It was the new players' role as "social persons" that was at issue, in contrast to their being competent players or animators of their characters. In discussing his university game club, Tim Kask emphasized that the welcome resulted from players' behavior:

There were perhaps half a dozen younger members who were made welcome; their peers were not. We made our decision on the basis of the individual's maturity and behavior. If he was continually loud and disruptive, he wasn't welcome. By the same token, when an older player showed the same traits, he was given the same choice as the younger: Clean up his act or leave. A couple of the youngsters became known as "characters" in the behavioral sense, along with a couple of their older counterparts.[41]

In local groups, the presence of teenagers (and even younger players) required consideration of what, exactly, constituted "adult themes" and whether (and how) these should be included. Larry DiTillio argued for greater awareness that *D&D* was not only a form of recreation but a domain of adolescent socialization:

In D&D we PLAY a character, but invariably that character contains elements of our own selves. For adults, those selves are already firmly fixed; for younger players those selves are still being shaped by EVERY experience they have, INCLUDING D&D. The game becomes not only a leisure activity, it becomes a teaching instrument as well.[42]

DiTillio emphasized that this was especially true when dealing with vicarious deviance as part of in-game adventures. Even if fantasy play, it might still affect the developing person. Adults would do well, he argued, to recognize that discussion of sexual orientation, gender, and race could shape younger gamers.

BOYS AND GIRLS TOGETHER

Incorporating women and girls proved a challenge for the nascent role-playing game hobby, arising from wargaming's legacy of male sociability, interests, and fantasies. At first, the large majority of fantasy role-play gamers were male, and many female players were the girlfriends of more committed men and boys; but women too found the game appealing. Not surprisingly, many experienced various forms of sexism, intended or not. This included challenges to women as persons, players, and characters. Harassment occurred, and while this was noted by women, men often did not acknowledge it as such. Much of this came in the form of sexualized joking and remarks which created a hostile leisure environment. For example, men often assumed that women would inevitably play female characters. Thus girls would not just play elves but would always play *female* elves, and their difference from males would be a salient part of the game.[43] For women who wished to be treated as equals, this assumption was offensive. As more women entered the hobby, the shared understanding of social expectations within the soft community began to change, but only slowly and imperfectly.

Jean Wells and Kim Mohan addressed the varying levels of acceptance of women in the hobby, presenting egregious examples of sexist behavior by male players.[44] By 1982, however, Roger Moore advocated for gender equality as a means to having a more enjoyable and better *D&D* experience: "Women are as capable of feats of heroism, genius, and cunning as men are in D&D games."[45] Calling for equality is easier said than done, and promoting the equality of gender, race, and sexuality has continued to be a heated topic of discussion in gaming narratives, in discussion around the table, and outside the leisure environment. Because many gamers are adolescents, with all their hormonal and cultural issues, gender equality has been a challenge.

ALIGNING THE PLAYER'S SELF

We turn from the framing of persons to that of players: persons actively engaged in role-playing games. In the context of the rules for gameplay, what constitutes appropriate or inappropriate behavior shapes whether the game is considered enjoyable. Persons who in their work lives or schoolwork are responsible and therefore used to acting in a nondeviant way may encounter difficulty as gamers where deviance is expected. This is more than a case of their playing disagreeable characters; rather, in the course of being a player, their actions can be considered disruptive by others. Often this involves slippage between the alignment of their characters (legitimate in the game context) and their performing this alignment within the group of gamers. In a series of articles, Gygax, as a cocreator of *D&D*, described alternate alignments.[46] Characters could act according to their "inner morality," being "Lawful," "Chaotic," "Evil," or "Good."

However, as Fine described,[47] the actions of characters can spill over into those of players. Players in their performances around the table often playfully embrace and magnify the alignment of their character. This suggests a leakage among layers of interaction. Despite difficulties in defining the meaning of alignment, these moral perspectives shape the experience of players and often bring pleasure, as imagining characters can lead to imagining selves in the framing of vicarious deviance. The "character of characters" shapes the style of interaction with other players. One player related a humorous story about two players in his group who went on a date. According to his account, nothing went right. They could not get theater tickets, and the man's car broke down. When another player learned this, he laughed gleefully, transforming himself into an evil character, "My spell worked." Alignment is regularly referred to as the basis for evaluating the appropriateness of a player's actions. The ability to play an evil or chaotic character raises the question of whether such gameplay changes the actions of the player as a player, and beyond this, whether it stains the person's "real-world" identity. The multiple levels of game framing permit a lawful good teenager and a conscientious player to enact a chaotic evil character. The in-game consequences for their character potentially provide lasting reputations for the player.

CHARACTERS IN A MORAL MILIEU

Not all forms of imaginative action were conceived of in the context of the rules for *D&D*. Some fantasy social situations expand beyond the easy structures that rules provide. Jean Wells, responsible for the "Sage Advice" column in *The Dragon*, was sometimes confronted with questions that might have been more appropriate for "Dear Abby." Wells was asked what should be done with a character who has gotten pregnant; or what a character should do if she is romancing a god, but the god insists that she divorce her current husband; or what the best ways are to thwart attempts by an assassins' guild to kill a player character.[48] The choices that characters faced could be expansive, as the imaginations of their animators knew few bounds.

Beyond questions concerning individual player characters, the imagining of some fantasy worlds that draw on *D&D* posit pantheons and societies that expected characters to display deviant behavior. In practice, this affords players opportunities for vicarious deviance. In other words, there is a fantasy world where the characters "reside." This local world, developed by the DM in conjunction with the *D&D* rules, has norms that are distinct from the gaming world (the world of the table) and the natural world (the world of the teenager), although the norms of the three layers often intersect.[49] The fantasy world that the characters inhabit permits the verbal accounting of hidden desires. In their gaming experiences, both authors "observed" sexual assaults—even at times, in the late 1970s, labeled rapes, and often occurring in medieval taverns. Crimes that these adolescents would never consider in the real world become possible when it is their characters who are acting, since these are actions embedded in imagination. The assumption within this accepting community is that such behavior is "part of the game": the membrane between layers will be unbroken. Acting in a way that is "evil"—as imagined—can be a means of being a "good" player, as role-playing involves imaginatively taking on another self.[50]

The three frames of social meaning, along with the dynamic linkages through which the real world, gaming world, and fantasy world intersect (what Goffman speaks of as up-keying and down-keying of frames), occur continually within role-playing.[51] This makes it difficult to provide universal examples of deviance without considering the level of performance. Still, deviance, primarily vicarious (but sometimes real), belongs to all three frames. The reality that most gaming groups are soft communities means that vicarious deviance is tolerated and local cultures are accepting.

SOFT COMMUNITIES AND VICARIOUS DEVIANCE

In this chapter, focusing on the early years of *D&D*, we have addressed the role of vicarious deviance in the context of soft communities. Soft communities are social spaces that tolerate eccentric behaviors and odd characters, as long as the participants reveal a commitment to the core activity—in this case, fantasy gaming. The presence of a soft community allows the gaming table to be a space where participants can imagine deviant selves while located in safe spaces where the imagining has few harmful effects. Around the table, these "acts" are recognized as fantasies, not realities with stigmatizing outcomes. This involves a playful envisioning of intriguing—but unacceptable—selves.

Role-playing games provide a theater of the mind that allows for the exploration of deviance. Rather than engaging directly in deviant behavior as themselves, players in a role-playing game are provided with norms and values that they can accept or transform through the actions and alignments of their characters. Through the interactive dynamic of the game, players explore the fictive consequences of their actions. Role-playing creates settings within a larger social frame.

Vicarious deviance centers on the idea that the characters engage in actions considered deviant in the framework of contemporary society. This includes blatant examples such as killing or looting dead bodies, but also more ambiguous forms such as talking back to authority figures, getting drunk, acting without regard for social consequences, or disrespecting the responses of others. This vicarious deviance is treated as legitimate in the game but is always considered within the context of the community's culture and is always separated from the "real world."

Although the frame of gameplay allows and even encourages character actions that would be deviant if enacted outside the fantasy context, the unfolding narrative of the game provides normative feedback. By taking on the role of a character, players can act in ways that they would not in their natural lives but are seen within the game as being permitted, and sometimes approved, by others. The game itself models a society where there are rules to be learned and norms to be observed. As Goffman observes in *Frame Analysis*, the frame of fantasy interaction suggests that the meaningful construction of the interaction order legitimates or outlaws particular kinds of action. This recognition ties back into the concept of soft communities. Role-play gamers are often derided as "nerds" or "geeks." For some, those terms are used as a badge of belonging and even a mark of status within the subculture. Gaming groups in their local context determine the amount of acceptable player-enacted deviance and the boundaries of that deviance. By examining vicarious deviance and soft communities, we have described how fantasy role-playing provides a site in which adolescents can engage their fantasies, grow, and mature. The conditions for vicarious deviance within a supportive group build shared pleasure and a sense of allegiance. Not every group condones vicarious deviance, but each group is a soft community with a sense that there are behaviors that group members consider appropriate because of mutual caring and concern. It is important to recognize the role of these soft communities in the socialization of players, in addition to the experience of individual gameplay. As the community of *D&D* expands and changes in the future, how players are socialized will change as well.

NOTES

1. *Mazes and Monsters* was subsequently made into a TV movie and served as a breakout vehicle for one of its actors, Tom Hanks.

2. Rona Jaffe, *Mazes and Monsters* (New York: Delacorte Press, 1981).

3. Joseph Laycock, *Dangerous Games: What the Moral Panic over Role-Playing Games Says about Play, Religion, and Imagined Worlds* (Berkeley: University of California Press, 2015).

4. Ernest Gary Gygax and David Lance Arneson, *Dungeons & Dragons* (Lake Geneva, WI: Tactical Studies Rules, 1974).

5. Joel Best, *Threatened Children: Rhetoric and Concern about Child-Victims* (Chicago: University of Chicago Press, 1990).

6. Jon Peterson, *Playing at the World*, 1st ed. (San Diego: Unreason Press, 2012); Laycock, *Dangerous Games*.

7. Daniel Martin and Gary Alan Fine, "Satanic Cults, Satanic Play: Is 'Dungeons & Dragons' a Breeding Ground for the Devil?" in *The Satanism Scare*, ed. James Richardson, Joel Best, and David Bromley (New York: Aldine de Gruyter, 1991), 107–123.

8. Mark Barrowcliffe, *The Elfish Gene: Dungeons, Dragons, and Growing Up Strange* (New York: Soho Press, 2007); Ethan Gilsdorf, *Fantasy Freaks and Gaming Geeks* (Guilford, CT: Lyons Press, 2009).

9. Howard Becker, *Outsiders: Studies in the Sociology of Deviance* (New York: Free Press, 1963).

10. The majority of participants we observed in the 1970s were White middle-class adolescent boys; women were present only on occasion. We subsequently note the demographic changes in the community as women and people of color became more numerous and visible.

11. Gary Alan Fine, *Players and Pawns: How Chess Builds Community and Culture* (Chicago: University of Chicago Press, 2015).

12. Examples include the "Golden Brigade." Gary Alan Fine, *Shared Fantasy: Role-Playing Games as Social Worlds* (Chicago: University of Chicago Press, 1983). Related social scenes included science fiction fan clubs, most notably the Minnesota Science Fiction Society (Peterson, *Playing at the World*), whose members were "early adopters" of role-playing as a form of leisure.

13. Jon Peterson, *The Elusive Shift* (Cambridge, MA: MIT Press, 2020).

14. Fine, *Shared Fantasy*.

15. Erving Goffman, *Frame Analysis: An Essay on the Organization of Experience* (Cambridge, MA: Harvard University Press, 1974).

16. Becker, *Outsiders*.

17. Timothy Kask, "Dragon Rumbles," *The Dragon*, no. 28 (August 1979): 2.

18. Theron Kuntz, "Up on a Soapbox: Wargaming; A Moral Issue?" *The Dragon*, no. 35 (March 1980): 17.

19. Timothy Kask, "Dragon Rumbles," *The Dragon*, no. 30 (October 1979): 41.

20. Timothy Kask, "Out on a Limb," *The Dragon*, no. 5 (February 1977): 14.

21. Fine, *Shared Fantasy*, 194; Daniel Mackay, *The Fantasy Role-Playing Game* (Jefferson, NC: McFarland, 2001), 54.

22. Chick Publications, *Dark Dungeons*, 1984, accessed August 1, 2021, https://www.chick.com/products/tract?stk=0046.

23. Martin and Fine, "Satanic Cults, Satanic Play."

24. E. Gary Gygax and Robert Kuntz, *Dungeons & Dragons Supplement I: Greyhawk* (Lake Geneva, WI: Tactical Studies Rules, 1975); David Arneson, *Dungeons & Dragons Supplement II: Blackmoor* (Lake Geneva, WI: TSR Hobbies, 1975); E. Gary Gygax and Brian Blume, *Dungeons & Dragons Supplement III: Eldritch Wizardry* (Lake Geneva, WI: TSR Hobbies, 1976).

25. Gregory Rihn, "Lycanthropy: The Progress of the Disease," *The Dragon*, no. 14 (May 1978): 5–6; Alexander von Thorn, "The Politics of Hell," *The Dragon*, no. 28 (August 1979): 2, 40–42.

26. Kevin Thompson, "Insanity, or Why Is My Character Eating Leaves?" *The Dragon*, no. 18 (September 1978): 9.

27. Harry O. Fischer, "The Finzer Family: A Tale of Modern Magic," *The Dragon*, no. 8 (July 1977): 8–20.

28. Arthur Collins, "Reflections of a Real-Life Cleric," *The Dragon*, no. 41 (September 1970): 6.

29. Collins, "Real-Life Cleric," 7.

30. Collins, 8.

31. Collins, 7.

32. Thomas Filmore, "The Play's the Thing," *The Dragon*, no. 11 (December 1977): 10.

33. Jake Jaquet, "Dragon Rumbles," *The Dragon*, no. 41 (September 1980): 3.

34. Jon Pickens, "Too Much Loot in Your Campaign? D&D Option: Orgies, Inc.," *The Dragon*, no. 10 (November 1977): 5–6.

35. Fine, *Shared Fantasy*.

36. Becker, *Outsiders*.

37. Kask, "Out on a Limb."

38. Fred Zimmerman, "Up on a Soapbox: When Choosing a DM, Be Choosy!" *The Dragon*, no. 48 (April 1981): 28–29.

39. Thomas Griffith, "Up on a Soapbox: Good GM Can Cure Bad Behavior," *Dragon*, no. 50 (June 1981): 52, 55.

40. Fine, *Shared Fantasy*.

41. Timothy Kask, "Dragon Rumbles," *The Dragon*, no. 36 (April 1980): 2.

42. Larry DiTillio, "Up on a Soapbox: Painted Ladies and Potted Monks," *The Dragon*, no. 36 (April 1980): 8–9.

43. Len Lakofka, "Notes on Women and Magic—Bringing the Distaff Gamer into D&D," *The Dragon*, no. 3 (October 1976): 7–10.

44. Jean Wells and Kim Mohan, "Women Want Equality—and Why Not?" *Dragon*, no. 39 (July 1980): 10–11.

45. Roger Moore, "Dungeons Aren't Supposed to Be 'For Men Only,'" *Dragon*, no. 57 (January 1982): 50–51.

46. E. Gary Gygax, "The Meaning of Law and Chaos in Dungeons & Dragons and Their Relationships to Good and Evil," *Strategic Review* 2, no. 1 (February 1976): 3–5; "Varied Player Character and Non-Player Character Alignment in the Dungeons & Dragons Campaign," *The Dragon*, no. 9 (September 1977): 5–6; "From the Sorcerer's Scroll: Evil: Law vs. Chaos," *The Dragon*, no. 28 (August 1979): 10–11; "From the

Sorcerer's Scroll: Good Isn't Stupid, Paladins & Rangers, and Female Dwarves Do Have Beards!" *The Dragon*, no. 38 (June 1980): 22–23.

47. Fine, *Shared Fantasy.*

48. Jean Wells, "Sage Advice," *The Dragon*, no. 32 (December 1979): 26–27; no. 35 (March 1980): 16; no. 36 (April 1980): 8–9.

49. Fine, *Shared Fantasy.*

50. Lawrence Schick, "Choir Practice at the First Church of Lawful Evil (Orthodox): The Ramifications of Alignment," *The Dragon*, no. 24 (April 1979): 34–39.

51. Goffman, *Frame Analysis.*

FUTURES

(*continued*)

Designer Vignettes IV (continued)

D&D is both the sum of its parts (roleplaying is fun, strategy is fun, dice are fun, telling stories is fun, etc.) and more than the sum of its parts (there's a magic that happens when you're at a table playing an RPG with friends or strangers, and it's hard to say exactly why and how it happens and where it comes from).

—**Sally Tamarkin**
Journalist, editor, writer, game designer;
alum of MCDM's *Arcadia* magazine; writer for *Dark Veil*

20

D&D&D&D&D: IMAGINING *DUNGEONS & DRAGONS* AT 150 AND BEYOND

Jonathan Walton*

This speculative chapter imagines what *Dungeons & Dragons* (*D&D*) will be like at age 150—a century from now. The second half of the chapter consists of a series of random tables—lists of entries meant to be randomly selected by dice rolls—that you can use to generate your own possible *D&D* futures. The table format reflects a common tool for procedurally generating content in *D&D* and also suggests that the future of *D&D* contains a wide variety of possibilities, many of which will coexist simultaneously. First, though, it's important to consider why we should imagine the future of *D&D*.

IMAGINING ALTERNATIVE FUTURES

MILES: Are you from another dimension? Like a parallel universe where things are like this universe, but different? And you're Spider-Man in that universe? But somehow traveled to this universe, but you don't know how?

PETER: Wow. That was really just a guess?

MILES: Well, we learned about it in Physics.

—*Spider-Man: Into the Spider-Verse* (2018)[1]

*Sincere gratitude to Dr. Melody Watson for her expert assistance in editing this chapter.

D&D, both when it was first collaboratively created and now fifty years later, is the way(s) it is because of how it came to be—because of the contexts, people, choices, and events that made it happen and continue to make it happen. But what if *D&D* was different? More to the point, what different forms can we imagine *D&D* taking in the future as everything continues to change?

Imagining future alternatives to existing *D&D* game texts and practices is a well-trodden path in tabletop role-playing. It's almost fair to say that modern role-playing as a form of media—in both its analog and digital forms—has its foundations in people trying to develop alternative ways to play *D&D*.[2] With this in mind, then, it's important to recognize that shifts in *D&D*—what *D&D* is and how audiences interact with it—are only partly driven by the commercial and publishing decisions of those who own the game's intellectual property. Indeed, the inability of TSR, WotC, and Hasbro to copyright game mechanics and the ease with which *D&D*-related concepts circulate in popular culture mean that the future of *D&D* will not be centered on the "nth edition." *D&D*'s future will instead be determined by the ways that different groups of designers and players will reimagine high fantasy adventures writ large in the decades to come.

Even the term *D&D*, with its broad popular influence, has already come—at least in popular discourse—to mean much more than just official products published and consumed under the name *D&D*. It also includes unofficial and derivative versions such as "old-school" games, *Pathfinder*, and *Dungeon World*, for example, as well as the broader *D&D* influences in media such as fantasy MMOs (massively multiplayer online games), the animated series *Adventure Time*, the console game series *Final Fantasy* and *Dragon Age*, various *isekai* media, and so on. When we speculate about the future of *D&D*, we are not restricted to a specific media property but are free to consider an entire genre of transmedia.

What kinds of alternative futures should people imagine for *D&D*? The short answer is: any ones that they want, any ones that speak to them, any ones that make them excited about playing games and sharing those experiences with others. As role-playing game (RPG) marketing materials frequently remind us, role-playing has "infinite possibilities," and we are "limited only by our imagination." But the longer answer to this question is a bit more complicated.

PREDICTING THE FUTURE?

Precognition allows your mind to glimpse fragments of potential future events. . . . However, your vision is incomplete, and it makes no real sense until the actual events you glimpsed begin to unfold. That's when everything begins to come together.

—"Precognition" (2004)[3]

Is it possible to accurately predict the future of *D&D*?

Future events emerge from the past and present in ways that can seem patterned and potentially predictable. Entire industries are built on this predictability, from weather and financial forecasting to risk management, policy making, design, technological innovation, environmental management, and—of course—the work of futurists.[4] On a humbler scale, people (and other organisms) perform many day-to-day activities with the expectation that their actions will lead to predictable outcomes. People assemble at a bus stop anticipating that a bus will eventually arrive and pick them up. A dog fetches a ball expecting the human player to throw it again. In *D&D*, a player might choose for their character to take a specific action because that action has either a greater chance of success or a greater chance of having a significant impact on the imagined events of the game. All these predictions, from the enormous to the mundane, are grounded in past observations—sometimes called data—as well as various kinds of anticipations, such as hopes, desires, hunches, and guesses.

As everyone knows from experience, however, not all predictions of the future are accurate. Many of them are wrong. Sometimes people wait for a bus that never comes, or end up riding a different bus that comes much later. Sometimes a dog fetches a ball only to discover that playtime is suddenly over. Sometimes, no matter how well a *D&D* player chooses their character's actions, the situation or the dice don't turn out the way they anticipated—for many, that uncertainty is one of the main reasons they play RPGs. Is this inaccuracy in prediction a problem of insufficient data or inappropriate hopes and desires? Perhaps. But the future is a slippery thing to grasp. Humans often face significant difficulties explaining the sequences of events that led to our past and present circumstances—as any historian or criminal investigator will tell you—even when there are historical records and eyewitness observations. The future is even more difficult to accurately discern. Alongside historical patterns and long-building developments,[5] individual and collective human choices matter—what we sometimes call *agency*, the bread and butter of role-playing. In addition, the immense complexity of material and social factors means that circumstances and events often emerge from idiosyncratic contexts that are impossible to predict or replicate. Philosophers sometimes talk about causation in terms of the necessary and sufficient conditions for something to occur, but J. L. Mackie famously recognized that any given event is caused by the combination of many smaller factors, or "INUS conditions," that are insufficient but necessary parts of an unnecessary but sufficient condition.[6] Consequently, determining the course of future events, even with extensive evidence concerning what might happen, is fraught with uncertainty.

This uncertainty grows the further into the future a prediction extends and with the complexity and scope of what is predicted. It is much easier for someone to accurately predict what they will have for breakfast tomorrow—given the limited scope of the prediction and the degree to which the circumstances of tomorrow's breakfast are under their control—than it is to predict the forms a complex transmedia phenomenon like *D&D* will take one hundred years in the future. After all, less than twenty-five years ago, the popular consensus was that tabletop role-playing was a dying form of media, overwhelmed by the rise of video games and new collectible card games, including a surprise breakout hit from a small company called WotC. How different things feel now, in the early 2020s, when *D&D* seems to enjoy greater popularity and cultural cachet than at any previous point in its history. How many forecasters would have predicted these events a mere twenty-five years ago, when the trends were very different? How much more difficult is it, then, to predict what will occur a century from now? Thankfully, making accurate predictions is not the only reason to speculate about *D&D*'s future.

EXAMINING THE PRESENT

Science fiction is the realism of our time. It describes the present in the way a skeet shooter targets a clay pigeon, aiming a bit ahead of the moment to reveal what is not yet present but is already having an impact. This gives us metaphors and meaning-systems to help conceptualize our moment.

—Kim Stanley Robinson (2017)[7]

Speculation about D&D's future can also be a way to explore contemporary issues in gaming. As a parallel, consider the social role of science fiction.

Science fiction occasionally seems to provide an eerily accurate view into the future, such as when the 1998 film *The Siege* portrayed a near future in which Arab and Muslim Americans were unjustly rounded up and imprisoned by police and military officers after a terrorist attack on New York City. But did the film anticipate the post-2001 domestic and international security policies of the United States? More likely it was simply grounded in an understanding—based on past examples—of how easily many Americans would give up their values of freedom and justice in favor of fear and xenophobia. The filmmakers and actors probably hoped to issue a warning about a coming future of rampant surveillance, securitization, and systemic racial and religious violence, but they were also commenting on aspects of the future that were already present in the daily lives of many Americans. As William Gibson is often quoted as saying, "The future is already here—it's just not very evenly distributed."[8]

In this sense, projections of the future are often, as Hamlet says, "the abstract and brief chronicles of the time"—representations of the present through particular lenses that clarify or emphasize certain aspects of contemporary existence. In the 1940s, when George Orwell wrote *1984*, the dangers of authoritarianism and totalitarianism were the focus of major political and popular concern. Likewise, when Margaret Atwood wrote *The Handmaid's Tale* in the 1980s, as well as when it was adapted for TV in the 2010s–2020s, women's rights faced new waves of attacks from the religious right in response to painstaking gains by feminist activists. Even earlier foundational science fiction texts such as Mary Shelley's *Frankenstein* (1818) and Karel Čapek's play *R.U.R.* (1920) embody and comment on contemporary issues of science, human anatomy, the self, humanity, and industrialization. Not all science fiction focuses so specifically on issues of the present, but it is certainly one of the genre's main strengths and one example of how speculation can be used.

With this in mind, when imagining the future of *D&D*, one thing people can do is reflect on its present and past. For example, one could propose a future in which *D&D* is an online pay-to-play subscription service that involves logging in to share an MMO-like experience with fellow players. What is being commented on when people propose primarily virtual or digital futures for tabletop role-playing? Unsurprisingly, this was a popular vision of *D&D*'s future when *World of Warcraft* (*WoW*, 2004) was the most popular game on the planet and virtual worlds were a core part of how many people imagined the future. It was a vision, in other words, largely about the dreams and anxieties of the present. That vision of a virtual future for fantasy role-playing has been reinvigorated recently by a new generation of *isekai* (other world) media in Japan and elsewhere, particularly *isekai* media inspired by both fantasy gaming and the imagined potential of virtual reality, following in the footsteps of media such as *.hack* and *Sword Art Online*. Perhaps, with Facebook and other tech companies attempting to push toward a nebulous "metaverse," other VR-focused visions for the future of *D&D* will also emerge.

Do these visions suggest, as they seemed to in the *WoW* era, that print media are doomed, and everything will eventually move online? Hasn't the recent outburst of *D&D*'s popularity been partly driven by players seeking "retro" in-person, face-to-face connections in an increasingly virtual society? Has the COVID-19 pandemic exacerbated a shift toward a style of online videochat-based play that will gradually become predominant, or are players hungry for a return to in-person experiences? Whatever the answer, fantasy role-players will continue to wrestle with their relationship to digital media, and imagining futures for *D&D* is one method they use to explore various possibilities—as well as to explore other issues such as race, gender, sexuality, and disability.

INNOVATION VERSUS RECOGNIZING EXISTING ALTERNATIVES

The D&D Next playtest has begun! . . . It's an exciting time for Dungeons & Dragons. We are happy to announce today that we are developing the next iteration of D&D, and will be looking to the legions of D&D fans to help shape the future of the game along with us.

—Mike Mearls, "Charting the Course for D&D" (2012)[9]

This one is for the queer, underprivileged, POC, and black creators that are trying to take and reclaim what that one company from the coast has forged. This one is for you. Take it . . . There's no limit to what your 6e should look like. Make it yours.
—Snow, "6e Game Jam" (2020)[10]

When thinking about alternative futures, whether in *D&D* or in human societies more broadly, it's easy to think that this requires pulling apart mainstream practices—whether dice mechanics or, say, gender roles—and then designing new ways to put them back together using innovative new approaches and ideas. That is certainly one way to do it, and one that is often extremely fruitful, leading to fascinating new approaches to games and life. But what about the alternative practices that already exist?

Designers and innovators frequently suggest that people must embrace new ideas, behaviors, objects, devices, systems, and—mostly importantly—new ways of thinking. People need to stop being so backward and become more advanced, need to not be left behind by their attachment to older, outdated approaches but continually seek out the next new thing, which will surely be better than what has come before. Game designers often fall into this way of thinking too, even when they are drawing inspiration from older, existing games—as is almost always the case. Even in the creation of "old-school" games—or when WotC's lead designers reportedly drew on *D&D*'s 1983 "red box" edition to design fifth edition—the point is usually not to exactly re-create the original but to improve on or change some aspects of it, to make it more compatible with contemporary approaches to gaming.

Unfortunately, an innovation-focused approach can sometimes serve as an excuse to avoid—or at least avoid giving credit to—the huge variety of alternative approaches that already exist. In contemporary society, activism and critical analysis from a range of sources—Indigenous and Black people; people of color more broadly; gender-diverse, queer, disabled, and poor people; people from immigrant backgrounds; and other marginalized people—have torn apart narratives of linear progress. Despite the claims of its proponents, innovation has led not to widespread human betterment and happiness but rather to persistent inequality and injustice, as well as creating new forms of inequality and injustice. Further, solutions already exist to many of the big problems facing humanity—from police brutality to oppressive gender roles to environmental devastation—if only the people and communities that have long cultivated alternative ways of being, outside of or in parallel to mainstream Western society, are listened to and empowered to change social norms.

In the context of *D&D*, one of the major discussion points in recent years has been how to deal with *D&D*'s history of racism, colonialism, sexism, ableism, homophobia, and elitism, much of which remains both baked into the rules and supported by swaths of the fan base. However, different groups of players have been identifying different ways of dealing with these issues since role-playing's beginnings, so the problem isn't so much that new and innovative techniques need to be developed—though those might also help—but that the existing alternatives have not typically been reincorporated into official *D&D* products and communities. In part, this is because cis white male designers have largely remained in charge at WotC, despite some notable efforts at changing that situation. Further, many designers have been hesitant to disrupt long-standing *D&D* traditions and risk angering the conservative white male portion of the fan base.

Even beyond issues of representation, power, diversity, and inclusion, other existing alternatives are worth pondering when thinking about possible futures for *D&D*—alternatives that involve different approaches to playing RPGs. *D&D* has always inspired "homebrew" alternative practices and rule sets, as well as "hacks" both large and small that alter existing rules and play guidelines. Other tabletop role-playing traditions, from *Call of Cthulhu* to *GURPS* to *Vampire: The Masquerade*, have long championed alternative approaches to role-playing. However, with the release of the Open Game License Version 1.0a (OGL) in 2000, WotC signaled to both fans and independent game publishers that it supported people taking *D&D* in new directions, creating both material for, and variant adaptations of, the game that went far beyond what official publications could possibly offer. Taking place around the same time, the rise of the indie games movement in tabletop role-playing—in a variety of forms, including "old-school" gaming, "story games," free-form LARP, and more—meant that large numbers of people were (and are) already playing RPGs in ways that are very different from what "mainstream *D&D*" is like, if that can even be understood as a single, unified thing. So when we imagine alternative futures for *D&D*, we don't have to start from scratch; instead we can draw on the vast number of alternatives that already exist, created by role-playing communities with various degrees of separation from official *D&D* products and practices.

PROCEDURALLY GENERATED FUTURES FOR TRANSMEDIA *D&D*

The future's not set. There's no fate but what we make for ourselves.
—*Terminator 2: Judgment Day* (1991)[11]

In the future, computers will procedurally generate alternative versions of *D&D* by the millions, based on the criteria you select, and then send you the top five results from simulated play tests with artificial intelligence (AI) agents so that you can pick which one you want to play today. At least, probably someday they will, though my colleague Matthew Guzdial, a scholar of computational creativity, always thinks my predictions for autogenerated tabletop RPG texts are off by an order of magnitude. In the meantime, though, I invite you—the reader—to procedurally generate some alternative *D&D* futures for yourselves.

Below I have included a series of random tables for rolling up your own *D&D* futures. Before we get to those, though, let me explain why these tables take the form they do. First, this format assumes that accuracy is not the most important or interesting part of imagining the future. These tables contain a host of possibilities—perhaps some of these predictions will come true, but the purpose is really to expand the range of possible futures that we can imagine. Second, the future—like the present—is never just one thing. Instead it is always a diverse field of multiple, contradictory things happening simultaneously, coexisting in some places, in tension in others. Rolling on these tables may give you a sense of what one game, one approach, one scene within future *D&D* might be like, but there will likely be dozens if not hundreds of thousands of different approaches and scenes that partly overlap. Third, the transmedia futures of *D&D* will not always be directly connected to each other but will instead show what Ludwig Wittgenstein called "family resemblance" to present practices, without necessarily having many formal features in common.[12] Even now, it can be difficult to spot the direct links between, say, *D&D*'s very first "white box" set from the 1970s and a single-session free-form LARP about the challenges and injustice faced by military interpreters—and that will be even more true a century from now.

With that introduction, have at it!

THE META-TABLE: A TABLE OF TABLES

To generate one possible future for *D&D*, roll a d100 (or pick!) 1d4+2 times on the "meta-table" below to determine which other tables you should subsequently roll on (or pick from). If the results tell you to roll on the same table multiple times, that's great—just combine the results. Or, if you prefer, just roll again or pick a different table. Beyond the results obtained from your limited set of 1d4+2 prompts, you're welcome to imagine that the other parts of your *D&D* future are more or less like some existing version of *D&D* or the broader role-playing tradition, but you get to choose which version.

D100	Table
Table Group 1. The Context and Form of Play	
01–06	1.1 The World
07–12	1.2 The Players
13–18	1.3 The Dungeon Master
19–24	1.4 Medium/Structure
25–30	1.5 Transmission
Table Group 2. The Premise and Characters	
31–36	2.1 Characters
37–42	2.2 Premise
43–48	2.3 Motivations
49–54	2.4 Complications

Table Group 3. The Setting	
55–60	3.1 Major Locations
61–66	3.2 The Wilderness
67–72	3.3 Monsters
73–78	3.4 Magic
Table Group 4. Rules and Procedures	
79–84	4.1 Resolution
85–100	4.2 Variant Rules

TABLE GROUP 1: THE CONTEXT AND FORM OF PLAY

Table 1.1 The World

When people think about our future on this planet, so much is currently up in the air, including human relationships with the natural world, the state of human societies, and the technological possibilities that will be open to us. Table 1.1 presents some possible worlds that we might inhabit in one hundred years, and will doubtlessly shape the kinds of games that people play.

D12	Detail
1	There's no electricity, either locally or more broadly, limiting many technologies.
2	There are constant natural disasters, due to shifts in climate or terraforming technologies.
3	Humans live in a permanent base or city on the Moon or Mars, dreaming of our distant blue-green planet.
4	It is a corporate cyberpunk future in which huge industrial groups operate with little oversight.
5	Play takes place largely in a bodiless cyberspace, virtually.
6	Humans live in the aftermath of a societal collapse, in small communities connected by trade.
7	Humans live in and among a variety of small microstates.
8	National borders have collapsed into a shifting sea of constant migration.
9	Societies have rewilded large portions of urban landscape and returned to a simpler existence.

(*continued*)

Table 1.1   (continued)

D12	Detail
10	As ocean levels rise, people have been forced to relocate to less populated inland regions.
11	Make up your own future for human societies, based on your hopes and fears.
12	Combine two or more of the above options.

Table 1.2   The Players

In a changing world, the people—or other entities—who play *D&D* may also change. Table 1.2 offers some possibilities for who future players might be.

D12	Players
1	Dolphins and other cetaceans, amid long ocean journeys
2	Posthumans modified by biotech, very different from humans now
3	Those ritually chosen by the Council of Ravens
4	Traveling theatrical performers in search of an audience
5	Internet creators who micromonetize their play, action by action
6	Struggling artists trying to revive an old art form, almost forgotten
7	Survivors in postapocalyptic refugee camps, keeping their spirits up
8	Prisoners playing in captivity, under constant interruption and surveillance
9	People living in a totalitarian state and hiding subversive political content in their play
10	Newly created AIs, being taught to interact with humans and each other
11	Massively Multiplayer Online Game nonplayer characters (NPCs), still working through procedurally generated content on abandoned servers
12	Hackers, trying to break into computer systems protected by interactive virtual worlds

Table 1.3 The Dungeon Master

The role of the dungeon master (DM) has transformed and proliferated into dozens of different approaches over the past fifty years, a process that is likely to continue in the future. Table 1.3 presents some possibilities, though these roles might also go by different names in your futures.

D20	DM Type	Details
1	Instructor	The DM teaches the game to the other players.
2	Host	The DM hosts the other players at their home or another location.
3	Facilitator	The DM facilitates play, helping it happen smoothly.
4	Opposition	The DM represents the forces opposing the player characters (PCs).
5	Rotating	The DM role rotates among the players, session to session or scene by scene.
6	Structured	The DM, like the players, has a specific list of actions they can perform.
7	Distributed	There is no DM, and their responsibilities are distributed among the players.
8	Phases	There is no DM, and play is structured by a series of set phases that the players follow.
9	Moves	There is no DM, and the players take turns choosing specific DM "moves" from a list.
10	Scenario	There is no DM, and play follows a specific series of events, set in advance.
11	Literal DM	The DM is just in charge of the dungeons, nothing else.
12	NPC Master	The DM is only responsible for portraying NPCs.
13	AI	The DM is an AI or machine-learning system that generates responses to player actions and questions.
14	Random	There is no DM, and random input (e.g., cards, an app, etc.) helps structure play.
15	Subaltern	The DM must be a member of a marginalized group (e.g., a woman, Black, etc.).
16	Textual	There is no DM, and players consult a booklet whenever they need outside input.
17	Character	The DM plays a single important character in the game, the center of the action.
18	Protagonist	The DM plays the protagonist, with the players portraying everything else.
19	Arbiter	The DM aspires to be a neutral judge who says what is most likely to happen.
20	Partisan	The DM actively tries to champion a particular cause, helping it achieve its goals.

Table 1.4   Medium/Structure

Role-playing isn't just 2d4 friends and a DM sitting around a table. Instead *D&D* could potentially take a wide variety of forms, with different structures and using different kinds of communicative media.

D20	Game Format
1	It's a solo game.
2	The game is designed for only two players.
3	There is a fixed number of players (e.g., 3, 4, 5, 6, or 8), perhaps with distinct roles for each.
4	The game is designed for a huge number of players: 12, 20, 50, or more.
5	There is a list of specific characters to choose from.
6	It's a board game or a board-RPG hybrid.
7	It's a card game or a game that uses cards in a core way.
8	It's a live-action game of some variety, like a LARP or an escape room.
9	The game takes place over video chat.
10	The game takes place over chat, text messages, emails, letters, or some other text-based format.
11	The game takes place over audio, like a phone call or podcast.
12	The game requires players to journal, blog, or vlog about the events of play.
13	The game uses metal or plastic figurines, which can be painted or not.
14	The game requires drawing maps.
15	The game requires collecting small items from nature or your house.
16	The game doesn't involve talking; players communicate with gestures and body language.
17	The game is a one-shot game, taking place over a single session.
18	The game takes place over a short narrative arc, say 3–6 sessions.
19	The game is some kind of digital game, app, or VR program.
20	The game uses an unusual medium or structure of your choice.

Table 1.5 Transmission

How will *D&D* be transmitted in the future, to new players? How do people come to learn how the game is played? How are traditions and practices passed on?

D20	Method of Transmission
1	It's transmitted by oral tradition, kept alive by the elders.
2	It's often played during important festivals, among family and friends.
3	It's a job that people learn to do, just like anything else.
4	Players are forced to make sense of it by consulting a series of contradictory texts.
5	Players need to apprentice themselves to a recognized authority and undergo training.
6	There are a series of video or audio recordings that teach players the game.
7	There is a collaboratively authored and constantly evolving digital text that explains the game.
8	New players can really only learn by playing, faking it until they make it.
9	It's not really something you learn; you just act like a normal person in fictional circumstances.
10	Once you have achieved the proper rank in the order, they induct you into the mysteries.
11	Honestly, everyone just makes it up as they go.
12	If you want to learn to play, there is coursework that is commonly recommended.
13	The guidelines are recorded in a media format that barely anyone still uses.
14	There's an in-depth VR training simulation that can be freely downloaded.
15	Any decent role-playing AI will be happy to practice playing with you.
16	Everybody already pretends to be different people all the time; this is the same.
17	People mostly learn from digital games and then port some of those skills over.
18	Mostly you just show up at special events, and the people there walk you through it.
19	The rules were carved onto metal tablets before the Great Disaster.
20	There's no real tradition; we just made this up ourselves, about a month ago.

TABLE GROUP 2: THE PREMISE AND CHARACTERS

Table 2.1 Characters

A set of player characters (PCs) is traditionally central to role-playing, but who are the characters in your future version of *D&D*?

D20	Identity of Player Characters
1	The PCs are all everyday people; roll on table 1.2 to determine what kind.
2	The PCs are all monsters; roll on table 3.3 to determine what kind.
3	The PCs are desperate people taking desperate actions.
4	The PCs are robots, trying to get by in a society in which they are often treated poorly.
5	The PCs are ghosts or undead, seeking vengeance, closure, or both.
6	The PCs are neighbors who are trying to help each other out through hard times.
7	The PCs are wandering merchants, traveling between communities and selling their wares.
8	The PCs are gig workers trying to make ends meet by taking on odd jobs.
9	The PCs are people who do this as a kind of hobby or side gig, not as their main work.
10	The PCs are members of a gang, illegal organization, or secret society.
11	The PCs are the wealthy and privileged, those with the most power and influence.
12	The PCs are activists and advocates, trying to change society for the better.
13	The PCs are all people who have not yet been fully accepted by mainstream society.
14	The PCs are all elderly people trying to figure out what to do with the rest of their lives.
15	The PCs are all parents and guardians, struggling to care for children or other dependents.
16	The PCs are all people with disabilities, trauma, or mental illness, just trying to live their lives.
17	The PCs are all humanoid insects of different species living in mixed communities.
18	There are no PCs; the story occurs at a higher level of abstraction, like a chronicle of events.
19	There are no PCs; gameplay consists of describing particular moments or images.
20	There are no PCs; different characters are portrayed by different players, as needed.

Table 2.2 Premise

So what do the PCs actually do? What is the premise of the game?

D12	Game Premise
1	The PCs build solidarity to tackle individually insurmountable problems.
2	The PCs sabotage the resources and capabilities of their opponents.
3	The PCs engage in direct action to halt injustice and create social change.
4	The PCs collaboratively create something together, working on some kind of large project.
5	The PCs refuse to go along with the local authorities and are currently being pursued.
6	The PCs help others escape from tough situations, providing a chance for them to start over.
7	The PCs are rivals and frenemies, competing against each other for something.
8	The PCs are just trying to make ends meet and survive their day-to-day lives.
9	The PCs are trying to become famous, either collectively or individually.
10	The PCs have one last job to do, and then they'll give it up forever.
11	The PCs are coworkers at the same company or organization; they don't have to like each other.
12	The PCs are honestly still trying to figure out what they're doing; it's a mess.

Table 2.3 Motivations

Whatever it is that the characters do, why do they do it? What are their motivations?

D20	Character Motivations
1	Out of desperation.
2	For shits and giggles.
3	It's their job.
4	It's their duty.
5	It's their inheritance.
6	To obtain something they want or need.
7	To find themselves.

(*continued*)

Table 2.3 (continued)

D20	Character Motivations
8	To impress their crush.
9	For love.
10	To get away.
11	Because no one else will.
12	To save the world.
13	To find someone.
14	For wealth.
15	For power.
16	To preserve their privilege.
17	To earn a place of their own.
18	To find out how it feels.
19	Because they've always wanted to.
20	Because they don't know anything else.

Table 2.4 Complications

Whatever the premise of your alternative *D&D*, complications always get in the way of the PCs' goals, because nothing is ever as easy as it seems.

D12	Character Complications
1	They don't trust their comrades.
2	They don't trust themselves.
3	They were never supposed to be here.
4	One or more of them are imposters.
5	They underestimate each other.
6	They don't trust each other.
7	They're not expected to come back.
8	They are cursed or doomed.
9	There's something wrong with them.
10	There's something fishy about this whole thing.
11	They intend to betray each other.
12	It's too heavy to steal.

TABLE GROUP 3: THE SETTING

Table 3.1 Major Locations

What is a setting without places? Table 3.1 lists places that could serve as a central location in your version of *D&D*, not just in a particular campaign but central to every iteration. What is it about this particular location that makes the game revolve around it?

D20	Location
1	A rocky outcropping emerging from the sea
2	A small village
3	A forest
4	A prison or dungeon
5	A crashed alien spaceship
6	Ancient biotech research labs
7	A domain of dreams
8	A doorway to the future or the past
9	An alternate dimension or outer plane
10	Inside a digital or technological system
11	An abandoned building
12	A secure facility
13	A wizard's tower
14	The palace or estate of a noble
15	A cove or harbor
16	A garden
17	A monastery
18	A series of aqueducts
19	A bandit's mountain lair
20	Deep beneath a frozen lake

Table 3.2 The Wilderness

A classic feature of *D&D* is the exploration of the wilderness, the area that exists beyond the edges of the known. Sometimes the wilderness is considered the antithesis of "civilization," although hopefully games can gradually move away from such colonialist models or at least problematize and subvert them. Table 3.2 suggests some different ways to think about the wilderness that your future *D&D* will explore.

D12	Nature of the Wilderness
1	The wildness in every human heart, more suppressed in some people than in others
2	The few remaining wild places of the world: sanctuaries from encroachment, settlement, urbanization, and enforced domesticity
3	The unknowable nature of the nonhuman or the Other, which scared Lovecraft but is actually something you can gradually come to know
4	Formerly settled or abandoned places, now rewilded
5	The unquenchable desire in the heart for experiences beyond one's limited imagining
6	The way the wild sneaks into everything: a flower in the sidewalk, coyotes in the streets
7	Chimeric creatures designed by biotech, mixing different species' DNA together
8	Wild things and places being steadily corrupted by human meddling
9	The desire of the wild to smash human hubris and retake places
10	The places that humans have made alien and unknowable by covering them with concrete
11	Space, the final frontier
12	The depths of the ocean, the other final frontier

Table 3.3   Monsters

Our understanding of the monstrous is prime for changing as we wrestle with ideas of justice and monstrosity. Table 3.3 suggests alternative ways to think about who monsters are.

D20	Nature of Monsters
1	Natural disasters caused by unjust human behavior, against the natural world or each other.
2	Manifestations of very personal fears and nightmares—of people feeling lost, alone, abandoned.
3	Caused by past crimes and evils, as in a horror movie; evil spirits that are not laid to rest.
4	Summoned by individuals to wreak havoc on those who harmed them.
5	Nonhuman others who are difficult to understand, who act without regard to their effects on us.
6	Basically animals, driven monstrous by human actions (see *Princess Mononoke*).
7	Like bad weather: not always predictable, impossible to control, something to be prepared for.
8	Results of biotech or magical experiments that mix the human and the nonhuman.
9	Manifestations of cruel divine or natural will, punishing humans for their hubris without distinction between the innocent and the guilty (see *Godzilla*).
10	Basically people; people who have been—justly or unjustly—banished from their communities and come back wild and strange.
11	Robots or other technological entities.
12	The 99 percent, the unwashed masses that the privileged always despise and fear.
13	Random or site-specific mutations that turn people or animals into monstrous things or combine them with the things around them (see *Annihilation*).
14	Visitors or invaders from the world of abstract concepts, given monstrous form or creating monstrous forms when they intersect with our world.
15	Celestial beings sent to enact the divine will and make the world more perfect or aesthetic in monstrous ways.
16	Monsters from the id, the manifested terrors of our own unconscious (see *Forbidden Planet*).
17	People or beings who have been unjustly wronged and seek righteous vengeance.
18	Things taking the form of modernist art and music or sound, disturbing our ideas about the world.
19	People who have been taught to hate us and everything we stand for.
20	The horrors of war or other forms of broad-scale organized violence.

Table 3.4   Magic

Magical spells, powers, and artifacts often play a prominent role in fantasy role-playing. Table 3.4 presents possibilities for the types of magic that might predominate in your particular alternative.

D20	Type of Magic
1	Necromancy
2	Portal creation
3	Biotech
4	Soul energy
5	Surreality
6	Dream manifestation and shaping
7	Nanotech manipulation
8	Terraforming
9	Spirit summoning and binding
10	Curses
11	The demon or monster inside certain people
12	The magic of a local place
13	The magic of a sacred artifact, rightfully possessed or stolen
14	The magic of lost science
15	The magic of alien forces
16	The magic of natural forces beyond the control of individuals
17	The magic of the monstrous; roll on table 3.3 to determine what kind.
18	The magic people were born with or that they inherited
19	The magic of the small gods
20	The magic of the hegemonic religious faith and its institutions

TABLE GROUP 4: RULES AND PROCEDURES

Table 4.1 Resolution

When things happen in RPGs and the players are not sure exactly how those things will work out, players traditionally resort to specific procedures to determine how the situation will resolve. These are often called "resolution mechanics." Contemporary *D&D* often calls on players to roll a single d20 with various modifiers to try to achieve a specific target number, but there are many other potential ways by which uncertain situations could be resolved. Table 4.1 suggests some that might be used in alternate *D&D* futures.

D12	Resolution Mechanic
1	Tarot or playing cards, randomly drawn from a deck.
2	Moving pieces around on an abstract board.
3	Attempting to solve puzzles within a limited time frame.
4	Answering a series of questions to help determine what happens.
5	Competing in physical challenges to see who wins.
6	Deciding who has the most to lose—they always prevail.
7	Flipping a coin, calling heads or tails in the air.
8	One player decides what happens, and another player decides the cost.
9	Bidding tokens to see who's willing to pay the most to get what they want.
10	There are no formal resolution mechanics; you just talk it out.
11	Dropping a leaf and seeing whom it points to when it has spiraled down to the ground.
12	Using some other short analog or digital game as a resolution mechanic.

Table 4.2 Variant Rules

Variants of *D&D* tend to have specific sections of rules that are noticeably different—more evocative, more specialized, or more elaborate—than the existing rules. Table 4.2 presents a range of areas in which the rules of your future *D&D* might be noticeably different—how do they differ?

D20	Table
1	Age
2	Armor
3	Beliefs
4	Communities
5	Curses
6	Death
7	Determination
8	Experience
9	Fate
10	Goals
11	Hit points
12	Levels
13	Love
14	Maps
15	Powers
16	Range
17	Resilience
18	Skills
19	Spells
20	Wounds

NOTES

1. Bob Persichetti, Peter Ramsey, and Rodney Rothman, dirs., *Spider-Man: Into the Spider-Verse* (Sony Pictures, 2018).

2. Of course, *D&D* itself was preceded by various other RPG-adjacent practices (*Kriegsspiel*, improv, Braunstein, etc.), and various non-RPG media, such as video games, have also had a strong influence on role-playing over the years.

3. Bruce R. Cordell et al., *Dungeons & Dragons: Expanded Psionics Handbook* (Wizards of the Coast, 2004).

4. Jennifer M. Gidley, *The Future: A Very Short Introduction* (Oxford University Press, 2017).

5. James Mahoney and Dietrich Rueschemeyer, eds., *Comparative Historical Analysis in the Social Sciences* (Cambridge University Press, 2003).

6. J. L. Mackie, "Causes and Conditions," *American Philosophical Quarterly* 2, no. 4 (October 1965).

7. Lauren Beukes et al., "Science Fiction When the Future Is Now," *Nature* 552, no. 7685 (December 2017).

8. William Gibson, in *The Economist*, December 4, 2003.

9. Mike Mearls, "Charting the Course for D&D: Your Voice, Your Game." *Legends & Lore* (blog), January 9, 2012.

10. Snow, "6e Game Jam," Itch.io, May 2020.

11. James Cameron et al., *Terminator 2: Judgment Day* (Tri-Star Pictures, 1991).

12. Ludwig Wittgenstein, *Philosophical Investigations*, trans. G. E. M. Anscombe (New York: Macmillan, 1953).

APPENDIX: A BRIEF SUMMARY OF *D&D* EDITIONS

Here we provide a brief overview of the various editions of *D&D*. We hope it gives unfamiliar readers and those new to the game an introduction to the timeline of *D&D* releases so far. Further information detailing specific supplements and campaign settings published for each edition of the game can be found online.

It is important to note that after the publication of the original edition of *D&D* in 1974, the game's rule set was split into two separate versions that were published at the same time: a rules-light system (the *Basic Set* and its iterations) and a rules-heavy system (*Advanced Dungeons & Dragons* and its iterations). This split ended with the release of the game's third edition in 2000.

ORIGINAL *DUNGEONS & DRAGONS* (1974)

The original edition of *D&D* (often called 1e or *OD&D*) was co-created by Dave Arneson and Gary Gygax and published by Tactical Studies Rules in 1974. *OD&D* was published as a three-volume boxed set commonly referred to as the three "little brown books/booklets": *Men & Magic*, *Monsters & Treasure*, and *The Underworld & Wilderness Adventures*. Multiple supplements expanding various areas of the game were published.

BASIC SET (1977–1994)

The *Basic Set* was the initial successor to *OD&D* and was released in 1977 while *Advanced Dungeons & Dragons* was being developed by TSR. The *Basic Set* offered players a more rules-light and easier-to-understand version of *OD&D*. This eventuated in the B/X (Basic/Expert sets, 1981), BECMI (Basic/Expert/Companion/Master/Immortals rules sets, 1983–1986), and *Rules Cyclopedia* (*New Easy to Master D&D* / classic *D&D* rules sets, 1991–1994) versions of the game, which TSR discontinued in 1994.

ADVANCED DUNGEONS & DRAGONS (1977–1995)

Advanced Dungeons & Dragons (*AD&D* 1e) was an updated successor of *OD&D* that was published by TSR between 1977 and 1979. It originated the three core rule books: *Monster Manual, Dungeon Masters Guide*, and *Players Handbook*. Multiple supplements expanding the game were also published. A second edition of *AD&D* (*AD&D* 2e), featuring new rules and character classes, was published in 1989. A revised version of *AD&D* 2e (*AD&D* 2e revised) was published in 1995.

DUNGEONS & DRAGONS THIRD EDITION (2000–2003)

Consolidating *D&D* into a single rule set once again, Wizards of the Coast (WotC) published the third edition of *D&D* in 2000. During this era, WotC also published the Open Game License (OGL), which allowed third-party content to be created for the game without breaching copyright.

DUNGEONS & DRAGONS THIRD EDITION (REVISED) (2003–2008)

Minor revisions to the third edition of the game were released in 2003 as *D&D* 3.5e (a half edition of sorts). Multiple supplements expanding the game were also published.

DUNGEONS & DRAGONS FOURTH EDITION (2008–2010)

The fourth edition of *D&D* was published in 2008. Differing from its predecessors, this version of the game published multiple volumes of the three core rule books, which were released yearly. As in the *Basic Set* era (1977–1994), "Essentials" versions of the fourth edition rule sets were published in 2010, intended for first-time players unfamiliar with table-top role-playing games.

DUNGEONS & DRAGONS FIFTH EDITION (2014–2024)

D&D 5e was officially released in 2014. Fifth edition reprises the three core rule books, and a number of supplementary play materials have been published—both original and inspired by previous adventure modules. The greater accessibility of *D&D* 5e's rule set, in comparison to previous editions, is commonly attributed to the resurgence of *D&D* play that is occurring today.

ONE D&D (2024 ONWARD)

Announced in August 2022, *One D&D* is planned to be released in 2024 as the latest edition of *D&D*. As of this writing, the new edition is undergoing play testing by members of the *D&D* community.

CONTRIBUTOR BIOGRAPHIES

Marcus Carter is an Associate Professor in Digital Cultures at The University of Sydney. With Drs. Kelly Bergstrom and Darryl Woodford, he edited *Internet Spaceships Are Serious Business: An EVE Online Reader* (University of Minnesota Press, 2015) and is the author of *Treacherous Play* (MIT Press, 2022). His research focuses on player experiences in games ranging from *Candy Crush Saga* to *Warhammer 40,000*.

Amanda Cote is Associate Professor and Director of the Serious Games Certificate in the Department of Media and Information at Michigan State University. Her work focuses on the industry and culture of analog and digital games, with an emphasis on gender, identity, and representation. Her book *Gaming Sexism: Gender and Identity in the Era of Casual Video Games* (2020) was published by NYU Press.

Mateusz Felczak is Assistant Professor at the Institute of Humanities, SWPS University, Warsaw, Poland. His research interests include modding, streaming media, electronic sports and religion in games. He is a member of the Center for Cultural Research of Technologies (SWPS University), the Games Research Centre (Jagiellonian University), and the Digital Games Research Association (DiGRA).

Gary Alan Fine is James E. Johnson Professor of Sociology at Northwestern University, having previously taught at the University of Minnesota and the University of Georgia. He received his PhD from Harvard University in Social Psychology and is the author of the early study of Dungeons & Dragons: *Shared Fantasy: Role-Playing Games as Social Worlds* (1983). He examines the culture of leisure communities, including Little League Baseball (*With the Boys*), mushroom collecting (*Morel Tales*), high school debate (*Gifted Tongues*), folk art collecting (*Everyday Genius*), competitive chess (*Players and Pawns*), and senior citizen activism (*Fair Share*). His current project examines U.S. Civil War history enthusiasts (tentatively titled *The Found Cause*).

Antero Garcia is an Associate Professor in the Graduate School of Education at Stanford University. His research explores the possibilities of speculative imagination and healing in educational research. Prior to completing his PhD, Garcia was an English teacher at a public high school in South Central Los Angeles. He has authored or edited more than a dozen books about the possibilities of literacies, play, and civics in transforming schooling in America. Antero currently co-edits *La Cuenta*, an online publication centering the voices and perspectives of individuals labeled undocumented in the US. Antero received his PhD in the Urban Schooling division of the Graduate School of Education and Information Studies at the University of California, Los Angeles.

David Harris is a PhD candidate at the Victorian College of the Arts and a teacher of interactive narrative and game design at Swinburne University of Technology. His research looks at the intersection of interactive or immersive theaters and the interactivity inherent in play and games. His inquiry looks at what a game or work offers an audience or player, and how these playful stakeholders respond to the situations these games or theatrical works provide. David is also an artist and theater maker, with a practice of immersive theater making and live game design.

Adrian Hermann is a Professor of Religion and Society at the Forum Internationale Wissenschaft, University of Bonn (Germany). He specializes in the global history of religion in the nineteenth and twentieth centuries and has recently begun to engage in the field of role-playing game studies. Over the last fifteen years, he has written on Christianity and Buddhism in Latin America, the United States, and South and Southeast Asia. After being an avid TTRPG player for most of the 1990s, he has recently taken up playing again but now also studies TTRPGs as part of his interest in contemporary audiovisual and digital media.

Zach Howard is the leading expert on Dr. J. Eric Holmes and his works. He is the curator of the Zenopus Archives website, an online repository for his Holmes research. He was instrumental in getting Holmes's Boinger and Zereth stories reprinted in the *Tales of Peril* (2017) omnibus collection, and Howard wrote *The Ruined Tower of Zenopus* (2020), a fifth edition (5e) update to the *Basic Set*'s sample dungeon. Holmes's *Basic Set* was Howard's first *D&D* rules set.

Michael Iantorno is a doctoral scholar whose research focuses on videogame modding, game industry labour, and intellectual property law. His dissertation explores the preservation, reproduction, and alteration practices that have developed around nineties consoles. In addition to his academic work, Michael hacks old videogames, develops TTRPGs as one half of Mammoth Island Games, and writes about games and the people who make them. You can find more of Michael's work at www .michaeliantorno.com

Daniel Heath Justice is a Colorado-born citizen of the Cherokee Nation who lives with his husband and their two sweet but slightly feral French Bulldogs in the traditional swiya of the shíshálh people. He is Professor and Distinguished University

Scholar in the Institute for Critical Indigenous Studies and the Department of English Language and Literatures at the University of British Columbia on unceded Musqueam territory. He is the author of numerous scholarly and creative works, including the epic queer Indigenous fantasy *The Way of Thorn and Thunder: The Kynship Chronicles*. He has played D&D since the mid-1980s; his preferred PC alignment is neutral good, his favorite character class is druid, and he is an unabashed halfling partisan.

C Liersch is a freelance artist and role-playing game enthusiast.

Josiah Lulham is a PhD candidate at the University of Melbourne, conducting ethnographic work with live-action role-playing game communities. His dissertation investigates the play of these communities and considers the ways in which the ambition to "be immersed" and have an experience in these bodily enacted yet fictional worlds "feels real," and the implications of this "real" feeling in the separated yet entwined everyday lives of those players. Josiah is also an actor, theater maker, and the co–artistic director of the Melbourne Playback Theatre Company.

Esther MacCallum-Stewart is a British author and Professor of Game Studies at Staffordshire University in the United Kingdom, where she specializes in player behavior and analog games—including tabletop role-playing games. Her work examines the ways in which players understand the worlds around them—as players, fans, producers, and consumers.

Jay Malouf-Grice is an anthropologist, tutor, and high school teacher in training at the University of Sydney. She conducted her Honors research on YouTube, analyzing the project of identity formation through role-play. For her PhD, she dove into Sydney's queer gaming scene and emerged four years later with a thesis and a newfound queer family. Jay is currently in five ongoing TTRPG campaigns, three as a player and two as a Dungeon Mistress. When she is not playing TTRPGs she can be found reading tarot or dying in *Dark Souls*.

Sam Mannell is a fiction writer and tabletop game designer. He currently writes and designs for MCDM and Ghostfire Gaming.

Dimitra Nikolaidou, PhD, is researching the relationship between TRPGs and speculative literature with a focus on representation and visibility. She is a member of HELAAS, FORS, and the international War/Game research project coordinated by the University of Tromso. Her work has been presented in international conferences both in Greece and abroad. Her papers have been published in the *WyrdCon Companion* (2015) and *Ex-centric Narratives: Journal of Anglophone Literature, Culture and Media* (2018). She has authored chapters in *The Palgrave Handbook of Global Fantasy* (Palgrave Macmillan, 2023) and *Wargames: Memory, Militarism and the Subject of Play* (Bloomsbury, 2019). Additionally, her speculative fiction has been translated in six languages and published in various magazines and anthologies, including *Beneath Ceaseless Skies*, *Gallery of Curiosities*, *Retellings of the Inland Seas* and *Andromeda Spaceways*.

Jon Peterson is widely recognized as an authority on the history of games. He is best known as the author of *Playing at the World* (2012), *The Elusive Shift* (2020), and *Game Wizards* (2021). He also co-authored *Dungeons & Dragons: Art & Arcana* (2018), *Heroes' Feast: The Official* Dungeons & Dragons *Cookbook* (2020), *Lore & Legends* (2023) and was the lead on the *Trivial Pursuit: Dungeons & Dragons Ultimate Edition* (2022). He has contributed to academic anthologies on games, including MIT Press's *Zones of Control* (2016) and Routledge's *Role-Playing Game Studies: Transmedia Foundations* (2018). Jon also has written for various geek culture websites, including *Wired*, *Polygon*, and *BoingBoing*.

Victor Raymond is a writer living in Madison, Wisconsin. He received his Ph.D from Iowa State University in Sociology with a graduate minor in Women's Studies. His current projects examine the early growth of interest in *Dungeons & Dragons*, and the imaginative role of dungeon creation as a part of game play. He is a founding board member of the Carl Brandon Society, and currently serves as the chair of the Tekumel Foundation.

Tony A. Rowe is an associate teaching professor at Drexel University instructing students in game design, production, and game history. He is a veteran of the video game industry with a twenty-year career as a professional game designer and is the author of numerous articles on the histories of digital and tabletop games. He is a California-born role player who shopped for games at the same Aero Hobbies in Santa Monica as Dr. John Eric Holmes. The first D&D rules set he purchased when learning to play was Holmes' *Basic Set*.

Emily Saidel studies the intersection of popular culture and politics through a feminist lens. She has previously held lecturer positions at the University of Michigan and Boston University. Her work examines narratives about the federal government in fictional American television, as well as issues of representation within televisual paratexts and video games. Before her doctoral education, she worked in performing arts administration and arts in higher education.

Premeet Sidhu is a high school English and History teacher and PhD student at the University of Sydney. Her PhD looks at the modern resurgence and learning potential of the tabletop role-playing game *Dungeons & Dragons*. Her broader research interests include investigating how meaningful player experiences in both digital and nondigital games can be applied in wider areas of game design, education, and media.

Evan Torner is an Associate Professor at the University of Cincinnati. He has published several articles pertaining to East Germany, critical race theory, DEFA Indianerfilme, science fiction, transnational genre cinema, and game studies, as well as coedited several books. His volume *Immersive Gameplay: Essays on Role-Playing and Participatory Media*, coedited with William J. White, was published by McFarland in 2012, and he is one of the founding editors of the *Analog Game Studies* journal.

Aaron Trammell is an Assistant Professor of Informatics at the University of California, Irvine. He is the Editor-in-Chief of the *Analog Game Studies* journal and Multimedia Editor of the journal *Sounding Out!* He is also the author of *Repairing Play: A Black Phenomenology* (MIT Press, 2023) and *The Privilege of Play: A History of Hobby Games, Race, and Geek Culture* (NYU Press, 2023).

Jonathan Walton is an Assistant Teaching Professor at Carnegie Mellon University's Entertainment Technology Center, where he teaches courses on game design and advises MA student projects. Jonathan previously worked for more than seven years in foreign policy, earning an MA in International Studies from the University of Washington and a BA in China Studies from Oberlin College. He has been involved in the indie RPG community for twenty years and wrote the post-2000 history of contemporary RPGs for *Role-Playing Game Studies: Transmedia Foundations* (Routledge, 2018).

Stephen Webley has over two decades experience in teaching games design, war and conflict studies, and applied psychoanalysis. During this time, he has used roleplaying games and play to teach how reality, play, and ideology are co-dependent and how the human instinct to play games can be used to foster learning, and empathic approaches to understanding crises. Steve has been an avid *Dungeons & Dragons* player since the early 1980s and his current research focuses on how play informs us of how fantasy and emotions shape everyday reality unbeknownst to rational and scientific world views. Steve currently teaches games design at Staffordshire University UK.

Kellynn Wee is a PhD candidate in the Department of Anthropology at University College London. Her research focuses on play, speculation, agency, sociality, and materiality in the emergent worlds of tabletop role-playing games in Singapore.

José P. Zagal is a Professor with the University of Utah's Entertainment Arts & Engineering program. He authored *Ludoliteracy* (ETC Press, 2010) and edited *The Videogame Ethics Reader* (Cognella, 2012) and, with Dr. Sebastian Deterding, *Role-Playing Game Studies: Transmedia Foundations* (Routledge, 2018). More recently, *Game Design Snacks* (ETC Press, 2019) is an edited collection of nuggets of game design wisdom with examples from commercial video games. Dr. Zagal is Editor-In-Chief of the peer-reviewed *Transactions of the Digital Games Research Association* (ToDiGRA). He was also honored as a DiGRA Distinguished Scholar and a Fellow of the Higher-Education Videogame Alliance (HEVGA) for his contributions to games research.

INDEX

Page numbers in italics denote tables and figures. Endnotes are indicated by "n" followed by the endnote number.

Jacquet, Gary "Jake," 63
Jaffe, Rona (*Mazes and Monsters*), 301
Jenkins, Duane, 34
Jones, Shelly, 5, 8

Kamm, Bjorn-Ole, 287
Kask, Timothy, 63, 305, 313
Keep on the Borderlands, The (1980), 71
Kennedy, Joy C., 181
King, Brad, 165
Knights of the Old Republic (1998), 165
Kriegsspiel (wargame), 24, 26

Lagace, Naithan, 7
Lameman, Beth Aileen, 7
Laycock, Joseph P., 187
Learning through *D&D*
    adolescent socialization, 313–314
    clinical contexts, 188–189
    educational contexts, 187–188
    leisurely play contexts, 189–190
    literacy, 180–182
    reflection, 182–185
    social development, 185–187
Legalities, open source games and, 82–83
Lensman (1969), 26, 32
Licensing. *See* Open Game License (OGL)
Liersch, C
    Classroom D&D, 228
    D&D Session, 118
    Forest Ambush, 14
Limited intelligence mechanics, 24–28, 37
Literacy and *D&D*, 180–182
Literature. *See* Speculative fiction
Little Wars (Wells), 25, 31
Live-streaming, 122–124, 126, 130–136, 288. *See also* Performative play
Lord of the Rings, The (Tolkien), 170, 241, 245, 285

Los Angeles Science Fantasy Society (LASFS), 66
Lovecraft, H. P., 69, 111, 148
Lowry, Sadie, 119–120

MacCallum-Stewart, Esther, 121–139, 164, 169
Mackay, Daniel, 6, 198, 200, 216
Mackie, J. L., 238
Magic
    as Eurocentric, 279
    in possible futures, *346*
    religion vs., 143, 146–147
"Magic circle," 111
Majkowski, Tomasz, 97
Makcik and Magicks (live game), 295
Manganiello, Joe, 165
Mannell, Sam, 13
Manual of Aurania, The (1976), 67
Marshall, Eugene, 265
Maze-driven gameplay, 27–28
Maze of Peril, The (Holmes), 68
Mazes and Monsters (Jaffe), 301
McCrumb, Sharyn, 166, 167
McElroy, Griffin, 200
McGonigal, Jane, 38
McLean, Will ("Papers & Paychecks"), 114, *115*
Mearls, Mike, 86, 240, 330
Media, influence of *D&D* on, 164–165
Megarry, Dave, 36, 63
Mendez Hodes, James, 233, 251
Mental health, 188–189
Mentzer, Frank, 72
Mercer, Matthew, 122, 130–131, 132
Mercer Effect, 124, 134–137
Meriläinen, Mikko, 183–184
Metheney, Brynn, 247, 250
Midway (1964), 32
Miéville, China, 166, 167
Mitchell, David (*Bone Clocks*), 161
Mitchell, Douglas, 21
Mizer, Nicholas, 4, 181, 286, 292